A MEMOIR

TIM PAT COOGAN

PHOENIX

A PHOENIX PAPERBACK

First published in Great Britain in 2008
by Weidenfeld & Nicolson
This paperback edition published in 2009
by Phoenix,
an imprint of Orion Books Ltd,
Orion House, 5 Upper St Martin's Lane,
London, WC2H 9EA

An Hachette UK Company

1 3 5 7 9 10 8 6 4 2

A CIP catalogue record for this book
is available from the British Library.

ISBN 978-0-7538-2603-4

Typeset by Input Data Services Ltd,
Bridgwater, Somerset

Printed and bound in the UK by
CPI Mackays, Chatham, Kent

The Orion Publishing Group's policy is to use papers that
are natural, renewable and recyclable products and made
from wood grown in sustainable forests. The logging and
manufacturing processes are expected to conform to the
environmental regulations of the country of origin.

www.orionbooks.co.uk

To the family and friends who bore with me

Contents

Acknowledgements

As this is a personal memoir my indebtedness to others may be taken either as being very small, or very great. Very small in terms of those whom I had to either consult or to interview. Very great in terms of those who in some way influenced my life or my memories.

To all in this category I say a heartfelt thanks.

No less sincere is my gratitude to those in the smaller category. My sister Aisling and my brother Brian who supplied me with family records, anecdotes and photographs. Barry Desmond who retrieved for me some of my mother's correspondence and, inveitably for anyone who researches a book in Ireland, the staff of the best club in the country – the National Library and its photographic archive.

I would particularly like to thank Gerry Lynne of the Manuscripts division for his courtesy in allowing me early access to John O'Mahony's invaluable collection of documents spanning the entire course of 'The Troubles' from the 1960s to the 1990s. The collection includes a selection of my *Irish Press* editorials on some of the happenings of those days, which, whatever their impact on the events described, were of use and benefit to me in the compilation of this book.

Irish archivists as a class have always been an enabling force in my writings and I am particularly glad to add to their roll of honour the Archivist of the Dublin Archdiocese, Noelle Dowling, who facilitated me in accessing my correspondence with the dominant Irish clerical figure of my early years, Archbishop John Charles McQuaid. Our preserved corrrespondence helped to recall the memories of living through the effects of an extraordinary compact between Christ and Caesar.

My thanks are also due to Bodley Head for allowing me to quote from Jonathan Powell's memoir *Great Hatred Little Room* and lastly, but not least, for the help of Gill Hess, Declan Heaney, Lucinda McNeile and Alan Samson for helping to transform this work from idea, though process into book.

Introduction

I found writing about myself a strange experience – no doubt there will be those who will say they found reading about me an even stranger one – because hitherto I have written only about my country or my people, not about my own activities. For the observer to become the observed is not an easy metamorphosis. The faces and places one has encountered swim readily through the mists of memories. But so do the continuous doubts.

Is this significant? Is that fair? How to balance truth against hurt? In a sense these are the same questions I have always had to answer in over a dozen books of history and biography, but they take on an added dimension when they touch on people you love, have loved or worked with. There is also the fact that to a greater or lesser degree we all go through life veiled and masked. One cannot, and should not, do this when writing a memoir. But one only realises the extent to which one uses masks to hide from oneself when one contemplates an elementary truth that inevitably emerges as one looks back on one's life through the arches of the years, which is that life is indeed a game of two halves. In the first half, one has too much time on one's hands. The labour associated with rearing a family and with work deceptively allow one the hope that some day one will be free to follow one's own instincts. But this deferment obscures the fact that time is passing, that it's not a rehearsal; it's the actual production. And then, in the second half, there's not enough time. One can't kid oneself any more by saying: 'I'll get through this challenge somehow. Plenty of time left in the future to do what I really want.' Even if there were time, what did one want? How many of us can truly say: 'I've always followed my own vision'? How much of life is role playing, playing the part one is cast in by circumstances, not choice?

Trying to analyse what I really felt in my various roles as a journalist, a family man, a writer, a broadcaster, whatever, I am reminded unwillingly of a pamphlet I once read as a boy. It was published by the Catholic Truth Society as part of the general effort by the Church to subject the idea of self to one of obedience to the doctrines of the Church. The clerical author purported to be commenting on a letter he had received from a young woman questioning some doctrine or other. Before even attempting a rebuttal of her argument, he seized on her opening sentence, 'I feel that …', and observed: 'I put from myself the thought that the use of the term "I" can often indicate pride and selfishness.'

Some of that sort of conditioning must have remained with me. While I do have a streak of rebelliousness, and a strong sense of outrage at what I perceive as wrongdoing on the part of individuals or society, I'm still wary of my own feelings, of the selfishness of 'I'. Uncertain of entitlement to its use in judgements. Like the ascent of Everest, I did what I did because it was there to be done, rather than through calculation.

Writing a memoir, however, requires some calculation. How, or how high, should the veil be lifted, the mask doffed? There are no easy answers to this question, but I have at least attempted to give honest ones. I have tried to be fair, but I have not tried to disguise the fact that I feel deeply about some issues – for example, the killing of a once-great Irish institution, the *Irish Press*, for which I worked for thirty-five years, or the killing of a more deadly sort that went on in Northern Ireland throughout much of my life. *Quod scripsi scripsi*.

So much for approach. As to methodology, through accident of birth and choice of career I have either been touched by or become involved in many of the significant happenings of my time, both in the Republic of Ireland and in the six north-eastern counties of Ireland frequently erroneously referred to as 'Ulster', although the province of Ulster actually comprises nine counties, three of which lie in the Republic. I have attempted both to treat of my own experiences and to give the historical background to the events.

I look back on my life in a mood of grudging gratitude that at least I have lived long enough to attempt the task. More importantly, as I do so I enjoy many friendships, with both men and women, my house is warm and comfortable, and there is an abundance of wine on my sideboard. How long this pleasant circumstance will last only God knows, but as matters stand, despite having encountered what, at times, appeared to be an unreasonable share of life's vicissitudes, a man in his seventy-third year with food, fire and drink in the house should certainly regard the glass of life as being half full rather than half empty. Particularly as my blessings have included six children, twelve grandchildren and three great-grand-children, and there is always the possibility that negotiations through the proper channels may increase this total.

The historical events that created the border affected my family, my childhood and my career. The complex issues of whose law, and whose order, impacted on both my mother's father and my own father. Both questions arose from the use made of the British Conservative Party of the resistance by Irish Protestants and unionists, particularly those in the north-east, to Catholic demands for Home Rule.

The Tory leader Randolph Churchill gave the Orangemen their watchword: 'Ulster will fight and Ulster will be right.' That statement is the reason Ireland is today partitioned and Home Rule did not occur. This despite the fact that from the mid-1880s to the general election of 1918 the Irish electorate had voted by huge majorities in favour of some form of Irish self-determination. Home Rule was placed on the statute books in 1914, but there it stayed as the Irish issue became engulfed in the Great War.

And so the constitutional approach to solving the Irish issue became ineffective. The physical-force school of Irish nationalism awakened in response to the Orange defiance. A wave of violence engulfed the island and there was a telling of the Sorrowful Decades of the Irish historical rosary. The 1916 Rising, the subsequent Anglo-Irish War, pogrom and partition in Northern Ireland resulted in the signing of a treaty between the British government and Irish nationalist leaders in 1921. The treaty agreed to the setting up of two separate states on the one small island. In the south, a Catholic-dominated Irish Free State with the same constitutional status as Australia and Canada. This meant that though the British left, the Irish Free State still had a London-appointed governor-general, and parliamentarians had to take an oath of allegiance to the Crown. In the north, Britain still ruled the six of Ulster's nine counties that had a local parliament dominated by Protestants.

The upheavals, the birth pangs generated by the emergence of the two states, generated lasting sectarian problems whose effects may, or may not, have been finally dealt with by the signing of the Good Friday Agreement of 1998. What is certain is that along the road to Good Friday Ireland had to traverse the Slough of Ambivalence in which many of the inhabitants challenged the legitimacy of either state, directly placing both my maternal grandfather and my father in the cross-hairs of history. They served in different police forces, but each in his time encountered equal measures of hostility from the community he was meant to be policing.

The armed Royal Irish Constabulary (RIC), to which my grandfather belonged, was regarded with hatred and hostility by the nationalists, who increasingly gave their allegiance not to the old constitutional Irish

Parliamentary Party, but to the more militant and republican Sinn Fein. As the Sinn Fein rebellion grew in intensity throughout 1919, the RIC more and more came to be the object of Sinn Fein and IRA wrath. Eamon de Valera put a motion to the Dail, a parliamentary assembly that in British eyes was illegal anyway, proposing that 'members of the police forces acting in this country as part of the British occupation and as agents of the British government be ostracised socially by the people'. The seconder of the motion, Eoin MacNeill, described the RIC as 'a force of traitors', and called the police in Ireland 'a force of perjurers'. The resolution was carried unanimously. It was effected by the IRA, causing multiple fatalities for the RIC and the destruction of many of their barracks.

Naturally therefore the nationalist rulers of the new state that emerged in 1921 saw the creation of a more acceptable police force as a number-one priority. The Garda Siochana, an unarmed force, which my father played a leading role in setting up, was the result. But the new force was born in the midst of civil war. Elements in the IRA, as well as de Valera and later the political party that he formed, Fianna Fail, denied the legality of the state, its police, judiciary and army. The police were in the front line of the conflict.

Throughout the treaty debates de Valera, who had stayed at home while the treaty negotiations were conducted in London, repeatedly expressed fury at the delegates signing without his authority, although he conceded that the delegates whom he had sent in his place (notably Michael Collins and Arthur Griffith) did have plenipotentiary powers. Despite having stayed away, he was fully aware of what was on offer as he had had the terms spelled out to him by Lloyd George in a series of tête-à-têtes in London earlier in the summer. At the debates, de Valera avoided the crucial issue of partition and spoke mainly about his objections to the oath and the governor-general. He continually interrupted the debates (250 times in all) and wound up covering a total of thirty-nine pages of the official Dail report as opposed to a total of twelve for Collins and eight for Griffith. In the end, however, the treaty was carried by a margin of seven votes, 64–57. After the vote de Valera led his followers out of the Dail in protest at the result, thereby apparently leaving himself in a parliamentary cul de sac. Erskine Childers, who admired him greatly, enquired of him where he now hoped to look for support. De Valera made a fateful reply: 'Extremist support.'

The quest for 'extremist support', combined with his smoke-and-mirrors approach to the core reality of the treaty – an acceptance of partition – led him inexorably towards courtship of the IRA and a policy that no bread was better than half a loaf. The people went for the bread. The margin amongst the public at large in favour of the treaty was far greater than amongst the more radical and ideological Dail membership.

However, de Valera's espousal of 'extremist support' drove him to take up a position that combined intransigence and stridency in equal measure. During the election campaign called to ratify the treaty he delivered a number of what became known as 'wading through blood' incitements to the IRA.

At Dungarvan, on 16 March 1922, he said:

The treaty [...] barred the way to independence with the blood of fellow Irishmen. It was only by civil war after this that they could get their independence. If you don't fight today, you will have to fight tomorrow; and I say, when you are in a good fighting position, then fight on.

The following day he told a crowd, a large section of whom were carrying rifles, that if they accepted the treaty, and if the volunteers of the future tried to complete the work the volunteers of the last four years had been attempting, they would have to wade through Irish blood, through the blood of the soldiers of the Irish government and perhaps through the blood of some of the members of the government in order to get Irish freedom.

These wild and swirling words were designed to further the cause of civil war over that of peace. However, de Valera refused to abate his course, saying, when it was pointed out to him that a majority of the people favoured acceptance of the treaty, that the majority have no right to do wrong.

Two factors should be stressed here. First, that even had de Valera not acted thus and absented himself from the treaty debate, a minority of republicans would probably have taken up arms against the treaty anyhow. Second, that a majority of this minority were not motivated by a mere bloodlust, but by a sincerely held dedication to the ideal of creating a thirty-two-county Irish Republic, with no British presence. Their successors were still fighting for this goal in Northern Ireland seventy years later.

However, it is also true that this minority would have been a very small one indeed had not de Valera added his presence and prestige to the extremist cause. He was ultimately forced to recognise the reality of the fact that most of the electorate opposed violence and that if he wanted to make political progress, the constitutional card was the one he would have to play. But even while playing it, he took care to do what he could to keep the IRA on side by adopting 'the snaking regarder' approach when addressing the inaugural meeting of Fianna Fail (at the La Scala Theatre, Dublin, on 16 May 1926). Stressing the need for careful planning in order to achieve Fianna Fail's objective by constitutional means, he nevertheless managed to work in an admiring reference to an IRA jailbreak a little earlier:

> I am willing to wager that when the boys who rescued Jack Keogh the other day undertook their task, they did not start by burying their heads in the sand. They started, I am sure, by finding out all they could about the conditions of his detention. They were then able to prepare their plans wisely and to set about their work with a real chance of success.

As Fianna Fail set out on what proved to be an inexorable march towards power, Fianna Fail spokespersons continued to strike an ambivalent note where militant republicanism was concerned. Speaking in the Dail on 12 March 1928, Sean Lemass stated:

> Fianna Fail is a *slightly* constitutional party. We are open to the definition of a constitutional party, but before anything we are a republican party [...] Five years ago we were on the defensive, and perhaps in time we may recoup our strength sufficiently to go on the offensive. Our object is to establish a republican government in Ireland. If that can be done by the present methods we have, we will be very pleased, but if not, we would not confine ourselves to them.

One of the most important statements in the ambivalence calendar was made by de Valera himself in the Dail the following year on 14 March. It contained a clear indication that he felt the police force was in some way an anti-democratic outcropping of an illegal State:

> I still hold that our right to be regarded as the legitimate government of the country is faulty, that this House itself is faulty. You have secured a *de facto* position. Very well. There must be somebody in charge to keep order in the community, and by virtue of your de facto position you are the only people who are in a position to do it. But as to whether you have come by that position legitimately or not, I say you have not come by that position legitimately. You brought off a *coup d'état* in the summer of 1922.
>
> If you are not getting the support from all sections of the community that is necessary for any executive if it is going to dispense with a large police force, it is because there is a moral handicap in your case [...] The setting up of this state put a moral handicap on every one of us here [...] Those who continued on in that organisation which we have left can claim *exactly the same continuity* that we claimed up to 1925. They can do it.

I know from my own researches into the IRA that the foregoing statement in particular gave many young men who joined the IRA a sense of historical legitimacy. Thus between erecting a framework of moral authority for the IRA and, at the same time, seeking to give himself the freedom to operate independently of the republicans, de Valera had delivered some pretty expensive hostages to fortune by the time, with IRA help, he triumphed at the polls in 1932. How he ransomed them and what befell my grandfather as a result of de Valera's strictures on the RIC is described in Chapter 1. The consequences for my father are outlined in Chapter 2.

My Parents and
Family Background

Generally speaking I regard childhood as another country which I only revisit when forced. It took the compulsion of writing this memoir to persuade me to seek an extended memory visa to return to what I recall as a place that was outwardly pleasant enough but inwardly permeated by anxiety.

I was born in 1935, and one of my earliest memories stems from an incident that occurred on a day in September 1939, when I was four years old and Germany was invading Poland. It symbolises much of my family's, and Ireland's, subsequent experiences over the next decades. As the tanks rumbled, my family and I were aboard a ship heading for a holiday on the Isle of Man. The *Irish Independent*, from which my father was reading aloud, had devoted its front page to the outbreak of war, displaying a picture of a helmeted German soldier. I remember that while some people listened gravely to my father, others ignored both him and the ominous photograph, preferring to be entertained by my resistance to my mother's efforts to crown me with headgear of her own, a frilly bonnet, so that a somewhat more light-hearted photograph might be secured. Later the ship would be sunk and Ireland, or at least the larger portion of it, in which we were fortunate enough to live, would react much as did those who chose to focus on the bonnet incident rather than the news of war. Our state would stay neutral in the conflict, which would not be termed a war, but 'the Emergency'. Tragedy would dictate that the frail vessel of our family prosperity would also be sunk and that we would be turned loose upon the waters of economic adversity aboard a smaller, leaky, unseaworthy vessel delicately redesignated 'Reduced Circumstances', rather than call it by its true name: Poverty.

Poverty was not endemic amongst either my maternal or paternal forebears, which, particularly in the case of my mother's father, Patrick Toal, was a considerable tribute to his intelligence, diligence and highly developed instinct for survival. He came of brainy, Catholic, well-doing, farming stock in an area of County Armagh, in and around the village of Moy, or the Moy, as it is known in Northern Ireland. The Moy straddles two counties, Armagh and Tyrone, which manage to combine a deserved reputation for scholarship, husbandry and neighbourliness with an equally well-deserved reputation for ferocity in the maintenance of the sometimes overlapping traditions of the IRA and of Gaelic football. In the later part of the twentieth century Catholic and Protestant animosities would place the Moy in what became known as 'the Murder Triangle', involving the Armagh towns of Lurgan and Portadown.

It was an appropriate setting for the young Patrick Toal to grow up in because his career straddled both Northern and Southern Ireland, and the overlap between politics of both the constitutional and the sanguinary variety. An incident in his early life provided the tipping point that sent him from North to South. Despite being a Catholic, Patrick had gained a toehold on the lower slopes of the civil service, to wit in the Ballast Office in Belfast, and was determined to make the most of his opportunities. He devoted much of his spare time to studying for various civil service examinations. But one fine day his superior, a man described, somewhat wonderingly, in the family folklore, as 'a *decent* old Freemason', came back from lunch 'full', as the Belfast expression goes. When he found Patrick with his nose stuck in a book as usual, the following dialogue is said to have ensued:

DOFM: Toal, what are you reading? You're always reading!

PT: I'm studying for the exams.

DOFM: Exams! Toal! Are you wise or what? You'll never get anywhere with exams. You're the wrong sort. Go away down south and get a job with your own kind.

Patrick realised that his superior was giving him good advice. He went south and joined the Royal Irish Constabulary. The RIC attracted what one RIC man's son described to me as 'the finest-looking and thickest body of men in Ireland'. Patrick could fairly have been described as good-looking, but he certainly wasn't thick, as his record shows.

By the time the sanguinary series of events known as the Anglo-Irish War, circa 1919–21 broke over his head, he had acquired a sergeant's stripes and a wife, Mary Guider, from Templetuohy, County Tipperary, where the Guiders, a farming family, have been recorded for centuries. Mary, or Marianne as she became known in later life, though Mary appears on her baptismal certificate, was tall, strikingly good-looking, and had twelve brothers and sisters. She and Patrick, however, restricted themselves to a mere seven children – four boys and three girls – of whom my mother, Beatrice, was the youngest. Patrick, in the manner of Irish policemen everywhere, had taken care to ensure that the day job did not get in the way of amassing a little capital. Stationed at a place called Hazlehatch, adjacent to the banks of the Grand Canal in County Kildare, he had realised that the canal's towpath and Hazlehatch's strategic location made it an excellent site for a pound. This he used not alone to impound stray animals but to provide lairage for cattle being driven along the canal en route to or from the Dublin market, and, most importantly, he also ran a post office.

The good news from all this was that the income he generated enabled him to provide his children with access to education – if they wished to apply themselves. The eldest and the youngest did not. The eldest, my uncle Joe, after a spell during the First World War in the Royal Army Flying Corps, opted for a lifelong quest to establish a world record for the consumption of whiskey. Thanks to my father, he ended his working life filed away in the fingerprinting section of Garda Headquarters in the Phoenix Park, Dublin, and cared for at home by the older of his two sisters, my saintly aunt Josephine, a nurse, who took him into her house and looked after him until he died. Something in Joe's rearing, and/or his mother's attitude towards him, may have had a bearing on his drinking. Marianne's first child, who had died in his second year of infancy, had also been named Joseph, and the first girl was named Josephine. There were suggestions in the family that the surviving Joseph was made to feel somehow inferior to the lost one.

The youngest, my mother Beatrice, born in 1905, exuded the most powerful force field. Along with a lively intelligence, and the most good looks and personality, not alone in the family, but among her contemporaries generally, she decided at an early age that it was a poor family that could not afford at least one lady. With Patrick's doting connivance, Beatrice duly cast herself in that role. She fought off all efforts to foist a formal education on her, complaining bitterly about her treatment at boarding school and teacher training college, but went on to become a prominent and much sought-after figure in Dublin society. With long brown hair streaming to her waist, in her day she was acknowledged as one of the best-looking women in Ireland. In fact, as we shall see, she was crowned a beauty queen in 1927. She also wrote a column for the *Evening Herald* and took part in a number of Abbey Theatre and Radio Eireann repertory productions.

The other children included Frank and Tim, who became priests, and Irene, who died at the age of seventeen following a mastoid operation. Her beauty was such that family tradition has it that when she died, the famous Dublin wit and surgeon Oliver St John Gogarty suggested that she should have been painted by the artist Augustus John. My mother's youngest brother, Patrick, is remembered for having obtained the best exam results of anyone in the family while he was at school. During the First World War he served in the Royal Army Pay Corps. The Irish authorities subsequently placed him in charge not of disbursement, but extracting money from the people of County Wexford as the county's income-tax collector.

The bad news broke over the family during the Anglo-Irish War, when my uncles Tim and Frank were away in Italy, studying for the priesthood in Genoa. It came in the form of an IRA flying column, which raided the Toals. Ireland being the small intimate society it is, I suppose it was not all that wild a coincidence that I would one day go to school with the son of a member of the column. More than thirty years later my schoolmate's father gave me a detailed account of what happened. The ex-column member, Sean Redmond, who was at the time a tailor in Dun Laoghaire, told me that it was well recognised amongst the members of the flying column that Patrick Toal was not one of those policemen who made it their business to harass the IRA. All that was sought were the takings from the post office, which were of course refundable.

However, according to Redmond my grandmother made a decisive, and disastrous, intervention. A member of the Mother Torrential school of Irish womanhood, who kept her vocal chords at a peak of operational, if not prudential, efficiency through constant use, she addressed the column's leader in the following terms: 'How well you would not have dared to come around here when my two fine sons Tim and Frank were at home – you *bastard*!'

Unfortunately the gentleman standing in front of Marianne happened to be the only commander of a flying column in O'glaigh na hÉireann (the Army of the Irish Republic) who had been born on the wrong side of the blanket – no easy situation in the Ireland of the time. Enraged at Marianne's outburst in front of his men, he ordered that the Toals be burned out. My mother used to embellish the story by saying that he also ordered that her pony and her little dog be immolated, and could describe her shock at seeing the smoking ruins the following morning in the most moving terms. However, as she was away at teacher training college at the time, did not have a pony, and Redmond strenuously denied the incineration of any livestock, I have to regard the jury as being out on that particular aspect of the family history. But what is unquestionable is that the burning left Patrick Toal, my grandfather, out of favour both with the Protestants of the North and his 'own kind' in the South.

However, his abilities ensured that his fortunes recovered within a few years and he ultimately took his revenge on Catholic, Protestant and dissenter alike by becoming an income-tax collector for the counties of Dublin and Wicklow, a post that in those days seems to have carried with it a percentage of the monies collected. At all events Patrick was able to buy a fine three-storey red-brick terraced house in Kenilworth Square, Rathgar, a fashionable district whose pretensions at the time gave rise to music-hall jokes about the 'Rawthgarh' accent.

An anecdote told to me by a former colleague of his in the RIC illustrates the quick-wittedness that took Patrick from the smoking ruin of Hazlehatch to red-bricked Rathgar. Apparently one Christmas Eve, while he was at the height of his income-tax-collecting incarnation, a young Garda walking down Rathgar Road noticed something odd about the way in which Patrick's car was slowly approaching him. Although not the brightest member of the force, the Garda deduced what was wrong as Patrick drew abreast of him. The car was being driven on the wrong side of the road! Excitedly the young Garda waved Patrick down. When he discovered the driver's identity, the Garda apologised for having had to stop him, but pointed out the not unsubstantial reason for his action, and began talking about needing to take particulars. Patrick, with his RIC background, was the epitome of understanding. He assured the young man that he understood perfectly, that he too was a man subject to authority, and opening the passenger-seat door, invited the Garda into the car so that they could drive to nearby Rathmines Police Station to speedily complete the formalities away from prying eyes.

Once inside the station, however, the courteous, genial Patrick Toal turned, in the phrase of my informant, 'as thick as bottled pig shit'. Not alone did he demand lawyers, doctors and suchlike, he seemingly also required the attendance of the archbishop of Dublin, the governor-general, the chief justice and, most important, the local chief superintendent, who was eventually, reluctantly, induced to leave a Christmas celebration and come to the station.

Somewhat curtly, he expressed surprise at seeing Patrick in such surroundings and enquired how he came to be there. Patrick replied that he had no idea, that his family would be distraught at his non-appearance at this most solemn of family occasions, and that the superintendent should address his enquiries to the young policeman who had brought him to the station. By now more than a little distraught himself, the young Garda burst out: 'You know very well why I brought you. You were driving under the influence of drink.'

'Oh!' exclaimed Patrick. 'And how did I get here?'

The victim led with his chin: 'You know damn well how we got here! Didn't you drive me here yourself?!'

Legend hath it that the superintendent apologised to Patrick, helped him on with his coat, escorted him to his car, made arrangements for the transfer of the young Garda to the Aran Islands, where, at the time, there was no vehicular traffic, and returned to his celebration.

At the time of the burning of Patrick's home, in another part of the forest my father, Edward, or Eamonn O'Cuagain, as he preferred to be known in the Irish form, was busily engaged on the IRA and Sinn Fein side of the argument. Good-looking, tall, strong-voiced, with reddish curly hair and a sense of humour, he was the sort of man who stood out in a crowd both because of looks and personality. A friend of his who attended St Kieran's College in Kilkenny city with him and later became parish priest of my father's native village, Castlecomer in County Kilkenny, told me that 'Ned', as he was generally known, was 'a big fellow and a great hurler. At the time there was a sort of loutish attitude towards studious pupils, "swots" they were called, and they were bullied. But no one bullied Ned.'

Loutish the students may have been, but Kilkenny itself is one of Ireland's castellated, courtly places, a Sarlat-la-Canéda set down in the Irish countryside. A countryside which in microcosm tells the story of Ireland through its architecture. The city itself contains an impressive reminder of the days of the English conquest, being dominated by the impressive Kilkenny Castle. A few miles away in the town of Callan there is a single-storey thatched house preserved in the name of a man who in his time was more prosperous than most of his fellow Catholics, Edmund Ignatius Rice (1762–1844). Rice was the wealthy merchant who in 1803 founded the Christian Brothers, the controversial movement that educated rural peasant and urban poor, and so helped to unpick the seams of conquest. Today Kilkenny seems an unlikely place to have given the world the description 'fighting like Kilkenny cats', commemorated by a local nursery rhyme:

There wanst was two cats of Kilkenny.
Each cat thought there was one cat too many.
So they fought and they fit
And they scratched and they bit
Till instead of two cats there weren't any.

The rhyme dates from the days when, in common with several other Irish cities, Kilkenny had an 'Irishtown', populated by the natives, and an 'Englishtown', behind whose fortified walls the planters sheltered. The mutual hostility between the two was symbolised by the way the cats from each settlement fought each other at every hand's, or paw's, turn. Bored Cromwellian soldiers took to enlivening their off-duty hours by tying together the tails of cats from the two enclaves and hanging them over a rope. In the ensuing fights to the death the Irishtown, or Kilkenny cat, inevitably won.

Kilkenny people and, in particular, its all-conquering hurling team came to be known as 'the cats' to symbolise a fighting spirit. During my Kilkenny boyhood holidays a hurley was the natural extension of one's right arm. Apart from playing with lads of my own age I would sometimes stand on a sideline, vying with my contemporaries for the honour of 'returning balls', striking an out-of-play ball back onto the pitch where the seniors were playing. When I first heard of this schoolboy role, I scornfully declared that I was going to play with the seniors, but after ten seconds of watching the ferocity of the 'clash of the ash' I was both profoundly grateful for the security of the sideline and imbued with a respect and admiration for hurling that abides with me still.

Where some branches of the Coogan clan are concerned, there would appear to be a bugle in the blood concerning what is known as the National Issue. A formerly widespread dig at Castlecomer people was to call them 'piss in the powders'. This stems mainly from the presence not so much of the locals, but of the large numbers of Yorkshire and Welsh miners who lived in the area during the 1798 Irish Rebellion. When tiredness and alcohol had sent the insurgents safely to sleep, the miners, and possibly some local sympathisers, rendered some of their meagre store of gunpowder useless by urinating in it.

My ancestors apparently stood aside from this display of liquid imperialism, a fact that my then employer at the *Irish Press*, Vivion de Valera, brought to my attention for his own purposes one evening at his home in Blackrock, County Dublin. Vivion had summoned me there hoping, with the assistance of a couple of props, to convince me that he knew, understood and sympathised with where I was coming from but – and it was a very forceful 'but' – that nevertheless I should tone down my editorials on Northern Ireland. The props were a bottle of Jameson Irish whiskey and a memoir of one of the 1798 leaders, who described how, as the defeated rebels approached Castlecomer, the inhabitants either fled or closed their doors, lest they be sent to the gallows for giving aid and comfort to the insurgents. Vivion had the memoir open at a passage that read that the only exceptions amongst the villagers were 'a family of Coogans who came out to welcome us and treated us most kindly'.

At least one member of the clan suffered terribly for his assistance to the rebels. On 25 June 1798 the Yeomanry, descendants of Cromwellian soldiers settled in the area, suspended a Patrick Coogan by his thumbs from the upturned shafts of a cart in his farmyard at a place called Coolraheen. He was then stripped and flogged with a cat-o'-nine-tails until his ribs showed and his entrails protruded from his stomach. Incredibly he survived. The floggers departed after his belly burst, and his mother was able to kick away the dogs, which were lapping up his blood, free him from the cart and somehow nurse him back to health.

Why some Coogans should differ so markedly from the majority of their neighbours, or indeed how they were able to survive such a public display of their difference, is a matter of speculation. The Irish branch of the clan goes back to the fifth century, when they were recorded as being followers of the Connacht king Maine Mor. But a Welsh branch of the sept sprang up as part of the legacy of what were euphemistically described as 'the companies of gentlemen' who joined Strongbow on his invasion of Ireland in 1169–72. The name Cogan derives from the village of Cogan between Cardiff and Penarth, and became common around Cork and Wexford. The unfortunate Patrick Coogan's father was born in Wexford, which may help to explain Patrick's empathy with the Wexford rebels. My father's presence in Sinn Fein is more easily explicable. There was a general move towards Sinn Fein amongst the young men of the time in the wake of the 1916 Rising, and the Black and Tans helped to underscore his sense of patriotism by beating up his father, Timothy.

To judge from what is known of the socio-economic history of the Coogans and of the various local families they married into – Joyces, Houlihans, Brennans, Pooles, Comefords, Shores and many other traditional Kilkenny patronymics – they were generally comfortably off, possessing either a little land or a small business, which would have put them a few degrees above the general standard of living of those present, but not of course anything near that of the great Anglo-Irish families of the county. Where Castlecomer was concerned, the most important family were the Wandesfordes, who at one time owned over twenty-two thousand acres in the area. Sir Christopher Wandesforde founded the town in 1635. He was apparently a man of taste who appointed an Italian architect to lay out Castlecomer, which is said to be modelled on the Italian town of Alsinore.

The Wandesfordes also founded the anthracite mines that brought the Yorkshire and Welsh miners into contact with the 1798 rebels. During my boyhood, although the British navy had long since gone over to oil, there was still sufficient industrial and domestic demand for the smokeless coal to keep several hundred men employed. A verse credited to an anonymous seventeenth-century scribe extols the virtues of Kilkenny city and of Castlecomer as follows:

> *Fire without smoke,*
> *Air without fog,*
> *Water without mud,*
> *Land without bog.*

The mudless water reference is to the limestone paving of Kilkenny city, which kept mud from the streets, but the other properties described concern the effects of the anthracite on Castlecomer. In fact while it is true that the anthracite did not smoke, some of my earliest memories are of sitting in my grandparents' kitchen, eyes smarting, an acrid sensation in my chest, waiting for the anthracite-fired range to draw properly. The anthracite was dangerous in other ways also. In the summer I spent holidays in the home of my father's uncle Johnny Joyce. The Joyces owned a pub and a farm in a small village near Castlecomer called Clogh, where the boys and younger men of the district swam in the Dinan River. Being accustomed to the suntanned bodies of people who swam regularly in the sea, I used to marvel at the extreme whiteness of the miners. Another memento of their underground lives was the peculiar scarring most of them bore. Coal wounds heal blue – if they heal. Another characteristic of the mines was that they took a regular toll of life. Every year it seemed that when I came down from Dublin for the holidays, some man with whom I had swum the previous year had been killed in a pit accident.

Another Dinan memory concerns trout fishing. My knowledge of this activity stemmed from reading stories of English life wherein people accoutred with flasks and split-cane rods expertly dropped flies into the mouths of rising trout. In Clogh, however, the rare white trout in which the river then abounded were killed differently, chiefly by spearing and snaring, although other methods were also sometimes used. One was to 'tickle' them gently upwards with one's fingers until they could be suddenly hurled onto the riverbank. A less skilful and altogether barbaric method involved dropping a sack of lime into a pool and collecting the poisoned fish as they drifted to the surface. I became quite skilful myself at snaring. This meant carefully slipping a loop, made from a strand of rabbit-snare wire tied to a hazel stick, over the head and body of a trout before striking upwards with the sudden expertise of any English fly fisherman. I was thirteen before I saw a fishing rod used in Clogh. It was carried by a man described to me as 'the Fianna Fail postman' and was my first introduction to the powers of that party.

Not surprisingly the fishing methods of my youth, coupled with modern agricultural chemicals, mean that the white trout of the Dinan have disappeared. So too have the Wandesfordes. They were archetypical colonialists, in their heyday brave, entrepreneurial, tough. The family used to boast that they never yielded to strikes or any other form of pressures to change the way they ran the mines. But they had to yield to the changes forced by time itself. During my boyhood a Captain Wandesforde, the master of the local hunt, could still be seen on his hunter, riding through the town his ancestor had founded. However, by then the mines were nearing the end of their days, and most of the land had been sold.

The Wandesfordes were responsible for one of the first incidents that as a child made me realise the split-level nature of my existence between the Wandesfordes, middle-class Dublin and my father's home environment. One St Stephen's Day when I was about eight I went with the wren boys, 'collecting for the wran' to the great Wandesforde house. I was uncomfortable in equal measure at entering such a grand place uninvited, a home far larger than any I was used to, as well as by the fact that most of my companions in the adventure, some fifty or sixty boys and men, were what in Dublin would have been termed 'common', coming from homes far less imposing than my own. In the summer these lads usually 'went in the bare ones'– i.e. barefoot, to save shoe leather. Not realising that shoelessness was an enforced condition, and not a custom to be emulated, I used to go barefoot myself in the summer and as a result picked up an endless succession of colds and cuts.

On that Boxing Day we stood on the gravel outside the house, where I joined somewhat uncomprehendingly in the chanting of various verses about 'the wran, the wran, the king of all birds', which on St Stephen's Day was caught in the furze. Then we waited. For what I did not know. Suddenly a second-storey window opened, a female hand emerged and

threw down a few coins. A very few. I picked up what later turned out to
be the most valuable one and, before a bigger boy took it from me,
recognised it as being an English threepenny piece. Though I did not realise
it at the time, I was witnessing a small part in a larger drama that was still
being enacted all over Ireland. It was entitled the Continuing Decline of
the Big House and the Remnants of the Anglo-Irish Ascendancy. That
particular big house fell into ruin and was eventually destroyed by fire.
There's an arts and craft centre there now and the public are free to walk
through what was once a walled demesne.

Despite proceeding unscathed through St Kieran's, my father decided, after
playing a hurling match at Knockbeg College in County Carlow, that its
facilities were preferable to those of the Kilkenny college and persuaded
his mother to part with the extra money needed to send him there. My
father's parents at that stage owned land, and a flourishing pub cum
general store. A native of the district, James Comeford, who became a
judge of the New York federal court and famously ran the great St Patrick's
Day Parade with an iron hand for many decades, wrote a history of
Kilkenny. In it he described my grandfather, Timothy Coogan, as 'a successful businessman'. Perspective is all. My mother's version was that 'Tim
Coogan drank out half the town of Castlecomer.' Anyhow, appropriately
enough, it is true that, although the family once owned more property
than most, it was the pub at the corner of Castlecomer's main square that
remained after his death. The survival of the pub is probably a tribute to
my grandmother, remembered as being a businesslike, devout woman
whose most noteworthy holiday excursion was an annual two-day retreat
in Kilkenny city, some twelve miles away. Thither she and a female companion would set off in a pony and trap each year, leaving Timothy to
comfort himself during her absence by immersion in the oral Irish tradition.
This included a mastery of the arts of Jameson and Powers whiskies,
Guinness's stout and the locally brewed Smithwick's ale. It may or may
not be safe to extrapolate from the fact that in that era of large families
and no contraception there was a lack of other forms of comfort in the
couple's life. They had only two children, my father and a girl, Mary.

St Kieran's and Knockbeg, founded, like other similar institutions, as
diocesan seminaries in the latter part of the eighteenth century, played an
important role in the development of the Church, both in Ireland and
internationally. The priests and bishops they produced spread the faith to
points as far apart as Australia, Argentina, Newfoundland and America.
By my father's time the colleges had expanded their role to cater for the

children of Ireland's small farmers, shopkeepers and publicans who wished to become upwardly mobile within the British system. After independence was secured these colleges built on the work of the Christian Brothers to provide the backbone of the administration, security and law-enforcement agencies of the new state.

The Irish educational system was the result of a tug of war between the forces of the two colonialisms, Mother England and Mother Church. The Irish national school system was set up to produce students who thought of themselves as loyal English children. The clergy and nuns who came largely to control the system saw to it that their pupils – along, let it be said, with receiving a good general education – were conditioned to ensure that Mother Church's empire would be strengthened both at home and abroad. Amongst the religious the Christian Brothers in particular sought to impart a distinctive sense of Irish nationalist identity. Ireland could only definitively be said to be throwing off both of these motherly yokes, and not always with the happiest of outcomes, in the era during which this book was written – for example, Irish society has not yet managed to adjust to the consequences of the departure of the Church from the running of the health services; in contrast to the strict but efficient authoritarianism of the nuns, there arose haphazard managerial systems in which respon-sibilities became less obvious than entitlements. Standards of hygiene fell, salaries increased, particularly amongst consultants, and there arose phenomena never known before, such as deadly hospital bugs and the scandal of patients, some of them suffering from cancer, awaiting beds on trolleys, sometimes for days.

In my father's time, though both educators and the educated were often rough-hewn, conditions harsh and discipline severe, to judge from the rows of his neat, carefully preserved schoolbooks the curriculum was impressive. My father could read and write in both Greek and Latin, spoke fluent French and Irish, wrote good English, enjoyed history and geography, and had what I considered a deplorable fondness for appalling things like calculus. When I was a boy, one of his frequent abjurations to me was 'If you don't pass your exams, I'll put you to break stones.' Being the type who could not pass an exam if they set it themselves, I spent many an agonised moment eyeing my father's schoolbooks and wondering where I was going to acquire experience in the theory and practice of sledge-hammers. I was much more at home with some of his other books, such as a complete set of the writings of Patrick Pearse, or works dealing with the lives of little-known figures in Irish history like Sir Cahir O'Doherty or Galloping O'Hogan, which helped to fire my own interest in history.

My father's sister, Mary, predeceased him in her early forties after contracting tuberculosis. She married a James Comeford, to whom she bore two sons, my first cousins James and Timothy. The family owned a farm, a shop and later a post office, which survived for much longer than did Patrick Toal's. Their home is located on the Dublin road outside Castlecomer at a place called Coolbawn, which on 18 June 1921 became the site of one of the last IRA ambushes in the county before the truce of 11 July of that year, which it was mistakenly hoped would mark the beginning of the end of Anglo-Irish hostilities.

My father used his influence with Michael Collins to have explosives sent down from Dublin to the local IRA column to make a mine for use in what was intended to be a large-scale ambush. In the event, it was the ambushers who were ambushed. Two volunteers were killed and another seriously injured. The IRA had detained passers-by in a holding site near the road so that no word of the ambush preparations would reach the barracks in Castlecomer. One of those held was a labourer who lived in terror of his fiery employer, a Protestant lady, a Miss Florence Draper, who owned a large farm nearby. The labourer persuaded the ambushers that he'd lose his job if he missed work. He was released, promising not to say what had delayed him. But his lateness to work led to his employer haranguing the truth out of him. She informed the police and a party of police and military took the IRA by surprise. Support for the Crown in Castlecomer at the time was not confined to the Protestant community. At the funeral mass for the dead volunteers, the parish priest preached a sermon in which he thanked God that it was only men of the IRA and not members of the Crown forces who had lost their lives.

Nevertheless Coolbawn, like the decline of the Wandesfordes, helps to explain why, after the Troubles had ended, so many Protestants left the South for the North, England and the colonies, thus helping to buttress the attitudes that sustained partition. After the funerals the IRA burned Miss Draper's house. Her sister, Rebecca, agreed to the IRA's request that she remove herself to an outhouse with her money and valuables, and members of the column actually re-entered the house, before the fire fully took hold, to rescue her good clothes. But the indomitable Florence, a Protestant version of Marianne Toal, refused to come out and threw hand grenades at the raiders. Then she took her dogs to the roof of the house, climbed into a large steel water tank and fired Very lights to attract the Crown forces. She was ultimately rescued, but the house was destroyed and the land was bought eventually by the Irish Land Commission and redistributed.

Before he went on the run during the Anglo-Irish War my father had taken primary degrees in commerce and law at University College, Dublin. His marks were such that he was awarded a travelling scholarship, which, had he taken it up, would probably have led to his becoming a high official in the British Colonial Service and ending his days as Sir Edward Coogan, OBE. The offer was delayed in reaching him because a landlady forgot to send it on. Even if she had not delayed it, there is doubt as to whether he would have abandoned his Sinn Fein colleagues at that stage. Family folklore has it that his response to a colleague who said 'I suppose this means you'll be leaving us now, Ned' was 'Sure I've put my hand to the plough and there's no turning back.'

He seems to have had a special aptitude for the work he was engaged in – intelligence-gathering, presiding over Sinn Fein conventions held to select candidates for the underground Dail and helping to set up an alternative system of courts and local government administration that hollowed out British administrative and legal control. My mother often quoted the works of Kevin O'Higgins, not a man known for the indiscriminate bestowal of praise, who wished publicly that 'Coogan had six brothers'. But I remember as a boy of ten, fired with stories about the War of Independence, being bitterly disappointed by my father's reply to my question as to what he did in the war. 'Tim,' he said, 'I'm delighted to say I never killed a man.'

Following a short stint as principal of the Commercial College in Limerick, he became one of the local government inspectors who set up the local government system in the new state in the teeth of peasant avarice and chicanery. For when the Anglo-Irish War ended, many a Paudeen not merely recommended fumbling in greasy tills; he would loot them where possible. In November 1921 my father set an exam for candidates for the post of secretary to the Kerry County Home. He was supervising it in Killarney when a number of masked and armed men burst into the hall, ordered that the examination be stopped, gathered up the papers and departed with much fulmination against 'cowards' and 'slackers'. These, it was averred, were getting good jobs, while decent men languished in jail. Decoded, this was Kerry-speak for the fact that a local candidate had the backing of an IRA faction.

However, my father sat up all night resetting another exam paper and the examination duly went ahead, with the post awarded to the candidate who came first. Alas, no sooner was my father's back turned than a local politician came to the unfortunate victor and 'suggested' to him that it would be best if he stood down in favour of another candidate. Kerry being Kerry, the request was acceded to. In the conditions of the time therefore, it was not surprising that an early attempt to create an unarmed police force after the treaty's signing collapsed when anti-treaty opposition, and inexperience on the part of its first commissioner, combined to produce a mutiny.

The man chosen to head a new, reorganised force was General Eoin O'Duffy, the then commander-in-chief of the army. Michael Collins had thought so highly of O'Duffy that before his death, in August 1922, he had spoken of him as his successor. But the cautious W. T. Cosgrave, who succeeded Collins as head of the government, had reservations about the able but mercurial O'Duffy. For one thing he had been the main protagonist of Collins's two-pronged approach to the dissident republicans. In the South, in order to uphold the treaty, they were hounded and harried. In the North, to undermine partition and *ipso facto* to secure the backing for the treaty of border-county members of the Dail, the IRA received money and guns with which to attack the Unionist administration. On Collins's behalf O'Duffy had overseen cross-border raids, the kidnappings of Orangemen, and lent his support to policies (which were officially denied) such as paying Northern nationalist schoolteachers not to cooperate with the British educational system. Cosgrave, however, deplored such measures, and abandoned them almost immediately after Collins's funeral.

Accordingly when circumstances dictated that O'Duffy had to be appointed the head of the new police force, An Garda Síochana na hÉireann (Guardians of the Peace of Ireland), Cosgrave sent for my father, in November 1922, and told him: 'Ned! You know we're setting up this new police force and we have to put Eoin in charge. But you know he's a wild man. I want you to keep an eye on him.' And so, on 1 January 1923, at the age of twenty-eight, my father assumed responsibilities for setting up an unarmed police force in the middle of a civil war. During 1923 and part of 1924 he actually ran the force while O'Duffy was out of the country.

A lasting legacy of that period is today's Garda monogram, the insignia GS. While O'Duffy was away, the government moved to change the insignia to SE, Saorstat Eireann, the Irish Free State. However, my father, a staunch believer in Irish unity, objected to this, saying:

We who are looking ahead look upon the guard as the Civil Guard of Ireland and not of any portion thereof. To treat the Guard as a portion of Ireland rather than a Guard for the entire country would be, to my mind, a great mistake [...] Surely it is not seriously suggested that we must change our badges in order to make it clear that we are a police force for only twenty-six counties of Ireland.

He proposed that if there was an objection to 'An Garda Siochana na hEireann', there was an even bigger one to 'Royal Ulster Constabulary', which would be more appropriately styled 'Royal Six Counties of Ulster Constabulary'!

'Keeping an eye' on O'Duffy, however, caused no difficulty – the pair became such friends that O'Duffy later acted as my father's best man – but the conditions of the time did, as the following (authenticated) story illustrates.

In October 1922 Garda Michael Conneally and two other members of the force were sent to Oranmore, County Galway, a strongly anti-treaty area. Here the small party lived by the generosity of a young couple who, with exceptional moral courage, gave them lodgings. This assistance combined with food parcels, money from home and working for local farmers enabled the three Gardai to survive in Oranmore for the next five months, during which time they received neither pay nor furniture for their empty barracks. The station records were kept in a biscuit tin. Showings of the flag such as appearances in uniform had to be largely confined to attending, and sometimes serving, mass on Sundays. It was not safe for members of the party to take to the roads alone.

One day in February 1923, as Michael Conneally was assisting the woman of the house to churn butter in the kitchen, a resplendent uniformed figure knocked on the kitchen door and enquired of the lady if she could get a message to the station party. Startled, the lady opined that she could. Conneally kept his back studiously turned to the uniformed apparition – the duties of a Garda are multifarious, but in the shock of the moment Michael did not feel up to explaining to Deputy Commissioner Coogan how these came to include butter-making. My father trained his gaze equally studiously on a point some six inches to the right of the policeman's ear and well clear of his blue police-uniform trousers, while asking the woman if she would be good enough to inform the missing party that Deputy Commissioner Coogan would be back in an hour to conduct an inspection.

An hour later Conneally introduced himself and his colleagues to the deputy commissioner, who gravely took note of all they had to say, promised that they would have all their requirements met with shortly and departed adjuring them to 'make friends with the people. Keep talking to the people. Stand by the people and they'll make friends with you.' Butter-churning was not discussed, and Michael Conneally would later say that my father's advice was the best he had ever received. A week later an army lorry, escorted by armed soldiers, drew up outside Oranmore Garda Station bringing the young men their arrears of pay and all the furnishing and bedding required to make the station habitable.

A few months later the Civil War ended, and though the country was still in a state of near-anarchy, a general election was called. It was in effect a referendum on the treaty. Conneally and his men were drafted in to the major polling centre of Athenry to ensure that the diktat of a local anti-treaty IRA warlord was not implemented. He had threatened that 'Anyone who votes in this traitors' election will have to deal with me.' Conneally, a very large man who, prior to the split over the treaty, had been an active IRA man himself, sent word to the warlord that anyone who interfered with voters would have to deal with him! Voting went ahead successfully.

But then the IRA commander vowed that the votes would never get to the counting centre in Galway. He lined up his men, armed with horse-whips, outside the gates, so that anyone emerging carrying the locked iron boxes containing the votes would have to run the gauntlet with, as Conneally afterwards told his daughter, 'the local parish priest roaring approval from the upstairs window of the presbytery'. Conneally, however, piled up the boxes in the well of a jaunting-car and then, with himself and his colleagues sitting protectively on the edges of the car, had the gates of the polling centre's courtyard unexpectedly thrown open and drove the frenzied pony through the off-balance, though whip-wielding, melee. Bloodied but definitely unbowed, the party got the votes to Galway, where they formed part of a landslide victory in favour of stability and an end to the destruction of life and property that now had to be paid for by the Irish themselves. As a measure of the straitened resources available to the new government to make such payments, it should be noted that at the end of 1921 the Cosgrave government made available £100,000 for local government. This was less than a tenth of what the British grants had amounted to.

The years of the High Heroic were at an end, and to underline their closure such unlooked-for by-products of revolution as Irish tax collectors and rate collectors made their appearance throughout the land. The latter were especially unwelcome, as the cumulative destruction wrought by the Anglo-Irish War and the Civil War necessitated the levying of higher demands than in the past. It might be remarked that another price that had to be paid for independence was a legislative tribute to Rome. The new Free

State government also dutifully introduced legislation bringing the twenty-six counties' laws into conformity with Catholic teaching on such matters as censorship, contraception and divorce. The Second Colonialism had rendered unto Christ.

Yet my father's lot as a policeman now grew somewhat happier, as did that of Michael Conneally and those like him. It took a while for the democratic penny to drop. Parliamentary proceedings were decidedly lopsided. Although de Valera and his followers contested elections, at which they consistently polled well, they remained outside the Dail because they refused to take the oath of allegiance to the Crown enjoined by the treaty. With de Valera and his supporters doing what they could to desta-bilise the new regime, the tiny Labour Party constituted the opposition, which tried, unavailingly, to curb the new government's zeal for balancing the books at the expense of the poverty-stricken.

De Valera did not begin the process of cutting free of his IRA tail until 1926, when he formed the Fianna Fail Party (Warriors of Destiny), and he took a further decade before severing it completely. However, he was forced to enter the Dail in 1927 after the murder of Kevin O'Higgins, the government's strongman minister for justice. The killing elicited emergency legislation which meant that he either passed under the yoke of the Oath or forfeited his seat. Thus the infant Irish democracy was allowed out of its Civil War crib and began to grow stronger, although unemployment and the continued presence of an IRA faction opposed to the government ensured that the two sitting tenants of the Irish political underbelly – murder and armed robbery – remained on the premises of Cathleen ni Houlihan. That indispensable tool of early Irish elections, the knuckle-duster, also remained in demand.

CHAPTER 2

A Policeman's Lot

M y father continued to enjoy the fruits of bachelorhood for almost six years after becoming deputy commissioner. Though his job was demanding, and frequently dangerous, he had the consolation of the officers' mess, police-driven cars and membership of Dublin's better golf clubs. My mother used to claim that he had the longest drive in Hermitage Golf Club. As he was nine years older than her, and one of Dublin's more eligible bachelors, I often wondered impiously in latter life if perhaps there was some underlying meaning to that claim which might have eluded her. In any event she told us children that she first met our father at a ball to which she had been escorted by a wealthy Dublin baker, Vere Downes. There was an immediate mutual attraction and, according to her, they hid from her escort in the cloakroom at the end of the dance and left together.

Around the same time (in 1927) my mother was crowned Dublin's Civic Queen of Beauty. Paris had recently selected a civic queen and the Dublin city managers thought that it would be a fitting thing for Dublin, the capital of an emerging new state, to have one also. So the Parisian lady was brought over to Dublin to assist in my mother's coronation. Sub-sequently my mother had two comments on the event. One, that she had only gone to it to cover the crowning for the *Evening Herald* and had not realised that someone had entered her for the competition until she won it! Two, that it was 'a dignified event in keeping with the dignity of the new state. None of that vulgar bathing-costume nonsense.'

The couple's wedding at the Church of the Three Patrons, Rathgar, in November 1928, with Eoin O'Duffy as best man, was one of the social events of the year. With their looks and personalities, for the early years of their married life they seemed a golden couple, destined for happiness if anyone was. Alas, the innocent and the beautiful do have more enemies than time.

At first they led a glittering social life. Dances, race meetings, tennis parties, Continental holidays and lavish dinner parties were the order of the day. By all accounts a dinner party hosted by my mother was an Event. Her taste in food, furnishings and literature was impeccable. A lady who taught English once told me that within a week of a new class's enrolment she could tell which students had come from homes where television predominated and which had grown up with books. I fear that my cultural persona imprint never properly reflected the impact of the many volumes that adorned the bookshelves of my parents' home. I remember in particular a complete set of the works of Galsworthy, bound in calfskin and printed on rice paper, which had been given to my mother by an admirer. The contents of the set at least remained with me to the extent that when *The Forsythe Saga* appeared on television I felt that I was seeing photographs of people with whose lives I was already familiar. Mother, or 'Mammy', as we always called her, blended cullings from upper-class English and European dinner tables with peculiarly Irish touches, such as the wearing of huge, ornate Tara brooches to fasten multicoloured embroidered capes, which, she averred, were once worn by the ancient Irish queens. She had a fondness for historical accounts of furnishings and décor, which she put to good use in her novel *The Big Wind*, which she would write some years later. Amidst the careful wives of cautious officials and conservative politicians she shone precariously, like a hummingbird in a bog.

In the theatre of her mind she was always the star. But star quality comes with both an emotional and a financial cost, and unfortunately where money was concerned the future was a country that no one paid heed to after my parents married. And, along with the consequent threat from within to their financial security, an external, political time bomb was ticking away. De Valera's star was in the ascendant and that of the now exhausted and ideas-bereft Cosgrave administration was waning. The government had successfully fought a civil war, overseen the implanting of democratic institutions in the new state and won considerable international respect, particularly in the Dominions, for the manner in which the Irish Free State had used Imperial Conferences to achieve an increasing measure of legislative independence from London. A loyal army, an unarmed police force, an incorrupt civil service and slow recovery from the waste and ruin of civil war were not inconsiderable achievements.

In other writings I have described how de Valera himself showed a belated awareness of what independent Ireland's first government achieved. He told his son Vivion that when he took power, and could study the files, he found that his political foes had done 'a magnificent job'. But that admission was made in private and in the future. As election time neared, de Valera and his spokespersons depicted their opponents as being British lackeys and cashed in on the fact that their achievements were not the sort of deeds that fired the imagination of a patriarchal peasant proprietorship. Nor could it be denied that part of the Civil War's cost had been the bitterness engendered by the government's ruthlessly successful policy of reprisal executions, which sent seventy-seven men to the firing squads. Moreover the cost-cutting measures necessitated by the era of the Wall Street Crash did not make for popularity, especially as said measures were frequently enforced in the most ham-fisted and insensitive way possible – for example, by cutting a shilling a week off the blind pension. Even half a century later the historian Joseph Lee would judge that the newly liberated Irish poor were made to feel 'the lash of the liberators'. That lash cut deep electorally.

Apart from his ability to manipulate economic issues, anti-British feeling and civil war passions with the help of his own mesmeric personality and the hallowed reputation of being the last surviving commandant of 1916, de Valera by contrast could offer a programme of doles, subsidies and protective tariffs aimed at both the poor and the industrialist. He also had the benefit of a fanatically loyal and efficient election machine in which his cultivation of 'extremist support' ensured that Fianna Fail cumainn, or branches, by day sometimes became IRA flying columns by night. Above all he had the *Irish Press*, first published in September 1931, of which he was both the editor in chief and the controlling director. It would be some sixty years into the future before my researches for biographies of both Collins and de Valera himself publicised the fact that he funded the paper largely through a manoeuvre whereby he got control of money subscribed by Irish emigrants in America during the Anglo-Irish War to help their native country win its freedom. In the early 1930s all ordinary people were conscious of was that the *Irish Press* was a brilliant political newspaper and, in pre-television Ireland, had a tremendous impact that tipped the scales of the balance of power in the 1932 general election. De Valera won enough seats to form a government with the aid of Labour and a year later he went to the polls again, this time to win an overall majority.

As I made clear in my introduction, de Valera's dependence on the IRA dictated that one of his earliest targets would be the police force, which had been at war with the IRA allies who had campaigned enthusiastically for him during the election campaign. Gerald Boland, who was minister for justice under de Valera, assisted me during my writing of my IRA book by allowing me to see Department of Justice records of the clash with the IRA and the sometimes very brutal response of the Gardai during the

1920s and early 1930s. The records reveal what I later described as 'an appalling sequence of events', which reached a crescendo as the general election neared.

> The year 1931 was notable for a tremendous upsurge in IRA activity, for killings, shootings and for continual seizures of arms and ammunition by the police, and by October it was obvious that the normal processes of the law could no longer deal with the IRA and a military tribunal was instituted. The shootings of jurymen and police witnesses made it almost impossible to get a verdict in an ordinary court, and the IRA paper, *An Phoblacht*, was continually stoking the fires with sentiments such as the following for 20 June: '*An Phoblacht* states that the members of the CID should be treated as "social pariahs" [...] that treatment must be extended to [...] judges and district justices, to uniformed police – to every individual who is a willing part of the machine, by which our Irish patriots are being tortured'.

De Valera's first major action on the day he took power was a gesture of conciliation towards the IRA. His ministers for defence and for justice, Frank Aiken and James Geoghegan, were dispatched to Arbour Hill Prison to hold talks with IRA leaders. The republican prisoners were released the next day. The military tribunal was suspended and, during a victory tour of County Cork, de Valera studiously avoided a welcoming party of Gardai drawn up to greet his arrival in Skibbereen. But he then took a salute from an IRA guard of honour on the opposite side of the road.

O'Duffy's was the first of the 'uniformed police' heads to roll. He was sacked, having refused to accept a civil service post on the grounds that if he was not fit to remain in the police, he was not fit to remain anywhere in government service. Eamonn ('Ned') Broy, one of Michael Collins's principal spies in Dublin Castle, succeeded him. Another key Collins agent in the Castle, David Neligan, the major 'social pariah' of the CID, also went. While *An Phoblacht* had demanded O'Duffy's sacking, it was also whispered in political circles that he had been trying to put together a group of like-minded army and police officers to resist de Valera's takeover by force if necessary.

Whatever the substance of O'Duffy's plottings, he literally gave colour to the Fianna Fail administration's propaganda about him afterwards by organising what became known as the Blueshirt movement. Early in 1933 he became director general of a group called the National Guard, which had the quite defensible aim of allowing Cosgrave and his candidates a hearing at election meetings, which IRA and Fianna Fail supporters systematically attacked, using the slogan 'No free speech for traitors'. A colleague of my father's, John Moore, told me what I consider to be the root-situation anecdote of the birth of the Blueshirts. Moore, who eventually became a chief superintendent, was then a sergeant. He was ordered on duty with only two Gardai to support him at a famous riotous meeting in Cork at which Cosgrave was denied a hearing. Moore told me: 'The place was in uproar. It was frightening. Ned Cronin came up to me and asked what I was going to do about it. I told him I had only two men and could nothing. "Well, I'll do something," he said and he went back into the crowd, and the next thing I knew Cronin came back out of the crowd holding a man over his head.' Cronin would later become a prominent Blueshirt. At the time word had gone out that the police were to go easy on the IRA, and uniformed Gardai were being jostled and spat upon in the streets by the more loutish amongst the IRA.

In August 1933 O'Duffy announced that he intended to lead a National Guard march to Government Buildings to revive a wreath-laying ceremony at the Cenotaph in the grounds, commemorating Collins and Arthur Griffith, which de Valera had banned. De Valera saw the march as a bow not merely to the state's founders, but to Benito Mussolini. Though he had not mobilised the forces of the state to protect Cosgrave's meetings, he now did so to attack O'Duffy. Along with banning the march, calling up the army and reintroducing the military tribunal, he set up a new armed police unit – from within the ranks of the IRA. On the day before O'Duffy's planned march, literally overnight IRA men, including some of those who had been breaking up Cumann na nGaedheal Party meetings, were drafted into what was officially termed the S-Branch, but became popularly known as the Broy Harriers.

The new police unit was initially deprived of an opportunity to deploy its lethal skills because O'Duffy responded to the government preparations by calling off the march. However, the Broy Harriers showed their kidney a year later. A lorry was driven through the gates of Marsh's Cattle Yard in Cork in an attempt to disrupt a cattle sale. The S-Branch, who operated independently of the Cork police authorities, opened sustained rifle and revolver fire on the lorry's occupants as they took cover. A fifteen-year-old boy was shot dead. Later, awarding damages to the boy's father, a High Court judge described the S-Branch as 'an excrescence' on the normal police force. None of the S-Branch stood trial as a result of the shooting, however.

The reason for the cattle sale lay in the fact that de Valera had helped to turn up the heat under the political stewpot by an exercise in the Robert Mugabe school of agricultural economics. This resulted in an economic war with Britain. Part of his election platform had been a promise to withhold payment from the British of the land annuities paid by Irish farmers. These annuities were a repayment of the loans that the British government had raised to buy out the Anglo-Irish landlords in the late nineteenth and early twentieth centuries, redistributing the land to Irish small farmers. Of course many of the rural electorate naïvely thought that this meant that the payment of annuities would cease. However, while de Valera reduced them, and funded arrears for small farmers, he nevertheless collected, and retained, the monies in the Irish exchequer.

This was a popular measure with the owners of smallholdings, but it had dire consequences for the larger farmers. As the annuities were not passed on to London, the British responded by slapping retaliatory duties on Irish cattle landed in England, thereby virtually destroying the cattle trade. In fact at the time de Valera boasted that the cattle trade was 'gone for ever'. He cushioned the blow by distributing free meat from the unsaleable cattle. But many of the larger farmers reacted by withholding their annuity payments. As a result their cattle were seized and offered for sale at public auction. They were bought at knock-down prices by government agents, using fictitious names, because ordinary buyers did not dare purchase the animals in such circumstances. After O'Duffy had called off his Cenotaph march, sales such as Marsh's became a main focus of the S-Branch's attention.

But O'Duffy's activities soon recaptured their attention. Appearing to epitomise martyred constitutionalism, he was appointed the leader of the United Ireland Party, better known as Fine Gael, an amalgam of opposition parties, which W. T. Cosgrave facilitated by voluntarily stepping down in favour of O'Duffy. However, O'Duffy's 'wild man' qualities persisted. His shirted followers looked like the Irish version of the European fascist brown- and black-shirted followers of Hitler and Mussolini, and were certainly represented as such by their political foes. Also, probably more under the influence of John Jameson and Co. than of the philosophers of the corporate state, the speeches he actually delivered, as opposed to the staid scripts issued from Fine Gael Headquarters, grew more and more inflammatory. The *Irish Press* sent reporters after him and reported what he really said as opposed to what his scripts contained. After he advocated that farmers withhold not merely land annuities but rates, the more conservative-minded in Fine Gael deserted him and Cosgrave reassumed the party's leadership.

After the split O'Duffy continued to lead the Blueshirt movement under various new titles, as the government's lawyers outlawed one successor to the National Guard after another. Both the Blueshirts and the IRA dissipated their energies in futile set-tos at cattle sales and election rallies, or when the Blueshirts began protecting British products that the IRA had boycotted as part of the general anti-English economic war feeling in the country. The IRA's standard of political nous may be reckoned from the fact that its chief economic target became Bass Ale. No spin doctor would advocate the gaining of political sympathy in Ireland by destroying barrels of beer! The two movements further weakened themselves through internal splits, and de Valera was able to use the public-order situation to cripple the forces of both right and left through a calculated use of the reinstated military tribunal. Although the IRA regarded itself as the legitimate authority within the country, a sort of home-based government-in-exile, de Valera chose at first to ignore the threat posed by this second authority and went for the Blueshirts, 349 of whom were put away in 1934. Then he turned on the IRA and, curiously enough, by 1937 the score of imprisonments handed down by the military tribunal was a draw: Blueshirts 434, IRA 434. Both were out of the game, the Blueshirts permanently so, petering out after a botched attempt by O'Duffy to intervene on General Franco's side during the Spanish Civil War, and remembered today only as a term of political abuse to describe Fine Gael.

De Valera thus emerged to tower unassailably over the political landscape; he did not suffer an electoral defeat (in 1948) until more than a decade had passed. He was able to bring forward a new Constitution in 1937 that bound Christ and Caesar even closer together through its reflection of Catholic views such as a prohibition on divorce and a recognition of 'the special position' of the Catholic Church. It also purported to deal with the causes of the Irish Civil War by dispensing with the oath of allegiance and with the governor-general. The border was of course unaffected by these cosmetic changes. As was the IRA. But now de Valera's freedom of political movement transformed his tolerance for the IRA into a stern hostility. Over the next decade the organisation was crushed by measures that included the hangman, the firing squad and the internment camp, backed by an indifference to death on hunger strike that Margaret Thatcher herself could not have bettered.

However, all this lay in the future. Through most of the tumultuous 1930s, as de Valera was establishing his grip on power, my father somehow held on to his position as deputy commissioner. Although he liked the man, he had not joined O'Duffy's abortive schemings. He disliked de Valera, holding him chiefly responsible for the Civil War, but he was a convinced democrat who believed then, as he had believed earlier when he inspired Michael Conneally, that the will of the ballot should take precedence over that of the bomb and the bullet. Some years after his death I learned the meaning of the word 'shibboleth' from him. I looked it up in a dictionary after coming across a trunk full of his papers (now, alas, no more) in which there was the handwritten original of a memorandum he had circulated to new members of the force telling them that for the first time in her history the country had native government and an opportunity of democracy. The Gardai were 'in the forefront of the battle to give voice to the democratically expressed will of the people. Let no threat or shibboleth dissuade you from doing your duty.'

He was popular in the force with both officers and men. In those days of stern discipline he found ways of breathing humanity into the strict letter of the law. The Garda drivers of the time always liked being detailed to drive him, because they never knew what excursion they might find themselves involved in at the conclusion of the drab business of inspecting rural stations, deciding where new bus-stops should be sited, what licences granted and so forth. Unfortunately, in one aspect of his jovial personality lay his Achilles heel. Ned Coogan was also Tim Coogan's son when it came to a fondness for alcohol. For him, the officers' mess now ceased to be a convivial place of elastic mess bills, poker games, easy camaraderie and discreet drinking. Strange promotions were being made, demotions and sackings imposed. Tongues had to be guarded, companions chosen with care because Things Went Back.

Things also Went Out. The regime of intrigue and suspicion stemming from de Valera's attempt to maintain IRA support for Fianna Fail was such that my father was particularly targeted in 1933. He had tried to have the famous Cork IRA leader Tom Barry questioned in connection with two murders that occurred in Cork in 1933 and for which Barry was the chief suspect. In a memo that came into my possession as this book was being written, my father instructed the local officer in charge of the investigation, Chief Superintendent Fitzgerald:

> The murder of this unfortunate young man, Hugh O'Reilly, and the murder of Cornelius Daly within a very short period, and practically in the same locality discloses a very serious state of lawlessness in that portion of Cork and every effort should be made to solve these mysteries and bring the culprits to justice [...] Parties believed to be in personal danger, whether for political or other reasons, should receive adequate protection.

Strangely the Garda superintendent resisted my father's attempts to get him to interview Barry, claiming that to do so would jeopardise an informant.

In those days of indulgence towards the IRA, Barry was ultimately sent to jail on the comparatively minor charge of possessing a Thompson sub-machine gun. After his sentencing he told Garda Sergeant Moore (mentioned above), who was charged with escorting him to jail on a train, that before travelling he wanted to attend a family wedding. He gave his word that he would give himself up afterwards. Moore accepted his promise and Barry duly turned up, slightly under the weather, directly after the wedding breakfast. Many years later Moore, who in the meantime had become a chief superintendent, and was placed in charge of the Special Branch, was having a quiet drink in a pub in Cork late one evening when a large whiskey suddenly materialised on the counter in front of him. He told me that before accepting it he enquired: 'Who is the donor?' The owner indicated a figure at the far end of the bar – Tom Barry. The two men toasted each other civilly.

However, both during his interrogation on the Thompson-gun offence, and elsewhere, Barry made it clear that he knew of my father's interest in pursuing him. As his knowledge could only have come from senior Garda sources, my father tried without success to get the leak investigated by the government. The government, or the Executive Council, as it was known at the time, took no action and referred the matter back to Commissioner Eamonn Broy. His response was ominous: 'The incident merely hastens a reorganisation of our headquarters branches that I have had in mind for some time.' My father was transferred from being head of the crime division, where he had been responsible for anti-IRA activities, to being put in charge of administration

Here, at the risk of digression, I might point out that the files from which these quotations are taken were suppressed until January 1999, a gap of over seventy years. Had the papers not been so delayed, I might have been able to discuss the affair with both Barry and Broy, both of whom I interviewed during my researches for my book on the IRA. During a particularly bizarre interview (recounted in Chapter 7), Barry was exceptionally forthcoming about another County Cork murder that I did ask him about, that of Admiral Henry Somerville in 1936. The retired, elderly admiral, a brother of the novelist Edith Somerville, had a habit of giving references to local lads, in Castletownshend, who wanted to join the British navy. Barry told me that, at the precise moment at which he had Somerville shot, he, accompanied by another prominent Cork IRA man called Kelliher, struck up a conversation with a Garda on duty outside the Metropole Hotel in Cork city, during which Barry pointedly underscored his alibi by asking the Garda for the time so that he could reset his watch.

Broy's memo, and the file that provided the facts given below, describing how my father's career ultimately did suffer a serious downward 'reorganisation', were given to me by my brother, Brian, while I was writing this book. He had acquired them through a combination of his own persistence over a period of years and the courtesy of the then minister for justice, Mr John O'Donoghue, a member of a Fianna Fail government, who finally directed that they be handed over several years before they would otherwise have been released.

I already had some insight into the background of what happened. Minister for justice under de Valera Gerald Boland, then a very old man, had told me, forty years after the affair: 'We knew that he drank, so we opened a file on him. With that and the Gresham incident we were able to get him.' What the file revealed was that, late in the evening, in the smoke room of the Dolphin Hotel, during Christmas week of the year I was born, 1935, in the presence of amongst others 'certain Garda witnesses' (unnamed), my father got very drunk and discussed 'political matters in a violent manner [...] referring to Mr de Valera [...] in a disrespectful and threatening way'. Not a good career move, even at a Dublin Christmas drinks party. But his standing was such that no immediate action was taken against him, although, for creating 'a grave scandal', he was formally warned that a repeat performance would get him fired.

Ironically 'the Gresham incident' that brought him down was not caused by alcohol. One evening the following July he made a brief call to the Gresham Hotel on his way home to give a friend a reference for a job he was seeking in London. Leaving the hotel, my father accidentally bumped into an American man, John Joseph Harrington. A row broke out, lasting about a minute. Following it, two Gardai (who happened to be passing the hotel) were called by Harrington. My father allowed himself to be searched to disprove Harrington's claim that he was carrying a gun. The Gardai who searched him found that he had no weapon, but Harrington later claimed that my father told him that he had a 'gat' and 'If it's trigger work you want, I'll give you plenty of it.' My father always denied uttering these words, which contain obviously American, not Irish, slang for gun.

At first the encounter appeared to be just a storm in a teacup. Neither man knew the other's identity, which only emerged later on. But, extraordinarily in view of the trajectory of my own later career, Harrington was the general manager of the *Irish Press*. Two stories about Harrington circulated in the paper. One, that he was appointed as a result of Irish-Americans' pressures to have someone in Dublin to safeguard their investments in the paper and so he came to the paper under a cloud, which his

personality did nothing to lift. Two, that it was because of his personality
that de Valera had him appointed. Not to safeguard the Irish-American
interests, but to further de Valera's. In any event at the time of the encounter
with my father Harrington told the two Gardai that he did not want to
pursue the matter any further and that seemed to be the end of the row.

Then, for reasons that were never wholly explained, everything changed
when Harrington got back to the *Irish Press* office in Burgh Quay and
discovered who my father was. A meeting of top-level editorial executives
was called at which – so a subsequent public inquiry was informed – it
was 'decided to write to the president of the Executive Council' formally
telling de Valera what had occurred. The inquiry opened before the month
was out. It was held in Kilmainham Courthouse, with lawyers appearing
for the state and for my father, though it was governed not by normal
court rules, but under Garda disciplinary regulations. The inquiry did not
reveal who made the decision to write to de Valera. Counsel for the state
denied not that the meeting had taken place, but that there was any
evidence to connect it with the instigation of proceedings.

He did not aver to the fact that de Valera was the editor in chief and
controlling director of the *Irish Press*. Nor was it mentioned that no
important formal communication would have been directed to him as
head of government, on *Irish Press* notepaper, by the decision of senior
Irish Press executives about to involve him and the paper in major controversy, without prior, and extensive, consultation with 'the Chief'. As I
would later learn full well, the unlisted black telephone that sat on the
desk once occupied by de Valera himself, while the paper was being
launched, and then by the editor of the day, was specifically intended for
upward communication as well as that of the downward variety by means
of which 'the Chief' kept in constant control of what went into the paper.
Another curious evidential nugget was the fact that the Garda sergeant
who had been called to the scene by Harrington had not thought the
incident worth reporting but had been subsequently encouraged to do so,
not through normal channels, but to an officer in the S-Branch.

However, the inquiry – swayed by my mother, my father had perhaps
unwisely elected to have it held in public – not alone disregarded such
matters, but the evidence of witnesses who flatly contradicted Harrington's
testimony. It found that my father had acted in a manner likely to bring
discredit on the Garda Siochana. And though it also found that he was
sober at the time of the incident, the state's counsel had been allowed to
make the insinuation that Harrington had found himself confronted by
somebody 'possibly inflamed by drink or something else'. The *Irish Press*,

though not the *Irish Times*, duly carried this on page one. Following that sort of publicity, it was a foregone conclusion that my father would be sacked as deputy commissioner.

But it proved unexpectedly difficult to remove him from the force. Broy wrote to the minister for justice, citing his record and suggesting that he be offered a civil service post. The file reveals official indignation and surprise at Broy's stressing of my father's good points. Forgetting that O'Duffy had been offered such a post and that Neligan had actually been given one, O'Duffy's argument (without of course attribution to its source) that if he wasn't fit to be a Garda commissioner, he wasn't fit to be any sort of public servant was brought forward. J. J. MacElligott, the secretary of the Department of Finance, in effect the head of the civil service, and a man not noted for producing proposals of which de Valera might disapprove, penned a particularly forceful memorandum to the cabinet not merely referring to my father's case, but containing a threat to bring the entire force to heel. He advocated extending civilian control (decoded Department of Finance control) over the appointment of Garda commissioners. MacElligott averred that the system whereby 'rankers', including Broy himself, were appointed commissioners meant that there was virtually no governmental control over the Garda and that the force did not have the administrative talent necessary to administer the monies voted to it. This of course conveniently overlooked the fact that Broy's had been a political appointment following O'Duffy's dismissal and that my father's administrative powers had made his reputation even before he joined the force.

However, the upshot of the affair was that my father remained in the force, but was demoted to the rank of chief superintendent, on the lowest pay grade of that scale. He stayed on for a further five years in unhappy circumstances. Men whom he had brought into the Garda were promoted over him, and being subject now not to feelings of gratitude, but to the political climate of the time, which favoured completion of the demolition work begun by the inquiry. It used to be said by my mother that at this stage he was offered 'a lucrative position' in Scotland Yard by Sir Norman Kendal, the deputy commissioner, but he decided on a new career away from policing. He completed his studies for the Bar, while at the same time reining in his fondness for bars. It was not easy. His Garda pension was small and to save on bus fares he – now in his mid-forties – had to cycle to and from Monkstown to the King's Inn on an old Rudge bicycle, a distance of some seven miles each way. But, with the aid of (limited) family assistance and an overdraft, he persevered. Though he occasionally fell off the wagon, sometimes in spectacular fashion, he successfully took his call to the Bar. I can still remember the shock I felt when I was about nine years old and, answering a summons to my parents' bedroom one day, was confronted by a strange, imposing figure, dressed in a long black gown, with a funny white thing covering his head. It was my father in his new wig and gown.

While securing his law degree, my father had also embarked on a career in politics, becoming a Fine Gael councillor on Dun Laoghaire Corporation. Subsequently W. T. Cosgrave again had a decisive effect on his career. After Cosgrave retired as Teachta Dala (TD), or deputy to the Dail, for Kilkenny, my father succeeded him, in 1944. For good measure he also became general secretary of Fine Gael, and his organisational abilities had a restorative effect on the fortunes of the party in the 1948 general election.

The night of his election in 1944 was apparently a memorable one in Castlecomer, with blazing tar barrels and cheering crowds creating unforgettable memories for those present. Unfortunately, although we children were brought down from Dublin for the occasion, some of the elders decided that we might come to grief in the crowds and we were sent to bed early, to my everlasting chagrin. It probably says much for Irish politics (and character) that my abiding memory of the great occasion is of a man who the next day sought compensation from my father because he claimed to have got tar on his clothes!

Along with his law degree my father also acquired a number of remark-able new friends amongst a group of fellow law students with whom, when finances permitted, he sometimes lunched or drank a bottle of stout. One of these friends was to have a marked effect on my own career. The group included Vincent Grogan, who later became the knight and chief knight of Columbanus, and helped to draft a Constitution for the new African state of Ghana. Vincent caused a considerable amount of eyebrow-raising in Catholic Dublin society after becoming chief knight because he set about modernising the hitherto closed and secretive Catholic pressure group and giving it an ecumenical air. He elevated even more eyebrows when one fine day he left his wife and large family and took off with another lady, who also had a large family, and into the bargain was Jewish! The other men in the group of friends were Sean McBride who, as chief of staff of the IRA, had been one of my father's chief opponents, and who would later win both the Lenin and the Nobel Peace Prizes, and, most remarkably, Vivion de Valera, Eamon de Valera's eldest son. I would later become friendly with all three. Vivion de Valera in particular, as we will see, had a marked impact on my own career.

CHAPTER 3

Home and Boyhood

The split-level motif seemed to permeate my early life. I was born (on 22 April 1935) as the great crisis in my father's career was beginning to build up. My brother, Brian, arrived almost two years later, and my sister, Aisling, four years later still. Although we were too young to understand why, as children we – and certainly I, being the oldest – were aware of an undertow of anxiety and tension to our lives in what appeared from the outside to be a world of gracious living. Despite the financial situation I remember my parents giving all sorts of parties: dinner parties, tennis parties, poker parties and performance parties, at which my mother sang and played the piano. Her favourite songs were the 'The Queen of Connemara', 'The Connemara Cradle Song', 'The West's Awake' and selections from Tom Moore's *Irish Melodies* and from Ivor Novello. My father's favourites were 'The Rose of Mooncoin' and '*Sliabh na mBan*'. The guests also sang, and sometimes recited poetry or extracts from plays. The most spectacular elocutionist was a local aristocrat, Sir Valentine Grace, who would at one moment declaim in a soft, melodious tone that I had to almost strain to hear and then, in the next, crash forth so thunderously that he frightened the life out of me.

Our home was a large house in Monkstown, County Dublin, which was, and is, an exclusive Dublin suburb. It had some twenty rooms, cubbyholes and cellars. Monkstown's street names, and those of the ground landlords, dated from colonial times: de Vesci, Longford, Pakenham. In our day Monkstown was a quiet, staid place of high terraced houses and walled gardens. Its inhabitants tended to be Protestant professional families either treading water or on the way down, and Catholic professional families on the way up. My family could accurately have been described as combining all three.

Our house was located not far from the sea, on an exclusive, horseshoe-shaped development called the Hill and was one of the largest and highest on it. It was built sometime in the 1840s as an exclusive hotel. In those pre-urban-sprawl days the view from it over Dublin Bay must have been one of the finest in Leinster. In our occupancy the house, approached from one side of the Hill, because it was surrounded by trees and bushes, appeared to stand alone. However, if one approached from the other side of the Hill, one realised that the grounds were split in two and that there was another, similarly proportioned, house adjoining ours. This was called Tudor House. The two must have been amongst the biggest semi-detacheds in the country. However, one day my mother decided that people should be made aware of the superior standing of our home, so she bought a brush and a pot of black paint and inscribed its name on the granite gate pillars: *Tudor Hall*. That was telling them.

During my early years servants were in plentiful supply, as befitted a Tudor hall. Generally speaking, we had a maid or two, a nurse and, as my father's time became more taken up with the law and politics, a gardener. We even had a boxing instructor at one stage, Battling Brannigan, a low-sized, leathery-faced man who apparently had been a famous boxer in his day. But it is the maids I chiefly remember. There is a book waiting to be written about the treatment of maids by the Irish middle class of those days. It wasn't merely that they were a constant prey to sexual molestation by the males of the homes they were employed in (not ours, may I hastily add), but that these unfortunates lived either in dark, often uncarpeted, basement rooms or in equally dark, cramped attics. I remember litanies of complaint from my mother about the selfish and unthinking behaviour of some of these girls who so far disregarded the interests of their employers as to insist on taking their weekly half-day off. The Reference was the great sword of Damocles held over their heads. Prospective new employers generally made employment decisions based on the references provided by previous employers. And as for their pay! One day I overhead my mother call out to my father the wording of an ad she wanted placed in the *Irish Independent*. I was intrigued to learn that she was seeking 'an experienced general' at an annual salary of thirty-six pounds.

Alas, the resplendent uniformed figure I was expecting turned out to be a young woman with a country accent and a battered suitcase. Epaulettes were not to be had for thirty-six pounds a year. One of my mother's pyrotechnical displays of temperament culminated in my father being brought in to lecture 'a general' who had committed the enormity of writing to her mother that 'Coogan himself is all right, but she is a wretch!' In the face of this dreadful insult no one thought fit to question the fact that my mother had suffered it through her normal custom of reading the maids' letters.

Mind you, some of these women got in their own licks. I remember one nurse, 'Shiela', for the severity with which she punished Brian and me when our parents were away, which was frequently. My father never learned to drive and relied on my mother to take him to political events in her little box Ford. In addition to inflicting her own punishments, when my parents returned Shiela would often present them with a long list of misdemeanours for which our father would also beat us. Even the fact that Shiela broke my leg one day did not provoke any undue outrage or cause her to be fired. The incident occurred somewhere approaching my fourth birthday. My foot had become entangled in the bars of my cot in such a way that when she yanked me to the floor the leg broke. In fairness it should probably be recorded that, as normally happens at that age, the greenstick fracture healed quickly. It all added up to the fact that Brian and I had to be careful about breaches of family discipline. During demonstrations of his 'sparing the rod, spoiling the child' philosophy, our father's response to our cries and protest was to tell us how benign our punishments were compared with those of his childhood. His father used to beat him in the shop window!

Despite this I remember him as being a kind-hearted man who elicited affection as much as respect. Two episodes stand out in my memory as symbolising the conflict between the tenderness he could show and the dictums by which he had been reared. In one he launched my swimming career in a manner that could just as well have put me off swimming for life. One fine afternoon, at the back of the West Pier in Dun Laoghaire, during a full tide, I was resisting his efforts to get me to enter the water when suddenly a large conger eel appeared. I will never forget the sight of the serpentine, greyish-black creature undulating a foot or so beneath the surface through the clumps of brown seaweed sprouting from white granite. It made me disobey my father's urgings and promptly bolt away from the water's edge. This made him forsake both cajolery and threat, pick me up and hurl me into the water. While scuba-diving in later life, I often thought of that episode as I finned along underwater rocks like a portly conger myself.

The second memory, however, makes up for such drastic initiation methods. About the same time as the West Pier incident I was standing with him in the garden as he burned rubbish when a gust of wind suddenly enveloped me in smoke and I started to cry. He put his arm round me and hugged me to him, saying: 'Tim, *amhic* [son], you don't think I would let anything happen to my little man?'

He loved sport and took me to see both rugby and hurling matches. I saw my first All-Blacks match with him at Lansdowne Road. My abiding memory of the game is of menacing black figures who emitted a disquieting air of violence as they moved at great speed around the pitch. It seems to me that that childhood memory still conveys an accurate picture of New Zealand rugby. For a number of reasons I remember the hurling, and in particular the last game my father brought me to at Croke Park. One was a general outburst of laughter in the stand after a loudspeaker message told the Kilkenny hurlers to assemble after the match outside a well-known pub. My father had commented: 'And tell them they can meet me inside it!' The second thing I remember says a great deal about that non-PC, faraway Ireland. It was a programme note describing how a famous goalkeeper used to keep his eye in by standing at a barn door on a summer's evening and stopping swallows. This conjured up horrific images: Blood. Feathers, SPLAT! The third memory involves a 'splat!' of another sort: a right hook from my father, following another hurling match, after I had incautiously burst out, during a row with him: 'I'm glad Kilkenny were beaten!' For a week a sore ear would remind me of a great truth about Ireland: criticism of Gaelic Athletic Association (GAA) teams should be administered cautiously and sparingly.

My father used to spend hours coaching me at tennis and, with less success, trying to develop my interest in gardening by having me dig and weed alongside him as he doled out horticultural instruction. Somehow Brian developed a genius for going missing when such lessons were in progress, but I never could. My father had all the ancestral lore of a countryman, stressing by example the need for thorough digging and manuring. I disliked having to fork in the manure, which he had delivered in great quantities, and I especially hated having to water the tomato plants. The water was taken from a barrel outside the green house in which he used to hang a sack of horse manure – that which issues from a horse's anus is far more fertile than that from a cow – which spawned hosts of fat, wriggling grubs. But even as a child I could see that his methods produced results. Along with tomatoes he grew things like artichokes and marrows in addition to beans, beet, celery, leeks, peas, potatoes, gooseberries, red- and blackcurrants, winter and summer pears, and a variety of salads and herbs, including parsley, which they say will only allow itself to be grown by whoever wears the pants in the house. I don't know if that theory was ever put to my mother, but we certainly ate a lot of parsley. My father must have been a very strong man.

The amount of work involved in all this horticultural activity was colossal. He added to his chores by dividing the various sections of the garden from each other by a series of low box hedges, which had to be clipped frequently and by hand. The extensive lawns too were cut manually, with a heavy push mower. But it was only towards the end of his life, when his professional interests began interfering with his gardening, that he took on Quinn, the gardener, to help him out.

It was an authoritarian age and both my parents had been reared by, with or from a set of values that, in the face of the evidence to the contrary all around them, thought of society as being hierarchical and ordered according to strict notions of right and wrong. Despite her peaks-and-valleys temperament my mother preached an unvarying code of ethics and a set of values by which one was supposed to live no matter what political or domestic upheavals occurred. She believed in effort and frequently quoted Browning's philosophy that a man's reach should be beyond his grasp. Even if the circumstances of the hour were bizarrely topsy-turvy, it went without saying that a gentleman should conduct himself with a certain style and be respectful to women, the clergy and authority generally. Her trump-card answer to any fulminations of mine against the Church was 'We must pay the homage of our understanding.' Beat that! One of her favourite quotations was a saying of the Fianna, the Irish Samurai, 'Be gentle in the house and rough in the gap of danger.' Delicacy of feeling and of expression were extolled as the ideal. 'Rarefied' was one of her favourite words. A favourite play or author was 'rarefied', as were the more cultivated expressions of upper-class society. Both my parents were strong believers in law and order, and in a disciplinary code for upholding it that included such unrarefied methods as the cane or a boot up the backside.

Throughout the period of the war and my father's legal studies, money was in very short supply. The war meant that there was talk about air raids, we ate black bread and my father listened to the BBC for news of the activities of someone called Churchill. He also spent time tracing the movements of armies across Europe and the Middle East on the coloured plates of a huge, linen-bound atlas. He was critical of the British because of what they had done in Ireland, but he wanted to see Hitler defeated and always seemed to be quite cheerful when he talked about the war. Consequently I didn't suffer any anxiety about its course until one morning, nearing its end. Sunlight was streaming in the windows as my father came down the stairs calling out for my mother after listening to the news. He looked unusually sombre and worried. I didn't know what he was talking about, but it seemed that the sunlight darkened and I felt worried also as he told my mother: 'Beatrice! They've got a terrible new weapon. It's called the atomic bomb.'

But our financial state touched me more directly. I was frequently sent down the Hill to Pakenham Road to the home of Desmond Bell, a senior counsel, to borrow legal texts. So frequently that I used to dread being given the instruction 'Go down to Mr Bell and ask him would he be good enough to loan me a copy of . . .' Even more humiliating was the Asking for Turf. We had an outside coal house, which was sometimes filled with turf, but was more often half empty. (Coal of course would have been scarce in any case because of the war.) Once, when the turf stock had dwindled to not much more than a thick carpeting of peat moss on the floor, Brian somehow managed to ignite a fire. For several weeks afterwards I used to be sent next door to ask Mr Bentley whether he would be good enough to loan us some turf, explaining that ours had been consumed in the fire and that yet again the new delivery had not arrived.

Mr Bentley, a courtly old gentleman, was the owner and headmaster of a Protestant boys' school, the grounds of which ran along the ends of the gardens of Tudor Hall and Tudor House. On his death, the place passed into the hands of two of his teachers, the brothers Evans. I remember one of these brothers as being much given to running through the trees and undergrowth of the school's extensive grounds, wearing a pair of shorts and a funny hat, at the head of a troop of 'Protestant Boy Scouts'. These were the Baden-Powell Scouts. They were viewed with such hostility by the Irish Catholic hierarchy that when de Valera was founding the *Irish Press*, he made use of the fact that English papers coming into Ireland contained recruiting ads for the Baden-Powell Scouts. These were the sort of influences that the foundation of the *Irish Press* would help to combat!

In the event the scouting activities, and much else that went on in the woods, were put to an end by a scandal that was only discussed when we children were supposedly out of earshot. Apparently, there *were* fairies at the bottom of our garden. History does not record whether these multiplied or decreased when, as happened, the Christian Brothers ultimately took over the school. For several years before the Brothers' takeover, the school and its grounds lay in dereliction, and were much used for the purposes of fornication and of the creation of mayhem by the youth of the district. It was frequented by gangs of 'common boys' from the council-house districts of Dun Laoghaire and the Farm. These vile young thugs' main ambition in life seemed to be to beat up Brian and myself. Being boys, we did not avoid these sanguinary encounters by simply staying out of the place, and sometimes invited attacks over the garden walls. Thirty or forty years later when I would encounter said thugs on the street or in the bar, they would invariably shake their heads and say things like: 'Jaysus, you and your brother were desperate young hooligans when youse were young.' Perception is all.

One of the money-making stratagems that my mother adopted while my father was studying law was to become a fishmonger. She travelled from Dublin to Castlecomer a number of times a week with the fish, either in her tiny car or, if this was hospitalised, as it very often was, in a bus. The fish were carried in specially designed straw bags. As these frequently leaked fishy, melting ice onto the other passengers, I particularly hated being brought on the bus journeys. Rarefied they most definitely were not. But the fish – sold in my grandparents' emporium – was in great demand. In those days inland Castlecomer did not normally get sea fish, although trout were plentiful in the rivers around the village.

My mother resented her fallen circumstances, resented having to sell the fish and above all resented a local chatelaine who dealt with her in what my mother felt was a condescending manner. There may well be something about buying fish that brings out the condescension and snobbery in a certain type of housewife. One of the great stories to emanate from Dublin's famous street market in Moore Street concerns Rosie, a legendary stallholder, who was angered one day by the persistent questioning of a bejewelled madam who wanted to be assured that the prawns were indeed fresh. Gesticulating so that everyone within range of the stall could see the flash of her rings, the housewife poked at the prawns for the umpteenth time and enquired yet again: 'But are you *sure* they're fresh? I'm having a *most* important dinner party!'

Rosie finally exploded: 'Listen, ma'am, them's prawns, not pricks! They won't grow, no matter how much you poke them!'

My mother was too ladylike to respond to her tormentor in similar terms, but she got in her retaliation one day after the Condescending One told her, before a crowded shop, that she wanted 'something special for an *exclusive* dinner party. Not the usual sort of thing you supply for the servants. This is for the *table*!' My mother promised the lady 'a great delicacy, rock sturgeon', and the following Friday sold her a straw bag full of fish: plaice, which went to the servants, and skinned dogfish, which went 'to the table'. Not rarefied perhaps, but in my mother's considered opinion 'Good enough for the stinking snob. A BIXYZ!' She had a stock of such euphemisms. Of a wasted endeavour she would say: 'I might as well have been rubbing my arm to a burnt brick, and I don't mean arm!' Of someone she disliked: 'She gives me a pain in the fundament!' Generally speaking the only near-obscenity she permitted herself was contained in a quotation, which she averred came from her mother, concerning small measures of gin. Holding out the glass, she would say: 'It looks like a ram's shit in a deer park.'

My father did not believe in small measures, a fact that became glaringly obvious when he sometimes reacted to the pressures of his existence by indulging in binge-drinking. His fondness for alcohol was far from being unusual in those days. Even as a small boy I learned to pick out the grown-ups who drank. They were the men whose whites of the eye had a yellow tinge. Those were the days of that widespread Irish custom 'the skite'. A casual drinking bout could, and often did, mushroom into a bender during which men took off from their homes, offices, farms, professions, whatever. Skites were of no fixed duration, continuing until ravaged livers, consciences, bank balances, or a combination of all three, drove the drinker home to the arms (or fists) of his family and into the ranks of the Pioneer Total Abstinence Association for a renewed bout of temperance, which could last months or even years until the next breakout.

In my father's case, most of the drinking bouts I remember were of short duration, generally hours rather than days. But I learned to dread the symptoms of a skite. Perhaps I'd wake up late one night to the sound of loud, angry voices and of things being thrown. Then my father would slam doors and go to the spare bedroom adjoining my parents' bedroom. The next morning he would sleep late, chamber pots would be filled with strong-smelling urine and, if there were none in the house, I'd be sent to buy my father's favourite hangover remedy, buttermilk. Once, the spare bedroom was unavailable for some reason and he climbed into my bed under a rain of books hurled by my mother. I got hit by a copy of the Bible and lay awake for hours terrified in case I might touch my fume-emitting parent *down there*.

My father did go on one Homeric skite which deserved mention in *The Guinness Book of Records*. It occurred a couple of years after he had become a barrister. From the first distant early warning storm signals of late homecomings and slurred speech to the purchase of the last quart of healing buttermilk it lasted for approximately a month.

Normally, when he was not drinking, my father was to be found in the company of professional people – army officers, senior civil servants, leading businessmen and so on – but when he drank, he consorted with a set of cronies who included a famous Garda detective called Dan O'Donoghue and, in particular, Mitchell, a fishmonger who had a shop near us in the village of Glasthule. Mitchell was a hard man. Late in life, long after my father had died, he developed facial cancer and a hole appeared on the side of one cheek. However, he still drank heavily and, when the pubs were shut, had a habit of calling on houses where he was welcome to continue his pursuit of the oral Irish tradition until the small hours of the morning. The wife of one favourite nephew objected to this custom, and one night the nephew had regretfully to inform Mitchell that he was not allowed into the house. Mitchell went back to his van and commenced drinking his bottle of Powers through the hole in his face. Eventually the wife relented and told the nephew to bring his uncle in from the cold before the neighbours became aware of the unseemly spectacle. But no, Mitchell's dignity was affronted at being refused in the first place, and like a grotesque version of one of the poets of old, who starved themselves to death outside the home of the chieftain who had done them wrong, Mitchell spurned the entreaties of his distraught relatives and sat in the unheated van all night emptying the bottle through the side of his face.

During the Great Skite we children were all pressed into accompanying my mother in a fruitless round of my father's known haunts, pubs, clubs and companions. On several bright May evenings my mother drove us to the Kilkenny bus-stop in Dublin, where I would be reluctantly forced onto the bus to check whether he was aboard. On one occasion my mother was informed that he had told someone that he was going to Castlecomer on the bus that evening, but we got to the departure point minutes after the bus had left. My mother's little box Ford had not the speed to catch up with the bus until it made a lengthy stop in the town of Athy, nearly halfway to Castlecomer. It was a beautiful evening, nature's mood in binary opposition to that in the car. We drove through fields filled with lambs and fringed by flowering chestnut trees, saying the rosary, my mother hoping, and I dreading, that my father would be on the bus. He wasn't. My mother almost had hysterics and sent me back for a second check, so that the bus began to move with me still on it.

After a couple of weeks the fruitless bus pursuits and my mother's rounds of the bars were given up in despair, although I was still sent to Dun Laoghaire occasionally to enquire in a number of likely premises if Mr Coogan had been in recently. For a time I developed such a hatred of drink that I learned to hold my breath in the pubs lest I might smell the evil aroma of alcohol. The numbers of novenas multiplied, as did the piles of brown paper envelopes with cellophane windows. The phone was cut off. I was instructed to tell the butcher and the milkman that their bills would be paid when my father returned from his holidays. My mother

took to her bed, imploring God to send her husband home and/or strike
him dead.

With every day that passed, my hopes for my father's return were more
and more outweighed by fears of the volcanic explosion that would surely
attend the homecoming. Then one day as I went through Dun Laoghaire
I saw him, standing on the pavement talking to two strange men. He
looked as he normally did, perhaps a little more flushed and animated,
and he stood in an unfamiliar stance with his hands clasped under his
coat-tails, but otherwise he looked exactly as he had when he said goodbye
to me on the morning of the day on which the Great Skite had begun. In
terror lest he might see me, I crossed the road and walked back a bit along
the way I had come. When I plucked up my courage to go back to where
I had seen him, he had disappeared. At the butcher's, I was given the meat
order but told to ask my mother to send a cheque before ordering any
more.

My return home interrupted my mother in a nap. I gave her the butcher's
message. 'Oh, God! Oh, God!' she cried. 'Was ever a woman so scourged?'
And then hopelessly: 'No sign of your father?'

'No,' I lied cravenly.

However, a few days later my father returned of his own volition.
Mounds of crockery were smashed. The spare bedroom reeked of brim-
ming chamber pots. Gallons of buttermilk were consumed, but as the days
passed the Pioneer pin made a reappearance on my father's lapel. He
returned to my mother's bedroom. The pinstriped, awe-inspiring man of
affairs reappeared. There was no further difficulty with the milkman and
the butcher. The tide of cellophaned envelopes receded.

My first school was Miss Stephens's. The classroom was the front room
of the home of an old lady who lived in a small house on a street known
as the Crescent, on the main road a few hundred yards from Tudor Hall.
The upstairs of the house consisted of the schoolroom, a parlour, Miss
Stephens's bedroom and a lavatory. The kitchen, again the split-level motif,
was downstairs, where there were a couple of other rooms, which, like the
kitchen, we never saw but constantly speculated about. The best feature
of the place was the long, hedge-enclosed garden at the back of the house,
where there was a lawn and a number of apple trees. We seemed to be
given a lot of playing time in the garden, and as Miss Stephens was both
an excellent teacher and an extraordinarily kind old lady, this introduction
to schooling was a pleasant experience. She charged ridiculously low fees,
something like three pounds a term, but she always gave every boy and

girl in the school – some thirty of us in all – a Christmas present. I was once sent to the toyshop to help with carrying the boxes of the Christmas annuals, snakes and ladders, Ludo and suchlike, and I could see from the prices that Miss Stephens was spending most of her fees on her pupils.

We learned to read, write, add, subtract, multiply and do long division. What we did not learn, as I would later discover to my cost, was the Irish language. Miss Stephens's only other defect was her method of teaching religion. Apart from making us learn our catechism and preparing us for confession and Holy Communion, she used to give us the benefit of her evidently extensive knowledge of the next world. We were thoroughly instructed in the horrors not merely of dying, but of the Particular Judgement that would follow this unpleasant event. After this we could look forward to the grand finale, the Day of General Judgement, on which, she informed us in solemn tones, the following would occur: 'Our Lord Jesus Christ will come with great power and majesty, and he will say to those who have led good lives: "Come with me, you who are blessed, to the Paradise prepared for you amongst the kingdom of my angels in Heaven.' However, to the rest of those present our Saviour would say: "Depart from me, ye cursed, into the everlasting flames of Hell prepared for you by the Devil and his angels."' All this, Miss Stephens assured us compellingly, would be accompanied by liberal doses of weepings and gnashings of teeth. 'Oh, think of it, children,' she would say. 'Think of it!' I did, frequently. Particularly, as I used to do often, when waking up in the middle of the night in the grip of nightmare.

Outside the school, the grimmer aspects of Church liturgy reinforced Miss Stephens's teachings. Lent was a time of increased mass-going, the enforced giving up of sweet things and the recital of more prayers and novenas. During the Easter-week Tenebrae ceremonies Monkstown Parish Church was darkened and all the statues including the Stations of the Cross were draped in dark purple. I remember one Good Friday when the prayers ceased abruptly and silence fell on the packed, darkened church. It was suddenly broken by the crash of what sounded like pieces of brass being smashed against each other. I realised afterwards that the sound was caused by two large books being clapped together, but at the time I was scared witless.

Not surprisingly, in view of her great generosity and the fact that as she got older pupils became fewer, Miss Stephens died in poverty, in a public ward. But she kept both her pride and her dignity to the end. When I was about sixteen, I heard that things were bad with her and organised a dance in the nearby Salthill Hotel. With the proceeds of the dance I bought a bottled gas heater and placed the remainder of the takings in an envelope. But when Brian and I arrived at the Crescent with our offerings, we found the house in darkness. As Miss Stephens was known to be pretty well immobilised, I realised that she was probably in bed and that we should not frighten her into attempting to get up. For some reason I thought of the downstairs rooms that we never dared enter during our schooldays, and on trying the window of one, found it was open and climbed in. I still wince when I think of my folly that night. I was in a state of sweating terror lest I made a noise that might give the old lady a heart attack or, worse, cause her to start screaming and attract the police. Yet, in the darkness, on my hands and knees, I managed to make my way through the damp, silent house, up the stairs and then noiselessly open the hall door from the inside. Brian and I had managed to manoeuvre the heater into our old classroom when the inevitable occurred. Miss Stephens woke up and called out: 'Who is it?' I managed to stave off cardiac arrest all round, stuttering out both our identities and our mission, and then, thinking that all was now well, lit the heater. 'No! No!' cried the old teacher. 'It gives me a headache. I can smell it. Take it away!' We left the envelope behind us, but had to remove the heater.

One of the great rites of transition during my schooldays was said to occur when you left the gentle shores of 'sums' and began to study geometry. Pythagoras's theorem was known as the *Pons Asinorum*, the Bridge of Asses. I found that a far greater transition occurred in my ninth year when I left Miss Stephens's apple-dappled garden and entered the tarmacadamed yard that encircled the functional buildings, designed after the best principles of the Your Basic Utility school of architecture, that housed the Christian Brothers' School in the nearby seaside town of Dun Laoghaire. The Christian Brothers were founded to help poor boys, and the teachers were also poor, without the financial backing needed to become priests. They were often looked down upon as 'other ranks' by the superior clergy.

By the time this book came to be written, the often harsh attitudes of clergy and nuns towards the laity had rightly been made the subject of fierce criticism, combated and put an end to. But a factor often overlooked was the equal, or worse, harshness frequently inflicted on nuns, brothers and priests by their superiors. Brothers, for instance, were often brought into the order at around twelve years of age. Recruiting Brothers would call to the home of a poor farmer or labourer with perhaps ten children, offering to take a bright boy who would be given a free education and trained as a Brother. Generally parents looked upon such offers as manna from Heaven. With some variations, this clerical equivalent of the British navy's press gang applied to poor girls too where certain orders of nuns were concerned. The children's wishes were not considered.

The potential Brothers were reared in a severely limited intellectual climate. One of their principal relaxations was the Sunday walk. Familiar sights on the roadways around Monkstown in my boyhood were the long crocodiles of black-clad boys with pudding-bowl haircuts and long red wrists protruding from their sleeves. What neither I nor the world saw was the fate that often awaited many of these unfortunates. Some did get the promised education, right through university. They were thus qualified to teach and could leave the Brothers and marry if they wished. But this eventuality was guarded against in other cases by removing the young men from the universities just before their final exams. Thus, while they were valuable as teachers in Brothers' schools they were not qualified to teach in other schools and were forced to remain in a cloistered world, with little contact with their families for the rest of their days. The miracle is not that the products of this system were often angry, resentful, celibate men, who took out their frustrations on their pupils, but that so many of them became good educators.

My first year at the Brothers' school was fine. Despite the possession of curls, which my mother carefully cultivated, and long eyelashes, which she claimed she was also responsible for because she spread Vaseline on my lids some hours after I was born, I did not suffer any great trauma at the hands of bullies during the ritualistic mayhem that passed for recreation in the schoolyard. Battling Brannigan's boxing tuition, and the God-given gift of a natural straight left, did something to make up for the harm done by the curls and the eyelashes. The superior was an imposing, white-haired six-footer with the same name as the Brothers' founder, Edmund Ignatius Rice. He was a thorough gentleman, even to the extent of having a distinctly upper-crust Anglo-Irish accent, a *rara avis* indeed amongst the Irish Christian Brothers. He managed to make his presence felt in every pupil's life, not by dispensing punishments, but by entering classrooms unexpectedly and calling out small groups at random to conduct prose and poetry readings or to answer mathematical problems. I was so much in awe of him that when he asked me to choose between reading a passage of prose or of poetry, I chose a poem, which was full of unfamiliar terms that I stumbled over, rather than the prose. I was one of the best in the class at reading aloud but I had never heard the word 'prose' before. I thought of such writing as 'stories' or 'essays' and I was afraid to ask Brother Rice what 'prose' meant.

Our class teacher, who took us for all subjects, was a Brother Behan, whom I also remember with affection. In terms of social origin he would have been a more typical Christian Brother recruit than Rice, probably coming from a labouring or small farming background, but he brought with him all the kindness of the Irish countryside. Tallish, well built, in his late thirties, smiles found no difficulty in settling on his face. Jokes were not unknown to him, and he ruled with a light rein, seemingly not overtaxed by keeping forty or so small boys in a state of reasonable attentiveness.

Alas, the Behan era was to be of short duration. I had entered the school at fourth class and somehow or another, at the commencement of fifth, had managed to get myself retained in Behan's class for another year, so as to catch up on my lack of Irish. But on the second day of this arrangement there entered the classroom, and my life, a classical example of the sort of man who got the Christian Brothers a bad reputation all over the world. We had been reading about the Fir Bolg (Bag Men), a race of fierce black-haired men who were said to have once inhabited Ireland and were supposed to have moved earth during building or farming operations by carrying it in bags. My initial reaction on seeing this Brother was that I had sighted my first Fir Bolg. First impressions are often correct. The Brother was certainly a primitive.

'I'm looking for my boys,' he said. He had a list of names of the boys in his class. Mine and that of two or three other boys who had opted to stay with Brother Behan were on it. And with no further advertence to Brother Behan, he read out our names, beckoned us out of our seats and bade us follow him to our new classroom – his. For the next year it was to be our little hell on earth. He used his leather unmercifully. Beatings were handed out for even the most minor slips at lessons as well as for real or imaginary breaches of discipline. Some mornings he would announce that as the wrong answers were not serious, he would not beat anyone, but then after lunch he would change his mind and lash about him like a demon refreshed. It was not unusual to be punished as many as three times a day, receiving clusters of up to a dozen hard slaps on each hand. My tenuous grip on the Irish language frequently put my hands in a condition where they could hardly grip anything at all. That Brother inculcated in me a hatred of the language that lasted all through my schooldays, and in adult life some sort of persistent block prevented me from learning it, even while living on the Irish-speaking Aran Islands. It wasn't merely his cruelty; it was the latency of cow shite about him that made me equate Irish with boshtoonery and ignorance. As a devoted reader about wildlife, I remember still the contempt I felt when he explained to the class one day that that synonym for grace, a black panther, looked like its very antithesis – a bear!

In one respect I was lucky. I escaped his special punishments, those wherein he took the victim into a room off the classroom, closed the door and lashed them on the bare buttocks. This custom, and some allied pastimes, may or may not have had a bearing on his departure from the Brothers, into whose ranks he – and many like him – should never have been admitted. Those of course were the days when authority was all and boys who allowed it to be known at home that they had been punished at school were at risk of getting a second beating accompanied by a diatribe on the iniquity of annoying the teacher when they should have been taking advantage of the good education that they were lucky to get.

But by the time his leaving took place, I too had departed. My parents, through a combination of my importunings and an improvement in my father's fortunes, had decided that my brother, who by then had also outgrown Miss Stephens, and myself should be enrolled in an exclusive day school run by lay masters. It was situated in the heart of Donnybrook, Dublin's most prestigious postal district, Dublin 4, and was so exclusive that after the election of 1948 had hurled de Valera and Fianna Fáil from power for the first time in sixteen years, partly because of my father's reorganisation of Fine Gael, the fathers of several of my classmates at St Xavier's College, as it was known, became cabinet ministers. A month before the election anyone looking at my father's career would have said that the barometer of his future was set 'fair'. Politically, because of his police and legal background, he was spoken of as minister for justice in what was obviously going to be a new government. Economically, he was on the crest of the wave. Apart from his growing Bar earnings the proceeds of the sale of the Castlecomer pub, after my grandmother's death, had freed him from debt. It fetched only £1,400, but that was a goodly sum in those days and the outcome was an afternoon that my parents spent sitting at my father's huge desk at one end of the dining room signing cheques, and smilingly crossing off yet another creditor from a long list of names. The list ran out just before the money did, but this brought joy rather than sorrow to my father. I remember him beaming at me as the last cheque was written and exclaiming: 'Timmo Shanko! I'm a free man. My debts are paid.'

Unfortunately, fate was soon to call in the biggest debt of all.

CHAPTER 4

A Death in the Family

'He's dead! He's dead!' shrieked my mother over and over again. These were the words to which I awoke at 2.30 a.m. on 22 January 1948. She crashed into the bedroom, half falling, half supported by my aunt Josephine. Behind them came the uniformed figure of the Garda who had come to the house to break the news. I remember thinking how awful it must be to be a Garda having to carry out such duties, while at the same time trying to comfort my mother. Auntie eventually got her to lie down. While she did so, the Garda said to me, at this point aged twelve: 'Now you're going to have to be the man of the house. You'll have to look after your mother.' It was the start of the 'Putting a Brave Face on It' phase of my life.

At first it seems that I succeeded only too well. In the morning when Brian woke up and went to my mother's room, where he was told the news, he burst into tears. My mother's reaction was to turn to me and say: 'How well you wouldn't shed a tear!'

My father's last illness was accompanied by all the intensity of Irish Catholic death. My mother 'storming the heavens', as she put it. This involved visits by priests, masses, endless rosaries, prayerful appeals for divine intercession via brown scapulars, green scapulars, a crucifix said to contain a fragment of the True Cross on which Christ was crucified, and a golden filigreed locket containing a picture of St Teresa, the Little Flower to whom my father had a special devotion. The locket also contained a major relic, a microscopic brown object said to be a fragment of the saint's bones. Part of my required reading was a biography of the saint, which contained details of her heroic life, such as the fact that once, while she was in bed suffering from tonsillitis, a wasp entered her mouth and stung her inflamed throat. The saint was reported to have thanked God for sending her a day on which she could endure such suffering for Him.

Some time after my father died I was given the locket to place under my pillow to help me over a bout of flu. In a fit of curiosity I prised open the glass cover and touched the relic, accidentally dislodging it so that it fell on the peeling, brown, varnished floor and disappeared. Miss Stephens's teachings echoed in my ears. Words like 'sacrilege', 'excommunication' and 'eternal damnation' passed through my mind. Realising, however, that I faced a more imminent threat than any of these dire eventualities – my mother's torrential wrath – I picked a tiny sliver from the wooden floor, replaced it in the locket and said nothing. Over the years the fears of hellfire and damnation subsided, but so, I am bound to say, did my scepticism about the relic's miraculous properties and the possibility of a portion of poor St Teresa being in the locket in the first place.

For, as I was writing this memoir, Irish house prices increased so much that Tudor Hall's value is currently estimated in millions. A truly miraculous transformation from the years following my father's death, as his beloved garden became overgrown with weeds and Tudor Hall began to suffer first from leaks in the roof and later from dry rot. When it rained, pots had to be placed even in downstairs rooms to capture the rainwater. Its constant flow created an ironic validation of my father's faith in the value of water in the encouragement of indoor plant life. The constant supply of rainwater nourished the growth of large, villainous-looking mushrooms that grew on several of the inside walls, even poking their unwelcome heads through the peeling wallpaper in the dining room and drawing rooms, three floors beneath the roof.

Alas, however, St Teresa created no miraculous change in the course of my father's last illness. As I think back to those days, recollections of religious iconography are enhanced by the sounds of running taps and flushings of the lavatory. My father had earlier contracted diabetes, which I thought merely meant that he could no longer eat sweets. One of his great pleasures during winter was to sit up in bed reading favourite works like Dickens's *Pickwick Papers*, dipping into a bag of boiled sweets, while outside rain and wind howled. In his last months, as the word diabetes came to be mentioned more often, he was afflicted also with frequency. This necessitated his paying an increasingly embarrassing number of visits to the lavatory in his office at Fine Gael Headquarters in Hume Street, Dublin. He stopped drinking and began going to bed early, but though he was taking better care of himself, he became a prey to colds and flu. During one of these illnesses, in the particularly harsh winter of 1947, there was flooding in Kilkenny. Some of his constituency workers came to Dublin to get him to view the damage. They waited in the avenue outside the house until my mother's car appeared and, after some recriminatory negotiation, eventually succeeded in getting access to his bedside. He left his bed and travelled to Kilkenny to inspect the flooding, getting a drenching in the process, which my mother would later say hastened his end.

So far as we children were aware, he had been his normal self over Christmas, although I had overheard him telling my mother in worried tones how embarrassing he found it to have to make such abnormally frequent visits to the lavatory. But, as the New Year of 1948 dawned, frequency turned into retention. It was thought that the sound of running water would help him to urinate and the bathroom taps were turned on continuously, but to no avail. Day by day the swelling of his stomach became more noticeable. However, there was no hint of what was shortly to befall as we went for what turned out to be our last family walk together from our home on the Hill to Seapoint, about a mile away, and back via Salthill, along the path separating the sea from the railway. It was unusually fine, what was termed a 'pet day', warm with a hint of spring that soothed the normally restless sea. Unusual too was the degree of affection that my parents displayed to each other, no friction or stridency – more, I diagnosed later with the benefit of hindsight, a drawing closer together in the face of threat. But there was no threat in evidence the next morning when my mother and father set off for St Michael's Hospital, Dun Laoghaire, in the little box Ford. My father carried his own case and appeared to be in good spirits.

At first it appeared that I was more ill than him, because I went down with flu. I have often wondered since whether that flu was psychosomatic. It meant that, being bedridden, I did not have to confront the sight of my father in the last days of his illness, yellowing by the hour, or to experience the bouts of emotion that took place in the hospital, before and after my mother's visits. The idea that my father might die, or indeed what death meant, was outside my comprehension, yet I could not but be aware of the deepening air of crisis in the house. Aunt Josephine, my mother's sister – though she always referred to her as 'Cissie' – had taken leave of absence from work and come to stay with us. Along with the increasing tempo of novenas, rosaries and priestly visits, there were the overheard conversations. 'He's getting very yellow. That's a bad sign.' A bad sign of what? I wondered, suddenly uneasily aware of the fact that Auntie was a nurse. Then talk grew of 'the tube coming out'; in his restless state, my father would sometimes dislodge the needle draining the urine from his system. In after-years my mother would heighten accounts of his suffering with lurid allegations about doctors being away drinking whiskey and playing poker when the dislodgements occurred so that there was no one available to replace the needle.

From St Michael's Hospital he was transferred by ambulance to the
Meath Hospital in Dublin to be treated by a famous kidney specialist of
the day, Surgeon Lane. The journey from St Michael's was horrific, the
ambulance crawling so as not to cause pain to my father, or to disturb any
drips or tubing, while in the tiny car following, the heavens were stormed
every inch of the way. The storming continued at home. Enveloped in an
atmosphere of impending doom, my mother and Auntie recited innumerable decades of the rosary, prayers and aspirations, in which we
children joined uncomprehendingly and to no avail.

The funeral was an awful business. First, as is customary, there was 'the
removal'. By prior arrangement the body had already been brought to
Whitefriars Street Church in Camden Street, round the corner from the
Meath. The church was packed to suffocation. It was the first time that
any of us children had even been near a coffin – for some reason, we were
not taken to the funerals of any of our grandparents or relations – and to
begin our acquaintanceship with one of these inevitable objects knowing
that our daddy was in it was a traumatic experience. The service itself was
short enough – a few prayers, some kindly comments about our father
and a decade of the rosary – but the hand-shakings and commiserations
must have taken at least an hour. Although embarrassed at being the centre
of so much attention, particularly by the fact that my mother kept on
crying *in public*, I found this phase of the obsequies rather comforting, as
Irish funerals often are. Now, almost sixty years later, I can still visualise
the faces of one or two of the older boys from school who attended the
church. As a result I make a practice of attending funerals whenever I can.
But the actual funeral the next day was ineradicably awful.

There was a lengthy funeral mass, conducted by several priests in sombre
black vestments and attended by what was apparently a distinguished, and
certainly an overflowing, congregation, all of whom seemingly commiserated with my mother, and most of whom told Brian and me that we
now had to look after her. Within me there grew a growing feeling of
resentment that everyone else now had a father except us. It wasn't *fair*.
The cortege took off from the church to Castlecomer. Our black limousine
followed the tricolour-draped coffin, and behind us stretched a long line
of cars, which grew longer with every town we passed through. Inside the
limousine, where we were joined by a priest, the rosary and other prayers
were recited incessantly. The long, slow procession was itself like a
sorrowful decade of the rosary, with the cars as the Hail Marys and the
towns we passed through the punctuating Our Fathers. Brian and I had to
get out and walk behind the coffin whenever we came to a town. At

Castlecomer, we were met by a band that played the dirge 'The Flowers of the Forest'. For a few seconds I became unmanned and for the first and only time the melancholy music caused me to break my resolution not to cry.

The mass and the subsequent drive had taken so long that it was almost dark when the interment took place, but it was still light enough to be aware of the scale of the crowd that attended. They said afterwards that it was the biggest funeral ever seen in Castlecomer, so although I missed the crowds who marked the beginning of our father's parliamentary career, I at least witnessed the scale of the turnout for its ending. Unfortunately, I would also have first-hand experience of the impact on my mother of the political fallout from that ending. Later she would say of the funeral: 'They rattled Ned's bones through every town in the constituency.' In those days the custom of widows standing for, and automatically winning, their late husband's seat was so widespread that an outside observer might have been forgiven for thinking that, along with the right to enter the Dail, deputies also acquired testamentary rights to their seats.

But my mother's case was to prove the exception to the rule. According to her, in a letter she wrote in June 1948 to Kevin O'Higgins's brother Michael, who was a minister in the coalition government:

> After Ned's funeral, various deputations awaited me to assure me of their support should I decide to stand in his place. A group of committee men, representing Fine Gael branches formed by Ned in every part of the county, met me and asked my permission to put forward my name, and they would do the rest. I agreed but was surprised and stunned when a man stood up at the convention and announced that I had phoned him my decision to withdraw!

She went on to say that her solicitor had advised her to sue, and that her supporters had urged her to stand as an independent, but that she had declined both suggestions on the grounds of not wishing to damage the party Ned had worked so hard for. Attempting to establish, or challenge, the truth of this description of the workings of provincial Irish politics of over a half-century ago would be fruitless. But one thing seems clear – the sparrows drove off the hummingbird. My mother always hated the mention of Kilkenny thereafter, and many years later she upbraided me for sending some of my children to a boarding school in the county.

The stream of callers to the house initiated by our father's death soon dissipated. The small amount of money collected by Fine Gael for his widow and orphans (£250 – far less than the cost of that very public funeral) also quickly dried up. My mother began to adjust to what would prove a lengthy widowhood. She would live in passionate celibacy for almost half a century. The Christmas after my father's death was the first when no turkeys, hams, spiced beef or Christmas cakes arrived from Kilkenny constituents, a striking early lesson in the short-lived nature of political generosity. We survived on the help of my uncles, Fathers Tim and Frank, in Australia and from the incredible aunt Josephine at home.

Even as I write this, sixty years later, I marvel at her goodness. She was a night nurse in what is now St James's Hospital, and in her time was called the South Dublin Union. As a young nurse, it had been her job to act as a midwife, delivering babies in the slums of Dublin around the Coombe and Sir Patrick Dunne's hospitals. In our childhood her job had moved to the other end of life's cycle, looking after 'the old grannies'. She always bicycled to work, rarely without 'a drop of stim' in her handbag – a small bottle of Hennessey brandy with which she soothed the fret of some dying old lady. It was not unknown for her to lay out as many as three old women in a night. When her stint on duty ended, she would normally attend as many as three early masses. Once home, she would see to her mother, clean the house and buy the groceries before permitting herself three or four hours' sleep and then cycling back to the Union.

Auntie never put her own interests above or even on an equal footing with those of her family. A very beautiful woman in her day, she had fallen in love with a submarine commander during the First World War. They wanted to marry because, as he correctly foresaw, a submariner's wartime life was likely to be short. But my grandparents' reaction was one of horror. How could she possibly be so selfish as to even think of marrying, when she knew that it was her duty to look after them in her old age? That attitude extended towards her brother Joseph also. I remember my mother recounting to a friend the shock and hurt her mother, Marianne, felt when Joseph married: '"Mama," he said, "I'll never leave you." Then a few weeks later he walked out and married *that* one!' It was of course entirely correct for my mother to have married. That was different!

Auntie made us constant gifts of money, which she could not possibly afford. She also altered the routine that had obtained in her mother's lifetime so that she came out to Tudor Hall almost daily, and did what she could to tidy it up. To bring in more money, my mother decided to rent out some of the bedrooms as bedsits, and Auntie would, single-handed, paint and paper one of the rooms ready for tenants. In addition it often fell to her to buy the furniture needed to make them fit to re-let after the previous occupant had departed. And all this despite the fact that on her right arm she carried to her grave a large radium burn that she received as a student nurse from what was described as an X-ray machine. The burn never fully healed and could be seen, blue-rimmed and ugly, when she rolled up her sleeves. But, though it must have pained her, she never complained, and worked so hard and so long in Tudor Hall that often she had no time for sleep. Having come out in the morning, with no stopping, save for mass and the purchase of bags of groceries for us, she would depart straight back to the hospital. Her generosity was such that when our clothes got shabby, Auntie would either take us herself or authorise us to see Mr Smith in Arnott's department store to be outfitted. When I protested once at the cost of a Crombie overcoat, Auntie replied with one of her favourite sayings: 'It's a good thing. Always get the good thing.' Sometimes she would say: 'It's a bargain if you never wore it!'

We augmented Auntie's charity by various stratagems. When the electricity was cut off, my mother would fill saucers with the oil normally used to burn wicks before a saint's statue and use the wicks to provide illumination. They did not give off much light, but at least we could see to say the rosary. Another stunt was to obtain from Boland's bakery in Dun Laoghaire unsaleable, misshapen loaves 'for the hens'. The 'hens' bread', as we called it, remained a staple diet for years. Less successful was a scheme of Brian's to make money by carrying cases for disembarking passengers off the mail boat. He set off on this mission with high hopes one morning and was gone so long that back at home we developed visions of impending wealth from tips. However, when his woebegone face appeared round the door, it transpired that there had been no tips – a bigger boy had chased him away.

My mother made incessant efforts to acquire a more reliable source of income than case-carrying. In one letter to Dr Michael O'Higgins, she wrote (in June 1948): 'I don't like to seem importunate, but what might look like a simple deferring of the matter for a week or two means so many hours of near-privation for the children and continued anxiety for me. I have no income whatever.' There were to be years, not hours, of anxiety and privation. At various times she had hopes of being appointed an inspector of female prisons, a member of the Radio Eireann Repertory Company and what she envisaged as a sort of social superintendent-type figure at Dublin Castle. The first two never materialised and she turned down the Dublin Castle job in outrage when it emerged that it would have cast her in a caretaker's role, living in a caretaker's cottage: 'Me!' she exclaimed. 'Me, a *caretaker* in Dublin Castle, where I attended balls and banquets with Ned. *Me*, having to look up to those snobby bitches walking past me!'

The feeling of unjust deprivation permeated much of our lives. The year after my father died Ireland was declared a Republic. My mother and her children were invited to attend the ceremonies marking the declaration at the General Post Office (GPO), the headquarters of the 1916 Rising. An army detachment marched past the reviewing stand on which were seated members of the cabinet and other important personages. The people we stood alongside must have been of some importance also, because I remember the Lord Mayor shaking hands with my mother. But, as the echoes of a *feu de joie* from the roof of the GPO died away, my mother commented bitterly in the brief silence after the rifle volleys: 'If Ned had lived, we'd have been in the stand.'

Of the many ministers she corresponded with, William Norton, a Labour member of the inter-party government of 1948–51, appeared the most sympathetic and thus furthered her hopes of a Radio Eireann job. In November 1949 he wrote what turned out to be an activity-without-movement letter saying that he had arranged to speak to the minister for the Department of Posts and Telegraphs because 'I am sure he will be sympathetic and, if the regulations permit, favourably disposed towards you.' Alas, the minister was not sympathetic and, as could have been foretold, the regulations did not permit. Towards the end of November Norton wrote to my mother about the outcome of his discussion, saying that the minister had informed him: 'The position in question will be dealt with by the civil service commissioners in the ordinary way and he will have nothing whatever to do with the selection of the candidate for the position.'

In the course of her correspondence with ministers my mother wrote that our father's children were 'worthy representatives' in whom he had 'inculcated deeply the highest principles of behaviour, national outlook and integrity'. Anyone watching Brian and me that year would have had to look deeply indeed to find those principles. The spirit of resentment that I experienced during our father's funeral – why shouldn't we have a father when everyone else had one? – soon carried over into antisocial behaviour. Much of the reaction was harmless enough, but some of it was actively malicious, going out at night to break streetlamps or, on dis-covering that a handkerchief could be turned into an effective slingshot, hurling stones from our, now overgrown, tennis court, over a high hedge and across a neighbour's garden so that they landed on the greenhouse of another neighbour two houses away. Fortunately the only casualties of this potentially lethal activity were some pieces of glass. But the flying stones could have destroyed a fine career – Peter Sutherland was a son of the greenhouse owner. He afterwards became an Irish attorney general, a European commissioner and, later, chairman of Goldman Sachs.

Our principal illicit indoor sport was shoplifting. I remember we carried off mounds of sweets from Woolworths in Dun Laoghaire. One of our pastimes when mitching school was to climb Nelson's Pillar, which, before the IRA gave its demonstration of its own version of the Rolling Stones in 1966, stood in the centre of O'Connell Street, Dublin. From this vantage point we would attempt to hit the Garda on traffic duty far below us with hard-boiled pieces of stolen liquorice. Fortunately the wind always carried these away and we never heard reports of them hitting anyone else, so they probably fetched up in the Liffey or on the roofs of nearby buildings.

Curiously, while we obviously to some degree became infected with delinquency during adolescence, we appear to have developed an immunity to other forms of infection. Tudor Hall attracted rats, some of them unusually large, which the presence of our several families of cats did little to discourage. We took to trapping the rats, and Brian and I had no compunction about handling their corpses, throwing them at each other or even swinging them by the tail in a rodent variant of conkers. We also appear to have been impervious to the poisons that laburnum trees are said to contain, causing them to be removed from some gardening catalogues. We had a couple of beautiful old laburnum trees, which were covered in yellow blossoms in the flowering season and dispensed multitudes of seed pods later in the year. Neither Brian nor I thought anything of chewing on these, and I was astonished to learn later in life that they are said to be highly toxic.

A more constructive pastime of those days I owed to Mr Gaffney, as we knew him, the librarian of the Dun Laoghaire Public Library. Within the limits of censorship and an attenuated budget he saw to it that the contents of the library were as varied and as enriching as he could make them. I could turn from *Tarzan of the Apes* to Dostoevsky, P. G. Wodehouse, Turgenev or works about the flora and fauna of the African jungle. The artist Tom Roche, who was destined to marry my sister, Aisling, herself a talented artist, also owed much to Gaffney. Both Tom and I were deemed worthy of being allowed to take out some of the library's really important stock of illustrated books, those that were kept in locked glass cases. Thus I studied the wonders of the Amazon and of astronomy, and Tom the works of the great masters.

I didn't acquire much of a reputation as a tearaway, but, probably unfairly, Brian did. He looked quite angelic, with a fresh open face and curly blond hair, but somehow from the earliest days he seemed to draw the lightning. One episode from our boyhood typified the sort of thing that befell him. After our father's death invitations to parties and high teas fell off sharply, but one kindly Protestant neighbour always made us welcome. In fact she was the first person to invite us out after the funeral. Her husband was the verger of Monkstown's Church of Ireland Church, and her two older boys were in the British navy. The youngest boy, who was still at home, was a particular friend of Brian's. He too had a penchant for getting into trouble, and my mother disliked him and deemed him a bad companion. Part of her motivation was class-based: a verger's son did not have the cachet of the old Protestant families who lived on the Hill. But as matters turned out, part of her antipathy proved to be a soundly based maternal instinct.

About two years after our father's death a series of arson attacks destroyed the hay belonging to a small dairy near us run by the two Lawlor brothers and their sister. The family's meagre income was augmented by one brother, who operated a horse-drawn cab. As both the dairying and cabbying depended heavily on hay, the fires were a very serious matter for the Lawlors, so the burnings that occurred at intervals of three or four months over a period of around eighteen months were the subject of much discussion in our area. One summer's morning, as I was setting off to a tennis tournament of all things, I saw Brian ahead of me, down the Hill, talking to a Garda. After the Garda had cycled off, Brian told me that the policeman had been instructing him to turn up at Dun Laoghaire Garda Station that evening to be charged with arson in the company of the verger's son. Apparently the lad had made a statement implicating both Brian and himself as being jointly responsible for the hay burnings. Hitherto that morning my principal worries had centred on the state of my tennis whites and the fact that my racket, an old one of my father's, needed restringing. But, although Brian swore that he had nothing to do with the hay burnings, his news put these woes into perspective. I warned him to say nothing to our mother and arranged to go with him to the station that evening. I performed disastrously in the tournament, probably meriting an entry in *The Guinness Book of Records* for double faults, thereby, *inter alia*, destroying the hopes I had entertained concerning the doctor's daughter, whom I partnered in the mixed doubles. But at some subconscious level my mind must have been functioning effectively.

For when we got to the station, where to my embarrassment we found the kindly Protestant lady waiting with her son for the charges to be laid,

I got a flash of inspiration that saved the day, or rather the night. After the desk sergeant on duty had read out the boy's statement, recalling incidents on the nights that the hay was burned, which included very damning details like meeting a courting couple and obtaining matches from the girl involved, who, it was noted, wore a red dress, it suddenly struck me that all the hay burnings had occurred on half-days or at weekends. The other boy, who had once worked for the Lawlors, would have realised that on those occasions the dairy yard would be shut and there would be no one around to observe him burning the hay.

I suddenly heard my own voice informing those present that Brian couldn't have been involved because at the relevant times he was taking art classes, at Mr George Colley's studio in faraway Dublin. As these were paid for by the hour, they were therefore written up in an attendance ledger, which was available for inspection. There was an uncomfortable silence after this announcement. It was broken by the other boy saying, to the horror of his poor mother: 'Ah, well, in that case I may as well admit it!' When the outraged sergeant asked him why he had implicated Brian in his statement, he simply shrugged his shoulders and said: 'I guess I felt I needed someone with me in the court.' It was said afterwards that the lying statement was in fact concocted by a member of the force who had a grudge against our father, but this was never established. Nor, fortunately, was Mr Colley's attendance book inspected. It would have shown that while Brian did indeed attend art classes, he did so for only a very brief period and then not on any of the dates in question. Necessity is the mother of invention. To this day I don't know where I got the inspiration for the alibi, but without it Brian would have joined the statement's signatory in his subsequent sojourn in a reformatory.

Apart from his artistic talent Brian was a gifted mimic, who during his teens became universally known as 'the Major' after concocting and delivering a satirical monologue on the exploits of a mythical British major negotiating the Zambesi. Even today, after more than fifty years have passed, most of them spent outside the country, schoolmates of Brian's still enquire fondly after 'the Major'.

We weren't at the top of the hit list when it came to invitations to parties at the homes of well-to-do young ladies, but Brian's pugilistic instincts guaranteed that we were at or near the top of the list of favourites to become involved in whatever brawls broke out at tennis-club 'hops' and so forth. It seems to be a rule of thumb that the more upper-crust, and beflannelled, the attendance at such playgrounds of the well-off, the more savage were likely to be the encounters when the young gentlemen involved met on dance floor or in car park to demonstrate the effects of alcohol and testosterone.

The clashes between young bucks at the tennis clubs, and those between the world of tennis clubs generally and the reality of our economic circumstances, were equally abrasive. The Tudor Hall tennis court became a mini rugby pitch. I often thought later that it played something of the role of the playing fields of Eton at Waterloo in the subsequent career of one of our best players. She was a particularly tall, leggy, attractive girl called Adrienne Ring, who afterwards, through her partnership with the designer Mary Quant, became one of the world's top models. During her climb to this glittering pinnacle her Tudor Hall-acquired hand-off proved its worth on many occasions.

Outwardly Tudor Hall itself maintained its imposing presence, but inwardly glaring changes occurred. The mahogany shelves and embossed wallpaper of my father's study yielded to plywood cupboards, kitchen units and greasy paint as bedsits sprouted in most of the available room space. None of the advertisements that were placed to attract these tenants actually stipulated that it would be mandatory for occupants to allow their rent to fall into arrears or to duff gas and electricity meters; the tenants just seemed to automatically behave in this way. Even as I write this, decades later, I still shudder at newspaper advertising phrases such as 'residential lettings' or 'rental income'.

My abiding memory of most of the unfortunates who we attracted to our 'bedsits' is that they had resonances of the bankrupt peregrinations of James Joyce's father, only without his erudition. My distaste for the business of landlordism was compounded by the fact of being frequently ordered to confront the tenants, not alone on the touchy subject of rent but on foot of various complaints of my mother's. Her resentment at having tenants in her house was so overwhelming that she was not prepared to concede any rights or entitlements to such creatures other than (perhaps) breathing. Enormities such as producing babies, cooking smells, boyfriends, prams or lines of washing fell, she considered, just barely short of meriting the death penalty.

Uncles Tim and Frank combined with Auntie to make a contribution to my mother's first major attempt at securing a commercial income other than from the bedsitters. This was a confectionery which necessitated large-scale commercial ovens being installed in the basement, along with some very pretty lady confectioners, and a calling in by my mother of useful contacts. Through one of these, Joseph McGrath, who ran the operation, she secured a contract to supply confectionery to the canteen of the Irish Hospitals Sweeps. The contract lasted for a couple of tempestuous years, punctuated by bouts of hostilities between herself and the catering managers over trifling irrelevancies such as quality control and late deliveries. As I was one of the principal delivery men, I was secretly delighted when this venture came to an end. I had found it embarrassing to have to carry trays of cakes not only to the Sweeps but to various confectionery shops. Even more embarrassing was often to be the piggy in the middle between my mother's demands to be paid yesterday and the shopkeepers obtusely failing to recognise that our cakes were superior to those of any other supplier.

Another formerly grand lady who lived in Monkstown and who had also come down in the world was Mrs Hempel, the wife of the former German ambassador to Ireland. Her position in Dublin society was plucked from her by the fortunes of war, leaving her with a bitterness which I one day experienced. The Hempels lived near us and, oblivious to politics, I sometimes played with the children. I had a dog called Boris, called after Borris-in-Ossory, the place from which it had followed my parents' car, and was ultimately brought home. One day, thinking to impress Mrs Hempel, I called to Boris to come away from one of her flower beds. I impressed her all right. She exclaimed: 'Ve vant no Russian fighters here!' and threw me and Boris out of the place.

The fact that Mrs Hempel managed to adjust to her new circumstances with more efficiency and success than we did was a constant source of annoyance to my mother, who unfairly referred to her as the 'Nazi BIXYZ' (the use of initials was a favourite euphemistic tactic of hers) put inferior ingredients in her cakes and should not have been allowed to trade anyhow. My mother's animadversions on confectionery matters did not prevent me becoming friendly with the Hempel boys, particularly Costa, who in later life worked for a time in Dublin as a reporter. Unfortunately Costa's very beautiful sister, Lief, was a few years older than me and, being a teenager, this placed her considerable charms well outside my range.

In between dealing with the iniquities of tenants and of competitive former ambassador's wives, my mother attempted to better our circumstances by attempting to write novels, to secure some sort of government pension for my father's services, and of course to 'storm the heavens'. Over a period of almost twenty years the heavens ultimately responded benignly. My mother secured a modified Garda pension and wrote the highly successful *The Big Wind*, which follows the career of the heroine, born on the night a hurricane struck Ireland, through the horrors of the famine and of the land war. The book took some twelve years to produce, and the *leitmotif* of my years at Tudor Hall following my father's death was the constant tap-tapping of her Borroughs typewriter. Apart from the phenomenal research, and the effort she put into writing the novel, she also encountered severe (and seemingly interminable) legal difficulties with her agent and publishers. Remarkably she successfully overcame these, although she had to fight her case, with no resources, through London chambers, but the effort and emotional intensity involved meant that she wrote nothing else of consequence. Witnessing her legal travails probably caused me to go in the opposite direction in later life, and get on with the next book rather than fight lawsuits. I don't know which of our courses was better. A writer's primary task is to write, but sometimes the philosophy of 'get on with it' can allow the unscrupulous to get away with much more than they should. This can result in loss of concentration, and output anyhow.

While it's true that my mother did a great deal of her own typing, she, like her eldest son, was not a good typist, and until my sister, Aisling, grew old enough to take over the chore, she engaged a series of amanuenses more distinctive for eccentricity than skill. Dickie Wyman was the most notable of these. He was the living embodiment of the Irish expression 'the relics of ould decency'. Tall and lean, he got his figure from malnutrition, his black hair from a bottle and his yellowing complexion from cigarettes and artificial light. He had a posh Anglo-Irish accent, around which he wrapped a stock, and a houndstooth sports jacket. A homosexual who enjoyed rough trade, he lived mainly by allowing his Dublin pad, the Catacombs, to be used by the literary layabouts who patronised McDaid's pub. The Catacombs had a sinister history, being used during the war by White Russians to beat up suspected Reds. Whatever services the McDaid's lot may have contributed to Wyman by way of beatings, they must have provided very little money. In those days none of them seemed to earn a penny other than by making the odd contribution to one or other of the literary magazines of the period. These included *The Bell*, an associate editor of which was Tony Cronin, who would one day become Charlie Haughey's literary guru, and *Envoy*, which was kept alive by the generosity of John Ryan. Ryan had inherited the Monument Creamery Company and also owned the fashionable pub the Bailey. Unlike the generality of the people he met and mixed with under his other hat, that of a keen yachtsman, John took an active and supportive role in the cultural life of Dublin.

So did Wyman, but at the far end of the scale. He subsisted by collecting the empty bottles left in the Catacombs by his guests and selling them – the bottles that is, not the guests, though I dare say he would have been capable of that too. Dickie also took odd jobs, one of the oddest being to act as my mother's typist. Two such very different stars could not long keep their motion in the one orb. When my mother soon decided that she could no longer afford his services, she gave me money with which to pay him off. I can still vividly remember the horror with which Wyman held out his palm containing the coins and in appalled tones asked: 'What is *this*?' His severance pay amounted to three shillings and ninepence. Not surprisingly we never saw him again.

One of the few pleasurable memories I retain of my mother's religious bent was the enjoyment Brian and I derived from placing kittens under her bedspread, somehow managing to keep straight-faced as they struggled to extricate themselves while we recited the rosary kneeling around the bed. Others concerned the large Christmas cribs filled with straw and figurines of the infant Jesus, Joseph, Mary and animals of all sorts. She had a special devotion to Mary, the mother of Jesus. One of her favourite hymns was 'Mary, Queen of the May', which I always like hearing. But it was her custom of decorating the May altar in her bedroom every year that I especially enjoyed. Apart from the copper beech, laburnum and lilac, interspersed with the few roses and bluebells that survived our neglect of our own garden, Brian and I provided enormous quantities of contraband summer flowers by laying waste to the opulent gardens around us. In the month of May the scents of summer vied with those of the bedsits and the confectionery. A tangible result of my mother's devotion to Mary lives on in the form of the hymn 'Our Lady of Knock', which is still sung at the basilica in Knock, County Mayo, built by her friend Major Eugene Horan, who succeeded in bringing the Pope to Ireland in 1979 to open it.

In the midst of this chaos my mother somehow managed to persuade the managing director of the Educational Building Society, Alex McCabe, to advance us a mortgage of £1,500 with which to buy Tudor Hall, so that we would no longer have to pay rent to the Longford de Vesci Estate. The names of these old Anglo-Irish landlord families are still commemorated around Monkstown. There is a Longford Road, a Longford Terrace, a Pakenham Road and a de Vesci Terrace. I used to play marbles along those then quiet thoroughfares, and many years later I had the pleasure of recalling both marbles and mortgage to Lord Longford over lunch in the House of Lords. Before he inherited the title, Longford, as Frank Pakenham, wrote one of the standard works on the Irish treaty, *Peace by Ordeal*. I wrote a foreword for a later edition of this work – even though it had a pro de Valera slant! Our lunch gave me an insight into how both the names and the fortunes of the Longford family survived. As we finished our meal, and I disposed of the last drops of our one shared carafe of house white, Longford called for the bill and then, looking at my empty glass, and fixing me with a particularly intent gaze, said: 'You don't want *another*, do you?'

However, to return to Alex McCabe, he was an old hero of the Anglo-Irish War and had taught my uncles Tim and Frank at the Jesuit college in Mungret, County Limerick. The foundation of the Educational Building Society was initially based on his idea of providing houses for teachers. He was the sort of maverick character whom one finds occasionally thrown up in the higher reaches of government, commerce or civil service by the ferment of revolution. In later life I got to know him quite well and he described to me in vivid terms how a turning point in the history of Irish democracy came about. It concerned the election of Joseph McGuinness as the first Sinn Fein candidate to win a Westminster by-election after the 1916 Rising. McGuinness was in an English prison at the time, and it was a piece of audacity on Michael Collins's part to put him up against the Irish Parliamentary Party candidate. However, Sinn Fein devised one of the most effective posters in Irish political history. It showed McGuinness in a prison uniform with a slogan reading: 'Put him in to get him out!' Alas, when the votes were first counted, it appeared that McGuinness was going to stay in. Then McCabe, a tall, striking figure dressed in a white raincoat and leather leggings, the very epitome of the Abbey Theatre's portrayal of an IRA man, leaped onto the platform. He placed a .45 Webley revolver against the returning officer's left temple and suggested to him, as he drew back the hammer, that perhaps the gentleman might feel inclined to check whether there were any other Sinn Fein votes lying about. The returning officer conceded that this was a reasonable proposal and, *mirabile dictu*, a bundle of a thousand first-preference votes for McGuinness was discovered. Such was the hinge on which Irish democracy swung. After McGuinness's victory a string of other by-election successes followed, including those of Cosgrave and de Valera, and Sinn Fein swept the parliamentary board in the 1918 'khaki' election.

McCabe was a long-striding, commanding figure. He told me once that his rapid gait both saved his life and almost killed him during the Black and Tan war. Because he could move so quickly, he got away from Tan patrols, but often as a result found that in darkness he stepped into many an icy bog-hole. He escaped the consequences of the flu and tuberculosis that killed more of his colleagues than the British ever did by a simple formula: 'It was all done on hot poteen,' he told me.

Moved both by my mother's importuning and the fact that at the time

Rome's Australianisation policy was uprooting him from his post, Uncle Frank decided to put McCabe's distinctive stride to good use. He approached the building society for yet another mortgage, this time for a project even less founded in reality than either the bedsits or the confectionery – the purchase of a farm. In his application letter Frank recalled how as a boy he and Tim had 'thrilled to the sight of your heroic figure striding across the playing fields of Mungret with that fearless carriage you made famous'.

McCabe genuinely must have been fearless, because he sanctioned the mortgage and, after months of driving around the countryside inspecting farms whose merits she was doubtfully placed to judge, my mother finally bought a property. It consisted of approximately a hundred and twenty acres and had been owned by a Protestant farmer named Willis in the town land of Timor, near Newtown Mount Kennedy, County Wicklow, about fifteen miles south-east of Dun Laoghaire. Later it would emerge that Mr Willis had retained the larger (and better) portion of his holding for himself. However, we were now farmers, and at the age of fourteen I set about becoming a skilled agriculturalist. One can never be sure of such things, and there may have been worse farmers, or families less psychologically fitted for the land than that of Mrs Beatrice Coogan of Tudor Hall, Monkstown, County Dublin, her two sons, Timothy Patrick and Brian, their eight-year-old sister, Aisling, and their uncle, Martin Francis Toal, DD, a distinguished Roman Catholic theologian, but tillers of the soil we were most emphatically not.

There are those, particularly amongst the unionist community and their sympathisers, who would claim that, in view of my later journalistic activities, there was a certain symbolism in the fact that, thanks to my father's guidance, the one farming operation in which I developed expertise was the spreading of shite – manure, as it was known in polite circles. We had a 'farm manager', Stephen, and a labourer, Billy. As befitted his exalted status, Stephen received thirty shillings more than the average agricultural wage paid to Billy, three pounds ten shillings a week. They, with my cack-handed assistance, attended to the scientific end of the farming operations – ploughing, milking, feeding the pigs and taking the cows to the bull. Not many journeys of this nature were required because we had only two cows. Our livestock was further depleted when some of the one litter of piglets that our sow produced died of swine fever and the rest were sold off. But I did have a number of turkey chicks, one of which actually survived long enough to be slaughtered for Christmas. What we had an unending supply of were bills – ordinary bills, civil bills and increasingly stentorian blasts from Alex McCabe, who must often have wished himself back in those simple days of Black and Tans, and forgetful returning officers.

Uncle Frank's dream of retiring from the parched landscape of an Australian Jesuit college to an idyllic green Irish farm nestling between the Wicklow Mountains and the sea soon faded. He and my mother fell out under the twin pressures of forceful personalities and ever-mounting debt. It had been intended that a Dutch farming family would take over the running of our holding, but my mother and my uncle Tim, the principal financial backer of the enterprise, baulked at the hard bargain that the Dutchmen attempted to drive. Stephen and Billy were one result, financial chaos the other. For a few years we drifted along, sustaining ourselves on the proceeds of the annual thrashing of oats and wheat, money from the bedsits in Tudor Hall and the occasional cheque from Auntie or Uncle Tim. Eventually, Uncle Frank wisely decided that theology offered a safer haven than Timor, and took himself off to the Collegio Teutonico in Rome, which was to pass into fame as the centre from which came Cardinal Ratzinger, the present Pope. At the college Uncle Frank produced his learned, multi-volumed and practically unsaleable series *Patristic Homilies of the Fathers*, based on the teachings of the founding fathers of the Church. The books were undoubtedly erudite – they were written in both Latin and English – and demanded a huge expenditure of effort, including the learning of German. But Uncle Frank was unfortunate in producing them at a time when the newer currents stirring in the Church were about to burst forth under the influence of Pope John XXIII. Under the conservative Ratzinger, poor Uncle Frank would have been a star, had he lived long enough.

While the farming venture cast Uncle Frank into scholarship, it had the opposite effect on me. I took care to ensure that my farming duties enabled me to miss an inordinate amount of schooling. I lived on the farm for months at a time, and can still remember how lonely a blackbird's call could sound over silent farmland at twilight. It was the era of the Korean War, and Brian, who like myself availed of the farm to miss school, but differed from me in managing to also avoid getting involved in its chores, commented one day that we were eating so much rice and raisins that we were in serious danger of developing slanty eyes. Despite the staple rice diet and the loneliness, the farm did provide some attractions. For example, I learned how to augment my diet by shooting rabbits and pheasants (in and out of season), and because I had learned to play tennis in Dublin, found myself a not unwelcome visitor to the local tennis club. I also enjoyed the annual threshings, when men came from neighbouring farms to pitch the sheaves into the threshing mill, bag the corn and store straw. There was one nasty side to the threshings. Myriad rats used to jump out of the sheaves and there was great excitement as the men tried – and generally succeeded – to impale the screaming creatures on their hay forks.

But eventually my mother decided that our future lay in Dublin, prompted in part by the disappearance of so much of the rents into Wicklow and in part by Alex McCabe. I remember Alex one night explaining to me why his wife never accompanied him to what was at the time a haunt of his and mine, Dublin's United Arts Club. 'An excellent woman,' he said. 'Connemara,' he said meaningfully. Then, as I obviously received this intelligence with puzzlement, explained: 'Takes a dismal view!' Alex himself was forced to take a dismal view of our mortgage repayments and to threaten the imminent disappearance of our entitlements to both farm and Tudor Hall. In this endeavour he would have been joined by a long line of process-servers operating on behalf of rate-collectors, butchers, suppliers of farm machinery and, in a word, practically anyone with whom we came into economic contact.

The sale of the farm changed our finances for the better for a while. Although land prices were ridiculously cheap by the standards of today, the prospect, however distant, of a European Economic Community was having an effect on farm sales. I think we achieved something like £100 an acre – at the time of writing, agricultural land in Ireland has been known to fetch over £40,000 an acre – which cleared the mortgage, reduced the debt on Tudor Hall and provided a couple of thousand over and above. As my mother kept this money in her handbag, both for security and ease of access when purchasing gin and tonics, this nest egg did not last very long, but it had a cheering effect nonetheless. Not so cheering was the return to school.

I have said that at the time of my father's death we were attending St Xavier's College in Donnybrook, an elite establishment concerning which many of its distinguished alumni have good things to say. I do not. The school had a system of merit cards, which gave a weekly assessment of pupils' progress. Mine were always either 'highly satisfactory' or at worst 'very satisfactory', chiefly because of my good behaviour. Said behaviour masked academic fraud. Somewhere along the line, through a combination of the transition from Miss Stephens to the Christian Brothers, and an unsettling tendency on the part of the school curriculum to progressively introduce subjects such as the Irish language, algebra and something monstrous known as geometry, a large black hole formed at the centre of my studies. Prior to my father's death I had managed to conceal this by judicious bouts of illness on the eve of the more damaging examinations, but now with my father's guiding hand removed, both bad behaviour and linguistic and mathematical shortcomings caught up with me. A series of mitchings from class and increasingly severe beatings were the result. The beatings were increased in severity by my mother's habit of bringing our domestic misbehaviour to the attention of the headmaster, a Mr Hughes, who apparently had once taught with distinction in Australia, a place wherein I earnestly wished he had stayed.

Some of my colleagues remember Hughes with affection, but to me he remains in memory as a snob, with an ever-ready leather, who insisted that Latin should be spoken 'in the Oxford manner'. Apparently he had it on good authority from some ancient Roman that Caesar should be pronounced 'Chezarrr'. In the year after our father's death Brian and I hit on ever more ingenious and destructive stratagems for missing school. I remember once trying unsuccessfully to frustrate my mother's attempt to make up for us missing our bus (deliberately) by driving us to school herself in a relic of the confectionery days, a green Ford van, by pouring a one-pound bag of sugar into the petrol tank. According to British comics like the *Champion* and *Hotspur*, this technique had worked wonders when used by heroic British saboteurs against Japanese warplanes, but in our case the sugar seemed to make the wretched van run better than ever.

While some might argue that strangulation and not departure should have concluded the St Xavier's experiment, departure was the option chosen. Brian and I, with our uncles' help, enrolled in Blackrock College, run by the Holy Ghost Fathers for what would turn out to be the first of two stints there. From the moment we entered the college I felt welcomed and at home, literally so, because the then president of the college, a Father Kennedy, put his arms round our shoulders and said: 'You are very welcome here, boys.' I had been feeling pretty miserable that morning. We were dressed in pinstripe suits, cut down from my father's clothing by Redmond, the tailor who had described to me how my grandparents' house came to be burned down by his IRA column. Our experiences at St Xavier's had not been good, and the place had been so snobbish that we had learned to look down on Blackrock as an inferior sort of establishment! Moreover Brian and I had had our ears filled for days with warnings that our iniquities at St Xavier's were not to be repeated in Blackrock. If they were, a combination of my father's dire warnings about breaking stones and the cat-o'-nine-tails would be brought into effect.

But in fact, although Brian continuously got into scrapes, I was extremely happy in Blackrock because of an amalgam of the attitude of the teachers, both clerical and lay, and the strong emphasis on sport in the college, which was, and is, one of Ireland's great nurseries of rugby. During my time there one of the imposing presences was a Father Hampson, the dean of studies and later president of the college, who trained the Senior XV. Father Hampson had a stopwatch on which he timed the number of seconds it took to get the ball from the scrum to the wing three-quarters. His favourite saying was 'Remember, boys, that the two most important things in life are the Grace of God and' – delivered with particular emphasis – 'the quick heel from the base of the scrum.' I am not quite sure why this, our first stint at Blackrock, came to an end after less than two years. Exam results and disciplinary problems at home may have played a role, but more likely Uncle Tim and Frank's Jesuit education had a bearing. In any event one day my mother drove us to Belvedere College. Here we sat an intelligence test that resulted in my being accepted into Belvedere and Brian being dispatched to Limerick to attend Mungret College as a boarder.

Any remote chance that the repeated dislocations of our school-going might have been somehow overcome by attendance at Belvedere was knocked on the head by the purchase of the farm around the time of our enrolment with the Jesuits. I took an instant dislike to the school, which was set in the centre of Dublin and, unlike Blackrock, was surrounded not by grass playing fields but tarmacadam. The one good thing I remember about Belvedere was that if one paid extra, which Uncle Frank did for a term or so, then it was possible to get lunch at the college. This was a very welcome addition to the somewhat haphazard culinary arrangements at Tudor Hall. I don't remember any of the Jesuits with affection, though I remember liking one of my fellow pupils with whom I went on a school cycling tour, Tony O'Reilly, who later became a rugby star and business tycoon. I would have thought that these accomplishments, coupled with the fact that he had had the honour of going on a cycling tour with me would have been sufficient distinctions for him, but he later accepted a knighthood from the British government and his newspapers are now instructed to refer to him as Sir Anthony O'Reilly.

The Jesuits' aestheticism appeared to me to be of a dehumanised sort, being summed up for me one day when I was suffering from an attack of sinusitis by a black-robed figure who looked at me quizzically before saying: 'Have a headache, do you? That's a pity!' I had been expecting that my distress would have merited being sent home in an ambulance, preferably with an instruction to take at least a month off to recuperate.

However, the farm provided me with a method of ensuring that I got time off. My diligent application to the role of SS man (shite-spreader) and its allied pastimes resulted in school reports arriving at Tudor Hall in which there occurred under the heading for 'Attendance' entries such as 'absent thirty-five days in term' and, in one glorious stand for liberty, 'absent seventy-five days'. I must have managed to stay away from school on days on which it wasn't open at all! At all events, as the farm departed us I departed Belvedere and Blackrock beckoned once more. Once again I found the priests and the establishment generally more congenial than the other institutions I had attended.

The Holy Ghost fathers have a reputation for being a cautious and extremely conservative order that catered for the elite of Irish society, but whatever the priests' theological standpoint, my observation of the congregation over the years was that it contained high quotients of kindliness and educational skill, and a marked tendency to temper the wind to the shorn lamb. The number of boys I encountered from poor backgrounds, or from families which fell on hard times, but who were not pressed for fees was quite significant. Certainly this was true in my own case, where both fees and discipline were concerned. Father Hampson was a much-feared figure because, as dean of studies, it was to him one was sent for punishment. Having been complained about by one of the lay teachers for disorderly behaviour, and put out of the class into the bargain, I expected that my punishment would begin with decapitation and then work downwards, but Hampson simply looked me in the eye and said: 'Tim, you don't want to become known as a notice box, do you?' and sent me back to the class, where my behaviour improved sharply.

Fifty years later I was talking to one of Father Hampson's principal beneficiaries of the quick-heel philosophy, Niall Brophy, a legendary wing three-quarter who played for the Lions with Tony O'Reilly, and was astounded to find that he had a very different view of Hampson to mine, despite being the sort of role-model pupil, excelling at both games and studies, whom the college extolled. Niall remembered receiving severe beatings from 'the Boose', as we called Hampson.

Perhaps the fact of the Holy Ghosts being a missionary order had something to do with the ambience of the college. While I never remember any of the fathers making comments about the various countries they served in, the cosmopolitan air of the place spoke for itself. I remember boys from Java, Argentina, Egypt, Malaya, Nigeria, America and even pagan England! Though the atmosphere of the place was heavily Catholic, when it came to what were termed 'religious knowledge classes' these foreign students either went to attend another class or to study somewhere else. Blackrock also provided me with an insight into the work ethic of Asiatics. In my last year in college I became a boarder and shared my room in the Castle, the residential house for final-year students, with a Chinese boy called Paul Wong, who came to the school after the Christmas term. Paul was a brilliant mathematician but he had little English and no Latin, both of which he required for entry to the College of Surgeons. I helped him with both subjects, and despite this he managed to achieve entry marks to Surgeons.

The intriguing thing concerning Asiatic students for us Irish boys was the way they studied, even when they didn't have to – i.e. when their parents were wealthy. One particular family from Malaya, the Eus, were apparently scions of a tin-mining dynasty. One of them told me that they had persuaded their father to abandon his plan to tour Europe with them and to buy them a Rolls-Royce and to give them the money instead. Even in bed the Eus continued their studies under the blankets with the aid of flashlights. Their lithe build was highly deceptive when it came to their physical strength. Badminton, which they played with a particular ferocity, had so strengthened their right arms that even the biggest members of the senior rugby team could not attempt to compete with them at arm-wrestling unless the Malayan lads agreed to use only their left arms. One of the prophecies attributed to the Irish St Malachy is to the effect that 'The yellow man shall stable his horses on the shores of Lough Neagh.' My days at Blackrock left me in no doubt that St Malachy knew what he was talking about.

Where my own studies were concerned, I gained some ground in English, history, Latin, commerce (curiously) and even went a certain distance with arithmetic and trigonometry, but such things as surds and geometry remained outside my ken, as did felicity in the Irish language, though I managed high marks in French. Not unsurprisingly, given my previous scholastic record, I was not an A student. In fact I was in class D for most things, only because the streaming system did not have a category E. However, I was in C for English, which did not study for honours subjects in the Leaving Certificate, but the English teacher, Father Sean 'Vicki' Farragher, still going strong as this is being written, decided to break with tradition and successfully argued with the college authorities that I should be allowed to take the honours course. I got an honours mark and subsequently C pupils became eligible to choose between pass and honours. Vicki gave his class two pieces of advice that I never forgot. In one, he told a classroom filled with either muddied oafs or would-be muddied oafs, hoping either to get on to some rugby team or some girlfriend, that 'Boys should learn how to dance. It's a valuable social skill and it makes for elegance of deportment.' And the other: 'Boys, if you're thinking of getting married and you want to know what your future bride will turn out like – look at her mother.' However, despite Vicki's kindly intervention I failed the Leaving Certificate examination overall and it was decided, with the assistance of my ever-indulgent uncles, that I should be given an extra year at Blackrock, this time as a boarder in the Castle.

The regime in the Castle was particularly benign. Provided I attended the classes for the subjects I was weak in, mainly mathematics and Irish, no objection was raised whenever I decided to skip a class and stay in my room reading. The president of the Castle was a Father Finucane, who had taught me Latin and French. He too had had an awesome reputation as a disciplinarian during his stint as dean of studies, but I remember him for two particular kindly actions. In one he accepted me back into the Castle with only a token reprimand after I had missed the Christmas examinations in order to work as a temporary postman. The other commercial activity I developed while at Blackrock was that of freelance sports reporter. My mother knew the editor of the *Irish Independent*, Frank Geary, and he put in a word for me so that I began doing sports reports for the *Sunday Independent*. This meant that I had to get special permission to leave the college on Saturday afternoons, and also that I missed playing in a lot of rugby matches. But despite his dislike of boys taking jobs that interfered with their studies, Father Finucane not only gave me permission but on one occasion, when he discovered that I would have to miss my lunch in order to attend an early kick-off, went to the school pantry himself and made me a pot of tea and brown-bread marmalade sandwiches. Respect for Father Finucane and other priests like him actually made me consider the priesthood myself – temporarily. One of the big events for final-year students was 'the vocation retreat', during which classes were suspended and we prayed and listened to lectures about the value of the priestly life. Powerful as these arguments were, acting on the minds of a captive audience of Catholic adolescents, I still maintained secret doubts about the reality of said values, as its cheques apparently could only be cashed in the next life.

The interviews to determine whether or not one had a vocation were held in the Castle's parlour. Father Higgins, the seminary director who conducted the retreat, temporarily banished my reservations by placing me in a large, brocaded, throne-like armchair, under a portrait of Cardinal d'Alton, and, looking up at the painting, he said with a smile: 'Now, Tim Pat, coming events cast their shadow.' I told him that while I accepted his argument that 'certain pleasures' that, at my age, might have a distracting effect would lessen as I progressed through life, and those of the priesthood would increase, nevertheless I still could not make up my mind. Happily Father Higgins made it up for me by saying that he thought Tim Pat Coogan seemed to be passing through a slightly 'selfish' stage and might not be willing to give the necessary amount of obedience required for the priesthood. Happily also the attractions of 'certain pleasures' have not borne out Father Higgins's forecasts by disappearing.

The priest who was destined to have the most far-reaching effect on my life was Father Michael O'Carroll, my history teacher. 'Doc', as he was known, was a tall, imposing figure who, theologically, would later became an admirer of the conservative Tridentine Archbishop Lefebvre, who defended the Latin mass against the ravages of the Second Vatican Council, but politically could have been described as both liberal and democratic. During the Second World War he attempted with limited success to highlight the plight of the Jews against the opposition of his fellow Holy Ghost priest the archbishop of Dublin, John Charles McQuaid and the Irish political and administrative elite generally. In those days the danger of offending the Nazis rated more highly than did succour for a race that had but a small presence in Ireland. Doc was also a moving spirit behind one of the first mass protest movements on a matter of public taste ever seen in Dublin. This was occasioned by a proposal by the Electricity Supply Board (ESB) to tear down a set of Georgian buildings that the Board owned in Fitzwilliam Square to build new offices. The issue convulsed people during the mid-1950s, dividing on typically irrelevant Irish lines, not merely by, with or from architectural heritage, but on republican arguments that the houses were a symbol of British oppression and that the Special Branch should be prosecuted for its treatment of the IRA during the war. Unfortunately, while it heightened public consciousness, judging from the course of subsequent town planning, this major controversy cannot be said to have led to a lasting improvement in civic pride.

However, Doc chaired the first, overflowing, public meeting in the Mansion House, opening with the words 'This is an exercise in democracy.' He veered off the main issue to praise the good work the ESB had done for the country, and then returned to the charge, via a thunderous 'But! In the present instance ...!' Disarming but effective, and confirming my own interest in heritage issues. Apart from encouraging my love of history, Doc had a significant impact at two major junctures in my career. He once asked me what I would like to do after leaving school, I replied: 'Journalism.' He replied briskly: 'Good! Plenty of room at the top.' There seemingly the matter ended. But some time afterwards a member of the college debating team fell ill and I was chosen as a replacement. The chairman of the debate was Major Vivion de Valera, Eamon de Valera's eldest son, and my father's companion of Law Library days. I was both attracted and repelled at the prospect of meeting a scion of the ogre de Valera close up. But the major, as he was generally known, turned out to be a rather nice-looking, silvery-haired man who was described as a scientist, but who listened respectfully to our informed opinions on the subject of the development of thermo-nuclear weapons. It was the only debate I had ever spoken in and the medal went to the captain of the opposing team, who had the advantage of speaking twice, but the occasion helped to provide me with a spring-board into journalism.

Without telling me, Doc rang Vivion de Valera shortly afterwards, when it was announced that the Irish Press Group of which Vivion was the managing director was about to launch an evening paper, the *Evening Press*. Doc told Vivion that he had a boy in his class who would either break his heart or turn out a genius. Either way he should be given a trial. When Vivion heard who the boy was, he recalled both the debate and those far-off bottles of stout with my father. My mother, who had also interceded with the paper for a position either for me or herself (not necessarily in that order), was advised to get me to send in an application. Doc never mentioned the call to me, and it would be more than twenty years later that Vivion did, but that was how my first regular job in journalism came about. Later still, when I had left journalism, Doc, who was then nearing ninety, intervened in my affairs once more in a manner, which will be described in context, that had an even more marked (and beneficial) effect on my career.

There were a number of reasons why Doc's first intervention was a godsend. One would have thought that my main difficulty would have been the getting of a job of any sort in Ireland at that stage, but curiously this was not my problem. Through a family friend I had actually obtained a post with the English firm Plessy's before the *Evening Press* came through. The job was intended to act as a springboard to a career in cost account-ancy, and in the circumstances of the time I was extraordinarily lucky to get work within, literally, a few days of leaving school, but I was about as well suited to accountancy as I had been to farming and, in addition to my dislike of the work, had to undertake what, in the state of public transport at the time, was a huge commute from Monkstown to and from the Cherry Orchard district of Dublin each day. However, I was only there a couple of weeks before the firm closed for summer holidays, and during these I received a letter telling me I was to start work as an 'editorial assistant' on the *Evening Press*, on 13 August 1954.

There were two reasons why the *Evening Press* was invaluable to me: Tulyar and the 'Blocker'. Tulyar was the name of a famous stallion whose purchase by the National Stud at the time had given rise to controversy in the newspapers. Unfortunately for me, the row over the wretched animal occurred to me one glorious July day as I sat my Matriculation Certificate examination in Blackrock College. I had already sat the Leaving Certificate exam in the preceding weeks and felt (wrongly, as it turned out) that I had obtained a pass in Irish. Resenting being cooped up as the sun shone, and knowing that I wasn't going to university and was only taking the Matric because everyone else in my class was doing so, when it came to the Irish paper I decided to enjoy myself. First, I answered everything, including the Irish composition question, in English. Second, the tone of my replies may be gauged from my response to the 'aisling', or dream poetry, section. In the 'aisling', Ireland, personified as a *spéir bhean*, or spirit woman, appears to a poet in a dream on a white horse and bemoans her fate. I wrote to the effect that the extreme impropriety of a lady appearing in a gentleman's bedroom at night on a white horse was to be deplored; that there was nothing new in the lady's message; that Ireland then, as during the Matriculation Certificate examination period, was in a state of chassis; and that understandably the poet had woken up sweating terribly, an odoriferous circumstance to which the lady had responded by promptly disappearing. I wrote that we were not told what happened to the white horse, but that very likely it had been purchased by the National Stud as had Tulyar. Presumably this answer, and others like it, had a bearing on the fact that for the Irish paper as a whole I received a mark of nought, thus failing the entire exam.

But it was the 'Blocker' incident that made it impossible for me to return to Blackrock, even had the college, and my indulgent uncles, thought it worthwhile to try again at my age (nineteen at the time). The 'Blocker' was a nickname for the only fly in the ointment I encountered at Blackrock. A dark-haired, lowering figure from South Armagh, I thought of him as a thick and obdurate man at the best of times, but then he made the crass misjudgement of dropping me from a rugby team. I immediately viewed him as a legitimate target, but I had to hold my fire until the final night of school. I struck by first pinning a satirical ode, based on Mark Antony's address on the death of Caesar, on the college notice board. The quality of this may be judged from a stanza that went:

But 'Blocker' is an Honourable Man,
A most renowned Gaelic Player,
And one who has the gift of prayer.

Then, while the unfortunate man was attending an end-of-school cele-bration, I removed every stick of furniture and carpeting from his room and dragged it into a classroom. To ensure that he got the message, I balanced his large china washing bowl, filled with water, on his partially open door and took off for home. Looking back, I will concede that there are those who would regard this reprehensible episode as being a piece of essential symbolism for someone contemplating a career in journalism: be sure to get your retaliation – and place yourself out of reach.

CHAPTER 5

Stoned on the Job

The *Evening Press* was a brave venture in the circumstances of the time. In 1954 the Irish economy was in an appalling state. My starting pay was four pounds a week and I considered myself lucky to have it. The levels of income and of social security payments prevailing at the time may be judged from the fact that if someone fell ill, it was a commonplace occurrence that a collection had to be taken up amongst his colleagues. When Michael Mills, one of the reporters, later a nationally known political correspondent, but at the time a news reporter, developed a long-term illness, it fell to me to take up a weekly collection for him. I consulted with Maurice Liston, who was regarded as the oracle of the newsroom because of his tendency towards Delphic pronouncements such as telling a colleague with a hangover that 'The worst wounds are self-inflicted.' Or advising that 'Drink when you're working creates a carnival spirit where there is no carnival.' I was thinking of seeking five shillings a week. Maurice snorted: 'Five shillings! Are you mad?'

'Two and six?' I enquired hopefully, albeit somewhat dismayed at an instantaneous 50 per cent cut in expectations.

'Listen, young man,' replied Maurice, 'you'll do well to get one shilling a week out of these fuckers!'

As, Delphi apart, Maurice was the best shorthand note-taker in Burgh Quay and, in addition to his professionalism, respected for the fact that he was one of the principal architects of the National Union of Journalists (NUJ), I accepted his advice. It was prophetic. By the time my collection stint finished, I was finding it progressively harder to round up the elusive shillings. The problem was not meanness but a scarcity of money.

Between them Vivion's father, his political associates and the opposition parties had created a situation wherein had the Irish bloodstock industry been treated as the people were, the Irish horse would be extinct. There were said to be some eighty-five thousand on the dole, but in fact many more were out of work, as female unemployment was not adequately reflected in the statistics. The state took no official note of those single women and widows who lived grey lives of toil helping out in the homes of relatives. It was only the safety valve of emigration that prevented the country exploding in revolution. A million people left the Republic during the 1950s, a cruel drain on a population of approximately 3.5 million, and even crueller for the emigrants themselves. They were bright and industrious, but their ability to develop either their minds or their careers was often severely circumscribed by the fact that in those days over half the school-going population finished with education at the age of twelve.

The older revolutionary generation, personified by Eamon de Valera, was incapable of leading or leaving the citadels of power. Wartime neutrality had left the country isolated from the rest of the world, an insulation deepened by the absence of the postwar Marshall aid that flowed into the rest of Western Europe. The presence of Catholic censorship, emigration and habits of deference amongst those who remained helped to stifle debate and the development of political or economic initiatives that might have helped the situation. So far as I was concerned, the encircling intellectual fog was penetrated by odd shafts of light from items in the *Irish Times* and the occasional BBC programme. Panellists on the BBC seemed to be able to talk with an assurance and fluency that in those days one rarely met with in Ireland.

In particular light shone from the array of Penguin books one could buy for half nothing in the Eblana bookshop in Grafton Street. It was here I made the acquaintance of Camus, Maupassant, Malraux, Ford Madox Ford, Hemingway, Fitzgerald, Waugh. My favourite newspaper was the *Observer*. Here one could read people as varied as Arthur Koestler, Katherine Whitehorn and Kenneth Tynan. There might be very little chance of seeing any of the plays Tynan reviewed, but one entered a theatre of the mind when he enlivened one's week with descriptions of performances such as that by the actress 'who swooped around the stage like a wounded pterodactyl'. You wouldn't meet the like of them in Dun Laoghaire!

But if you did go for a walk along Dun Laoghaire's East Pier on a winter's day, the view you would see, on looking back towards the town, accurately portrayed the depressed state of the economy. The houses along the seafront were generally unpainted, and inevitably the hall doors were either black or dark green. The waters of the harbour itself were green also, of the Joycean snot-green hue. In the winter the sailing boats of the better-off were on dry land, and the most regular activity in the harbour was the comings and goings of the mail boat between Holyhead and Dun Laoghaire. Daily the boat took away the hopes and dreams of a generation, to be crushed between the realities of Camden Town, Kilburn, the building site, the avarice of the subcontractor, the doss house and the dead-end job.

Those were the days when London's Black Marias, as the police vans were known, were also called 'Paddy's taxi', when British lodging houses frequently displayed signs saying: 'No dogs, blacks or Irish.' The pubs, which were largely responsible for the behaviour that put the Irish on the bottom of that list, did a roaring trade. The Irish, many of them, merely roared, briefly, and broke their strength for the 'subbie', as the (generally Irish) subcontractors were known. Irish labourers who worked for subbies often paid no tax, stamped no cards and prepared no future. Of course, being the indomitable Irish, a large percentage, possibly the largest, both men and women, broke out of the ghettos and made successful careers for themselves. But in historical terms the 1950s were the last major high-water mark of the two colonialisms, Mother England and Mother Church. In England the surge of cheap labour built the dams, roads and factories, and completed the work of postwar reconstruction.

In Ireland there were few factories, and church steeples were the dominant feature of the skyline. In the streets one saw priests and nuns in all sorts of robes: long-robed brown friars, black-garbed priests and blue and white 'butterfly' nuns, with their huge flyaway headdresses. The priests read their missals and said their prayers. No one appeared to read the unemployment statistics. The commercial climate of the country therefore was not propitious for the launching of a new publication. But somehow Jack Dempsey, the general manager of the company, had already persuaded Vivion de Valera that a company was like a tree or a family; it either grew or it died. The result had been the successful *Sunday Press*, published in 1949, and now logical, organic growth demanded the creation of an evening paper, to keep the giant printing presses running on a twenty-four-hour basis. The paper was edited by Douglas Gageby, a Belfast Protestant who was educated at Trinity, served in the Irish Army Intelligence Corps and after the war got a job on the *Irish Press* via his brother officer, Vivion de Valera. His knowledge of German earned him an assignment to write about postwar Germany and the resultant series of articles catapulted him up the ranks. His reputation was such that Vivion de Valera brought him back from the Irish News Agency after he had been head-hunted by that short-lived organisation. Normally people who left the *Irish Press* were not welcomed back, but the caustic, talented Gageby merited a breaking of the rule.

He interviewed me, less than two weeks after I had completed my disastrous Matriculation examination and, fixing me with one of his celebrated brown-eyed glares, told me: 'You realise of course that in journalism you can be fired at any second. A general manager of UPI' – United Press International – 'has just gone through Europe and fired every second man in the News Agency.' After letting this sink in for a while, he added: 'I think you might be the sort, though, that could survive.'

The *Evening Press* provided an excellent assault course in survival techniques. 'Casuals', as freelancers were known, shoaled in and out of the office. Staffers had to contend with the threat of suspension as well as that of firing. Yet there was an enormous camaraderie and energy about the place. The staff were much younger than the journalists on the group's other two papers, the daily *Irish Press* and the *Sunday Press*, and regarded the *Irish Press* in particular as a bastion of obscurantism.

De Valera's dead hand still rested on the morning paper, a fact that I feel was symbolised by the manner in which the death of the pioneer of research into sexual behaviour, Alfred Kinsey, was reported, and by the personality of the senior paper's children's editor. Kinsey's death was recorded in a one-paragraph story which mentioned that he was a world-renowned authority on gall wasps and left out the rest. The children's corner was run by a mythical 'Captain Mac', who in real life was a Captain Keogh and had been an officer in the brigade that Roger Casement had attempted to recruit during the First World War from Irish prisoners of war in German camps. The captain used to come into the office wearing his Casement uniform and proudly displaying a long sword. I can't imagine what effect he would have had on any children he encountered, but he certainly scared me.

Reporters were generally recruited from provincial papers, some of the younger sub-editors because they had managed to sell particularly large numbers of small ads for the new paper. Douglas Gageby was in his mid-thirties, at the time the youngest editor of a national paper in the country – a title I was delighted to take from him some fourteen years later, when I was appointed editor of the *Irish Press*. But to begin with it was hard to know what my own title was. Officially described as an 'editorial assistant', I was neither a copy boy nor a journalist.

Journalism is a calling situated somewhere between that of the artist and the artisan, and I had an even more anomalous position because my first job lay halfway between that of a copy boy and a sub-editor. A writer in the *Irish Press*, Aodh de Blacam, once described a sub-editor as being someone who crossed out other men's words and went home in the dark. Workers on an evening paper go home in daylight, but sub-editors still had to cross out superfluous words, check for inaccuracies and generally prepare reporters' copy for the typesetter, with what was meant to be a catchy headline. However, my principal task was to sit beside the chief sub-editor and note the time that each piece of copy went into the out-tray, from whence it was taken to the typesetters by a copy boy. When the copy was set, I had to fill in the time at which it appeared in proof form. No one explained to me that this was a form of unacknowledged work study of the hair-trigger printers' union. I would have been safer playing hopscotch on a motorway. But somehow, during the interminable con-frontations between unions and managements over late starts and missed deadlines, the statistical source of the management's accusations was never revealed. My other duties included making tea, which I was good at, and ensuring that the comic strips and the horoscopes appeared in sequence, which I was very bad at. On a number of occasions either February's horoscopes appeared in June or Taurus's predictions appeared instead of those of Sagittarius or some such. Readers should remember this anecdote when next they look up their own horoscopes in their favourite journal.

My becoming a sub-editor depended on two things. One, a continual bearing in mind of the fact that, like rugby outside halves, sub-editors were of two species, the quick and the dead. The other, on my pleasing John O'Donovan, the chief sub-editor. Although as time passed I came to realise that O'Donovan was the kindest of men, winning his approval proved a difficult assignment on many levels. He was a Shavian devotee, who modelled his meticulous handwriting on that of George Bernard Shaw. My handwriting was (and is) appalling, a serious drawback for an aspirant sub-editor. He was also a vegetarian and a health fanatic, who was so hygiene-conscious that he always held his penis in tissue paper while urinating. I remember one day a shocked casual from the sports department, who did not know O'Donovan, excitedly telling his colleagues that they should 'run down to the jacks quick – there's a fucker using toilet paper to take a piss!'

O'Donovan once tried to further the career of a copy boy who declared himself to be a socialist but whose socialism largely took the form of not getting out of bed in the morning. O'Donovan tried to enrol the copy boy's mother in the cause of improving the lad's time-keeping, but with a shake of the head she replied: 'Ah, sure you can't do anything with him – he's like his da, daft!' Thereafter, by way of gratitude for O'Donovan's solicitude, the lad used to ceremoniously pause outside the editor's office wherein Gageby and O'Donovan ate their lunchtime sandwiches and, lifting the lid of O'Donovan's sterilised earthenware teapot, spit – copiously – into the lapsang souchong. Fortunately the boy was fired for some other misdemeanour before O'Donovan found out about the spitting.

Even more fortunate for me was the fact that O'Donovan never found out that, despite the extra year as a boarder, I had again failed Irish in the Leaving Certificate and been awarded the lowest mark recorded that year in the accompanying Matriculation examination. My file in the editor's filing cabinet contained a note: 'Leaving Certificate to be produced.' I was asked to produce the certificate on a couple of occasions and somehow managed to fob off O'Donovan with promises to do so. Several years after the exam results had become known, I became a temporary columnist for the paper and was given the use of the office, which was empty at night, to type my copy. Finding the filing cabinet open one night, I removed the note.

We had very little to do with the staff of the other two newspapers, whom, with the arrogance of youth, we regarded as fossilised old party hacks, engaged in turning out propaganda for de Valera and the Fianna Fail Party. The early success of the *Evening Press* owed much to youth and to two innovations, which say a good deal about the low level of coverage by the electronic media of the time and the general innocence of society. Transistors were of course unknown, as were hourly news bulletins. Emigration, as I have said, drew off much of the energy and potential revolutionary violence of the society – there were only two murders in the country in the year in which the paper was founded. (At the time of writing, there are often more than that number in a week.) One innovation involved leaving portions of page one empty for the country, or first edition. Then, as sports results and breaking news reports reached the office, these were phoned to a series of depots around the country where the new information was stencilled into the blank spaces. Thus country towns, remote from Dublin, were supplied with the bones of the news available to Dubliners who bought the last edition of the day.

In order to give an impression of large-scale editionising, the three main editions of the day were labelled second, fourth and sixth. Nobody ever seemed to realise that there were no first, third and fifth editions. While the Bush innovation, as the stencilling process became known, gained country readers, the success of the paper in the city editions owed a great deal to three babies belonging to three Dublin working-class families, the Ashmores, the Berrigans and the Brownes. At different times, for different reasons, the babies disappeared from their homes and fetched up with new parents. An *Evening Press* reporter, Jim Flanagan, somehow discovered the whereabouts of one of these infants, the Ashmore child, and then while the women of the city were still agog at this development, amazingly the cases of two other missing babies turned up also, one of them initially in the columns of our rival evening paper, the *Evening Herald*. Sales rocketed as the papers vied in a baby war.

But as all the children involved were from working-class backgrounds, Vivion de Valera became anxious that the paper's preoccupation with the offspring of the lower orders might damage the upmarket image of the paper. Once the initial excitement had died away, reference to the missing babies, even in conversation, became unwelcome in Burgh Quay. Having a bent for mathematics, Vivion was much happier with the calculations of the geologist Morough O'Brien, who under the pseudonym Moon Charter drew diagrams that enabled marvelling readers to follow the progress of the Russian *Sputnik 1* across Irish night skies during the month of its launch, October 1957.

The *Evening Press* was largely apolitical and majored on breaking news stories and encouraging new trends in the country such as angling and the spread of the amateur drama movement. Both of these trends were fastened on by a remarkable journalist, John Healy, in whom Douglas Gageby saw a talent that had escaped other employers. Healy had the brains of his native County Mayo and an American accent, honed by a three-month stay in the US on a journalistic scholarship. He also had the physical appearance of a Guinness barrel wrapped in a cardigan and topped by a large bald head. His mannerisms, such as buttonholing someone and (literally) bouncing them off-balance with a thump of his belly while commencing a monologue (he did not hold conversations) with the words 'Say, fella', made him a number of enemies. But he was the classical example of the truth of Cyril Connolly's aphorism that inside every fat man there's a thin man trying to get out. In later life he became a fashionable painter. As a journalist, he had one of the finest instincts for impending changes in society that I ever encountered. He revolutionised Irish political journalism after he left the Irish Press Group, developing first a political column, under the pseudonym 'Backbencher', which had much to do with bringing the *Irish Times* to its present position of influence in Irish society, and later a pioneering TV programme, *The Hurler on the Ditch*, which changed Radio Telefis Eireann's (RTE) hitherto deferential attitude towards politicians. He also wrote two classic books on emigration and poverty in his native County Mayo, *Nineteen Acres* and *Nobody Shouted Stop*. Both of these owed their publication to the fact that Douglas Gageby often sat across the table as Healy typed, pulling pages of typescript from the machine and uttering soothing words of encouragement such as 'Come on, you lazy bastard, you can do better than that.'

Fishing is one of man's least talked of and yet most popular activities. Once Healy began writing about the topic, the readers poured in. But until he began to cover the amateur drama movement, practically no one in Dublin had realised its potential. In pre-television Ireland the movement attracted a huge following and, along with the Gaelic Athletic Association (GAA), was one of the chief sources of entertainment in rural Ireland. The paper also attracted attention for a social column, 'Dubliner's Diary', written by Terry O'Faolain under the pseudonym Terry O'Sullivan. Terry was immensely proud of his daughter Nuala, whose achievements in academia and television he used to extol in our watering hole, the Mucky Duck, a pub that had incautiously been christened the Silver Swan by its owners. Nuala later became a distinguished print journalist and an author. Her autobiography revealed that the O'Sullivan–Whelan household was one of the most chaotic in Dublin. It contained little in the way of furnishing save books and a record collection, largely because Terry's wife cracked and took to the bottle under the pressure of the Great Disappointment, the realisation that, after the early days of what the poet termed the blood's millrace and the body's thunder, relationships frequently crumble into coldness and anger under the strain of marriage, mistresses and child-bearing.

To me Terry became the embodiment of 'the split-level syndrome'. He always appeared immaculately dressed in public, coming to work via the barber, the dry-cleaner and the laundry. To the outsider he appeared to glide effortlessly through the phoney world of the gossip columnist: plush places, glittering receptions and fawning head waiters. As invariably courteous as he was immaculately dressed, Terry never missed a deadline, although the dawn frequently found him weary and half-drunk, finishing his column just as the first of the day staff came to work. I sometimes acted as stand-in columnist while he was sick or on holiday. And, knowing his difficulties, felt that he met Hemingway's definition of courage: 'Grace under stress.' Terry was not allowed to drive, his licence having been taken from him following incidents in which telegraph poles stepped out in front of him and cars became embedded in shop windows. Gageby and Jack Dempsey between them converted this drawback into an asset by convincing Vivion that the image of the 'Dubliner's Diary' column would be furthered by having the columnist appear at functions chauffeur-driven in an Austin Princess limousine.

Nowadays newspapers tend to be produced by corporations, which in turn produce a cautious political and social ethos in which strange beings flourish: joggers, teetotallers, golfers. This was not the case during the first

decade or so of the *Evening Press*'s existence. The sub-editors' desk was
normally peopled by men – no women were employed in this role until
well after I had become editor of the *Irish Press* and appointed a young
woman, Helen Rogers. Most of the men had a pack of twenty cigarettes
beside them and at regular intervals sent out a copy boy for top-ups. They
topped themselves up by slipping out for quick ones to the neighbouring
pubs, Mulligan's, the White Horse, the Mucky Duck and the Scotch
House. On one celebrated occasion, coming up to edition time, O'Donovan
stormed through all four pubs brandishing a sheaf of proofs and bellowing:
'Time, gentlemen, please,' his face a deep shade of purple, his mien terrible
to behold.

Even O'Donovan, or JOD, could not cow the sub-editors into giving
up their cigarettes. However, he ensured that the smoke was kept as far
from him as possible by staging pieces of theatre such as overturning tables
and chairs shouting: 'I smell a smoulderer!' and finally jumping up and
down for several seconds on any butt incautiously dropped near his chair.
He insisted on ventilating the huge smoke-filled newsroom, or at least his
end of it (the reporters puffed away happily in their end), by keeping the
windows open in all weathers. I remember one January seeing snowflakes
drifting in from the Liffey onto shivering sub-editors. Part of the shivering
was caused by sheer fear. I once measured the distance from the case-room
door to O'Donovan's throne at the head of the sub-editors' desks: ten paces.
O'Donovan could cover the distance in three huge bounds. Frequently, as
edition time neared, the door from the case room would crash open
and O'Donovan would emerge, in puce-tinted rage, waving a proof and
screaming things like 'Sweet fucking Jesus! What fucking eejit subbed this
piece of illiteracy?'

Generally speaking the first *Evening Press* sub-editors tended to be of
two kinds, tyros and skilled old lags, many of whom had learned their
trade, and developed their thirsts, in Fleet Street. If a letter came to these
men at the office, it tended to be from their wives' solicitors seeking either
a new divorce or an old alimony. Some of the tyros had applied for a job
on the paper thinking vaguely that journalism would be a stimulating
career. I can still vividly recall the day when one of them discovered just
how stimulating.

Slim, shy, Anglo-Irish, elegant of speech and appearance, the tyro,
mistakenly believing that the first edition had safely gone to press, had
begun eating his cucumber sandwiches when suddenly the case-room door
crashed open and O'Donovan erupted onto the scene in such a fury that
he covered the distance to his chair in only two bounds, enquiring, in

stentorian tones, as to the identity of the adjectival cretin who had subbed a certain court case. Paling with shock and embarrassment, the unfortunate tyro put up his hand as though he were in a classroom: 'Here, sir!'

O'Donovan liked the young man, and his choler lessened somewhat. However, like Magnus Magnusson, he had started so he would finish. Accordingly he entered into the following dialogue on sub-editing with the tyro:

o'donovan: Put the main news in the heading – 'Judge shits himself in Dublin court!' Do you understand?

tyro (weakly): Yes, sir!

o'donovan: Then bring up the best copy into the first paragraph – 'You're a cunt,' says judge! 'I am you bollocks,' says defendant. Do you understand?

tyro (weaker): Yes, sir.

o'donovan: Then you catch-line the thing properly – piss one, piss two, piss three! Do you understand?

tyro (barely audible): Yes, sir.

o'donovan: And put in plenty of catchy cross-heads – 'Fuck a duck! Fuck two ducks! Fuck a swan!' Do you understand?

tyro (inaudibly): Yes, sir.

O'Donovan then left for the case room like a departing tsunami. The tyro merely departed.

My early days in the *Evening Press* were a classic example of split-level syndrome. On one hand I was inordinately delighted to have a job, and a job moreover wherein things seemed to eventually turn out as planned, despite the inevitable chaos involved in producing a new evening newspaper. By contrast life in Tudor Hall had tended to prove that plans were an offence in God's scheme of things and inevitably broke down in such a way as to cause the maximum distress and disappointment. But at a deeper level of my mind I had troubling doubts and regrets that I had entered on a path that had high walls on either side and would be difficult to leap over and become my own man. From the word go I knew that the hustle and bustle was not conducive to the production of serious writing. However, the bustle certainly kept introspection at bay.

Progress in technology has spelled the death of an amazing variety of once skilful trades. There were the klishographers, who turned photographs into metal plates, which were then placed on pieces of carefully cut metal that brought the plate level with the print on the page, 'type high', as it was known. Then the whole confection was imprinted on a matrix by the stereotypers. Molten metal was then poured over this and the resultant curved plate was bolted onto the giant printing press, which ran off the finished paper. The aristocrats at the top of the pyramid of crafts were the typographers, proud men with a powerful union, who were conscious of the fact that in the days when only gentlemen could carry broadswords, printers were allowed short swords and were so respectable that they were allowed to conduct their union meetings in chapels. It was from the Church connection that the term 'father of the chapel' derived, as did the names for typefaces such as 'Revere', a reminder of the days when the bulk of a printer's work were things like Bibles, hymn sheets and prayer books. There was very little call for prayer books in the *Evening Press*.

The two greatest crises I suffered in my first months on the subs' desk were not over issues of journalistic integrity, but John O'Donovan's underpants and my beard. Even though I was now a junior sub-editor, and (in my own eyes) a person of some consequence, John had a habit of sending me for errands as though I were still a copy boy. One day he directed me to a nearby shop with a set of new underpants which were too small for him and which he wished to have exchanged. I did so and walked back to O'Donovan in a state of mixed anger and terror at the prospect of losing my job. Nevertheless I informed him that such errands were demeaning and I would perform them no more. He was genuinely hurt, considering me an ingrate who did not appreciate all he had done to further my career, but he never sent me for messages again and we ultimately became the best of friends. I was saddened when he suffered a stroke and died some years after he had left the *Press* to become a full-time writer, achieving success through, amongst other things, writing the long-running children's TV series *Wanderly Wagon* for RTE.

Douglas Gageby was another matter. Unlike the emotional but soft-hearted O'Donovan, who trumpeted his wrath, Gageby's weapons, developed in officers' training courses, were the vitriol bottle and the rapier. He began deploying both when, after I had been on the subs' desk for six months, I let it be known that I intended growing a beard as part of my preparations for my first visit to Paris. Any subsequent mistakes in my work were met with icy comments about people who concentrated on growing fucking beards, not on their jobs. I was warned to have my stubble shaved off when I came back from Paris, but by the time I did return I had quite a respectable growth. Gageby did not come into the office that morning. He phoned from home to enquire of O'Donovan: 'Do we have a beard amongst us?' When told: 'Sadly, yes,' he issued instructions that it was to be gone when he came in after lunch. I don't know what insane stubbornness made me defy the order, but I underwent a very nerve-racking six months before the tickling caused by fine weather, and Gageby's literally face-saving absence on holiday, brought about the beard's disappearance.

A feature of the *Evening Press* at the time was the material 'from Mogobulaland', as John O'Donovan christened it. This was agency feature material that was sent out to the case room a day in advance to fill up the early edition of the *Evening Press*. The fillers were replaced as fresh city news came in. Preparing this material was priceless training for a young sub-editor, although it got boring after a while. I tried to enliven the hours, and the copy, either by slipping unsuitable material into the out-tray when the chief sub-editor on duty was looking the other way or by putting more lively headings on the copy than those supplied by the agency. The level of these offerings may be gauged from the report of a court case in Kenya in which a man was charged with raping a woman at a well. He had taken her from the rear, and when the judge asked the victim why she had not protested or struggled while the offence was being committed, she replied: 'I thought he was a friend!'

Part of a sub-editor's duty in those days was to supply letters to the editor. I often had two or three controversies running simultaneously. In one such I was both a fictitious brigadier general and an old IRA commandant who conducted a spirited exchange over the brigadier's assertion that the IRA were far worse than the Mau Mau. Several innocent correspondents contributed to the issues thrown up by the bogus controversy. But my finest hour as a sub-editor came somewhat later in my career when the Russians put two cosmonauts into space and I led the paper with the headline 'Red Males in the Sunset'.

Journalism is a peaks-and-valleys occupation. Periods of intense activity are followed by bouts of mind-numbing boredom. Then there are the harmful effects to health of shift work. A combination of these factors caused a lot of journalists to burn out or hit the bottle, or both. With the cruelty of youth I once seized on a senior colleague, Tommy Hennigan, a victim of the peaks-and-valleys syndrome, as the butt of a prank that I regretted ever afterwards. Tommy was actually the chief sub-editor of the *Sunday Press* but was making a little extra money moonlighting on the *Evening Press*. The *Sunday Press* at the time was a highly successful publication, run on strict military lines by the editor, Colonel Matt Feehan. Feehan had a habit of pounding his desk with a fist as he made a point as to how he wanted a story covered, or castigated someone for covering it the wrong way. Tommy was once asked how he put up with the pounding-fist routine and he replied: 'Arrah, it's not so bad. Like knocking your head on a stone wall, it's great when you stop.' Tommy had come to a stop on the *Evening Press* on the afternoon of the prank. As was his wont, he had dozed off, and I surreptitiously slid a seemingly genuine report in front of him, stating that President de Valera had collapsed and been taken to hospital. To add credibility to the thing, I included a paragraph containing an alleged quotation from a doctor son of de Valera's saying that it appeared that the president had had a heart attack.

Tommy woke up after a short doze, looked around him to see whether anyone had noticed that he had been sleeping and saw the earth-shattering piece of copy before him. Normally a sub-editor would be instructed on what typeface to use in processing the report, but I had given no typo-graphical instructions on the bogus copy. Tommy had to use his own initiative. After scratching his head for a couple of seconds, he decided that the chief sub-editor must have given him verbal instructions which he had not heard and wrote a cautious single-column heading: 'President has heart attack – report.' Then he placed the copy in the in-tray and went back to sleep. The assistant chief sub-editor never even glanced at the copy before throwing it into the out-tray, and I had to run after the copy boy and destroy the item, which would have been the *Irish Press* equivalent of an item in the *Tehran Times* falsely stating that the Ayatollah had suffered cardiac arrest. Tommy was bated unmercifully about the incident sub-sequently, but it cured me of practical joking.

Not long after the Hennigan incident Gageby and O'Donovan decided that it was time for me to experience heart-attack territory myself. I was promoted to the position of stone sub-editor. This was the most onerous sub-editing task of them all, an invaluable training ground and a position of great responsibility, which literally carried health risks as it involved reading sheaves of poorly inked proofs at high speed, which eventually had a bad effect on my eyesight. However, the management refused to recognise working on 'the stone' as a special category, so there was no extra money going with the post.

Although it was Ireland's newest journalistic venture, the *Evening Press* was a maelstrom of archaic trades and work practices. The *Irish Press* building where the paper was produced was originally Daniel O'Connell Conciliation Hall. Later it became the Tivoli Music Hall and it was commonly said that the spirit of the Tivoli rather than of O'Connell animated the building. Certainly anyone who looked at the manner in which the paper was made up on the stone would have agreed with that judgement. The air was foul from the fumes of molten lead in the type-setting machines and in the stereotype department wherein the pages were cast before being bolted onto the printing presses. There was oil everywhere because the stone, where the pages were made up, had to be slippery in order to slide the iron chases containing the pages on and off the wheeled bogey that took them to the stereo. The floor of the case room was uneven. It was made from baulks of timber like railway sleepers. Though still strong, they had become eroded and warped with the years, so that one could look down between them at the huge linotype presses roaring away below our feet (and of course sending ink spray into our lungs).

Not surprisingly, working in these conditions, Nicky Rossiter, the man who pushed the heavy bogey, developed agonising pains in his hips and lower back. Not surprisingly either, approximately as much effort went into placating the officials of the various unions coming up to edition time as into the design and content of the paper. I remember one day desperately trying to coax a compositor, who was also the printers' father of the chapel, to fetch a couple of galleys of type needed to finish off page one, but instead having to listen to a stream of invective directed at anyone and everyone within sight. Finally, in a desperate effort to interrupt the spew and avert the lateness, for which I would be blamed, I pointed towards a particularly popular member of the staff who happened to be passing and said: 'Well, at least you'll agree that he's a decent man.' The printer, who had the height, physiognomy and malicious outlook of a troll, was flummoxed for a second. 'Yeh, yeh,' he conceded uncertainly, but then finished triumphantly: 'He'd take off his fucking boots to kick you!'

As well as strong nerves the stone sub-editor required strong arms. It was his job to carry the metal bases of the photographic blocks from the stereotype department to the stone. Many a time I cursed the inspiration that led me to blow up a picture across six columns when it fell to my lot to carry the resultant inch-deep, metal 'mount', as it was known. The copy boys were supposed to perform these duties, but the first talent that they seemed to develop was a genius for going on some other errand when edition time approached. If any big event required full-page pictorial coverage, which in those days was common practice, the physical toll on the allegedly creative stone sub-editor was massive. Certainly keeping fit was never a problem in those frenetic days. Skill levels were such (and, equally important, the lawyers had yet to develop the litigation culture that now prevails) that serious mistakes were rare and libel suits infrequent. Somehow in the chaos leading up to production deadlines, what was known as the 'back-desk' system ensured that the smudgy proofs were thoroughly read and most howlers caught in time. The back desk was where the editor and his assistants sat performing the journalistic equivalent of a wicket keeper in cricket.

My first article was published a few days before my twentieth birthday in 1955. I didn't care what I wrote so long as I got something into print before that day – I didn't count my earlier sports reports as 'real' journalism! – so I successfully submitted a piece for a regular historical feature that the paper ran under the title of 'Yesterday'. It was a seemingly innocuous topic, an account of a duel fought by Daniel O'Connell in which he mortally wounded his opponent, but its reception was a salutary introduction to the sort of reactions that journalism can unwittingly stir up. The first reaction came from my mother. I thought she'd be delighted, and would congratulate me when I got home, but instead she rang me up at the paper to administer a tongue-lashing for what she termed a theft of *her* material. She was engaged in the lengthy historical research for what eventually resulted in the publication of her fine historical novel *The Big Wind* and thought that I had taken the material for the feature from her. The continuing resentment she felt at the bad hand she had been dealt by life sometimes manifested itself in unfairnesses like that. Outbursts of unreasoning jealousy directed not merely at her children but anyone who enjoyed a piece of good fortune denied her.

That first article that she objected to also brought a tirade from Douglas Gageby, who bitterly upbraided me for its tone and muttered dire warnings about that being the last time my name would appear in the paper. I later found out that the 'Yesterday' feature was a favourite of Eamon de Valera himself, who had it read to him each day. He got on to Vivion to complain. Vivion in turn roasted Gageby, and Gageby passed on the rocket to me. My offence? In the piece I had posed the question 'How did the "bloodless Liberator" come to kill a man?' and then gone on to describe what happened. The use of the term 'bloodless Liberator' was held to be disrespectful to Daniel O'Connell. From that incident one may judge the reaction to the use of real or imaginary disrespectful references, headlines or photographs considered offensive either to Fianna Fail luminaries or to friends of the de Valera family. In those days the path of an *Irish Press* editor was truly a thorny one, and generally short-lived into the bargain. Yet somehow throughout the *Sturm und Drang* I managed to maintain an upward trajectory.

Douglas Gageby moved off to become editor of the *Irish Times* and one of the greatest editors in the history of Irish journalism. His gift for sensing new trends in society was a particularly priceless asset at the time. For the times were indeed a-changing in Ireland, as elsewhere. Some of the influ-ences that were of particular interest to Ireland during the 1960s were the currents flowing from the Second Vatican Council called by the great Pope John XXIII. The liberalising effect of the Council on clerically dominated Ireland is hard to imagine in this, the twenty-first, century. As late as 1951, three years before the *Evening Press* was founded, a government had fallen because of the bishops' opposition to a health scheme that would have given women access to gynaecological information. One of the major figures in that controversy, Archbishop John Charles McQuaid of Dublin, was still one of the most powerful figures in Ireland. He was a vigorous defender of the Irish hierarchy's long-standing ruling that it was a mortal sin for a Catholic to attend Trinity College, Dublin, without permission. How vigorous may be gauged from his reaction to the fact that Trinity students shared the facilities of Dublin's Veterinary College with those of University College, Dublin, which was mainly attended by Catholics. But because McQuaid decided that the teaching of biology had a moral basis, 'a Protestant cow' and 'a Catholic cow' had to be provided, along with 'a Protestant horse' and 'a Catholic horse'. I understand that the piety of the Catholic pig was a particular source of edification to all who witnessed it. McQuaid's influence permeated University College, Dublin, where student societies had to be very mindful of the need not to invite speakers of whom His Grace might disapprove. John Charles's influence was such that he could, and did, decide what plays Dublin audiences should or should not see. Football too came within his purview. He once tried unsuccessfully to have the communist Yugoslavian soccer team banned from playing in Dublin. John Charles's influence was of very particular moment in Burgh Quay partly because, as president of the college, he had been particularly kind to Vivion during Vivion's time in Blackrock. But there was also the small matter of his having helped to draft de Valera Senior's Constitution, which passed into law in 1937 and had a distinct bearing on his being appointed archbishop subsequently. Therefore any news item involving the archbishop's activities had to be handled with a reverence reserved only for God, de Valera and the Irish language.

Two of Vivion's worst outbursts of wrath were generated by complaints from 'John Charles'. They were caused by (quite accurate) reports that, in the wake of the Second Vatican Council, evening mass was to be introduced to Dublin and a Catholic chaplain was being appointed to Trinity College. The offence lay not in the veracity of the reports but in the fact that the *Evening Press* had had the temerity to publish them before His Grace had made the official announcements.

Douglas Gageby was succeeded by Conor O'Brien, and in the resultant reshuffle I became features editor. Shortly afterwards I received job offers from the newly founded radio television station RTE and on foot of these was given more money and a higher rank (assistant editor) to induce me to stay with the *Evening Press*. Years later I would have cause to wonder at the wisdom of my decision, but the fact is that from the time I first joined the group in 1954 to my leaving it in 1987, only on one occasion did I make a serious effort to leave. It confirmed me in my general, half-formulated resolve that I would only quit the company if one of two things happened: a) I entered politics, and b) I quit journalism altogether to become a full-time writer.

On the occasion when I considered leaving, I applied for an attractive post as director of Publicity and Publications for what was at the time a prestigious Irish body, the Confederation of Irish Industries. The post carried a high salary and fringe benefits. Understandably it attracted a large number of applicants. After a series of shortlistings the race came down to a choice between me and a man called Michael Sweetman, who had a large young family, as did I by this time. The job went to Sweetman. It caused him to board a Trident jet at Heathrow a few years later, on 18 June 1972, with a party of Ireland's top businessmen, bound for Brussels. It got only as far as Staines before it crashed, killing all 118 persons onboard. After missing that appointment in Samarra, I stayed with the *Press* for most of my working life.

I liked the people I worked with and had a special regard for Vivion de Valera from the time I first met him. I recognised that in many respects he was an eccentric whose behaviour around the time of a full moon was not entirely predictable, but in quiet moments he could show a good side, recognising that he owed his position to heritage rather than natural ability and showing a proper, albeit private, contempt for the attitudinising and falsities of party politics. Of course there was a basic falsity about his own position, which, as we shall see, I discovered later, and it had the effect of cancelling out much of the goodwill I once felt for him. But I must give credit to Vivion for his early influence on my career.

Both he and Jack Dempsey went out of their way to warn me of the dangers of allowing rancour to develop because of the politics of the past. Vivion in particular frequently and shrewdly played on my already strong consciousness of being Irish. He used to stress the fact that though Fine Gael and Fianna Fail were the results of the sunderings of the Civil War, both had their origins in Sinn Fein, united in a common resolve to do what was best for Ireland. Both he and Jack apologised for the attitude of the

Irish Press towards my father in the 1940s, Vivion in particular stressing that the campaign had not been his father's wish. Later I would learn, alas, that a great number of things could be done, and profited from, in the de Valera family and then disowned as not being wished for. However, in my early years as editor of the *Irish Press* I accepted Vivion and Jack's guidance, and in particular Dempsey's, who, on discovering that I had not actually read the *Irish Press* coverage of the period but intended some day to go to the National Library to look it up in the files, advised me with great force and obvious sincerity: 'Never read those files. Never read them!'

CHAPTER 6

Marriage of a Teddy Boy

Three years after joining the *Evening Press* I entered into an even more significant long-term relationship – marriage. I first met Cherry O'Brien when she was nearing thirteen years of age and I fifteen. She worked in Cassidy's department store in Dublin and formed part of a group of girls who used to frequent what passed for nightlife in the Dun Laoghaire of our time, Teddy's Ice Cream Parlour on the seafront. I was part of a group of boys who sought to frequent the girls and, looking back, was incredibly lucky to survive to do so.

My father's possessions included two revolvers from his Garda commissioner days, one a .45 Webley, the other a .38 Smith and Wesson. There was also some ammunition for both. After he died the Gardai began calling to our house, looking for the guns, but my mother always denied knowledge of their existence, not because she either thought she might have use for them or wanted to pass them on to the IRA, but because she hadn't received a Garda pension. One day, seeing the Gardai coming up the avenue, she hid the guns under a pile of her bras and knickers in a drawer of her dressing table. This she left embarrassingly open, while locking the one above it. Needless to say, this was the drawer the cops fastened their attention on, following a fruitless search of the house. After much protest, and feigned hysteria, my mother finally yielded the key to the locked drawer, where nothing was discovered save more lady's unmentionables. These provided a fine pretext for further histrionics on my mother's part concerning matters such as 'the violation of my intimacy' and the Gardai withdrew from the house gunless, but with their vocabularies considerably enriched.

However, as we grew a little older, Brian took to displaying the weapons in Teddy's, as I discovered to my horror one night, when I saw the guns being passed around a group of fascinated teenage boys. I immediately snatched back the .45, but the Smith and Wesson was in the hands of our friend Ronnie Drew. I tried to wrench it away from Ronnie but his grip proved unexpectedly strong and he held on to the revolver as we tussled. Fortunately, though I did not know it at the time, Brian had unloaded the weapon and it could not go off. Brian later sold the weapons to another, older friend, and he, Ronnie and another friend did go off – to Spain. The three intended to study the guitar, bullfighting and, in the case of the third friend, Pat McMahon, painting. All three intended to survive by teaching English, a language that none of them spoke particularly well but which they at least knew better than Spanish. Ronnie later put his strong fingers to good use by becoming the guitarist (and lead singer) with the famous Irish group the Dubliners. Their career began in the Widow Donoghue's pub in Merrion Street, Dublin, where an important aspect of mine developed also – it was there I bought my first pint of Guinness, at the age of nineteen.

Guns apart, the Teddy's interlude was unbelievably innocent. If one was lucky, assignations agreed on in giggling sessions over cups of coffee, whose contents were made to last for hours, could result in further giggling sessions 'courting' in the back rows of one of the four cinemas Dun Laoghaire then possessed. These were the Adelphi, the Astoria, the Pavilion and the Picture House, which was more generally known as the Bug House. In place of the four separate cinemas there is now one omniplex and the Pavilion is now a live theatre.

As I was a boarder, I had to sneak out of the college on Sunday nights to accompany Cherry to the pinnacle of Dun Laoghaire social life, the weekly 'hop' in Sandycove tennis club. In order to scale the college walls, I had to climb down, and up, a telegraph pole, the only academic post I would ever hold. The nature of the petting, or 'having a court', as it was known, was of the sort indicated in the immortal story of the man who, at the age of forty-eight, left his west of Ireland village of Cloonishlan for the first time to visit, of all places, Paris. On his return, he was asked how was the sex life in Paris and replied wonderingly: 'Fucking is only in its infancy in Cloonishlan!' We all lived in a Cloonishlan of the mind during the Teddy's era.

Cherry, her sister, Moya, and her brothers, Michael, Desmond and Niall, were the children of Maureen and Michael O'Brien, a small builder who lived in nearby Dalkey. The building trade, an accurate barometer of the state of the economy at any time, was not merely stagnating but putrefying. Maureen was the dominant member of the family, a classical Irish mother figure, viewed with affection and awe by her children and, later in life, venerated by her multitudinous grandchildren. She now came to a momentous decision. The family would emigrate to Canada. So, while I was back in Blackrock for my final year, the O'Briens set off for Toronto.

As with so many Irish families touched by emigration, the departure from Ireland inaugurated a period of disruption of the O'Briens' family life. Maureen did not like Canada and soon returned to Ireland with four of the children, leaving Cherry to look after Michael. Later I would realise that Michael was the epitome of the type of Irish emigrant who kept Irish society going with what were known officially as 'invisible remittances' from all over the globe. It was a more apt phrase than its coiners realised. Economically, the money was tangible; politically, its earners were out of either sight or consideration. During almost a decade of intermittent emigration, first to Canada, then America, Michael sent back what he could to Maureen.

In Canada Cherry was much sought after. An attractive, vivacious redhead with an infectious smile, in an environment wherein money was more plentiful and social life more varied than in Dublin, she soon became engaged, to Bobby Thomas, another Dalkey emigrant and a noted rugby player. Michael, however, was finding no pots of gold at the end of the Canadian rainbow and was considering moving to America. Maureen told me later that she decided that Cherry should return to Ireland, to ensure that she had me out of her system, before marrying Bobby. Whatever about that, within a short time of her return we took up where she left off and decided to get married.

Conor O'Brien and his wife, Mildred, gave sustained practical application to the saying 'A friend in need is a friend indeed' and supported us through the emotional turmoil preceding the marriage. Our main concern was what would our families say. The thought of telling my mother kept me awake at night. Very little thought was given to the small matter of what we were going to live on. My salary at this stage (1957) was seven pounds a week, augmented by an occasional two pounds twelve and sixpence for subbing on the *Sunday Press* on Saturday evenings (about twelve euros in today's currency). We had endless confabulations about what faraway church we would be married in and what priest we could get to marry us. The nearest priest to hand was the last one we could turn to. Uncle Tim was back on holiday from South Australia and the news had to be kept from him until he was safely back in Australia. In order to minimise the attendance of friends and relations, we decided to get married in the Church of the Star of the Sea, Sandymount. When we finally broke the news to Cherry's mother, Maureen, I told her that we were getting married, denied that there was a baby on the way, and inflated my income to twelve pounds ten shillings a week, with the *Sunday Press* as a regular, not an occasional extra.

The greatest problem of all was the prospect of telling my mother. I thought constantly about an incident that had occurred two years earlier. In July 1955 I had enjoyed my first paid holidays and gone hostelling and hitch-hiking around the country, hostelling in a Kilkenny castle, gazing at the little lily-filled lakes around Inchigeelagh and Ballyvourney in West Cork that were shortly to be obliterated by a dam-building project, sleeping in a hay barn on the slopes of a Kerry mountain, and eventually making my way along the coast to Kilkee in County Clare. In Kilkee I encountered members of the University College, Dublin, Drama Society, who included Lelia Doolan, later to become one of the country's best-known theatre and TV producers. Another attachment to the group was Dickie Harris, who, as Richard Harris, would become a film star. He read aloud a short story of mine. He was a good swimmer, and we used to swim out from the low cliffs at a place called New Found Out in an unsuccessful attempt to get near the dolphins that seemed to continuously leap and play about a kilometre or so out in the bay. At night, after the normal show in a local theatre, we would sometimes stage impromptu performances in a natural amphitheatre in the cliffs. One night the star of the show was a tall, handsome young man who gave a powerful rendition of 'The Volga Boat Men'. As the final echoes died along the cliffs, I asked who he was and a girl told me, sadly, that his name was Tom Stack and he was shortly to be ordained a priest. I didn't meet him then, but Cherry and I later struck up a lifelong friendship with Tom.

After this time-out-of-life holiday I had returned home full of such memories and ready to give an account of my travels, only to find Mother sitting up in bed, in the late afternoon of a bright July day. She was consumed by misery at her lot generally, and enraged at me in particular for my selfishness in leaving her, 'not caring whether I lived or died'. Holidays, she decreed, were only for married men with families, who had been working several years. It had always been customary with her, if I ever mentioned emigration, to comment fiercely: 'Don't leave it to *them*!' How much of this attitude was based on a feeling that I should take my rightful place in society, and how much on an understandable desire to keep both her son, and his potential for supporting her, near to hand, I never knew. What I did know with certainty was that telling her that I now intended leaving home permanently was not going to be a pleasant process.

I was in such a state of dread that I left it to the last moment, pulling out a chair after tea one Friday evening and telling her that she should sit down in order to receive some news I had for her. The fact that I intended to get married did not provoke any undue reaction. It was my answer when she asked: 'When?' that set the heather blazing. The answer was 'Wednesday'. Apart from the understandable shock at the fact of my imminent departure from Tudor Hall to marry someone whom she didn't know, there was the very real financial problem that this would cause her. I gave up half my weekly pay. Although it wasn't much, the loss of this slender prop was a serious matter. But fair play to her, she turned up at the church on the morning of the wedding, on 10 August 1957, grim-faced but there, with a somewhat bewildered Aisling alongside her.

Rarely was there such an economical wedding. The most significant contribution I had received towards my new status from the Irish Press Group was a 'knock down' from the printers. This was an unusual honour for someone not of their ranks. On a prearranged signal, just as I prepared to leave the case room on the last occasion as a single man, everyone began banging together the metal galleys used to hold type. The noise rang in my ears for a long time afterwards, but unfortunately it did not ring in any tills. Conor O'Brien and Mildred acted as our best man and matron of honour. Our wedding breakfast was a fry served on the Galway train, and by nightfall we were installed in a chalet on the shore of remote Lough Atorick, near Woodford, County Galway.

Apart from being the scene of our honeymoon, that boggy, beautiful part of County Galway was also the setting for Brian Merriman's classical poem 'The Midnight Court', in which the women of Ireland arraign the men for their lack of sexuality and the fact that so many of them become priests. The action takes place on the shores of Lough Greaney, a short distance from Lough Atorick. While I would like to think that our honeymoon did something to redress the women's complaints, I have to confess that the poem had nothing to do with the choice of a honeymoon site. My habit of reading everything and anything had paid off. The chalets had been advertised in a small ad in the rival *Evening Herald* and appealed to me both on the grounds of economy and because they were on the opposite side of the country from Dublin and our families.

An episode from our honeymoon days illustrates both the rural inno-cence and the poverty that lay behind the emigration figures of the time. We had become friendly with the people of the area, a remote townland about five miles from the village of Woodford. One of the families had two daughters, aged thirteen and fourteen, who were shortly to fly from Shannon to begin a new life with relations in America. As a pre-departure treat we included them in a group of locals with whom we visited the one hotel in the area. During the evening the girls asked to be shown the toilet. We had forgotten about them when suddenly from overhead there came screams and the sound of running feet. They had been panicked by 'the flood of water coming up through the floor'. It was the first time that the children had encountered a flush toilet.

Our return to the city was marked by ribaldry and respectability. The ribaldry was provided by Brendan Behan, whose trademark was embarrassing people. On the day I returned to work he hailed me – loudly – in the crowded street outside the *Press* building: 'Hey, Tim Pat! How was the honeyer? Did you feel as though your arse was eating chocolate?'

Poor Brendan. His biography should be entitled *Portrait of the Artist: Destroyed by Dublin*. The last time he and I were in a pub together, about a year before his death in 1964, was in the White Horse beside the *Press* building. I was acting as Terry O'Sullivan's stand-in on 'Dubliner's Diary', and intended procuring a few Behanisms to enliven the column. Instead I found myself consoling Beatrice, his wife, as she gazed miserably but helplessly at Brendan standing at the bar with two well-known Dublin soaks. Every so often he would tell the barman to give him a ten-shilling note from the till. Then he would roll up the note, suck it for a while, like a lollipop, and then spit it out. There was a ring of ten-shilling notes around the trio's feet. I offered to get the barman to stop, but Beatrice told me it was useless. All he would do was go to another pub and indulge in some similar caper, accompanied by the soaks, and probably there'd be more like them at the next venue. Either way the pub management knew that within a day or so, when he had sobered up, he would return and, unquestioningly, settle his bill, whatever its size. In the event the only help I could offer Beatrice was to send her home in a taxi alone.

So much for the perilous spontaneity of Brendan's alcohol-fuelled ribaldry. The respectability came from number 11 Marine Drive, Sandymount, where I had taken a flat. It was owned by a nice middle-aged couple who were very good to me in the few days I spent there before the wedding. The woman of the house washed my shirt and pressed my wedding suit – my only suit. After the honeymoon we shared the facilities with another newly married couple. The husband was a Cork man given to looking at his wife meaningfully and declaring: 'I feel de urge. De urge is coming on me.' Cherry did not like the place and we found another home, consisting of a romantic, but undecorated, annexe to a large house in nearby Sandymount Avenue. Sandymount is a much sought-after area, and our new home was very convenient to Burgh Quay, but when we walked along the strand we thought not of Joyce and walking to infinity, but looked longingly at distant Dun Laoghaire and Killiney Hill as though we were a pair of banished Syrians gazing at the Golan Heights.

The banishment did not last long. While I was still decorating the annexe, Maureen found us a house called Lohengrin, on the slopes of Killiney Hill, next door to the home in which her own married life had begun, Clanaber, above Torca Road, which she had helped Michael to build. It was a fairy-tale location, overlooking the Vico Bay, Ireland's Bay of Naples, but before we could begin enjoying the fairy tale I had to finish painting the annexe. I dislike decorating work at the best of times, but painting that annexe for the next tenant was one of my least rewarding experiences. However, the Lohengrin interlude was a happy one, enlivened by the arrival in February of Thomond, our eldest daughter, who, even as a baby, showed promise of her later good looks. The only problem was that, unlike the Lohengrin of legend, who was pulled along by swans, prams had to be pushed up a steep hill.

Another steep hill that had to be negotiated was reconciliation with my mother. It proved easier than I had expected. I borrowed a typewriter and wrote to her from the *Evening Press* newsroom. Forty years later, after she had died, I discovered that she had kept the letter all that time. Read today, it appears less an exercise in reconciliation than a demonstration of how the portcullis of the inarticulate falls between the generations:

Evening Press
Burgh Quay

14 September

My dear mammy,

This is a difficult letter to write because there is so much to say that I have no words to say it all in. First, however, I want to thank you for coming to the wedding. That took a lot of courage, you must have felt like hell. I did not write to you while we were away because I did not relish the thought of sending chatty postcards! I did send one to Auntie however and asked her to say something to you on my behalf. I hope she did.

How are Brian and Aisling? Is it true that Uncle Tim has gone to England? I hope he put his hand in his pocket before he did so. What sort of health are you having? Is anything coming of the book? I don't want to alarm you but Liam MacGabhann is getting a job as news editor on the *Sunday Review* which is coming out in November. He was lucky to get it because I heard that he was under notice with the 'People'. I can't vouch for that but it seems that if the Knock articles are his baby you had better see about referring them to another foster father – no successor has been appointed to him on the 'People' and he does not leave for a while yet so there may be still hope if you move fast.

And now I am near the end of this letter, leaving all the things I ment [sic] to say unsaid, which is probably just as well since I might not have seid them in the right way. I don't think that as things stand that any chatty teas or visits would be wise for anyone's sake but I'll write to you every week with a similar enclosure (at least).

Love from Tim

P.S. How are Brian and Aisling? I know I asked before but I miss them! Please give them both my love. God bless you all and I really mean it.

I forget how much I sent my mother but it would have been a tiny sum. To say that I had very little money would be to understate the case by a factor of several hundred per cent. Eamon de Valera had created a doctrine of frugal living, which meant in effect that he took a vow of poverty and the electorate observed it. Vivion de Valera espoused his famous father's teachings in so far as his employees were concerned. On top of this, those two pillars of society the banks and the Church had a mutually exclusive attitude that added to the problems of living. The Church actively encouraged large families, and the banks equally actively discouraged the correspondingly large overdrafts that any attempt at comfortable living on an Irish income inevitably created. At a stage when we had three children I could have acquired the tiny mortgage on a detached three-bedroom bungalow, with a garden, in Dalkey for a deposit of £150 and repayments of only £3 a week, ten shillings less than I was paying in rent. It would have been a godsend, but the manager of the Munster and Leinster Bank, where I had had my account for five years, refused to lend me the £150, even though I made regular lodgements and was never overdrawn. His method of refusal was particularly unsettling. He first asked for time to consider my request, then after weeks of shilly-shallying finally declined, telling me: 'The boys in the back room wouldn't have it.' Then he laughed and began singing a snatch of 'The Boys of the Old Brigade' as he condemned me and my family to years more of badly maintained rented accommodation.

It was not until Cherry's father, Mick O'Brien, returned permanently from America that we acquired a home of our own. He built it despite an ever-mounting series of obstacles, the most inexcusable being the obstruction of the Dun Laoghaire Corporation, who delayed the planning permission outrageously. Once, after I had thought all objections had been met, the plans were returned to me for 'elucidation and reorientation'. When I asked the relevant official what this meant in practice, he hummed and hawed and refused to give me a straight answer. Finally I asked would it help matters if I proposed to build a bungalow rather than a two-storeyed house. He replied: 'It doesn't matter – whatever you build will be an eyesore!' Whether acting on the advice would have helped or not I cannot say, of course, but throughout these delays I refused to pay heed to those friends who suggested I have recourse to that well-known Irish method of solving planning problems, the brown paper envelope. I finally took the risky step of availing of a provision that then obtained – appeal over the heads of the local bureaucrats directly to the minister for local government. The appeal was ultimately allowed, but the corporation got in what it thought was a last decisive blow. I was instructed that the house was to be built at road level, but it was to be set more than twice as far back from the road as we had originally planned. The effect of this was to create a Catch-22 situation. The site, an old railway siding, fell sharply the further one went from the road. So if the house were built on the spot sanctioned by the council, it would be a) well below the level of the road, and b) have a very large crater where the front garden should have been.

Mick solved the problem by a) building the house on pillars rising from the granite foundation of the railway, and b) opening the space between road and house as a dump! Initially the crater attracted everything from old cars to builders' rubble, but then fortune smiled on the venture and a huge source of fertile earth became available. A prominent Dublin developer, Paddy Belton, commenced work nearby on a large estate, Arnold Park, and a vast accompanying pub and car park, the Graduate. My school friend Kevin Delaney, who was married to Cherry's sister, Moya, and our friends and neighbours the Kelly brothers, John and Mick, ran the site. They directed that the huge lorries carrying away the bulldozed topsoil should deposit their loads in what is now my front garden. I later repaid their kindness by giving my most generous support to the Graduate.

Unfortunately, the corporation's delaying tactics rendered me liable for new taxes and wage increases that were introduced by Sean Lemass at that time in an effort to buy trade union peace. Building costs shot up dramatically and I was extremely lucky to be introduced to a legendary Dublin bank manager, Michael Tierney, who was in charge of what was then the Provincial Bank in O'Connell Street and is now the Allied Irish Bank branch used by the Taoiseach, Bertie Ahern. Tierney allowed my overdraft and my home to go up. But then a credit squeeze hit, delaying the granting of the mortgage, which was a particularly severe trial for Mick as he built the house in between working on other jobs. He had a custom, in the summer, of taking work that commanded a good view, such as a renovating job overlooking Killiney Bay. In the winter he preferred to refurbish pubs.

Then, as the house eventually commenced, Mick contracted the leukaemia that eventually killed him. His hands swelled up from the cortisone treatment and made it difficult for him to use a trowel and a level. But he met this setback, as he had all the other delays and obstructions, by saying: 'Don't worry, we'll get it up. Eventually.' I worked with him as a labourer and we did get the house up, moving in 1964, the year I was commissioned to write my first book, *Ireland Since the Rising*. I called the house 'Eventually' and this memoir is being written in 'the bunker', as I christened the den I established in the basement area that Mick O'Brien's ingenuity created. The book too was completed, eventually. One of the first letters of congratulation I received came from the bank manager who had let me in for all the heartache in the first place by turning down my application for the loan on the bungalow. The bungalow is worth around €1 million today.

But in those days nobody had any money worth speaking of. Very early on in my career in the *Evening Press* I had discovered that even an editor could be broke. Douglas Gageby asked me to run over to the accounts section of the GPO with an envelope containing a cheque for his phone bill. The girl behind the grille first accepted the cheque, then came back to announce loudly that the Department of Posts and Telegraphs did not accept post-dated cheques. I crawled back to Gageby in great mortification, wondering what I should say, but he showed his nicer side when I broke the news to him, replying: 'That must have been very embarrassing for you. Don't worry about it.'

I did worry about my own finances, though, constantly. Things like holidays were what other people did, or more accurately what, in our circumstances, we should have left other people to do. I had acquired a Lambretta motor scooter from one of the *Evening Press* reporters, Jim Downey, by simply taking over the repayments, and Cherry and I decided to use it for a trip to Wicklow and West Cork. We borrowed a tent from Ronnie Drew. I remember thinking that his gravelly voice was as nothing to mine after the first sleepless night spent camping in Glendalough. St Kevin, to whom the place is dedicated, made his name by, amongst other things, hurling a temptress from his cave into the waters of the lake. If the saint could have had access to the Lambretta and Ronnie Drew's tent, no such drastic measures would have been needed. The lady's ardour would have been extinguished by a combination of wind-chill by day and, at night, by the fact that the tent door was missing. Nevertheless we pressed on from Wicklow to West Cork and returned safely, having travelled for the best part of five hundred miles on a scooter that had a top speed of twenty-eight miles an hour.

Our first holiday on Aran, in 1959, was slightly more successful. Our finances had not improved in any way; in fact they had disimproved, because we now had two children, one of whom, Jackie, our second daughter, we took with us in a carrycot, while Maureen looked after Thomond. How Jackie survived the trip to grow into the fine person she became I do not know. I had heard myriad stories about Aran from my mother, who had been brought there by my father. There they met, and became friendly with, Pat Mullen, a tall, incredibly good-looking islander who had acted as adviser to Robert Flaherty when he was making the pioneering documentary *Man of Aran*. Pat was the father of Barbara Mullen, who appeared in a number of films and starred as Janet in the long-running BBC TV serial *Dr Finlay's Casebook*. Brendan O'hEithir, whose father had taught on the island and whose mother was a sister of the Aran-born writer Liam O'Flaherty, was the Irish editor of the *Evening Press* and he added to my mother's fund of Aran stories. The general impression I gained from Brendan and other friends who had visited the Irish-speaking island was of a cross between the legendary Hy-Brasil, the Island of the Blessed, and a semitropical paradise of blazing white beaches where fish were so numerous that they hurled themselves into the islanders' canvas canoes, known as currachs.

In fact I was to be bitterly disappointed when the *Naomh Eanna*, the ferry that sailed from Galway, remained in sight of land – that is when the rain and mist slackened – for most of the three-and-a-half-hour journey. Long enough to create seasickness but not a real sense of remoteness. However, the gods had decreed that if we wanted remoteness, remote we would get, as I discovered from a group of wild-haired, and even more wild-eyed, fishermen who lined the quay wall to check out the day's haul in the way of tourist women. In fact it turned out to be the week's catch, because there were but two scheduled sailings in the week and then only when weather allowed, which it had not been doing recently. Their pleasure at Cherry's appearance was more than offset by their displeasure at mine, but I eventually stirred sufficient speech out of one of them to discover the whereabouts of our guesthouse. It was in Kilmurvey, four miles away! A jarvey man agreed to take us there in his pony and trap.

It now began to rain so heavily that had we not poured the water off, Jackie could easily have made it into *The Guinness Book of Records* for being the first infant to drown in a carrycot. The misting rain cut visibility to something approaching fifty yards, which was quite enough. All we could see were vistas of black, streaming rock, grass tinted orange by salt spray and, through occasional gaps in the downpour, a grey, snarling sea that no self-respecting fish would be found dead in. You could see at a glance from whence came the west of Ireland fisherman's saying 'What the sea gives it takes back.' Our depression was added to by the fact that there was no possibility of getting the ferry off the accursed place for at least four more days, more if the wind increased, which it showed every intention of doing.

However, when we got to our guesthouse, the kitchen was warm, as was our welcome and a badly needed cup of tea. Our room was candlelit. Bottled gas was only in the early stages of being introduced to the island. Economically and psychologically, Aran in those days was to Ireland as Ireland was to Europe. However, the bed was comfortable and Cherry decided that she and Jackie would take a nap before being exposed to any further tropical delights. The rain stopped and I went for a walk along Kilmurvey Beach. Here I met an islander in his sixties, dressed in the traditional homespun tweed, woollen Aran sweater and pampoties, the home-made, cowskin, Aran version of what are today known as trainers. The islander had little English but a great deal of anxiety. His nets, it seemed, were in danger of being swept away and 'the other fellow' hadn't turned up to help him row his currach out to retrieve them.

Being used to rowing boats, I immediately, and incautiously, offered to stand in for 'the other fellow'. The difference between boating on Aran and along the Dun Laoghaire coastline was considerable. First we had to *carry* the heavy currach from where it lay in sand dunes, over a stone wall and then across an exhausting expanse of soft sand to the water's edge. I will never forget the crushing weight of the currach's gunnels on my shoulders. The prow of the boat blotted out my vision and I had no idea of distance, or of obstacles underfoot until I stumbled over them, wrenching my back and drawing not sympathy but roars of disapproval from the boat's owner behind me.

The word 'currach' in Irish means 'giddy', and I soon found out why. It takes time to get acclimatised to the narrow poles with which the craft are rowed, even in the best of conditions. These were not the best of conditions. The rain had stopped but the wind had increased, putting up the waves so that my efforts at guiding the craft from the position in the bow, to which the older man had assigned me, resulted in us spending an exhausting half-hour getting from the beach to a pier that jutted out from some rocks less than 200 yards away.

Sitting at the edge of the pier was one of the finest-looking men I had ever set eyes on. In physique and demeanour he resembled one of the pagan kings of yore. He and the currach's owner exchanged a barrage of strange-sounding, idiomatic Irish, which I could not follow, but eventually the exchange resulted in the pagan king assuming the bow position, my moving to the centre of the boat and the owner continuing to man the third set of oars astern. Again we set off along the shore, keeping about a hundred yards out from some of the most evil-looking rocks and snarling, breaking waves that I had ever seen. The wind was dead against us and rising, and though we now rowed with far greater precision and speed than before, we still made very little headway. My strength began to give out as both wind and waves rose in ferocity, my condition being worsened by the fact that my companions continued to call out to each other in evidently growing nervousness. Even though I was a good swimmer, I began to wonder about my ability to make it back to the shore. I guessed, as it turned out correctly, that neither of my companions could swim and, as I had done life-saving courses, I felt that if we overturned, then I would have an obligation to attempt to rescue at least one of them, an endeavour which, in that tempestuous sea, would inevitably have ended in drowning.

Finally, as I neared exhaustion point and the snarling rocks drew closer, I became sickeningly aware of the fact that I had all our money and our return tickets in my wallet. If I drowned, how was Cherry going to get off the island with Jackie? The thought made me speak out (in English). Keeping my voice a lot calmer than I felt, I suggested that it might be better if we turned for home before the conditions worsened any further. To this the pagan king replied, not very reassuringly: 'Sea. Sea. Tá mud ag dul abhaile' ('Yes, yes, we are going home – if we're able.') But then, while I was digesting this alarming piece of information, the pagan king directed that we stop rowing and turned the boat almost broadside-on to wind and waves. He used the prow of the boat as a sail, to keep us slightly up in the wind, pulling strongly on his left oar as he did so. The effect was magical. With him steering and the other two sets of oars extended like trapeze artists' poles, we skimmed across the waves and got back to the beach in less than twenty minutes.

The strand had been deserted when we left, but now quite a crowd had gathered. They cheered and clapped as we came ashore. I couldn't understand what they were saying. The only English spoken came from the currach's owner. As I shook hands with him and commiserated with the loss of his net, he said: 'Ah, 'twas too breeshy, 'twas too breeshy.' When I got back to our guesthouse, I found the woman of the house and her two daughters in a state of high emotion. Word had reached them that I was in imminent danger of drowning and they had been wringing their hands at the prospect of breaking the news of my death to Cherry. Like Mark Twain, I airily assured them that the news was much exaggerated and told them we were never in any real danger with the pagan king aboard. They seemed puzzled at my description of this heroic figure and wondered aloud who it could have been. Just then I spotted him through the window as he cycled past the house. When I pointed him out to the women, they let out little screams and blessed themselves. My Homeric friend had only returned to the island that very morning from one of his (frequent) lengthy spells in Ballinasloe Mental Hospital.

Yet we were as desolate leaving Aran on that first occasion as we had been shattered on arrival. The weather had improved so much that on the morning that we left the sun was blazing and the sea was blue. In the fields, the wild flowers danced goodbye to us and the glare from the beaches was dazzling. As our pony and trap took us to the harbour, we met the currach owner on the road. We said our goodbyes and he repeated his refrain 'Ah, 'twas too breeshy, 'twas too breeshy.' I again commiserated with him on the loss of his nets and he replied: 'Ah, sure no. I didn't lose them! I waited until the next day when the wind went down and at low tide I went out along the rocks and pulled them in.' So for once it appeared the sea had not taken back what it had given. Or had it?

During that first stay I taught twelve-year-old Michael McDonagh, the only son of the landlady, how to swim. He, like the men I had been out with in the currach, would probably otherwise not have learned to do so, because of the general superstition that it was unlucky to attempt to cheat the sea of its prey, and that in any event if you went into the water in bad weather, it would be impossible to survive the Atlantic waves and swimming would only serve to prolong the agony. Nearly thirty years later Michael and his friend and neighbour Brian O'Flaherty went out in their sturdy lobster boat, the *Lively Lady*, on a day similar to the one I have described; the boat was swamped and neither of the bodies was ever found.

CHAPTER 7

Authorship Beckons,
TV Flickers

Television came to Ireland on New Year's Eve 1961. It literally shed a strange light on Irish society. I remember one evening in particular, a couple of years after RTE opened, driving through a sprawling council estate on the outskirts of Dublin and seeing the flickering blue light coming from almost every front window. Knowing that the same light was also flickering in cottages and mansions throughout the country, those windows gave me a sudden insight into the fact that a new force was abroad in the land. Political platform, pulpit and press were all facing a fresh challenge.

It did not take long before I found myself involved in the fallout from that challenge. Cherry had suffered a miscarriage, which led her to form a women's group whose objective was to get the Irish hierarchy to raise the question of contraception at the Second Vatican Council, which opened in 1962. The chances of this objective ever being achieved may be gauged from a non-conversation I had with a nun in St Michael's Hospital, Dun Laoghaire, after the miscarriage had occurred. Lean, antiseptic, her starched habit glistening white and cold, a symbol of her untouchability and remoteness from bloody sexuality and death, the nun instantaneously dismissed my query as to whether steps could be taken to prevent women from being constantly at risk from the sort of trauma Cherry had just endured: 'Mister Coogan! Mother Church does not allow any form of contraception!' And, with a snap of her long, spatulate fingers and a swirl of white, she was gone. Those were the days when Church attitudes to the dangers of contraception were such that the symphysiotomy operation was still carried out in Catholic hospitals, including the National Maternity Hospital in Holles Street, Dublin. Symphysiotomy involved sawing through a woman's pelvis, so that it 'opened like a hinge' and remained permanently opened and widened. The consequential discomfort and permanent pain militated against further pregnancies.

Television, however, provided an opportunity for a somewhat longer discussion of the issue than that with the nun. I was invited to take part in a panel discussion with a prominent physician, Dr William O'Dwyer, who at the time was the president of the Irish doctors' representative body. I asked him what was the Irish medical position on the Pill. It was the first time that contraception had been discussed on Irish television and the panel were so stunned that I had to explain to the viewers what the Pill was. My abiding memory of the episode is that the Irish doctors' position on the issue appeared to be one of marked embarrassment combined with equally marked inactivity. Vivion de Valera, who disliked the word 'pregnant' appearing in his publications and had not seen the programme himself, did not want for reports of it. They poured into his office from all points of the compass. 'And the worst of it,' he said, 'was that apparently you didn't just raise the indelicate subject, you kept on after Dr O'Dwyer, trying to pin him down – in *public*!'

Afterwards some of my *Evening Press* colleagues took to referring to me (behind my back) for a time as 'the Menstrual Boy'. But I was invited to become a freelance interviewer on one of the earliest current affairs programmes, *Newsbeat*, which went out after the *Six O'Clock News*. The interviewers had to arrange their own interviewees and suggest discussion topics. For this they received seven pounds an interview, a vital addition to my household budget. As so much of the subject matter discussed was initiated by the interviewers, I found *Newsbeat* an invaluable vehicle for getting in contact with some of the more interesting people in the country. One of these was the writer Flann O'Brien, real name Brian O'Nolan, one of the great comic writers of the twentieth century. O'Nolan had actually done some work for the Irish Press Group and drank in one of the *Press* pubs, the Scotch House. But he generated a 'keep-off' force field that I always hesitated to breach. However, in 1964 he produced *The Dalkey Archive*, which dealt with amongst other things St Augustine, bicycles that turned into humans, humans who turned into bicycles and the secret life of James Joyce in Dalkey. This existence, known only to O'Nolan himself, he located in the house adjoining Lohengrin, the Crag, owned by his friend Niall Sheridan. The Dalkey connection caused me to seize the opportunity of meeting the great man with particular vigour. I arranged with family friends, the Murphys, who owned Cliff Castle Hotel, to be allowed to conduct the interview on one of the hotel battlements overlooking Dalkey Island.

O'Nolan, who had a reputation for being a difficult man, turned out to be full of charm and humility, warning me that I would have to attack him to help him over his terror of the camera. Then his wife, Evelyn, rang me to implore me not to give him any drink. 'He's very good,' she said, 'only if he gets drink into him, he'll let himself down.' I used my friendship with the Murphys to arrange to conduct the interview at 8.30 a.m., so that we would be gone long before either the pubs or the hotel bar opened. O'Nolan was to be picked up by the RTE cameraman at 8 a.m., myself shortly afterwards. It was a beautiful summer's morning, which made the chosen interview setting an idyllic one. The only problem was that no one turned up to collect me until 9.15 a.m., when the distraught cameraman pulled up at my home with his worried-looking son and helper sitting beside him in the front seat. So far as I could see there was no O'Nolan aboard. However, as I descended on the cameraman, my fists clenched, a bleary-eyed figure sat up on the back seat – O'Nolan as drunk as I had ever seen a man.

The photographer explained that O'Nolan himself had opened the door to them, immaculate in his charcoal-grey pinstripe suit and sober as one could wish. However, the kindly Evelyn herself had unfortunately provided an opportunity for him to get at alcohol by insisting that everyone sit down to the traditional hearty Irish. As the rashers and scrambled eggs were disappearing, O'Nolan did so also to answer 'a call of nature'. Breakfast continued. Suddenly realisation dawned on Evelyn. She screamed: 'He's at it again! Go upstairs and get him out!' Understandably the photographer demurred at the prospect of extracting Ireland's (and possibly Europe's) greatest comic genius from his own lavatory. In the end, though, when the problem was explained to him he banged on the WC door until O'Nolan emerged – drunk. Behind him there rolled on the floor an empty bottle of Powers Gold Label whiskey, which he had secreted in the cistern.

Now, however, slumped in the back seat, O'Nolan spluttered into life, saying: 'Don't mind him. He thinks I'm drunk! We'll do the interview splendidly. To the battlements.' As the camera was being set up, O'Nolan and I attempted to rehearse the points that would be covered. The rehearsal was not a success. 'Nolan alternatively insisted that I a) attack him, and b) get him a ball of malt, or else no interview. Even though the hotel bar was shut, I managed to persuade one of the hotel waitresses to get me a small whiskey, but this was spurned on the grounds that 'small ones are an abomination' and on the equal, and correspondingly abominable, circumstance that O'Nolan refused to drink alone. So back I had to go to the rather stressed waitress and purchase two large whiskeys. In those days the idea of drinking raw whiskey in the morning was an anathema to me, but I had to gag through my drink while O'Nolan put his away in one gulp, throwing down the abhorred half one for good measure. The interview began, with me attempting to attack O'Nolan and also keep to the extraordinary subject matter of the book. O'Nolan, however, wanted to discuss his ambition to defend the Church against its enemies and particularly those given to buggery. St Augustine, he opined, was a bugger. Not a lot of people knew that in the Ireland of the time, particularly not in the Ireland of Dr John Charles McQuaid.

Then the camera broke down, and he refused to carry on afterwards until two more balls of malt were produced. The interview continued along labyrinthine paths o'erhung with delirium tremens until the Camera Failed the Third Time. O'Nolan demanded further balls of malt, but instead the by now very flustered waitress produced two large gin and tonics. Interview or no interview I refused to drink mine, but O'Nolan remarked that 'it's got the same grain base' and, topping up the gin with tonic, downed it in a few swallows. For a moment the sunny morning darkened. Although alcohol had not played the happiest role in my childhood, my own experience of the stuff was largely associated with parties and jollity, and I found it profoundly depressing to watch the bluey-tinted liquid pass through that brilliant man's almost equally blue-tinted lips.

Somehow we stumbled through the rest of the interview, packed up the gear and got O'Nolan back into the car, intending to decant him at his doorstep before the pubs opened. Alas, a true alcoholic always knows where his drink is. As we drove through Dalkey, from the apparently somnolent O'Nolan there came a stentorian 'STOP! THEY'RE OPEN!' We had no choice but to let him out of the car outside Searson's pub, where, they told me later, he remained drinking, as he normally did, until four in the afternoon, when they put him in a taxi. His hangover the next day must have been horrific, but somehow his column appeared as usual in that morning's *Irish Times*.

When I rang up Frank Hall, the editor of *Newsbeat*, to check what the interview looked like on film, I was, mistakenly, at first delighted with his reaction: 'Congratulations,' he said, 'you've taken part in a classic. One of the all-time great TV moments.' And then dispiritingly he went on: 'Of course, it can never be used!' So I never got my seven pounds, a serious matter for me at the time. I was not at all surprised when, some years later, Hall was appointed film censor and energetically set about safeguarding public morality with his scissors. His performance could well have served as a metaphor for the times. A married man, throughout his TV and censorship incarnations he also conducted an affair with Frankie Byrne, the country's first agony aunt. Do as I say, not as I do was the order of the day.

Nowadays when I think of the O'Nolan episode and look at the thesis industry busily churning out uncomprehending bumf about him and artists like him, the poet Patrick Kavanagh or Brendan Behan, what I remember is people crossing the street to get away from them. By chance I was seated at the bus-stop across the road from Goggins pub in Monkstown on the afternoon of the first Bloomsday, 16 June 1954, with a son of the house, when a horse-drawn cab drew up outside the pub and decanted the original Bloomsday crew, Brian O'Nolan, Patrick Kavanagh, John Ryan, Sam Leventhal and Anthony Cronin, who made the first retracing of Leopold Bloom's footsteps on that famous day in world literature. At the time neither of us knew anything about Joyce or Bloomsday, but we could tell that the group had made a number of pit stops before this one. The reaction of my companion pretty well summed up that of the bulk of the citizenry towards literati at the time. Looking in particular at the agricultural, swaying figure of Patrick Kavanagh, he exclaimed: 'Jaysus, I hope that crowd are not coming into *our* place!'

Arrears of rent caused similar sentiments on the part of Kavanagh's landlord, and for much of his tenure the poet trembled on the verge of eviction from his Pembroke Road rooms. I remember his standing on the stairs outside the *Irish Press* editor's office, before I became editor I hasten to add, and tearing up an article that he had tried unsuccessfully to sell for two guineas. 'Pure shite,' he exclaimed. 'Pure shite!' So is much of the thesis industry.

Not all my television experiences were as catastrophic as the O'Nolan one. In fact one episode, which at the time appeared to threaten my livelihood, actually led to my becoming an author. I had appeared on a panel discussion about a report of a commission into the Irish language. The then president of Maynooth, Tomas ÓFiaich, had chaired, and in the course of the programme he made it abundantly clear that both the report and the language policies of the day were disastrous. At this stage, with emigration and unemployment rampant and half the school population receiving no further education after the age of twelve, I was outraged at the amount of time devoted both to teaching the catechism (Christian doctrine, as it was known) and to Irish, which was so badly taught that very few people learned it anyhow. After the programme the hot lines to Burgh Quay were turned incandescent by language enthusiasts. Old de Valera himself was outraged and for a time no bookie would have given odds on my remaining in my job, never mind being promoted.

But one of the people who agreed with my viewpoint and admired what he wrongly assumed was my courage (which was not in fact courage, but

A mother's love . . . The author, aged four, kitted out by his mother in a Little Lord Fauntleroy outfit for a fancy dress ball.

The infant author and his mother.

Patrick and Marianne Toal, the author's maternal grandparents, with two of their sons, Tim (right) and Frank, on the day of their ordination to the priesthood. Tim became a Monsignor in Australia, Frank a noted theologian in Rome.

Beatrice Toal, the author's mother, at the time of her crowning as Dublin's Civic Queen.

The author's father, Eamonn Coogan, in his hurling days.

Eamonn Coogan, in mufti, seated beside General Eoin O'Duffy and the officer corps of the newly formed An Garda Síochana na hÉireann.

'Who said farmer?' The author's father, then Deputy Commissioner of the Garda, with a group of other senior colleagues, attempting to free their pot-holed official car with a gate, which they had removed without permission, from the entrance to a farmer's field. One of the party captured the picture, and created the startled expressions, by shouting, 'Farmer!'

The author's father at the wedding of his sister Mary to John Comeford.

The author's parents in their early Tudor Hall days.

The author in 1966, the year of the publication of his first book,
Ireland Since the Rising.

At the annual Jacob's Awards dinner at which presentations are made to outstanding TV and radio performers.

At a dinner organised by the author for Terry O'Sullivan's twenty-fifth anniversary as the *Evening Press* diarist, at what was then Dublin's best restaurant, the Mirabeau, run by Dublin's first celebrity chef, Sean Kinsella. Douglas Gageby (left) with Terry, Vivion de Valera, Sean Ward and Conor O'Brien.

The author and Terry O'Sullivan cut a cake baked to mark the twenty-fifth anniversary of Terry's Dubliner's Diary column in the *Evening Press*.

The Loose Alliance . . .! Outside Paddy Burke's pub in Galway with some of the Irish editors who came together during 1978–9 to discuss the possibility of having a Freedom of Information Act and a Press Council introduced to Ireland. The group includes Vincent Doyle, *Evening Herald*, on the author's left. To his right, Senator Maurice Manning, Aidan Pender, *Irish Independent*, Roy Lilley, *Belfast Telegraph*, the columnist John Healy, the editors of the then *Cork Examiner* and *Cork Evening Echo*, Fergus O'Callaghan and Tim Cramer, representatives of the provincial papers. Kneeling in front are Ben Bradlee, the editor of the *Washington Post*, and Michael Hand, left, the editor of the *Sunday Independent*.

The author surveys a mock-up of the *Irish Press* which he had re-designed, during a period when it was off the streets during a strike over the introduction of new technology. The new-look *Irish Press* was to be its last incarnation as a broadsheet.

(Eamonn Farrell/Photocall Ireland)

ignorance: I simply hadn't known the strength of the enemy who lay in wait) was Father F. X. Martin. Martin was a distinguished medievalist historian and an Augustinian friar. FX, as he was generally known, later successfully evaded huge costs awarded against him for leading a protest movement that delayed the building of new county council offices at Wood Quay, Dublin, one of the world's great Viking sites. He pleaded that he had no assets as he was simply a mendicant friar. Although, despite his protests, the building went ahead, the controversy did a great deal to heighten public consciousness about environmental and heritage issues. Martin, a keen horseman, suffered no worse consequences of his actions than being nicknamed 'the Beggar on Horseback' by university colleagues. When he was consulted by an emissary from the London publishing house Pall Mall about the commissioning of a history of Ireland to mark the fiftieth anniversary of the 1916 Rising, he suggested that I be approached.

There is some X factor in life whereby things come to one at certain stages. I was beginning to find the *Evening Press* horizons were narrowing and I had a strong but vague desire to 'write a book'. I had written a number of articles for the London *Spectator*, and short stories both for the *Evening Press* and for a Canadian magazine called *The Montrealer*. I remember writing to the editor of this publication telling him that I thought two of his contributors should be encouraged. One was a Canadian, Mordecai Richler, and the other Brian Moore. I loftily informed the editor that if Moore in particular got over his tendency to morbidity, he would have a future!

The idea of writing an account of what had happened in my own country between 1916 and 1966 appealed to me. Like practically everybody else of my generation, I knew little about the course of events. It struck me as a very good idea that I should be paid for finding out more about things like the reasons why someone should have set fire to my grandfather's house, or what lay behind the hushed tones and the use of the word 'pogroms', which, as a boy, I had heard in my elders' conversations about Northern Ireland. The formal teaching of history in the Irish school system of the time generally ended around 1916. Very few insights were available as to what had been at stake in the Civil War, or how the ruling Fianna Fail Party and the main opposition grouping, Fine Gael, had emerged from that conflict, let alone why the IRA had begun to raid barracks in Northern Ireland again during the 1950s or why it was that the Irish legal system seemed to be so extensively permeated by the morality of the Roman Catholic Church.

There were two chief reasons for our ignorance. One of them was Civil

War sensibilities: toes stepped on in classrooms could belong to a neighbour or, even worse, to the Boss! The other was the inertia of Irish historians who rarely strayed outside safe territory like the Middle Ages. A widely heard excuse for this laziness (and cowardice) was the fact that in 1922 during the Civil War the IRA had destroyed a great number of irreplaceable historical documents at the fall of their headquarters, the Four Courts, the seat of the Irish legal system and site of the Public Record Office. Apparently it never occurred to the academics, more notable for their complexions of port wine and sirloin hue than for their rigour, to take the trouble to interview the survivors of the revolutionary period. Being a journalist, this was exactly what I did, and although interviewing and spending time in the National Library while holding down my job nearly brought about a breakdown, I nonetheless found the exercise extraordinarily interesting.

One stroke of good luck helped me with my work. Industrial relations in the *Irish Press* were always gladiatorial. Along with the quite extraordinary levels of camaraderie and professionalism there was a paradoxical antagonism towards 'the management'. Though the staff gave of their all, there was a strong element of those who, in the Dublin phrase, 'hated the Boss as a duty'. The management was able to get away with a regime of low pay and casual working for two reasons: first, the general level of unemployment in the country, and second, and even more important, because in those days the *Irish Press* formed part of a cartel, so that if a strike occurred in one Dublin newspaper, the others ceased publication also. A strike that helped to sound the death knell of this unholy alliance (which mainly benefited the *Press*, as the other newspapers treated their staff better), occurred in 1965. For an entire summer the appalling climate of industrial relations proved a godsend to me. The journalists were not on strike, so our contracts enabled us to report for duty every day with nothing to do.

I worked feverishly on my manuscript by day and by night, managing to avoid being allocated any of the soul-destroying tasks that Vivion thought up in order to shed the distasteful obligation of having to pay people to do nothing. I use the term soul-destroying advisedly. Vivion had a fixation about areas of the company being allowed to operate independently in any way. One such area was the library run by the saintly, and scholarly, Aengus O'Dalaigh, a bachelor who was both one of the best research resources in Ireland and a man of infinite charity. The only slight difficulty in obtaining information from Aengus that anyone ever encountered was a gentle 'Would you mind waiting a moment? I have a poor man I have to see in the front office.' Decoded, Aengus was running downstairs to share some of his meagre income with yet another toucher. Such 'poor men' came to him at all hours of the day and night.

However, Aengus, whose brother was another noted Irish scholar, Cearbhall O'Dalaigh, who afterwards became president of Ireland, had incurred Vivion's wrath by compiling a magnificent library both of cuttings and books. Instead of giving Aengus additional space, as he sought, Vivion wanted him to be more ruthless in his keeping of material, and during the printers' strike of 1965 he got his chance. The managing editor, Bill Redmond, the journalistic hit man who was charged with the Sisyphean task of encouraging things like punctuality and creativity amongst reporters (while discouraging it in their expense accounts), was instructed to see to the winnowing of Aengus's treasured files. One bright July afternoon I had occasion to witness the fruits of his labours. Two sports sub-editors had been chosen – being sports sub-editors, it was assumed that they would not have any scruples over destroying news reports – to go through the filing cabinets and cull two out of every three items.

In those days newspaper cuttings were pasted onto bright yellow linen paper, folded and placed in large, strong envelopes that might contain as little as two or three, or as many as a hundred items. The library, which occupied what must have been the front rows of the balcony of the old Tivoli, looked down on the now silent case room some twenty feet below. When I got to the area, Aengus was running around like a bird whose nest has just been devastated by magpies. He seemed to be on the verge of hurling himself into the case room. The normally drab library area now had a floor of bright yellow that shone like some sort of vandal's tapestry in the sunlight. The cuttings, which minute by minute were remorselessly added to, under Redmond's gimlet eye, were by then a foot deep. As I waded through this tide of destruction, my sandal caught on something and I almost fell. I picked up the obstruction and found that it was a thick envelope that contained the entire, unrivalled, coverage of the Blueshirt movement by *Irish Press* reporters.

It had been the *Irish Press* reportage of what the leader of the movement, General O'Duffy, actually said when, Jameson-fuelled, he got in front of a microphone, as opposed to the more anodyne scripts which his staff issued, that turned the public against the Blueshirts. But before this happened, during that short-lived but turbulent period of street politics in the 1930s, it seemed for a moment as though a shirted organisation, with resonances of Continental fascism, might become a force in Irish politics.

God knows what else was thrown out, but certainly Aengus never got over the loss.

I didn't realise it at the time, but such bloody-mindedness was a part of *Irish Press* managerial philosophy. I witnessed another loss of a similar type a quarter of a century later. The art department was frowned upon because it had a semi-independent existence and an effort was made to bring it under the control of the newsroom with the post of art editor regarded as an avenue of promotion from the newsroom. Part of the downgrading attempt lay in denying the department, which contained the best photographic team in the country, the facilities it needed to properly store negatives. Irreplaceable glass negatives were placed in shallow, open shelving, built along one of the busiest corridors in the building, which served the newsroom, amongst other departments. Inevitably each day saw some of the negatives brushed from their unsuitable storage area and crushed underfoot.

The power of the *Evening Press* was attested to by the manner in which the 1965 strike ended. A group of city-centre traders representing the then largest shops in Dublin – household names like Arnott's, Clerys, Switzers and many others – came to Jack Dempsey's office one day and told him that as a result of the strike their business had on average dropped by 30 per cent. They asked how much would be required in increased advertising to meet the printers' demands. A deal was hammered out and the strike ended. It had lasted just long enough to enable me to meet my deadline of 31 October of that year. The book was called *Ireland Since the Rising*, and apart from giving a linear history of the fifty years that had elapsed between 1916 and 1966 it also contained chapters on topics such as the Church, the GAA, the IRA, culture and Northern Ireland. It made quite an impact on a generation that puzzled over, but never quite understood, the forces that shaped our society.

My researches also gave me an insight into the power of those forces – in ways I had not anticipated. Late one night I had returned home from Belfast, feeling almost exhausted physically, but mentally exhilarated, having secured a very good interview for the book from Captain Terence O'Neill, the Northern Ireland prime minister. This was quite an experience for a journalist from the *Irish Press* stable, but my exhilaration disappeared when, sitting in my silent home, I read a letter that had been left lying for me on the kitchen table. It was Cardinal Conway's response to a questionnaire I had sent him and other Church leaders. Conway had specifically asked that I put down my questions in writing and I had done so reluctantly, pointing out that a person-to-person interview gave the subject a better chance of assessing an interviewer's bone fide questions than did a reliance on the coldness of written questions.

Conway assigned me no bone fides. He was clearly outraged. His long letter spoke of my questionnaire betraying a bias and prejudice that made him fear for the objectivity and integrity of my book. He of course refused the interview, and despite my tiredness I lay awake much of that night in a state of mingled anger and fear, pondering how I would meet my mortgage if, and when, the cardinal contacted Vivion and had me fired.

Next day anger got the better of me (for a time only) and I wrote an equally lengthy reply to Conway, hotly denying either bias or a lack of objectivity. After a few more drafts I came up with a more temperate reply, but one which contained the point that by coincidence I had received his letter on returning from an interview with the Unionist prime minister, who, while disagreeing with my views, had at least agreed to meet me.

My reply may have had the effect of confining the cardinal's reaction to the Church, rather than the temporal arena. For, as the weeks passed, it became evident that Vivion had not been complained to. However, as I discovered more than forty years later, Conway did deal me 'a belt of the crosier' by sounding alarm bells amongst his colleagues. Remarkably, as we shall see in Chapter 8, it emerged from the papers of the ultra-conservative archbishop of Dublin, Dr John Charles McQuaid, that he had actually answered my questionnaire before attending a meeting of the hierarchy at Maynooth. Here, a handwritten note on his typed replies (dated 27 April 1965) states: 'Only yesterday the bishops informed me that this man's going to write a book of flaring criticism.' The typed replies to the questionnaire were apparently prepared by one of his aides, either the diocesan press officer Osmond Dowling or his influential assistant Father Ardle McMahon. The archbishop had then added comments in his own handwriting. Neither set of replies was ever sent, but, surprisingly enough in view of the foregoing, I managed to secure face-to-face inter-views with three members of the hierarchy: Michael Browne of Galway, Cornelius Lucey of Cork and Peter Birch from the Kilkenny diocese of Ossery. Years after Conway's death I was invited into his old study, in his residence at Ara Coeli, Armagh, by his successor Tomas ÓFiaich and spotted a copy of *Ireland Since the Rising* on his shelves. Tomas took it down for me and we discovered that Conway had gone over the book literally line by line. Almost every page carried underlinings or handwritten annotations in the margins.

Vivion de Valera did hear dire things about the book. He came to me not long after its publication at Easter 1966 with a copy under his arm and told me that he was going to read it, and if there was what he phrased as 'anything in it', he would have to 'cut the painter' between the two of us. Conway does not appear to have got in touch with him, but as Vivion was a great attendee at foreign affairs receptions, to judge from papers released by the Department of Foreign Affairs as this book was being written, his fears were probably stoked by members of that department who corresponded about me to each other for a month beginning on 14 March 1966. The Irish ambassador to London had started the hare with a communication to the department about an article on the IRA he had heard I had written for a forthcoming edition of the *Daily Telegraph* colour magazine.

On Tim Pat:

> Although I do not know him personally, I gather his judgement is somewhat faulty and I hope he will be discreet in what he says about modern Ireland. I gather he can be quite critical, though strangely enough for a journalist he is well disposed to our department.

Magnanimously, Keating continued: 'I do not suggest that we try to nobble him in any way.' But he went on: 'If you have a means of persuading him that statements one can make easily at home are liable to be greatly distorted abroad, it might do no harm.'

The persuasion process was undertaken by a home-based diplomat, Frank Coffey, who noted that he did not know me, but fell in with the view *du jour*, saying he suspected that Keating's comment on my judgement was correct. He then described how he went about the process of persuasion without 'nobbling':

> I telephoned Mr Tom [sic] Pat Coogan and spoke to him bout [sic] the date of publication of his book. The conversation came round to his other writings and to his article on the new IRA for the *Telegraph*. He said he had sent in the article some time ago and it was to be published very soon. (It would appear that it was in train well before the recent bombings[1] and was not inspired by them, as suggested by Mr Keating.) Mr Coogan said he had the reputation of the country very much in mind, particularly as he was writing for an influential British publication.

Coffey's boss, Sean Ronan, wrote to Keating summing up the press

---

[1] The bombing referred to was the blowing up of Dublin's Nelson's Pillar, described in Chapter 8.

coverage of the 1916 fiftieth-anniversary celebrations and reporting on Coffey's contact with me:

> The overall reaction in the foreign press to date is quite god [sic] and we stand to gain enormous publicity abroad through coverage of the celebrations. An exception of course was Tim Pat Coogan's article and photographs of the IRA in this week's *Daily Telegraph* supplement. He was contacted about his proposed article by an officer of the department who knows him but he did not give much change.

Coffey, of course, had already told Ronan that he did not know me, but, as can be seen from the correspondence, civil servants' concern for journalistic accuracy is not always paralleled by their own observance of this desirable trait. Keating, still in persuasion rather than nobbling mode, ended the correspondence on 13 April, saying:

> My own view is that the article is coloured by adjectives and tendentious. Interpretation to put it on a par with the same paper's description of the flag as 'orange, green and white' in its report on the 1916 commemoration. It is of course now too late to do anything about it. I had not thought of an official reply but if [sic] by some Irish historian if we could forment [sic] one.

Even if the department could have found one of the Irish historians of the day with sufficient energy to write such a letter, it is unlikely that he or she would have found anything to justify a correspondence. The article, which had been commissioned by the *Telegraph* and, because of the requirements of colour printing, had been delivered weeks before the bombing, was a straightforward account of the IRA's background and its position in contemporary Ireland. However, using the persuasion, not nobbling formula, the department did take revenge. Although my book was the pioneering work, indeed the only one, on post-1916 Ireland, it was not included on any of the recommended reading lists that the department issued in its brochures. But, as we shall see, another Department of Foreign Affairs, the American State Department, was to rate the book more highly than did the Irish mandarins.

Vivion too liked it, and after reading it asked to be shown the proofs of the review that the *Irish Press* was planning to run. It had been written by the secretary of the Department of Local Government, Tom Garvin, who had a reputation as a Joycean scholar. It was so hostile that Vivion ordered that the review be killed and a more favourable one obtained from some other quarter. By a curious irony of the fate that decreed that Vivion and my father should become friends, and that I would one day edit a newspaper that was only allowed into our house when suitably doused in holy water, it would be Garvin's son Tom, a professor of politics in University College, Dublin, who much later launched my unflattering biography of Vivion's father, Eamon de Valera.

Ireland Since the Rising attracted such interest that I received a number of enquiries from other publishers. I got myself an agent, Murray Pollinger, who had lived through the IRA bombing campaign in England, which had preceded the outbreak of the Second World War. The memory of this abided with him and it was he who suggested that I write a book on the IRA. Of the various sections of Irish life that I had examined during my research, I too had found the IRA people extremely interesting. They were quite unlike the fearsome thugs I had been led to expect, and though some were clearly merely narrow-minded chauvinists, many turned out to be high-minded, well-read and good-living people in every facet of their lives save their belief that physical force was justified in getting the British out of Northern Ireland. I fell in with Pollinger's suggestion, and he negotiated a contract for £3,000 with Pall Mall, payable as various tranches of manuscript were delivered.

This was of course a milestone development for me, although it was not apparent at the time. The event that struck me as being of the greatest significance that year was the Great Trip. In those days travel opportunities were few and far between. The demands of my work and of a growing family literally circumscribed horizons. I had been to America once, in 1961, when Trans World Airlines (TWA) brought over a party of journalists to mark the opening of a new route to New York. It was meant to be a forty-eight-hour visit, but I stayed on for a week with Cherry's relations the McDermotts in Fordham, who treated me with great hospitality and ensured that I saw every tourist attraction in the city. However, my abiding memory of the trip was the outward flight. Over the Atlantic at 36,000 feet the captain informed us that Alan Shepard had just become America's first astronaut. We empathised with the achievement and toasted it so liberally that many of us could have walked in space ourselves.

That first trip, with its glimpses of the architectural tone poem that is New York, was literally a horizon-expanding experience for a twenty-six-year-old Irishman emerging from the still over-encapsulated Ireland of the clergy, the porter, the poverty and the officious, self-satisfied civil servant. But it was a glimpse as seen through the windows of Irish-Americana, the police, the graduates from Fordham, the Irish pubs, a mould that would crumble as the decade wore on but that was still largely intact during my first visit.

The Great Trip, however, was something akin to my being invited to leave the TWA Boeing and join Shepard in space. This time the invitation came to me because, after *Ireland Since the Rising* was published, the American embassy nominated me flatteringly, if undeservedly, as 'the outstanding Irish journalist'. I and a group of similarly chosen European journalists were invited to see America from the inside.

Our hosts were the White House, the State Department, the Pentagon and the United States Information Service (USIS). We were given our own aeroplane, a Caribou, in which to crisscross America and we saw sights denied to ordinary mortals, such as the interior of the Cheyenne Mountain Complex. This mountain shielded a giant underground bunker, mounted on springs, from which the Americans controlled their Strategic Air Command nuclear bombers, which remained in the air for twenty-four hours a day. Here, as in other parts of the American defence network, giant screens marked out in latitude and longitude gave the precise position, name and speed of every ship heading towards the US. Elsewhere similar screens did the same for aeroplanes. That was in 1966. Given the growth of technology subsequently, one can only marvel at how a primitive determination could circumvent the vastly improved contemporary shields and create the Twin Towers atrocity.

One object of the trip was to reduce the risk of misunderstandings between the US and the Soviet Union. By being open to journalists about its defences and its society, the Americans hoped to let the Russians know exactly where they stood so as to reduce the risk of Armageddon by Accident. Apart from visiting the State Department, the White House, the great cities and all the time zones of America, we visited leading newspapers, magazines and television stations, including the *New York Times*, CNN, NBC, *Time*, *Life*, *Fortune* and universities like MIT and Tufts. During our visit to Time-Life the editor in chief of *Time* magazine, Hedley Donovan, known as 'Deadly Hedley', made a remark I never forgot concerning newspaper control. 'We,' he said, 'are not a dictatorship. We are a *non-democratic* organisation.'

The second great objective of the trip soon also became clear – to prepare public opinion for the Washington view of the Vietnam War. The number of academics we met who had either returned from or were going to Saigon was highly significant, giving an insight into how the university system fed into the war effort. I would later have an even better insight into this phenomenon. The publishing house Praeger, which printed *Ireland*

Since the Rising in the States, was owned by Frederick Praeger. Praeger, a former intelligence agent, had become aware of the vast number of academic treatises that had been written for the State Department and the Pentagon concerning various world trouble spots. He realised that, say, a paper on North Vietnam's rice-growing potential, while it had an obvious military implication, could also, with a little editing, be turned into an arcane but useful economic text. Accordingly, as such documents became declassified Praeger would publish them, and subsequently many other things originating from the State Department, and thus built up a lucrative publishing empire.

During the Great Trip we were brought to press conferences and meetings with American decision-takers who included the joint chiefs of staff and Dean Rusk, the then secretary of state. I remember the State Department visit, during which I was introduced to the august figure of Averell Harriman, less for what this scion of American aristocracy had to say about Vietnam than for what an aide told me about him. The official had been tidying up Harriman's desk and was shocked to discover that an open drawer contained $500,000 in large-denomination bills. He urgently sought out Harriman and asked him what he should do with the money. Harriman's only reply was 'Leave it there.'

After an interview with the joint chiefs of staff I was sounded by a Marine general on Irish public opinion towards the Vietnam War. I told him that in all honesty I felt the bulk of public opinion existed in a state he might find difficult to understand, namely pro-American but against the war. A sober, highly intelligent man, he seemed to be even more sober after our conversation. As a military man, he knew only too well what he and his troops were getting into, but he was equally aware that he could be going into battle, with the most advanced weaponry in the world, lacking the most important weapon of all, the support of public opinion.

Whether that conversation, or a number of interventions that we touring journalists made at press conferences and briefings, had anything to do with it I cannot say with certainty, but shortly after the Pentagon visit we were given the opportunity of flying to Vietnam. Even though I had been away from home since late October and it was now early December, I jumped at the opportunity. Amongst those who also did so was Arnie Gunnarson, the Icelander. Arnie, a tall, godlike figure who appeared to have stepped straight out of one of the Viking sagas, was impervious to the ravages of alcohol. The group collectively and individually suffered all through the trip from atomic hangovers. American hospitality is as lethal as its method of prosecuting war. Arnie, however, could generally be found on the morning after not in repentance, but the swimming pool. He attributed his invulnerability to 'B witamins'. As a contribution to scientific research on the subject of booze, I should record the fact that the magic witamin never worked its alchemy on me. I visited Arnie and his wife, Hefner, many years later in Iceland, on the eve of the millennium. We toasted both the century and a friendship cemented in the steaming, triple-canopied jungles of Vietnam, while seated in a heated thermal pool near his home, surrounded by snow and ice, with hailstones pelting down on our heads. Next day Arnie was his usual unforgivably healthy self and I had the flu.

Apart from the friendship of Arnie, and other companions on the trip, like Emile Bourgraff, the Luxembourg representative, the trip had lasting consequences for me and is the reason why today my major ambition is to see an Irish government take active steps to mobilise the Irish diaspora into a coherent, united group. For the trip taught me the difference between the America I love, that of myriad friendships, of life, love, liberty and the pursuit of happiness, and America as empire. I realised that America is not simply a country but a complex continent, held together by an innocent and oversimplified notion of patriotism typified by the Stars and Stripes that flies on so many front lawns, the daily affirmation required of children in schoolrooms and the respect for the president, which is not short of a latter-day acceptance of the Divine Right of Kings. America's different time zones, climates, foods and variations in wealth go along with a similar variation in attitudes. What interests them in Idaho differs from the preoccupations of California, which in turn are not those of Boston, Chicago or Milwaukee. The further one gets from Washington, the less the place influences Americans' thinking. The states have their own legis-latures, and their own populations, frequently far larger than Ireland's.

What they do not have, and badly need, is decent media. For the most part American journalism is insular to the point of being parochial, and foreign coverage, even by the wealthy electronic corporations, is very poor. America is so vast that the contents of the *New York Times* or the *Washington Post* scarcely have any influence in Kansas. Approximately one congressman in five holds a passport, which is higher than the percentage of Americans who travel abroad – even before 9/11 further curtailed the numbers. As a result, the formulation of foreign policy is largely determined by the powerful Washington lobbies. The industrial-military complex, oil, the supporters of the state of Israel, and latterly the exiled Cubans all have more influence on what America does abroad than do its citizens, at least until the body bags start coming home.

Much blood was to flow in Vietnam between my visit at the end of 1966 and the ending of the war in 1975,[2] but I can honestly say that within an hour of landing in Saigon I realised that the Americans hadn't a hope of winning. Emile Bourgraff had a contact aboard a Red Cross ship moored on the Mekong River, a few hundred yards from our hotel. The medics treated victims of the war impartially. As a result the Vietcong would warn medical personnel to stay clear of areas in which ambushes were planned. The level of contact was such that Emile and I were in a position to interview Vietcong sympathisers in the heart of supposedly secure Saigon. We were intended to be what are now known as 'embedded journalists' and were issued with American uniforms. I found the concept deplorable and had no intention of being subject to it. I wore a uniform of my own, an Australian digger hat, to keep the sun off, and a white shirt. Bad for camouflage, but good for the soul. I must admit that I did like the soft leather Marine boots and brought them home with me. Even though we were under military protection and flown about the place in military planes and helicopters, I found it quite easy to learn what was really happening behind the sanitised briefings, the daily 'Five O'Clock Follies', that the Americans put on for the benefit of journalists in Saigon. The only good thing to be said for these briefings was that they took place in air-conditioned rooms, a godsend in humid Saigon.

Sometimes I would plead diarrhoea, and drop off the officially planned schedule of events, to use my Irish citizenship to prise information out of either an Irish-American combatant or a priest. I found the Vietcong situation reminded me of that of the IRA. Universally condemned, they are not impervious to bullets or shrapnel, which create what are legally described as 'notifiable injuries'. Yet one never hears of an IRA man being treated for wounds in an Irish hospital being turned over to the authorities. The situation was visibly worse for the Americans, because they were obviously two feet taller and infinitely more prosperous than those whose hearts and minds they were supposed to be winning. Moreover they had to contend with guerrillas who had the assistance of triple-canopy jungle.

I realised the significance of this when talking to an Irish aerial reconnaissance expert one afternoon. It was his job to analyse the photographs taken after bombing missions and submit the results to the generals. At the time the great cant was that the war could be won if the Ho Chi Minh Trail bringing supplies from North Vietnam was 'interdicted' – i.e. blasted

[2] The Peace Accords signed in Paris on 27 January 1973 ended the US military involvement but did not end the war between North and South.

out of existence. With classical American candour he rubbished this theory: 'Bullshit. *Any* trail in Vietnam is a Ho Chi Minh Trail. We're bombing these people from seven miles up through triple-canopy jungle. Half the time we either hit nothing or hit the wrong people.' Yet meanwhile, as we spoke, back at the 'Five O'Clock Follies' the American public were being fed lies and disinformation about the conduct of the war, and its eventual outcome. One of our mentors on the trip was a tough American colonel who had fought in the Second World War. I became friendly with him and was invited to his home to eat hotdogs and watch American football. He told me: 'My great fear for America is the influence of illiterate wealth. You get some fundamentalist, nutty Texas oil millionaires influencing the White House and Christ knows what might happen.' We now know what happened. It's called Iraq.

However, with all its imperfections the American system did get me to Vietnam, and on my return to Ireland I wrote a series of articles that won me high praise from one of the best writers on the war, Martha Gellhorn, who was once married to Ernest Hemingway. She told RTE's *Late, Late Show*, which at the time had the highest viewing figures in the state, that Irish people wanting to find out what was going on in Vietnam should read my articles.

I got no such encouragement from the IRA when I attempted to write my book. Cathal Goulding, the then chief of staff, issued an instruction to the movement that I was to receive no cooperation and sent an emissary advising me to lay off the project. However, I was younger then, so I told the emissary, Eamonn McThomas, that the IRA's history was not the property of Cathal Goulding alone, but of the Irish people, and that I intended to write the book anyhow. McThomas visibly blanched at this, and advised me to be careful, that Goulding could be dangerous. I replied something to the effect that I would have considered such a quality as being part of the job specification for the position of chief of staff of the IRA. An accepted (and spent) advance doth make us wondrous courageous, particularly when one has a large and growing family.

I commenced my research in January 1967, largely circumnavigating Goulding's ban to a great extent by using a simple technique. In effect I asked everyone I approached to conduct two interviews: one with me, to make up their minds whether or not I could be trusted, and the second, or subsequent, interviews to be devoted to the book. It was slow, but in nine cases out of ten this technique worked and the book duly appeared three and a half years later, in June 1970. It has remained in print until the time of writing, growing through various editions until it is now larger than

War and Peace. The gestation period was not entirely due to the difficult subject matter.

In July 1967 Vivion de Valera took me out to Jammet's, which for years was Dublin's only fine-food restaurant, and offered me the editorship of the *Irish Press*. I was flattered to be asked, but shied away from the idea of becoming involved with what was then a dull, declining, party-political newspaper. However, in typical de Valera fashion Vivion had brought along a prop to help me make up my mind. It was a copy of the first editorial of the *Irish Press*, written, he told me, in large part by his father from a draft supplied by Frank Gallagher, the paper's first editor. He drew my attention to two statements in particular. One: 'We are not the organ of an individual, or a group or a party. We are a national organ in all that that term conveys.' The other: 'We have given ourselves the motto "Truth in the news." We shall be faithful to it. Even where the news exposes a weakness of our own, or a shortcoming in the policies we approve, or a criticism of individuals with whom we are associated, we shall publish it, if its inherent news values so demand.'

At that stage the paper could have been judged by the extent to which it had fallen from these admirable standards, and the idea of restoring editorial independence and professionalism overcame my reservations about taking the job. I accepted on the spot, without even enquiring what my salary might be. It took six months before I found out because, also in typical Vivion fashion, he warned me that the offer would only take effect in six months' time, 1 January 1968, and that in the meantime I was not to mention the offer to anyone, including Cherry. Subsequently I often wondered what would have happened had I been able to finish the IRA book before that date. Its success might have decided me to resolve the constant conflict within me as to whether I should continue as a journalist or become a full-time writer. As things turned out, Jammet's became the theatre in which Vivion and I would resolve our many subsequent battles.

The first of these was both hilarious and prophetic. A few days after that first Jammet's dinner Vivion called me into the *Irish Press* editor's office, which was vacant at the time, because, as indicated earlier, morning paper personnel work at night. Even had the unfortunate editor been present, I think Vivion would have commandeered the office anyhow, so great was his anger. With voice and finger shaking he pointed out an item on page one headlined 'Coffin Falls into Paradise' and snarled: 'That's the sort of thing I *don't* want in the *Irish Press*.' The story described how a coffin carrying the remains of an old nurse who had died in Boston had fallen to the ground as it was being taken by helicopter towards the poor woman's native Aran Islands. The townland into which the coffin fell was called Paradise, and as far as I could see the sub-editor had done a good job. I rashly said as much to Vivion and to put it mildly a certain frisson resulted.

The coffin incident had two major consequences. One, it taught me that Vivion de Valera had to be handled like a woman: listen attentively to her complaints for an hour and she'll become yours for the night. The second lesson to be derived from Nurse Folan's fall was the light it shed on the way power was exerted in the Ireland of the time. A few days after the Paradise story appeared, worse befell the coffin. This time it fell from the sling that attached it to the helicopter and disappeared for ever into the Atlantic, midway between the Cliffs of Moher and Inishmaan, the middle of the three Aran Islands. The incident attracted a certain amount of comment at the time but had faded from memory by the following October, when I stepped off the Dublin train in Cork to conduct an interview for my book with the famous IRA leader of the Anglo-Irish War, Tom Barry, who, as indicated in Chapter 2, I would later learn had been my father's adversary. I of course knew nothing of this at the time and for the moment had more immediate concerns. To my consternation, Barry met me at the station to inform me that he could not do the interview because he had to go straight to Shannon Airport to perform an urgent favour for his friend Gene Sheehan. Gene turned out to be a well-known character in both Boston and Ireland. He liked the company of journalists and I had seen him frequently in Mulligan's pub buying rounds for everyone in sight.

Though I was friendly with him, I had always been wary about accepting his hospitality, the money for which derived not merely from his lucrative undertaking business in Boston, but also, it was said, from an agency for slot machines, obtained from the Mafia. The puce-faced Gene carried before him the visible evidence of a lifetime devoted to the oral Irish culture (Messrs Jameson, Powers, Paddy Flaherty, Guinness, etc.). His large and pimpled nose appeared to have grown to a point where it normally occupied at least a third of his face, but when I met him in Cork that day, it had expanded to cover at least a half. Gene had been drowning his sorrows copiously ever since the Paradise incident, and with good reason, as we shall see. However, he recognised me at once and welcomed me to join the party for Shannon. Along the way Barry, one of nature's story-tellers, gave vivid descriptions of every murder, ambush and skirmish that had occurred between Cork city and Shannon Airport. I was then placed in the care of a driver while Barry and Gene disappeared on a mysterious mission. When they reappeared, about an hour later, one look at their smiling faces was enough to tell me that whatever they had been up to things had gone well. Barry rubbed his hands and exclaimed in broadest Cork: 'Dat's it. De bizshness is done. Now we can have a few halves.' In fact we had no halves, but a great many large ones, which led to my discovering both what lay behind Vivion's agitation over the Paradise report and how the old republican Mafia operated.

Hitherto I had assumed that the reason for the coffin's tendency to part from the helicopter had been the weight of the coffin compared to the size of the helicopter. I had seen it parked at Shannon and it was tiny. Too light, I thought, to be able to maintain its course and at the same time remain in control of a heavy, swinging coffin. However, over the 'few halves' Barry gave me the 'Boston Version'. According to this, there had been no Nurse Folan in the coffin. After a lifetime of saving and prudent investing, she had died in Boston some time before the Paradise episode. After attending at her bedside for some weeks, like a great pot-bellied vulture, Gene had convinced the wealthy spinster that she should allow herself to be buried on her native island. At first she had demurred on what I thought were quite reasonable grounds. At the time Aer Lingus, which Gene always referred to in his radio ads as 'the friendly Irish airline', had indeed a reputation for ferrying Irish-Americans home 'to be buried in the old sod'. But there was no way that the friendly Irish airline, or any other airline, could land on Inishmaan, because in those days the island had no airstrip.

However, one night in a pub in South Boston a great light dawned on Gene as he watched the TV news from Vietnam – helicopters! The next afternoon he got the now rapidly failing Miss Folan's agreement to having her corpse flown to Shannon by Aer Lingus and then onward to Inishmaan by helicopter. The poor woman was properly waked, and the Irish consul general, seeing her ensconced in one of Gene's most expensive coffins, naturally made no bones (so to say) about signing the necessary papers. However, it seems the good lady subsequently made no journey. There were, and possibly still are, links between the Irish and Italian Mafias in the Boston building industry, an area in which the term 'cementing relationships' has a special connotation. Each side takes care of the other's problems. Anyhow, I was given to understand that Miss Folan's remains remained in Boston and Gene's large, expensive, rosewood coffin was used to ferry another, unspecified but definitely illegal, cargo across the seas to Ireland, as had been done many times, both before and afterwards.

But though the coffin landed safely at Shannon, Gene began having doubts about the wisdom of the Inishmaan venture when a member of the airport staff remarked to him: 'They'll have a great wake for the poor woman when she's landed amongst her relations.' Suddenly Gene had a fearful thought: 'Sure they'll never open the coffin at this stage?' he enquired. 'Of course they will,' was the answer! It was then, according to Barry, that Gene hit on the idea of having the coffin fall from the heavens over some deserted townland en route to the island. Unfortunately, the chosen wasteland turned out to be called Paradise and Tommy Browne, the alert press correspondent stationed at Shannon, promptly circulated the item to every known news outlet in the English-speaking world, including the *Irish Press*. What I didn't know at the time was that Vivion's annoyance had been caused by the fact that Gene had got on to his old friend Frank Aiken, a former chief of staff of the IRA and now minister for foreign affairs and one of Eamon de Valera's closest friends. Aiken had lifted the phone to President de Valera, who had in turn phoned his son with some sharp comments on the unseemly levity of the story and its positioning on page one.

The unexpected publicity had panicked Gene. He had intended to use the fall as a pretext for keeping the lid shut during the obsequies: 'Did a lot of damage. Not nice to look at. Upsetting for the relations. Keep the lid shut at all costs, etc., etc.' However, after the Descent into Paradise, and the provision of a new coffin, Gene learned, from the man who had reminded him about the wake custom in the first place, that the Aran Islanders were unlikely to be prevented from opening the coffin by 'a few injuries. Sure they do be dragging bodies out of the sea over there weeks after the crabs do be at them – a few bangs here and there would be no bother.' And so, on its second attempt to land on Inishmaan, Miss Folan's coffin somehow became detached from its sling and slid into some of the deepest and most turbulent waters off the Irish coast. The navigator of the helicopter followed the coffin into the water, a happening that caused various theories to surface, if I may use that term. One such was that at first the coffin obstinately refused to sink and needed some encouragement. However, the navigator later explained that he had gone in to 'mark the spot'. Whether this was to be done by carving an 'X' on the third wave from the right or some such, I don't know. But the most likely explanation for the navigator's presence in the water is that after the coffin fell, the crew, who of course would have known nothing about Gene's scheming, made what, in the circumstances, was a courageous attempt to reattach it to the helicopter, but that the coffin sank before they could do so.

But it transpired that the reason for our journey to Shannon lay in the fact that the Department of Transport and Power had ordered an inquiry into the affair and Sheehan had called upon Barry to ensure that the verdict arrived at would be the correct one. After the repeated volleys of large ones had worked their tongue-loosening alchemy, Barry confided in me that a Certain Important Figure at Shannon Airport would have a considerable influence on the inquiry's outcome. The gentleman in question had also been a member of Barry's flying column during the Black and Tan days. Whether or not our journey had any bearing on the outcome I cannot say with certainty, but it is a matter of record that the following July, the minister for transport and power, Erskine Childers, brought the curtain down on the Folan affair without any further controversy. He spoke during the adjournment debate in the Dail, which is a traditional time in Irish politics for disposing of potentially embarrassing business, because no one wants to precipitate a lengthy debate that could interfere with the holidays. Reading from his prepared brief, the minister, who later became president of Ireland, informed the House that a) the melancholy event had occurred because of a defective shackle, and b) there need be no fear of any repetition, because the helicopter company had gone out of business.

Looking back on the incident, I must say I prefer the Boston Version explanation to that of either the helicopter's size or of a defective shackle. But whatever way one judges the incident, one thing is certain – poor Nurse Folan never got to the Aran Islands, but she did wind up on page one of the *Irish Press*.

CHAPTER 8

Editing the Shambolic

The shambolic manner in which I took over the editorial chair in the *Irish Press* says much about the condition of the paper and its staff at the time. One afternoon in January 1968 the existing editor, Joe Walsh, then in his late fifties, was unexpectedly called over to Vivion de Valera's large office in Irish Press House, O'Connell Street. The office doubled as a boardroom and he had to walk to Vivion's desk across an expanse of floor space that Mussolini, who specialised in such theatrical effects, would have approved of. Then he was told that he was being replaced and that he had the choice of either objecting, and being fired, or accepting and remaining in employment with some other title. He opted for the latter. Fintan Faulkner, the deputy editor, who was in his late forties and was one of the most loyal and hard-working journalists in the company, was then called in and informed that I was to be placed over him. I was present at this interview and it was left to me to answer the bewildered Faulkner's response. Normally Fintan had the yellowing coloration of the night worker, but now his face turned red with shock and disappointment, and he asked unsteadily: 'Where did I go wrong?'

There was an embarrassed silence, which Vivion chose not to break, and then I replied: 'You didn't do anything wrong; everyone knows your reputation. It's just hard luck on you that we are living in new times and a new generation.' Faulkner remained as my deputy for the best part of twenty years, and in all that time he behaved with impeccable loyalty and professionalism.

Vivion had told me that he was going to inform the staff of the change, but, as he would do a thousand times, he changed his mind. It was left to Joe Walsh to break the news to his colleagues and introduce me to them. The walk back to the editorial offices in Burgh Quay with Joe was not the most cheerful perambulation of either his or my life, but an element of farce descended when we got to the editor's office, where the staff was assembling for the nightly conference. Walsh went ahead of me and, as he did so, stumbled, caught his arm in the door and locked it. I had to go down on my knees and appeal through the letterbox to be let in. As I entered the room, Walsh finished telling the staff that he was no longer the editor and would be moving to O'Connell Street, 'to the management side of things, as planning editor'. There was a deathly silence, and then his direct (unlisted) phone rang. The minister for transport and power, Erskine Childers, hero of the vanishing-coffin episode, was calling the editor to inform him that he was making a speech that evening, for which he wanted good coverage. After Walsh had finished assuring the minister that his speech would be well looked after, an assistant editor, Jack Jones, finally broke the ensuing silence and enquired: 'And who may we ask is the new editor?' 'I am,' I told the shocked staff, suppressing both my embarrassment at the cack-handed way the thing had been done and the fact that I had just taken a private vow that henceforth no minister was going to feel entitled to ring me up and dictate coverage to me. At thirty-two, I was the youngest national paper editor in Ireland and time had yet to make breaches in my ramparts of defiance.

The *Irish Press* had been neglected so badly that (at first) it was fairly easy to make improvements. Some of these were simplicity itself. Pictures that normally would have been used over skimpy three columns I cropped and made larger. Before I arrived, it had been standard procedure to cut, alter or add to the copy from the political correspondent, Michael Mills, as those in authority thought fit. I directed that Mills's copy was never to be touched without my authorisation, which in effect meant never. The change cost me a good deal of flak from traditionalist-minded readers who regarded any breath of criticism of Fianna Fail as akin to heresy, but Mills eventually blossomed into becoming one of the country's most respected political correspondents. He wound up being appointed Ireland's first ombudsman by a Fine Gael Taoiseach, Garret FitzGerald, which of course confirmed the older readers' suspicion of my editorship. In our pre-take-over conversations Vivion had admitted to me that he had used the *Irish Press* like a shield, while building up the *Evening Press* and the *Sunday Press*. I took this to mean that, along with diverting resources to the other two papers, he had deliberately attempted to head off Fianna Fail criticism of the fact that the newer papers were propaganda-free zones by allowing the *Irish Press* to become slavishly party-political. As a result the paper had lost much of its standing in the wider community, particularly to the *Irish Times*, where Douglas Gageby was responding effectively to the fresh currents stirring in post-television Ireland.

One of the best people in the company was Padraig O'Criogain, who had been with the paper since it was founded and knew every road, railway and boreen in the country. A classical example of the old-school Irish nationalist (God, de Valera and the Irish language) Padraig was unmercifully mocked behind his back by the younger journalists of the *Evening Press*, myself included, before I got a little older and wiser and came to appreciate his qualities. But to anyone who didn't know him well, his style of nomenclature could appear as simply comic. For example, from the start the *Evening Press* used to appeal more to younger readers than to the more staid inhabitants of the older parts of Dublin. Sometimes when we were having a drink in the Mucky Duck, Padraig would vigorously scratch his left armpit while exclaiming, equally vigorously: 'Any place Cromwell went we can't sell a copy!'

I had forgotten the impact this style of speech could have when one day I arranged for Paddy to address the *Irish Press* staff. He began by giving a historical account of how the *Irish Press* network grew up. The paper actually had only one delivery van and the existing newspapers fought a costly legal battle to prevent the *Irish Press* from being allowed on the newspaper train that brought the early editions of papers to the country. But the *Press* helped to overcome this by printing pictures of the newspaper van from different angles, with the number plate obscured, under headings like 'The *Irish Press* Van Is Coming Your Way' or 'Watch for the *Irish Press* Van in Your Area'. But as Padraig explained to the staff, the reality was that the paper would somehow be got onto a train. Then it would be removed onto a bus, which would penetrate further into the outer reaches of rural Ireland. Eventually it would reach some small town where bundles would be collected and distributed by a local Fianna Fáil councillor or some such. Other parcels would be taken to remote crossroad shops 'by the local Fianna Fáil postman' and eventually, in the case of one mountain hamlet in Kerry, the papers were taken up into the hills by 'a farmer with a good Fianna Fáil ass and cart'.

To younger journalists, the thought of that good Fianna Fáil ass was not altogether reassuring. Most of them understood that not alone were the farmer and his ass long gone, so too were the mountain communities that once read the *Irish Press* so avidly, and with them many another rural community that once supported the paper but whose sons and daughters had either emigrated or now lived in cities where, depending on which end of the social scale they occupied, they had developed a pernicious habit of reading either the *Irish Times* or the *Daily Mirror*. Gone were the days when in any country town one could tell at a glance the affiliation of the newsagents. If they sold the *Press*, they were Fianna Fáil; the *Independent*,

Fine Gael. This fierce loyalty died slowly, but it died as readers died and
the paper failed to move into the towns or the universities to find their
replacements.

The really surprising thing about the paper's following was not that so
much of it dropped off but that so much remained. The respect and
affection some people had for the paper was extraordinary. When my
bank manager's father died, one of the gifts that the family brought to the
coffin was a copy of the *Irish Press*. The paper was literally a unique Irish
institution. Amongst the various luminaries who worked there were three
presidents – de Valera, Erskine Childers and Cearbhall O'Dalaigh – Sean
Lemass, who succeeded de Valera as Taoiseach, Sean McBride and various
cabinet ministers. A sizeable portion of the Irish Bar paid for its studies by
day by working for the *Irish Press* by night, as did a great number of other
people who later distinguished themselves in the arts, commerce and
various other branches of the media.

I had been swayed into taking the editor's job both by Vivion's production of the first editorial and by his subsequent frequent assertions that
I should not regard the *Press* as a Fianna Fail paper but as a de Valera one,
and hence open to newer thought and innovation of all sorts. I did not
understand at the time the distinction Vivion was drawing between Fianna
Fail and de Valera. He told me an anecdote once that summed up both his
inner clarity of vision and the circumscribed nature of his inheritance. He
and Liam Cosgrave, W. T. Cosgrave's son, who had succeeded his father
as leader of Fine Gael, were invited on a parliamentary delegation to India,
where they enjoyed the friendliest of relationships. But on the Aer Lingus
plane from London on the final leg of the trip home, a hostess offered the
two men newspapers. Vivion selected the *Irish Press*. Liam, who would
not be seen in public reading the Organ of the Infidel, ostentatiously
selected and opened the *Irish Independent*. When the hostess had passed
out of earshot, Vivion remarked to Liam: 'You know, Liam, each of us
could write a book and it would have the same title – *Growing Up in the
Shade*.'

It was one of the great inhibiting factors of the *Irish Press*'s development
that Vivion felt it incumbent upon him to play less the role of a newspaper
proprietor than of Nicodemus. I thought that his motivation was merely
a misplaced zeal to attempt, in changing times, to ensure that the shade of
his father's stultifying philosophy would continue to obfuscate the paper.
But there was a deeper, underlying cause. As we shall see, it would take
me more than twenty years to discover the intricacies of how de Valera
Senior had managed to manipulate monies from a bond drive in America

mounted to further Irish independence during the Anglo-Irish War, and later divert Irish taxpayers' money into securing his control of the paper. The average member of Fianna Fail had been encouraged to regard the *Irish Press* as the party paper, and had subscribed money towards its foundation, without realising that the paper was not controlled by Fianna Fail but by the journalistic equivalent of the Roman Catholic concept of three divine persons in one God. There was God the controlling director, God the managing director and God the editor in chief, all united in the person of Eamon de Valera.

However, this information, though contained in the articles of association of the Irish Press Group, appeared in very small print, which one would have had to go to the Companies Office in Dublin to read. Accordingly, for so long as it suited him de Valera allowed both the party and the public at large to regard the paper as the voice of Fianna Fail. After he succeeded his father, Vivion was constantly haunted by a fear that somehow a Fianna Fail-inspired rebellion against his legal but morally dubious control could lead to his ouster.

Now, in January 1968, the paper was losing circulation at a rate that it was expected would exceed 20,000 copies by the end of the year. So it did seem reasonable to expect a fair degree of latitude from party constraints, and I accepted the job without ever enquiring what my salary would be. It turned out to be £3,000 a year, which in those far-off days was a not inconsiderable sum, and in any event 50 per cent more than I was receiving as deputy editor of the *Evening Press*. After some months of taking taxis home in the small hours of the morning, Vivion agreed that I should have the use of a car – a leased Volkswagen Beetle – for which I received a mileage allowance to pay for petrol based on the assumption that I would cover 10,000 miles in a year. In fact between speaking engagements around the country and visits to Northern Ireland I did that much in under six months. Meanwhile Vivion drove a Mercedes, and Jack Dempsey a Jaguar.

The low ebb that the *Irish Press* had reached was for a time a help to me. People soon spotted that something new was happening, and instead of sliding remorselessly the circulation began to go up. This development was not viewed by the establishment as an altogether unmixed blessing. One of the first people to write to me was Cardinal Conway, who, after first congratulating me on my appointment, went on to warn me of the heavy responsibility that lay on my shoulders to ensure that the values of the Church were upheld. The contents of his letter were almost identical to the messages that both Conway's predecessor, Cardinal d'Alton, and Eamon de Valera himself had issued when RTE began broadcasting at the start of the decade. All three noted the potential power of the medium and expressed concern that it be used to maintain and uphold traditional beliefs. Over the years I would attract criticism from many quarters, but one of the heaviest charges laid against me was that I introduced feminism to Ireland! There is, as we shall see, a degree of truth in the accusation. Those were the days when one still made a sharp distinction between the contents of the women's page and the rest of the paper, a male-dominated world of sport, politics, the professions and the Church, not necessarily in that order.

In fact very definitely not in that order. The reality of Ireland from the 1960s practically to the signing of the Good Friday Agreement in 1998 is that there were two revolutions going on. One was the armed struggle centring on Northern Ireland, the other the almost equally hard-fought campaign by the women of Ireland to wrench back from the Church control over their own bodies. Traditionally, the Church did particularly well out of the subjugation of women. The census of 1961 showed that Irish women's fertility in marriage was the highest in Europe, as it had been for the previous hundred years. But at the same time the population of the Republic was dropping. Emigration thus both drew off potential revolutionary ferment and strengthened the power of the Church world-wide, particularly in England, America and Australia. In a number of key areas the Church was implacably imposed to altering laws and circumstances that could affect this position, in particular the laws governing censorship, contraception, divorce, abortion and, most important, the control of education. The Church's position on these issues was reflected in the Constitution, which referred to 'the special position' of the Catholic Church and directed that no law permitting divorce could be enacted in the Republic. The Constitution located women's place in the home, and this view was reinforced by a ban on married women being employed in the civil service.

The terror that the male-dominated legislature (the Dail) experienced at the notion of legalising contraception may be gauged from the fact that when Mary Robinson introduced a bill in the Seanad to legalise contraceptives and get shut of the censorship into the bargain, she could not get the necessary six of her fellows to sponsor the bill so that it could be published and debated, never mind voted on. And so parents who might just about have had the economic and psychological resources to care for one or possibly two children continued to have ten, and sometimes more. To the credit of journalism, it should be noted that one of the two senators willing to co-sponsor the bill was a journalist, John Horgan, then religious affairs correspondent of the *Irish Times*, who had begun his journalistic career as an *Evening Press* sub-editor. The other was Trevor West, who was that dreaded combination (in the eyes of the Church), a Trinity academic and a liberal. The year after Mary Robinson proposed her contraception measure a young mother, Mary McGee, who had a heart condition that could have killed her if she had another child, brought a constitutional case against the ban on contraceptives and ultimately won her action (in November 1973). The Supreme Court ruled in her favour and ordered that the government ban be dropped.

But it took the politicians another six years to work up the courage to do this. One of the sleights of hand used along the way was the introduction of a measure whereby the Pill was sanctioned not for contraceptive purposes, but for regulation of the cycle. Of all the reactionaries in the Dail responsible for this delay, none turned out to be more reactionary than Vivion de Valera. I reckon that the wasted energy and effort that I put into arguing with him on the topic would have yielded several fair-sized books had I devoted my energies elsewhere. He adopted an extraordinary debating position. Looking at me meaningfully, he would point to the fact that he and his first wife had only two children, and he would say, in man-to-man fashion: 'There was nothing wrong with either of us.' He would then go on to insist that he was anxious to have something done about the contraception laws but that 'This Robinson lady makes it very difficult.' And finally he would say that it wouldn't do 'to come out in favour of condoms, *at this stage*'. When the right stage might arrive I could never fathom, nor would any intelligent outsider looking at the Irish body politic's general reaction to legislation affecting faith-based matters.

Divorce was not tackled full-frontally until 1986, when a Fine Gael–Labour coalition sponsored a referendum on the issue. This went down in flames despite the fact that there was a very sizeable broken-marriage problem building up in the Republic. The referendum failed for two reasons. First, the government had not brought in ancillary legislation to provide for the upkeep of divorced spouses, and it was easy to deploy the argument, in an agricultural nation, that 'Divorce would mean that a young woman would get the farm and the former wife would be left with nothing.' The second factor was that while the leader of Fianna Fail, Charles Haughey, took the public stance that Fianna Fail would not oppose the referendum, privately Fianna Fail TDs and party officials canvassed against the referendum so as to embarrass the government. The divorce proposal was overwhelmingly defeated – 62 per cent of those who voted were opposed. Divorce was not sanctioned until another referendum was held in 1995, and then by only a tiny majority: 50.28 per cent voted 'yes'. Abortion of course is a horrendously divisive topic in any country, and in Ireland during the period under review the divisiveness was added to by one of the Irish Church's last great shows of strength. This was a successful campaign in 1983 to have a constitutional amendment introduced that seemingly made abortion impossible in the Republic.

The 1983 proviso really came back to haunt the leaders of both Church and state when in 1992 the ghastly X case occurred. The 'X' concerned was a fourteen-year-old girl who had been raped and was taken to England by her parents to have an abortion carried out. However, the parents checked from London with the Irish police whether or not a DNA sample from the foetus could be used in evidence against the rapist. The state's reaction to the query was to warn the parents that if they went ahead with the abortion, a prosecution would follow. The parents and the traumatised girl returned to Dublin. The High Court then issued an injunction forbidding the child to leave the jurisdiction for the duration of her pregnancy. A storm of controversy broke out – a storm, let it be noted, that did nothing for Ireland's reputation in Europe. However, two weeks later the Supreme Court issued a convoluted judgement that allowed the girl to travel to London to have the abortion, lest she commit suicide, as appeared likely at the time.

Then, as right-wing groups struggled to force the government into holding another constitutional referendum that would combat the effect of the Supreme Court ruling, the Church itself, unexpectedly and embarrassedly, came to the aid of the 'right to choose' lobby. It was announced that one of the most prominent Irish bishops Bishop Eamonn Casey was leaving his bishopric because he had fathered a son. During the heated debate on the X case a prominent priest, Father Michael Cleary, suggested on television that the parents of X could have arranged her abortion in London without publicity but that the phone call to the Irish police had given the pro-abortion lobby a huge PR bonus that had not been unforeseen. Not long afterwards the priest was discovered to have fathered not one but two sons. During the Pope's visit to Ireland in 1979 Casey and Cleary had been the two most visible faces of the Irish Church. In warm-up ceremonies prior to the Pope's appearance they had made speeches, led audiences in prayer and even in sing-songs. The revelations about the pair served to hole the Church's authority well below the waterline.

While all this was happening, some six to seven thousand Irish women were known to travel to England each year to have abortions. In fact they still do.

Against this background, the accusation, in the late 1960s and subsequently, that I was helping the feminist cause exposed me to what nowadays is known as collateral damage. I had brought in Mary Kenny as woman editor. A Dubliner, working on the London *Evening Standard*, she was one of the most brilliant young journalists of her time, but she was also one of the founders of the Irish Women's Liberation Movement. Mary arrived in Burgh Quay like a comet exuding in its wake a shower of flaming particles from burning bras. On the day she arrived in the place she found that no office had been provided for her, and with a stamp of her foot and a toss of her head informed the managing editor, the formidable Bill Redmond, that she needed an office, and until one was found for her she too could be found in Mulligan's. Redmond was a very tall man with a mop of dark hair and the biggest and blackest eyebrows in town. Staff normally faded before him like chickens fleeing a hawk. But in this instance he promptly found an office for Mary, and thereafter she used it as the headquarters of the Revolution. She surrounded herself with a coterie of talented young women, like Ann Harris, Nell McCafferty, Rosemary Sweetman, June Levine and Maire de Burca, all of whom shared the view that Ireland would be immeasurably better off once the feminist revolution and/or the socialist millennium was achieved and the power of Fianna Fail and the Irish Church overthrown.

Explosive terms like contraception began finding their way into a paper that carried on its masthead the Irish inscription '*Chun Glóire Dé agus onóir na hEireann*' ('For the Glory of God and the Honour of Ireland'). The masthead also carried, in English, the mass of the day and whatever saint's day it was. Mary did not allow herself to be influenced by saints' days. Out went cooking recipes and in came articles about a strange un-Irish activity called sex. By way of emphasising her point of view, Mary would sometimes come into the office, and even the Dail, dressed in her battle gear: huge Elton John-like spectacles, a long cigarette holder and hotpants.

Another first-class journalist whom I was able to attract to the *Press* at the time was Joe Carroll, an ex-Blackrock man and a contributor from Paris to both the *Guardian* and the *Irish Times*. Joe eschewed hotpants but he did make readers aware that there was something called the European Economic Community (EEC) in the offing and made trips to Europe to alert the Irish public as to what lay round the corner. Carroll and Kenny apart, I think I can justly claim that in those days the Irish Press Group had a greater number of outstanding personalities on its books than any other institution in the country.

John O'Shea, for example, could have been taken as a perfect example of the saying that when the Lord was making Kerrymen he left out the reverse gear. John grew up near me in Monkstown and, knowing his parents and family, I reckoned, correctly, that, all appearances to the contrary notwithstanding, he too would turn out well. Accordingly John became a sports journalist. He had been a fine athlete, competing in student Olympiads, and might have become a rugby international had a knee injury not ended his career. One of his sports was javelin-throwing, which stood him in good stead in the *Evening Press*. The playwright Jean Genet used to say that whenever he made a friend he felt it was his duty to betray him to the police. John seemed to feel that it was his duty to speak his mind forcefully to anyone who came across his path, friend or foe.

My presence at one social occasion helped to prolong his longevity after he informed a mutual friend, a former famous Kerry All-Ireland footballer of legendary fiery temperament, that he was 'the worst fucking player, on one of the worst fucking teams, ever to come out of Kerry'. On another, his comments on the Dublin Gaelic football team led to a strike. The *Evening Press* editor, Sean Ward, a keen 'Dubs' supporter, meeting John on the stairs shortly after reading his column, became involved in an altercation that escalated to warnings about John's future employment prospects should the sacred reputation of the 'Dubs' again be sullied. The NUJ backed John, the management Sean, and, ludicrously, the row became magnified to a point where both the *Evening Press* and the *Irish Press* were briefly taken off the streets, a comment more on the poisonous industrial-relations climate of the group at the time than on the argument.

Along with the abrasiveness John possessed incredible energy. He was one of the hardest workers on the staff and, in addition to the high blood-pressure levels he contributed to, he contributed to high circulation levels also. But the most remarkable thing about him was that for most of his journalistic career, spanning approximately a quarter of a century, he was creating and running a Third World aid agency, GOAL. Teams and individuals that he castigated in his articles willingly staged events for GOAL. International sportsmen became patrons of the association. From a corner of the *Evening Press* sub-editor's desk, in between meeting news-paper deadlines, John mastered the intricacies of international politics, airline schedules, running an ever-growing army of volunteers and the fund-raising necessary to maintain an organisation internationally acclaimed for its rapid response time to humanitarian crises. To me he always seemed a throwback to the old Irish missionary monks who main-tained civilisation in Carolingian Europe. Querulous and rebellious, bishops and kings frequently found them a royal pain in the arse and expelled them from their domains. But in their wake grew schools, monasteries, hospitals and tangible demonstrations of Christianity.

Eventually even John found the strain of continuing his journalistic work while running the agency too much for him. Some years after I had left the *Irish Press* he called to me looking for advice. He had always managed to keep his administration costs unusually low for such an organisation, one reason being that he had never taken a salary from GOAL because he 'would not give it to the bastards to say that I was making money from the Third World'. Without hesitation I told him that it would be better for him, his family and the agency if he gave up the *Evening Press* and devoted himself full-time to the poor. And so it proved. Needless to say, he was not earning much with the paper anyhow, and the modest salary he allowed himself was more than made up for by the increased energy he devoted to GOAL. I reckon I did good work in both bringing him in and getting him out of journalism.

A complete contrast to O'Shea was another John, who joined the *Press* at a later date. This was the writer John Banville, one of the best craftsmen ever to grace the sub-editors' desk. He brought the same mastery of detail displayed in his novels to checking and rewriting copy in his neat, quite beautiful script. Sometimes he looked exhausted, pouched-eyed and white-faced, but he maintained an easy camaraderie with his colleagues, taking his pint with them at 'cut line' and becoming in turn deputy and then chief sub-editor, which necessitated his remaining on duty into the small hours of the morning. Then, not so many hours later, he would get up, rinse his mind of journalistic pressures, research, write his books and then head back into the *Irish Press*.

He was fortunate that, in those pre-Booker Prize days (1977–81), a particularly fine US ambassador came to town, Bill Shannon. Bill had been with John F. Kennedy on his visit to Ireland, wrote his speeches and was present when the American president and President Eamon de Valera set up the Ireland Fund. This was later taken over by Tony O'Reilly. An offshoot of the Kennedy initiative was a literary fund, which, as ambassador, Bill became responsible for nearly twenty-five years later. During his tenure Bill appointed me the judge of who should be awarded prizes from the fund. By 1981 John had written *Nightspawn*, *Copernicus*, *Birchwood* and *Kepler*, so I make no apology for deciding that one of the prizes should go to him. It was, I think, his first major cash prize (something in the order of $3,000), but neither I nor, I should imagine, anyone else, including John, can be certain of the amount, because a feature of the award ceremonies was the Homeric lunch that accompanied them.

The *Irish Press* had a good literary tradition. Its first literary editor, M. J. MacManuus, set standards that were followed through the years by a variety of editors. Figures like Lennox Robinson, Brendan Behan and Ben Kiely were frequent contributors, and this tradition was immeasurably strengthened when one day Sean McCann, who had been seconded from the *Evening Press* to help in the re-Vivification of the *Irish Press*, as I termed it, brought the novelist and literary editor David Marcus into my office. David, a Cork man, was one of Ireland's small but immensely valuable Jewish community. His uncle, Gerald Goldberg, made history by being elected the first Jewish lord mayor of Cork. David had run the highly thought-of *Irish Writing* magazine. He had an ingenious plan for reviving the tradition of Irish literary journals – *The Bell*, the *Dublin Magazine*, *Envoy*, etc. What he suggested was that I devote a page each week to a short story, poetry or an extract from a work in progress.

At first Vivion was inclined to resist the idea, through an uneasy set of worries as to what his old mentor, Archbishop John Charles McQuaid, might make of the sight of troublesome writers appearing in the chaste columns of the *Irish Press* under the tutelage of a Jewish editor. McQuaid had shown himself as being anything but supportive about Jewry during the Second World War. But with the help of Jack Dempsey I eventually succeeded in selling Vivion the idea and it is literally true to say that for the next two decades every Irish writer of consequence either had their first work published in the *Irish Press* or made a contribution to the 'New Irish Writing' page, as it was known. There was a slight glitch at the start. Vivion had grudgingly accepted the page with a stipulation – it should not be used to further the aims of either 'the wild, wild women', by which he meant the likes of Mary Kenny and her friends, or for 'the sort of thing that that lady Edna O'Brien comes out with'. Just before the feature began I happened to ask David who was his first author, and he replied: 'Edna O'Brien'! Edna was rescheduled for a few weeks further down the line.

Mary was eventually lured back to Fleet Street by a lucrative offer from the *Evening Standard*. By then I had become so sick of Vivion's harping on about her activities that I decided to shut him up once and for all. For her replacement I selected a man! Liam Nolan was a well-known broadcaster and journalist alert to what was happening in society, but compared with Mary he could justly be termed a conservative. I guessed that his appointment would result in a good deal of publicity and interest, which would help to offset the loss caused by Mary's departure. And so it proved. Liam eventually turned his hand to other things, but his sojourn put an end to Vivion's fixation with the women's page.

One of Vivion's central problems was of his own making. In his role of editor in chief his position as a Fianna Fail backbencher was untenable. He disliked political life, and had little empathy with ordinary electors, but the complaints and pressures he inevitably sustained through hanging on to what was, in essence, merely an extra source of income greatly accentuated his Nicodemite tendencies and placed obstacles in the way of developing the *Irish Press* as an independent, influential voice. He used to justify his position to me by saying: 'Oh, it's far better to take the load and stay inside in case *they* ever make a move.' It was not until I had left the *Press* and begun researching his father's life that I discovered that what he was really doing was retaining his place in the political arena so that he would have distant early warning of any serious threat to his hold on the newspapers from Fianna Fail. There was always a school of thought within the party that wanted to turn the paper into the party organ which, their fathers were led to believe, they had helped to set up in the first place.

Vivion's near-pathological obsession with retaining control of the group also inhibited growth. Shortly after my appointment a programme of rebuilding commenced at Burgh Quay. It took for ever. Vivion financed the operation not through a bank loan or a share issue, which would have been normal business practice, but by slowly saving monies over the years and from day-to-day revenue. Meanwhile the staff worked in awful conditions as a new building slowly took shape around them. One night, some time after the internment camp had been opened outside Belfast in Long Kesh, an old Second World War airfield, I took the then *Sunday Times* editor, Harry Evans, on a tour of the paper. When we succeeded in threading our way through the paint pots, ladders and scaffolding that surrounded the sub-editors' desk, we were greeted with a banner that read: 'Welcome to Short Kesh!'

Irish humour resembles Jewish humour, in that its basis is rarely funny. In the case of the *Irish Press*, though of course I did not realise it at the time, the de Valera control-freakery that led to the Long Kesh joke would one day lead to the death of the paper. One of the few serious rows Vivion had with Jack Dempsey arose out of his objections to a son of Jack's joining the commercial section of the company, even though there was a vacancy and Dempsey Junior had already proven himself in a senior post with a multinational. I remembered this incident one night after my son, Tom, had put his foot on the first rung of the journalistic ladder by becoming a copy boy, at the age of eighteen. Vivion appeared in my office one night, remarked on Tom's joining the staff, and then suddenly hissed with great vehemence: 'Of course you know he doesn't have rights to any inheritances or entitlements, or anything like that!' A little later in the night he suddenly manifested himself alongside Tom and, in the most kindly fashion, publicly wished him well in his career. 'What a very nice man,' commented Tom to me later. I simply smiled and thought of my own first reaction to meeting Vivion in Blackrock.

One of the sections I attempted to improve, against a wall of opposition based on managerial disinclination to employ staff, was financial coverage. The basis for the opposition was succinctly spelled out by Jack Dempsey's anguished response to my plans: 'You want to hire a financial editor *and* three reporters? Do you realise that an ex-bank official used to do the whole page by himself, subbing the stocks and getting the page off the stone?!' Speaking more confidently than I felt, I replied that I knew that the page had been run on a shoestring, that we were losing readers because of it, and that actually I felt we needed four, not three new reporters. However, when Jack finished the mandatory war dance, he did agree to go so far as to allow me to pay a fee to John Mulcahy, then editor of an excellent fortnightly called *Hibernia*, to advise on setting up a financial section. Mulcahy was one of the more interesting people in contemporary Irish journalism. His financial skills were such that he had been financial controller of Aer Lingus before he decided to follow his instincts and go in for journalism on a full-time basis. This was facilitated by the fact that he had chosen his ancestors with care and came from a well-off family.

His unusual combination of financial and journalistic expertise soon made *Hibernia* a force to be reckoned with in the 1960s. He took his inspiration from Thomas Davis's paper of the 1840s, *The Nation*, which in its day was the leading Irish nationalist opinion journal. John showed me a leather-bound volume of *The Nation* and, pointing proudly to its mission-statement first editorial, said: 'That is what I want to do with *Hibernia*.' He succeeded so well for a time that, after some anti-government criticism appeared in its columns, Vivion de Valera ordered that *Hibernia* join the long list of taboo subjects that were not to be mentioned in the *Irish Press*. For a time the sound of these taboos splashing into the Liffey after I took over had helped to attract attention to the paper. John's produced a blueprint for a new-look *Irish Press* financial section, which envisaged four finance reporters and a financial editor. This reactivated the war dances and was resisted for several years on the grounds of cost.

Eventually I did manage to get three young reporters installed in a small office above my own, in whose stifling conditions they markedly improved the financial coverage. Eventually also, after several bouts of interviewing and losses of suitable applicants because the money on offer was so paltry, I managed to hire a financial editor. Shortly after I had brought him up the stairs to the dingy little office, which now contained four people, three with desks, my phone rang. It was the new editor tendering his resignation: 'I'm sorry,' he said, 'but I realise now that I have taken on something that I should never have become involved with!' You, I told myself silently, are not the only one.

The transient one was succeeded by a former bank official, Joe McAuley, whom I later discovered I had caused to be fired from the Bank of Ireland. I had printed a picture on page one of the *Evening Press* showing a hapless queue waiting outside a Labour Exchange for money, which was not forthcoming because the local bank had not yet opened. Many years later I learned that Joe, who had the keys of the branch, had been on such a bender the previous night that he woke up several hours late. McAuley, a brilliant man, subsequently went to Africa to place his financial expertise at the service of Irish missionaries. When he returned, slim, tanned, square-jawed, a touch of grey in carefully combed black hair adding a note of distinction to his looks, his appearance added weight to his assurances that he had 'drunk himself out' and was now 'on the dry'.

As I was to discover, rather painfully, over the next few years, this was not quite the case, and Joe too subsequently marched into the pages of *Irish Press* folklore. On the very first night he joined the staff, the journalists walked out because he was not a member of the NUJ. At that time I was sitting in the restaurant of the Gresham Hotel trying to persuade Basil Chubb, a distinguished Trinity political scientist, to become a contributor to the paper when I got a phone call informing me of this interesting development. Accordingly I finished telling my guest how stimulating he would find the atmosphere of the *Irish Press*, arranged to continue our dinner a week later and went back to the paper to sort out the row.

Vivion de Valera had of course been responsible for the situation wherein the financial editorship was so unattractive that the post had fallen vacant through its incumbent walking out five minutes after he saw his working conditions. I had also fully briefed him about McAuley's background, and he had then called for and carefully studied his CV, noting the number of important positions he had held in the Bank of Ireland. Nevertheless, his first reaction to the NUJ action was: 'How could we possibly come to hire a non-journalist?'

As one of my precautionary moves had been to get Joe to apply for membership of the NUJ and to have his nomination backed by two chapel officers, the fire was soon put out. Joe, however, continued on an incendiary path for some years, well liked by those he dealt with but obviously, sometimes spectacularly, losing his battle with the bottle. We eventually came to a parting of the ways and he left for Cork, where he married a very nice woman who had had the good sense to inherit not one but two farms. Joe made an enthusiastic contribution towards drinking out both holdings before dying in his sleep of a heart attack.

Under his successor, Brian O'Connor, the financial section of the *Irish Press* became not alone respected in its own right but something of a nursery of talent. Brian moved on to greater things in Fleet Street. One of the young men traumatised by the fleeting financial editor's five-minute tenure, Joe Murray, became a hugely successful PR consultant and Damian Kiberd, who also followed in Joe McAuley's footsteps, founded the influential and lucrative *Sunday Business Post*, ultimately selling his interest and moving on to become one of the country's leading columnists and broadcasters.

But probably the most extraordinary career trajectory of all those connected with the *Irish Press* financial department was that of John Mulcahy. On a visit to London I bumped into him in Fleet Street one day. John was like a man who had seen the beatific vision. He had just come from the offices of the satirical magazine *Private Eye*, then in its comparatively early days, but already a success. 'Do you know,' said John, 'the cover price alone pays for everything, newsprint, journalists, the lot? They have the advertising revenue clear!'

John went back to Dublin, where *Hibernia*, which had now become a weekly, was folded, Thomas Davis's memory given a discreet burial and a new publication, *Phoenix*, was born, modelled on *Private Eye*. *Phoenix* has probably had a far greater impact on Irish society than has *Private Eye* on Britain's. Apart from its scurrility and disclosures, one cause of that success is its financial coverage.

Curiously enough, the one facet of my editorship in which I was able to keep a promise I made to myself without too much difficulty was on the political front. Possibly my TV reputation helped, but to begin with, apart from a few major exceptions I will come to later, I simply refused to take calls from TDs, senators or ministers. Almost invariably it proved possible to head off pressures by having a secretary say sweetly that Mr Coogan was not in that night but would it be possible for the minister to set down his complaint in writing and she would see to it that Mr Coogan responded to it as soon as he came in the following day. Of course, once a politician is reduced to committing himself to paper, half the battle is won. And for those who choose to go ahead and make their verbal complaint to 'whoever is in charge in his absence', there was the doubtful solace of having their complaint duly taken down in shorthand by someone on the news desk, while being informed that of course the note-taker could not guarantee anything in the absence of the editor. Eventually the politicians simply stopped phoning. Even at the height of 'the arms-trial affair', described in Chapter 9, I only received one phone call from a minister and that was from the minister for defence, who was in a panic because someone had told him (wrongly) that we had a story about a cargo of guns being landed illegally somewhere in Ireland.

My secret weapons were my secretaries and the loyalty of the staff, particularly Fintan Faulkner, who could have been forgiven for taking an opposite line. The two secretaries most involved were the Two Eileens, Eileen Tubrid and Eileen Davis. Eileen Tubrid was a staunch republican. Her husband, Patrick Fleming, had unwittingly helped to propel me towards writing the IRA book. He was one of the principal driving forces behind the IRA bombing campaign of England that had sparked my agent's imagination. A quiet, shy, religious lady, Eileen, who was in her sixties when I took over, was the soul of loyalty and discretion and possessed practically instantaneous shorthand and typing skills. Eileen Davis, who succeeded her, was a complete contrast. Equally efficient, in her early thirties and very good-looking, she had a better political brain than any minister and a financial expertise that she inherited from her Huguenot ancestors. Eileen didn't only watch my back, she foresaw the pitfalls ahead.

She demonstrated this skill in memorable fashion one night at the height of a national debate on capital punishment that took place during 1975–6, arising out of the sentencing to death of two anarchists, a husband and wife, Noël and Marie Murray, for the murder of a Garda. The couple had been interrupted in a robbery by Garda Reynolds, who was off-duty and in plain clothes when he courageously tackled the pair. A shot was fired, which was probably not intended to be fatal, but Garda Reynolds died on the spot. The case aroused tremendous controversy. Capital punishment was *de jure* still possible in Ireland at the time for the murder of either a Garda or a prison officer, but de facto a thing of the past. The Murray debate was not merely about the rights or wrongs of capital punishment itself, or the issue of hanging a husband and wife, but it also revived bitter memories of the executions of IRA men during the Second World War by de Valera. Vivion always referred to these last executions not as 'de Valera's executions', but as 'Gerry Boland's executions', after the minister for justice of the time.

Vivion's position on the death penalty was a flat 'maybe'. He averred that he was personally against it, but 'on the other hand there may be certain circumstances in which the safety of the state, etc.' In other words the possibility that the gospel according to de Valera Senior might some day have to be upheld had to be provided for. His views on IRA violence in Northern Ireland were equally ambivalent: 'I'm not against slaughter, but let it be organised, like in a proper army. We don't want to fire any shots ourselves of course, but if some shots come from them and hit the right targets, then we shouldn't complain too much.' But in so far as I as editor, trying to interpret policy, was concerned the 'maybe' posture left him in a position where he could declare that he was either an abolitionist or a hanger, as occasion demanded. On the night in question, the occasion of the rejection of an appeal by the Murrays against the death sentence, he became decidedly pro-hanging.

I was out of the office, attending a function, when the Supreme Court's verdict was delivered, but, as arranged, Eileen rang me with the news and I dictated a suitably forthright, anti-hanging editorial. Then, unusually for her, Eileen began hemming and hawing, hesitating to ring off and type up her shorthand notes. Finally she came out with it: 'I think you might want to think over what you've said. The Major [Valera] has been on. He said that he wanted to find out if you're writing about the Murrays.' 'If' I intended to comment on the most controversial topic of the year ... I interrupted her to reply to the effect that he'd find out in the next day's paper and delivered a few accompanying observations on the unsuitability of Nicodemus to the running of a daily newspaper. She waited patiently for my adjectival flow to cease and replied diplomatically: 'I don't think that's a good idea. He said something about the editor knowing what the policy is and he'd like to know what you're saying.' As I fumed and fretted, she commented further: 'Maybe I shouldn't say this, but I think he's got someone with him in the room. I think he's up to something.' Very uncharacteristically she continued to impress on me that I should be careful, so I finally decided to abandon my editorial and leave the chore to one of the assistant editors, Michael Mahon, who had been at the paper for decades and was used to Vivion's vagaries.

Wearing his editor-in-chief hat, Vivion subsequently had several conversations with the unfortunate Mahon, and the ensuing editorial was a slithery but perfect example of the 'maybe' policy. While it stopped short of recommending the death penalty, it did leave open the possibility that in certain circumstances it could be quite good for society. Particularly, I commented to Eileen, in the case of persons suffering from constipation. But she continued to aver that I had taken the wisest course, Vivion had been up to something.

One would not have thought so the next evening. He frisked into the office for a brief visit, all smiles, barely pausing to reply to my protestations about the inadequacy of the editorial that at least it was better than the *Independent*'s. This was true, but it was embarrassingly inferior to that in the *Irish Times*. However, Eileen was proved right a few evenings later. I was on the phone to Richard Cooke, a senior counsel, and a friend of Vivion's, about a libel matter when for some reason it occurred to me to ask if he'd had many queries to deal with on the night of the Murray verdict. 'Oh, yes,' he replied. 'Vivion was here in the house. He was very worried about someone in the office.' When I told Cooke that the 'someone' was me, he affected to be surprised. According to him, Vivion had not said who the someone was.

I never unearthed Vivion's motive in behaving as he did that night. The most likely explanation is that a kind of emotional firestorm had built up inside him at the possibility of a challenge to his authority on an issue on which he knew public opinion would be against him, but on which at the same time he was not prepared to be seen to differ from his father's policy. Even though the legal minuet of their trial, sentencing and appeal had to be gone through, it was a foregone conclusion that the Murrays would ultimately be reprieved and, as ultimately happened, given long prison sentences. If, as seems likely, Vivion was trying to stage a confrontation in the presence of his lawyer, so that he would have grounds for firing me, he had picked a bad issue. Nevertheless, blind intransigence in the face of a perceived public challenge remained a de Valera characteristic and, as it turned out, created the *causa proxima* that finally brought down the paper.

Vivion apart, I suffered from very little political pressure along the lines endured by Joe Walsh, though there were, as we shall see, a couple of notable exceptions early on in my stint, neither of which came to anything substantive. It should be understood that when Sean Lemass retired in 1966, while I was en route to Vietnam, the two main contenders for the role of Taoiseach were Charles J. Haughey and George Colley. Neither of them got the post. Jack Lynch, a legend of the hurling field, was appointed as a compromise candidate between the two rival factions. Lynch was a diffident Cork man with all the charm, politeness, shyness and slyness of his native county. He was the sort of person the Frenchman had in mind when he said that an Irishman was like a peach, soft on the outside, but with a very big stone at the centre. I know of a hurling adversary of Lynch's who, for the greater part of an All-Ireland hurling final, had 'given the timber' to Lynch at every possible opportunity without retaliation. But with a few seconds remaining, Cork safely ahead and, most important, the referee at the other end of the field, Lynch suddenly struck his unsuspecting tormentor a blow so mighty that the injury still 'came against him' on winter mornings fifty years later. When his hurling career ended and the kingmakers from the various parties came calling, Lynch told me that he could as easily have joined Fine Gael as Fianna Fail had it not been for his admiration for de Valera.

Lynch had studied law and worked as a civil servant before beginning a fairly effortless cruise to the posts of minister for education and finance, which he held before entering the governmental driver's seat. He had been reared in modest circumstances. His mother was the widow of a tailor, a brother became a parish priest and his horizons were those of a twenty-six-county Irish nationalist. Cork is about as far away from the border as one can get, and Lynch was of a generation of which it could be said that partition had worked. This fact would assume considerable importance as the Northern situation worsened. Lynch, like most of the population he represented, had grown up in a society in which Northern Ireland did not figure in normal daily conversation and sectarianism was quiescent.

When I took over the *Irish Press*, such incidents of sectarianism as occurred were at a relatively low level of intensity. Generally these centred on issues such as domestic strife over the dictates of the Catholic Church's *Ne temere* decree of 1908, which stipulated that the children of a 'mixed marriage' should be brought up Catholic. Irish society was heavily Roman Catholic in ethos, though in matters such as housing or employment there was nothing remotely resembling the apartheid state that the Orangemen had created in the Six Counties. Of course no one saw as sectarian the Catholic censorship or the religious provisions in the Constitution, such as the reference to 'the special position' of the Catholic Church or the prohibition of divorce. The fact that contraceptives could not be purchased in the Republic was not seen as being sectarian either. Such things, like the weather, were intrinsic features of Ireland, as were episcopal eruptions of varying frequencies from figures like Archbishop McQuaid or the bishop of Cork, Connie Lucey. Connie was a loquacious but fundamentally decent man. During the contraception controversy that wracked the Church following the issue of the papal encyclical *Humanae vitae*, it fell to him to silence a priest of his diocese, Father James Good, who did not agree with the Vatican line. Father Good left Ireland and set up a mission in the

Turkana Desert in Kenya, one of the world's most inhospitable places. When Connie retired as a bishop, in his seventies, he moved to Kenya also to serve under his old friend Father Good.

I got on well with Jack Lynch, and I feel that he might have made a greater contribution to political life if he had not literally developed an Achilles heel. One summer, on holiday in Cork, he stepped out of a boat while on holiday with his wife, Maureen, and landed on a pointed rock, which shattered a web of small bones in his heel. The injury, which developed as he was facing the crises of the Northern situation, left him in constant, debilitating pain, which he tended to dull with the aid of Paddy whiskey. The only difficulty I ever had with him occurred when he rang me up one night not to say he wanted such and such in the paper, but to say that he wanted to take back his promise to contribute to it! His decision was based on the fact that in a forthcoming special issue, marking the fiftieth anniversary of the founding of Fianna Fail, I had also obtained a contribution from John A. Murphy, another Cork man, and a professor of history at University College, Cork. Murphy's overall contribution to Irish political debate might fairly be described as being acerbic rather than profound, and Lynch refused to appear in the supplement with him. However, after a couple of phone calls I succeeded in keeping my lions in separate cages.

But the two rivals whom Lynch defeated in the race to succeed Lemass were a different matter. Neither Charles Haughey nor George Colley thought the best man had won. Haughey was the epitome of what I had in mind when I coined the term 'the Men in the Mohair Suits'. His father had fought on the opposite side of the Civil War to de Valera, and was one of those whom Michael Collins used to smuggle guns into Northern Ireland during the Civil War to help the Catholics who at the time were under heavy attack from the Orange element. Haughey had studied law and accountancy before entering politics, and had married a daughter of Sean Lemass's. Self-confident to the point of arrogance, he never allowed his wife to interfere with his marriage, and conducted a very public affair for several years with Terry Keane, the wife of Ronan Keane, a prominent barrister, who later became the chief justice. When I first met Haughey, in 1965 while I was researching *Ireland Since the Rising*, I was both impressed and repelled by him. I thought then, and subsequently, that he had the best brain of any politician of his time, but there was something disturbing about his arrogance and his obvious lust for power.

Shortly after I became editor, Haughey asked me out to dinner. We had a lengthy interlude in the Shelbourne Hotel after which we drove out to his huge home at Abbeyville in Kinsealy, North County Dublin, where the worship of Bacchus continued. Haughey had a simple agenda. He wanted the new-look *Irish Press* to back him. The reward for this would be a formula whereby a journalist could be supplied with 'nuggets of information'. I made it clear that he could expect fair coverage and nothing more. Finally Haughey looked at me sadly, shook his head and said: 'Tim Pat Coogan, you're going to be no use to me!'

The approach from George Colley was more subtle. It came through an *Irish Press* staffer, Tony Gallagher, one of the top reporters of his day, who was married to a sister of Colley's wife, Mary. Tony told me that Colley would like to have a chat with me, and acting on the general principle that I should be prepared to chat with anyone, I cheerfully went to meet him in his home. Colley was an intelligent man, without Haughey's extra cutting edge but with an obvious fundamental decency. There was no guile about him; he just wanted the new *Irish Press* to support the old traditional values, the Irish language, the Catholic religion, Fianna Fail and George Colley, not necessarily in that order. His relationship with Haughey before his untimely death in 1983 was turbulent in the extreme, but he never caused me any difficulties and was always polite when I met him socially. The nearest we ever came to hostilities was over an incident involving Major, my mother's African Great Dane. A woman who strongly upheld the principle 'Love me love my dog', she insisted on taking Major on a flight to the Aran Islands in the tiny nine-seater Britain Norman aircraft. Major sat in the seat behind the unfortunate Colley, and in the course of the short flight managed to deposit a couple of quarts of slobber down the minister's neck and back.

As indicated earlier, the influence of Archbishop John Charles McQuaid was all-pervasive. His catechism was taught in schools throughout the country. It laid a heavy emphasis on man's fallen nature and emphasised the need to avoid 'occasions of sin'. Vivion de Valera had a famous anecdote from his days at Blackrock concerning what McQuaid viewed as one of said occasions. While still a student, Vivion was made a director of the *Irish Press*. Hearing this, McQuaid called him to his room and, producing a bundle of *Irish Press* back issues, warned Vivion that he had a responsibility to wipe out the sort of grave evil they contained. He then drew the startled Vivion's attention to the full-page Clerys's ads they contained. The famous Dublin department store used to highlight its bargains with tiny pen-and-ink drawings of raincoats, suits, dresses, swimwear, whatever. After Vivion had failed to find evil lurking in any of these, McQuaid produced a magnifying glass and told him to look again at the women's swimwear ads. When Vivion did so, he found that he could (dimly) see the outline of a mons Veneris in the drawings.

After becoming editor I felt that the safest course for me was to keep as far away from this extraordinary man as possible. *Irish Press* folklore included stories about McQuaid's treatment of a predecessor of mine, Bill Sweetman, a few years after being appointed archbishop in 1940. The stories were confirmed by the release of McQuaid's papers over sixty years later. Sweetman had incurred McQuaid's displeasure by not giving space (because of wartime restrictions on newsprint) to McQuaid's Lenten pastoral of 1943. McQuaid complained to de Valera. The Taoiseach delivered a rocket to Sweetman and instructed him to placate McQuaid. Sweetman immediately asked to see McQuaid in a letter that indicated that he probably intended to reassure the archbishop on the paper's policy toward the Church while at the same time pointing out the difficulties caused by newsprint rationing. Significantly, and bravely, Sweetman gave no hint of apology.

McQuaid's reply says much about his contempt for journalists and the relationship between Christ and Caesar in neutral Ireland as much of the rest of the world was being consumed by war:

> My dear Taoiseach,
>
> I think it well to send for your information the letter of Mr Sweetman and my answer.
>
> An interview with Mr Sweetman seems to me an affair not to be lightly given I do not know the man at all. His position is one of subordinate to a board. And he has supplied no evidence that his board even knows that he has asked to see me.
>
> Besides, to discuss policy with a *mere editor* [author's italics] is something I cannot do, in my present position, chiefly because policy is not my affair at all.
>
> I trust you will approve of the caution I have given Mr Sweetman to feel in my reply. On Saturday perhaps we could discuss it.
>
> With my kind regards,
> I remain, my dear Taoiseach,
> Yours very sincerely,
> John C. McQuaid

However, an initiative of Cherry's led to my becoming quite friendly with McQuaid. She wrote to John Charles looking for assistance with some of the lame dogs she was helping over stiles at the time and received an invitation to Archbishop's House by return of post. The interview was a success. Under the influence of Cherry's personality, the archbishop immediately agreed to provide the assistance sought. One of the deserving cases involved quite a long-term commitment, paying for the university fees and other expenses of a lad who had both been orphaned and contracted polio at an early age. The archbishop kept in touch with him during his university days. He invited him to Archbishop's House from time to time to check on his progress and, if he looked particularly shabby, sent him to Arnott's department store to be outfitted at his expense. There was no sexual dimension to the archbishop's interest, but the lad told me that he was often astonished at the extent of his questioning, and knowledge, of student personalities and societies. McQuaid's intelligence sources kept tabs on the Ireland of the morrow as much as on those of the day.

On her visit to him the archbishop remarked to Cherry that 'Tim hasn't come to see me.' Cherry explained that this might have something to do with the fact that I was not a practising Catholic. I would have thought that this marked me out as something worse than a Protestant in the archbishop's eyes, but he brushed off the observation with an airy 'Oh, don't mind about that. He'll come back, he'll come back!' He repeated his wish that I call on him and I duly did so. Lean, above average height, robed in visible scarlet and black, and clothed in his invisible reputation, McQuaid close up was a commanding figure who could have given Coleridge's Ancient Mariner lessons in the use of the 'glittering eye'. He had had tuberculosis in his youth and this may have accounted for a certain sibilance in his tone and a lower than average speaking voice. He used the latter to great effect, as it meant that people had to bend their heads respectfully to listen to him.

I felt that talking with him was a bit like entering a house in which certain rooms were off limits – those marked 'divorce', 'contraception' or 'censorship', for example. Although I would have acknowledged that it was a large house and there were other rooms – those marked 'international affairs' and 'Northern Ireland', for instance. Concern for the poor, the effects of unemployment and the aspirations of trade unions also commanded his attention. I knew nothing about his replies to what I took to be my unanswered questionnaire of course and he never mentioned them, which was a great pity because, in the climate of the time, to put it mildly, they would have provided material for interesting dialogue. For example, I had asked whether the Irish Church was preoccupied with sex at the expense of concern for other matters such as poverty and equal educational opportunity. The typed party-line reply was:

No. There is probably a saner attitude to sex in this country than almost anywhere else. Family life is stable, woman are respected, vocations are esteemed. The problems you mention are very important. The founding of the Catholic Social Services Conference in the early dark days of the Emergency showed an awareness of this. The country as a whole is now more concerned with social issues.

McQuaid's handwritten note included:

Sex, in the sense used here – illicit sex – is a sin and is the concern of the Church. The other comparisons are not sins, and there is evidence [...] that so far from poverty leading to sins of damnation the reverse is often the case.

He felt that the typed reply to a question on censorship and the inhibition of ideas did not go far enough – it had attributed the inhibition mainly to a lack of university education – and added: 'Speaking purely personally, I'd be inclined to go strongly here in defence of censorship.' But the typed replies also denied that the Church was responsible for censorship, saying: 'Censorship of publications and films is governed by Acts of the Oireachtas.' The same hand-washing approach governed his replies to my questions about the Mother and Child Scheme controversy and about the separation of classes for Catholics and Protestants in the state's veterinary college (the Protestant cow, Catholic cow syndrome). The answer to the first question pointed out that at the time the government fell the archbishop was out of the country, but did not mention that he had piled up the powder and lit the touch paper before doing so. The second supported the separation of classes but said it was an arrangement made by the civil authorities, which he supported as an act of 'reverse justice for the University College, Dublin, students'. He was obviously stung by my putting to him the allegation that he was responsible for the state-backed Voluntary Health Insurance (VHI) not providing maternity benefit. He said this was 'completely untrue'. The question was an 'insult to everything I have stood for'. The other question that seems to have struck a nerve was one about his favourite books and authors. The typewritten answer gave a list of the classics, Latin and French. He then inserted Greek, theological and spiritual writers, works on psychology and medical research. His favourite authors were said to be John of the Cross, Acquinas, St Teresa of Avila and Francis de Sales. But then in his own hand he bracketed my questions and wrote: 'These are an intrusion into my personal life.' Bill Sweetman would have understood!

There was much more, but suffice it to say that the most significant churchman of my time had one view, I another and that for many of my formative years his was the view that prevailed in the archdiocese of Dublin, government circles and beyond. I could not say that we ever became close – he resigned in 1971 and died two years later – but we never fell out either. Any notes he sent me about things he disagreed with in the paper were temperate and couched in sorrow rather than anger. I admired the charitable streak in his character and his shrewdness of judgement. One comment of his that has abided with me was: 'My friend, never let yourself become a prisoner of someone else's nerves.'

Bishops are independent rulers of their own dioceses, particularly so when a bishop is as forceful as McQuaid, and moreover in charge of the most important archdiocese in the country. But in theory the cardinal of Armagh is the most important figure in the Irish Church. Tomas O'Fiaich, the former president of Maynooth, was one of the more interesting characters that I encountered throughout my career. Low-sized, fat, sweaty and overweight, he epitomised Cyril Connolly's fat man/thin man dictum. Tomas publicly had to toe the Church's line during the controversies on divorce and abortion that raged in these years, but privately he told me that divorce and such matters of conscience should be left to the individual, not passed into public legislation as a result of pressures from the Church. Being from the North, he understood only too well how Catholics could practise their religion without the assistance of the state.

He was a linguist, speaking several European languages fluently, and above all an Irish scholar, who delighted not alone in Irish history generally, but in particular that of his native County Armagh. He and I owed our reconciliation, following our joust over the Irish language, partly to the *Sunday Times* and partly to Shrove Tuesday. Other countries have Mardi Gras. In my early days as editor the Irish equivalent was the president's dinner at Maynooth, which says all that needs to be said about the Ireland of the time. Those were the days when paedophile scandals had yet to come to light, and it was not to be foreseen that one of ÓFiaich's successors as president would be sacked, and later laicised, for sexually abusing students. On Shrove Tuesday the president's friends, who constituted a Who's Who of decision-taking Ireland and its clergy, would gather in the president's study for a few pre-dinner drinks and then troop, or totter, to the main dining hall for what was always a magnificent feast. The corridors we passed along told the story of the Irish Church. They were filled with huge framed collections of the photographs of newly ordained priests going back to the previous century. Over the years the frames stayed the same size, and if anything the smiles on the young priests' faces grew larger, but so did the scale of the pictures inside them, to fill up the space created by falling vocations. As this was being written, only one priest had been ordained in Maynooth the previous year. Under Tomas O'Fiaich the hospitality was particularly lavish and widely availed of. He and I had had no difficulty in burying the hatchet after our Irish-language joust, but his nationalism continued to make him a particular hate figure with the anti-republican Dublin 4 elite. After his nomination to the See of Armagh in succession to Cardinal Conway, who died in 1977, the *Sunday Times* carried an article (on 28 August) by Muriel Bowen attacking what was termed the Vatican's 'appalling choice' by an unnamed Irish senator. The problem with O'Fiaich was that he was 'steeped in nationalist sentiment and constantly goes back to Crossmaglen where violence is ever present and Gaelic culture matters'. The article bemoaned the fact that British politicians would feel obliged to extend private invitations to O'Fiaich to dine in Downing Street, an access that 'leading politicians and industrialists might well envy'. That night I wrote a strong editorial pointing out that there was a difference between someone who cherished their culture and their traditions and a bigoted chauvinist. The truth was that, outside of Dublin 4 and the leadership of Fine Gael, ÓFiaich was practically a cult figure amongst the North's Catholics. In addition he always went out of his way to extend the hand of friendship to Protestants, both typifying and encouraging the feelings of a majority of his Catholic County Armagh brethren. Although the county was one of the worst affected by the Troubles, one of my abiding memories of O'Fiaich's ordination is of the spontaneous outburst of applause that greeted the appearance of the Protestant archbishop of Armagh, Dr George Otto Simms, and a group of his fellow bishops.

His fondness for ecumenism helped to cast a cloud over one of the last Maynooth dinners I attended before he received the red hat. It was arranged that I would pick up the former provost of Trinity College, the mathematician Dr J. G. McConnell, at his home in Killiney and bring him to and from the dinner. When I called for McConnell, I was greeted by a stern-faced housekeeper who instructed me in decidedly frosty tones that I was to bring the 'the doctor' back in some impossibly short space of time, because he had a very bad hip and needed rest. Later that evening, while we were still in the president's study with the dinner yet to come, I realised that the housekeeper's deadline had already passed. Somewhere approaching three o'clock the following morning I decanted McConnell and a couple of other passengers into my car and set off for Dublin. It was around 4.30 a.m. when I arrived at his home. I remember the prospect of facing the housekeeper vying with speculation, as I slipped past Archbishop McQuaid's official residence, near McConnell's home, as to what the archbishop would have said had he seen me bringing home a Protestant.

On the journey I had practised using words for which I only needed to breathe in, should the housekeeper be still awake, but the coast seemed to be clear as McConnell got out his latchkey and attempted to aim it at the lock. He did not need it. The door swung open and there stood the housekeeper – with a broad smile of welcome on her face! She insisted that I come in for 'one for the road'. I discovered that another lady had joined her in our absence. There were a large number of obviously well-patronised bottles on display and, after filling our glasses, the pair insisted we dance to the music of a record player. After some half an hour of decidedly wobbly dancing McConnell decided that we needed 'a real tune'. First he unlocked an escritoire, then he unlocked another drawer and, pulling out a metal box, unlocked this also and took from it a set of the old 45 records. These contained recordings of Orange bands, which played marching tunes like 'The Boys of Cullybackey' and other such airs. 'Now there's *real* music for you,' said McConnell as, hip or no hip, he twirled the housekeeper round the room to the sound of fife and drum.

After my IRA book was published in 1970 I had a taste of the Burgh Quay version of the saying that a prophet is not without honour save in his own country. Hector Legge, the editor of the *Sunday Independent*, serialised the book. Vincent Jennings, the editor of my sister paper the *Sunday Press*, did not. Showing more prescience than I did myself at the time, Hector divined that perhaps things were not as they should be in the Irish Press Group and got permission from his board to approach me with the suggestion that I should succeed him, as he intended to retire shortly. Our supposedly private meeting was held in the Mirabeau restaurant in Dun Laoghaire, run at the time by Sean Kinsella, Ireland's first celebrity chef. Just as Hector finished putting the proposition to me, who walked in but Sean McGarry, who was the agent in Ireland for the publishers of the IRA book, along with those of many other English publishers. Presumably none of them had checked into his background. Had they done so, they would have discovered that he had been an active Nazi supporter. A brilliant salesman, McGarry was also one of the more talkative men in Dublin, and enlivened my meeting with Legge considerably by exclaiming: 'Oh, oh, what's going on here? Wait till I tell Major de Valera about this!' In the event I stayed on but Conor O'Brien went in my stead.

His decision to accept the *Sunday Independent* offer after I had turned it down was to have far-reaching consequences for Irish journalism. Conor was always out of sympathy with the old revolutionary generation. Apart from the backwardness of the country in those years, for which he blamed Fianna Fail, he described himself as a Redmondite and thought that 1916 and all that happened subsequently were an unnecessary mistake. His mother, Hilda, lived in a house overlooking the Rotunda Gardens, where the 1916 rebels were rounded up and held overnight in the open air before being marched off to prison. This experience coming on top of a week of fierce fighting, with little food or sleep, obviously left the men bedraggled and unshaven-looking. His mother used to say: 'Nobody would have called them heroes that week. They were a pretty hang-dog lot.' Of all the 'hang-dog lot' and their contemporaries who emerged as rulers of the country after 1916, Conor had particularly little time for the McGraths, who controlled the Irish Hospitals Sweepstakes.

The 'Sweeps' were a particularly Irish institution. Like the *Irish Press* itself, the Sweepstakes grew out of the soil of Irish revolution. Building on Michael Collins's old gun-running network from America and England, the head of the family, Joseph McGrath, had developed one of the most efficient smuggling networks in the world. The actual running of the Sweep was quite above-board. The people to whom the receipts were consigned in Ireland, by an ingenious variety of routes, made sure that both counterfoils and monies reached their proper destination. For example, although he had been on the opposite side of the Civil War to McGrath, Liam Pedlar, who had organised gun-running routes during the Anglo-Irish War, and was a staunch de Valera supporter, and circulation manager of the *Irish Press* into the bargain, saw to it that the many counterfoils contained in outer envelopes addressed to members of his staff at Burgh Quay were punctiliously forwarded to the Sweepstakes' headquarters in Ballsbridge.

The Sweeps gave a good deal of employment to widows, women who, in job-starved Ireland, would otherwise not have worked at all. The actual Sweeps draw was performed in the presence of a uniformed senior Garda officer and the counterfoils were drawn by nurses. My aunt Josephine used to tell a story about her experience of the draw. She inadvertently picked up two tickets while her hand was in the drum and for a few seconds had to agonise over which one to drop, thereby costing the anonymous loser a fortune. The Sweepstakes' stated *raison d'être* was to raise money for Irish hospitals. Hence the name Irish Hospitals Sweepstakes. They did as the title suggested throughout their early years. The radical health minister Dr Noël Browne once told me of his amazement and delight at finding how much money had been deposited in Department of Health accounts by the Sweepstakes. His predecessors had let the money pile up, spending some of the interest but not the capital. Browne used the money in his successful drive to, as the old Dublin lady described it, 'bring in the free TB', in other words to virtually eliminate tuberculosis.

But what was not generally known was that over the years circumstances had arisen whereby the Sweeps raised only a tiny fraction of the amount needed to run the hospitals, possibly as little as a per cent. Competition had increased as various American states had founded their own lotteries and sweepstakes. A newer generation of Irish-Americans did not have the same enthusiasm for the Sweeps and there were fewer and fewer old IRA men to turn blind eyes in the customs and postal services and so on. However, the Sweepstakes still made a very large amount of money for the McGraths and their associates.

Accordingly, in one of the most famous episodes in Irish journalistic history, Conor authorised a mutual friend of us both, Joe McAnthony, a fine reporter, to write a series of articles that said in essence that although some of the Sweeps money did indeed still go to Irish hospitals, very large sums lined the pockets of the McGraths. Knowing that there would be tremendous fallout, Conor decided to run all of McAnthony's articles in one edition of the *Sunday Independent* lest the first article should also be the last. While the paper was being put to bed, and for some hours afterwards, on the excellent principle that a good editor can never be found when the hounds are pursuing, Conor and Mildred stayed in my house chatting, and drinking gin and tonic with myself and Cherry, as if nothing out of the way was happening.

On the Monday morning the fertiliser hit the fan. Tommy Murphy, who controlled Independent Newspapers, was also a prominent stockbroker. Within the first half an hour of opening for business his firm lost many of its most important clients. In addition a great deal of advertising was withdrawn from the *Independent*. Some of the firms who pulled out were directly controlled by the McGraths; others responded to their pressure. The following Wednesday at Leopardstown Races, when Murphy approached Paddy McGrath (a son of the Sweeps founder) with his hand out to apologise for any hurt caused by the articles and to assure McGrath that he had nothing to do with their publication, McGrath, who like Murphy was a steward of the race meeting, publicly abused the older man, calling him amongst other things 'a fucking traitor'. The courtly Murphy, more stockbroker than newspaperman, was devastated, and so began the process of divesting himself of his newspaper empire, which led to Tony

O'Reilly taking over the Independent Group. 'Reilly's reign began with a sit-in by journalists. Industrial harmony was ultimately restored through a combination of increased pay and assurances to the staff that Tony was not taking over on behalf of Paddy McGrath.

Joe McAnthony subsequently carved out a successful career for himself, but across the Atlantic, with the Canadian Broadcasting Corporation. Some years after the series appeared, Conor O'Brien, whose nerves had suffered as a result of the episode, was replaced as editor of the *Sunday Independent*. I am no medical expert, but what I have seen of cancer over my lifetime leads me to believe that it sometimes develops as a result of stress. At all events, Conor O'Brien, admittedly a heavy smoker, died of lung cancer a few years after his demotion.

Another form of cancer that was to affect me profoundly during my career as editor, as it did the political life of the country as a whole, was the Northern Ireland situation. When I became editor, in 1968, the IRA was largely an extinct volcano. A campaign against the border, led by Southern republicans, had sputtered on and off between 1954 and 1962, generating huge publicity, but fortunately creating little loss of life. Two of the most spectacular events of that era held a particular interest for me, the Armagh Barracks raid of 1954 and the blowing up of Nelson's Pillar in Dublin, in 1966, four years after the campaign had officially ended. Friendships formed as a result of researching the former led me to accidentally solve the mystery of who was responsible for the latter.

The Armagh raid prompted Brian O'Nolan to open the 'Cruiskeen Lawn' column he wrote to mark the first Bloomsday as follows:

> This is a small, shy and simple article. It can be written only within the week or so in which a number of courageous men made off with about two hundred rifles and a lesser amount of other lethal gear. Every man concerned could have been shot dead. Why did they risk so much for so little?

Why indeed? Without going into a dissertation on the IRA's philosophy, it can be said that the Armagh raid occurred because an alert IRA intelligence officer noted that, owing to the peaceful state of the country at the time, the sentry on duty at this key British barracks did not have a magazine in his Sten gun. Following this discovery, the IRA managed to infiltrate one of their men, Sean Garland, into the garrison and later, using his information, to drive a lorry into the place, overpower what little resistance they encountered, and get away with a huge haul of guns and ammunition. The bloodless coup was a turning point for the IRA. It led to an increase in funding and recruitment, and contributed significantly to the rebirth of an IRA campaign that sputtered on and off for a further eight years. On the fiftieth anniversary of the raid, the participants, now long retired from physical-force activities, held a commemorative dinner in a Dublin hotel to which I was invited. Amongst the many fascinating pieces of information I gleaned during the meal was the fact that I was sitting beside the man who blew up Nelson's Pillar.

Prior to the meal I had accepted the general theory that a wing of the IRA led by Joseph Christle Senior, whose wife was French, had been involved. The bomb-making expertise was said to have been supplied by a Breton nationalist and the fact that nobody was killed in the blast was attributed to the IRA's having hustled people off the street moments before the explosion. My dinner companion confirmed that Christle was involved, but only in so far as he gave his consent to the operation when his permission was sought.

Dislodging Nelson, 'that symbol of British imperialism', from his perch in O'Connell Street, Dublin's main thoroughfare, opposite the GPO, the hallowed site of the 1916 Rising, had been an ambition of successive generations of IRA men long before 1966. In fact I had already interviewed a would-be bomber. This man, in 1938, together with a similarly booby-trapped companion, had walked through the busy thoroughfare with sticks of gelignite strapped to his chest, liable to be blown up at any moment if someone had bumped into him, only to discover that, because it was wintertime, the pillar had closed early that day.

My dinner companion decided to take on the successful operation of 1966 for two reasons. First, it was now the fiftieth anniversary of the Rising, and second, a friend of his in the IRA who was planning to commemorate the anniversary by blowing up the pillar had himself been accidentally blown up a little earlier. My companion decided that it would be a nice gesture to carry out his friend's wishes! He had to make two attempts. In the first, the alarm clock that he used as a detonator to set off the explosive charge failed to strike. Nothing daunted, he made a second ascent of the pillar a day later. This time he took his small son with him, to deflect suspicion should the porter at the entrance to the pillar recognise him from the earlier visit. Those were pre-security-check days, and he found the bomb undisturbed where he had left it, in a small ventilation slit about halfway up the pillar. He fixed the fault in the alarm clock and reset it for the small hours of the following morning. This time the bomb did go off and the top half of the pillar collapsed under its own weight. Nobody was hurt, and there was no other damage caused. Dublin was then a very different city to what it is now and there were no passers-by in O'Connell Street at the time.

But there could have been an appalling carnage. For what the bomber did not know was that the lord mayor's ball was being held that night in the Metropole cinema complex (now a branch of Marks and Spencer), only a few yards from the pillar. The ball ended just ten minutes after the explosion. Had the dodgy alarm clock gone off a few minutes later than scheduled, tons of rubble could have fallen on the emerging dancers. As it was, the only injuries caused by Nelson's abrupt departure were a few small cuts and bruises suffered by some German photographers.

The photographers were friends of the great *Irish Press* photographer Colman Doyle, who was also the *Paris-Match* representative in Ireland and had an international reputation. The Germans offered Colman a place in the premises they had rented on the corner of Henry Street and O'Connell Street to record the final act in the Nelson drama – the destruction by the Irish army of the rest of the pillar and its large plinth. At the time the Irish political elite were preparing to commemorate the 1916 Rising with a huge parade past a specially erected viewing stand outside the GPO. The prospect of having to inspect the parade in the shadow of what looked like a giant amputated phallus, reminding people that the 1916 leaders had fought for a united Ireland, not a partitioned one, both appalled and outraged the decision-takers, who wanted the world to believe that the border was no longer an issue and that the IRA was a thing of the past. (This was why my article in the *Sunday Telegraph* demonstrating the organisation's continued existence aroused controversy.) Consequently the army was instructed to remove the remains of the pillar and its plinth by any means possible.

Knowing this, Colman turned down the proffered vantage point on the grounds that it was too near to the detonation area. 'Ah, Colman,' said the Germans, shaking their heads sadly, 'you don't know news photography.' 'No,' replied Colman, 'but I do know the Irish army!' and he stationed himself some one hundred metres away from the Germans. In the event, because of the size of the plinth, the explosion turned out to be the Dublin version of Bikini Atoll, and Colman's superb pictures subsequently went around the world. The German photographers and their cameras went head over heels across their expensive eyrie. Also sent flying was the glass from practically every window in O'Connell Street. Next day two bruised German cameramen turned up in the *Irish Press* offices, where Colman graciously agreed to give them some of his spare prints.

CHAPTER 9

Rebel Airs and Places

Unfortunately the subsequent history of the IRA, with which I was to become all too familiar, was far more sanguinary than the death of Nelson, although no one could have foreseen this in 1968. When I took over the *Press*, Belfast scarcely showed up on Dublin's radar screen. The South suffered from emigration, inflation and unemployment, and was trying both to cope with these problems and to pursue two policy goals that, more than any other factors, gave rise to the birth of the 'Celtic Tiger' economy later in the century, namely overhauling the educational system and laying the foundations for entry (in 1973) into what was then the EEC. Apart from the fact that de Gaulle vetoed the country's first effort to enter the EEC, the difficulties involved in fast-forwarding a backward-looking, clerically dominated society to EEC speed may be judged from what befell one of the top civil servants involved in the effort, Sean O'Connor. Much of the 1960s were devoted to debate over the introduction of what was known as 'the free education'. This involved huge state investment in secondary education, which by definition necessitated greatly increased governmental intervention in the building and running of schools. O'Connor was the man chosen by the Department of Education to bell the cat, in other words to inform Archbishop McQuaid, on behalf of the hierarchy, that henceforth the Dail, as well as Maynooth, would have to be reckoned with in education. He told me himself that on the morning he was to see McQuaid he suffered a massive heart attack.

The Republic had looked up briefly from educational preoccupations in 1965 to welcome Sean Lemass's courageous gesture in going to Stormont, the seat of the Northern parliament, to meet with the prime minister, Captain Terence O'Neill. Public opinion was also pleased by O'Neill's reciprocal visit to Dublin later in the year. But in 1968, although the civil rights marches had begun to attract headlines and TV coverage, Northern Ireland was hardly the topic *du jour*. By and large the Republic had missed the significance of the fact that Ian Paisley and other fundamentalists had thrown snowballs at Jack Lynch's car when, after he had succeeded Lemass, he too drove into Stormont.

O'Neill himself was fully alive to Paisley's dangerous potential. 'It's the Book,' he told me during the interview I conducted with him in 1965. 'He does all this with the Book in his hand, and the Book is very important up here.' In those days Paisley did indeed carry a Bible on protest marches, which grew ever larger and more menacing. And, unlike the trendy suits he wears as this is being written, he wore dark clerical garb. Southerners understood neither the significance of his trappings nor the equally dark sectarian passions he had stirred into life again by threatening a protest march on a dingy little inconspicuous red-brick side street off the Falls Road where a Republican candidate in the 1964 Westminster election had placed a small tricolour in his window. In those days unionist control, and *ipso facto* nationalist inferiority, was such that displaying the Irish flag was forbidden by law. Catholics were virtually disenfranchised at local elections, in which there was a property vote. As a unionist with, say, three houses thereby acquired three votes, it was a simple matter to outvote Catholics who had none. Thus the resulting unionist-controlled local councils were able to exclude Catholics from both state housing and jobs. Paisley wanted things to stay that way.

His activities resulted in the Royal Ulster Constabulary (RUC) smashing down the door of the candidate's house, forcibly removing the tricolour, and triggering the first major rioting of the Troubles. It was the first time that TV viewers saw cars being petrol-bombed in Ireland. To Southerners, Paisley appeared to be no more than a blinkered but harmless bigot when he led a demonstration to Belfast City Hall to protest at the lowering of the Union flag when Pope John XXXIII died. But the man with the Book had discovered a great truth: the detritus of centuries of colonialism, dispossession and of Catholics and Protestants learning to hate each for the love of God had created in Northern Ireland a seemingly inexhaustible political bedrock of dementia.

Paisley would mine this lode assiduously for more than forty years. He got rid of O'Neill, his successor and cousin Major James Chichester-Clarke, and Brian Faulkner, who followed Chichester-Clarke. Finally he succeeded in bellowing his way into the leadership of the biggest segment of Protestant opinion in the Six Counties, at the head of the Democratic Unionist Party (DUP), which he founded in 1971. But despite all this, at the time of writing most Southerners regard him as a benign old gentleman who graciously accepted the position of First Minister and, in tandem with Sinn Fein, created a peaceful Northern Ireland. Like de Valera, Paisley has made a transition from the role of loose-lipped demagogue, tearing society apart, to that of democratic elder statesman. Nothing succeeds like success.

In 1968 Paisley's activities were very much viewed as noises off. In fact, because he has a sense of humour, he was regarded in the South as a 'character' rather than a threat to the peace of the entire island. I interviewed him in the run-up to the Twelfth of July celebrations of 1967 and experienced his charm at first hand. We met at his home, which had all the bare-walled austerity of the lowest of Low Church. My abiding memory is that there seemed to be a great number of huge, leather-bound Bibles lying about the place. Later we drove to the site where his Martyrs' Memorial Church was in course of construction, on the Ravenhill Road, one of Belfast's most prestigious addresses. Paisley posed for Colman Doyle with his arms round two of the workmen. As the picture was taken, he told them: 'You'll be on the front page of the *United Irishman*!' The men visibly stiffened and looked scared at the mention of the then IRA newspaper. It was a good example of his technique. The smile, the jest and the inculcation of fear.

After concluding the interview Colman and I went for lunch in the Central Hotel, which had a large Catholic clientele. The waitress was intrigued by our accents and tried to guess where we came from and what we did. I jokingly offered her a clue, holding out my hand, saying: 'Guess who that hand has just shaken hands with.' After suggesting a number of Northern dignitaries, including 'the cardinal', she gave up and I told her it was Paisley. She looked shocked and, blessing herself, burst out: 'Oh, God forgive you. That man's after getting the bowels shot out of a young lad who works here.' Paisley in fact had nothing to do with the shooting, which was carried out by members of the recently re-formed Ulster Volunteer Force (UVF), for no other reason than that the young barman was a Catholic. But Paisley certainly contributed mightily to the stoking of Protestant fears against Catholicism and nationalism. The British set up an inquiry into the causes of rioting in Northern Ireland, under Lord Cameron, which discovered that two organisations founded by Paisley, the Ulster Constitutional Defence Committee (UCDC) and the Ulster Protestant Volunteers (UPV), had behaved in a fashion that 'readily translated into physical violence against civil rights demonstrators'. One of the tactics he used to arouse Protestant fears against the Civil Rights Association was the potent slogan 'CRA equals IRA.'

The civil rights movement was in fact the outcome of the British educational revolution caused by the Butler Acts. After these began to benefit the Catholics of the Six Counties, they gained the confidence to start speaking out for their rights. Figures like John Hume, Austin Currie and Bernadette Devlin emerged from the universities. In Belfast an ex-merchant seaman called Gerry Fitt articulated the grievances of Catholics in the Dock Ward.

For most of the 1960s there was no IRA in the physical-force sense. From the official ending of the border campaign in 1962 the organisation had eschewed the gun, apart from the occasional funding of a bank robbery, which all sections of the IRA traditionally regard as a legitimate activity: 'balaclava banking', based on the theory of withdrawals. The movement had embarked on a Marxist course of infiltrating trade unions and media outlets and exploiting where possible issues such as housing, mining or riparian rights. The first petrol bomb, explosions and shooting deaths (in 1965) of what are now known as 'the Troubles' were all caused by Protestant militants. So were the first major explosions, most notably the Silent Valley bombing of 20 April 1969, aimed at Belfast's water supply and followed by two further such attacks, which proved to be the tree trunk that broke the camel's back of Captain O'Neill's premiership in 1969. People took the bombing of the water supply to be the precursor of a campaign of loyalist incendiarism. The first policeman to die in the Troubles, Constable Arbuckle, was killed by loyalists on the Shankill Road in 1969. Republicans did not begin killing members of the RUC until 1970, and the first British soldier was shot in 1971, six years after the Protestant Ulster Force had started killing people.

For, as the strains of 'We Shall Overcome' began to be drowned by those of 'The Sash' and the thud of RUC batons on civil rights dem-onstrators' heads, pressures had built up within the ranks of republicanism for a physical-force response to the situation. Unlike the marching on the streets, the impassioned debating on television by nationalist and unionist spokespersons, the IRA debate was largely an underground one. It did not become public until after that watershed year of 1969 in which British troops appeared on the streets of Northern Ireland in response to periods of sustained rioting in Derry and Belfast during August. In Belfast Orange elements were outraged by the spectacle of Catholics staging their own version of the siege of Derry by successfully withstanding a sustained assault by Protestants. They attempted a pogrom in the Clonard area of the Falls Road adjoining the Protestant Shankill. Had the Catholics of the area not organised themselves into defensive units, the Clonard Monastery and its surrounding schools and convents would have been destroyed. Some of the Ulster Special Constabulary (USC), or B Specials, members of a force ostensibly set up to defend the border against IRA incursions from the South, were incautious enough to be captured on TV taking part in the rioting. The RUC simply disappeared from the Falls Road a couple of hours before the petrol bombing began.

The Belfast IRA's armament consisted of approximately ten handguns, one of them a Wild West Colt with a defective chamber. It had to be moved forward manually after each shot. An uncle of Gerry Adams, Liam Hanaway, who had used one of the guns, gave me a tour of the Clonard area and showed me how he had fired a shot at one corner, then dodged down a side street to fire a shot at another, so as to give the appearance of a large presence of IRA men. The presence of Hanaway, his approximately five companions and hordes of stone-throwing Catholic youths (one of whom was shot dead) restricted the burnings to one street, Bombay Street, alongside the Redemptorist monastery. The monastery survived, and as we shall see, it was from there, over thirty years later, that the main initiatives of the peace process emerged. However, in the wake of the burnings the letters IRA now appeared on gable ends as 'Irish Ran Away'. The bitterness behind this slogan, the Belfast Catholics' version of 'You can never find a policeman when you want one', was caused partly by the demilitarisation of the IRA that had taken place since the 1962 ceasefire and partly by a determination to ensure that if the Protestants came back, they would be met by gunfire, not stones.

The events of 1969 led to the physical-force wing of the IRA led by Sean MacStiofain, Rory O'Bradaigh and Daithi O'Conaill splitting from the Goulding-led constitutionalists. The genie of Irish physical-force republicanism was now out of the bottle, and neither Hell nor the Devil would succeed in getting it back in again for more than thirty years. Indeed the genie can still make an occasional deadly foray, as the Omagh explosion and various lesser atrocities that occurred after the Provisional IRA's ceasefire of 1994 amply demonstrate. But it is extremely unlikely that the Provisional movement would have grown to anything remotely resembling its subsequent strength had that never-failing source of fuel for Irish grievances, British government policy, not made one of its more disastrous interventions on the Irish scene.

In June 1970 Labour was ousted and the Conservative and Unionist Party was returned to power at Westminster. Within a matter of days the Tories began implementing the unionists' wish list. The election occurred on 20 June and on 3–5 July portions of Belfast's Lower Falls area were cordoned off and the army embarked on a search-and-ransack operation that closely paralleled General Massu's interdiction of the Kasbah in Algiers during the Algerian War. However, no searches took place in loyalist areas, although at the time the IRA had killed nobody and Protestants had been doing so assiduously. The deaths, the destruction occasioned by 'the Rape of the Falls', as it was instantly termed by nationalists, resulted in a tidal wave of recruiting for the Provisional IRA and created real bitterness between Dublin and London.

When the Irish minister for foreign affairs, Dr Patrick Hillery, visited the area in secret on 6 July 1970 to see the destruction at first hand, his British counterpart, Sir Alec Douglas-Home, declared that Hillery's action was 'a serious diplomatic discourtesy'. The British, and indeed the Irish, were completely unprepared to interact with each other over the Six Counties. Hillery told me afterwards that when he ordered a search made for relevant files in the Department of Foreign Affairs, all that turned up were a few dusty, obsolete memoranda that had no bearing on the issues of the day. The files, or the absence of them, were a telling illustration of the amount of real time devoted by successive governments to what was supposed to be Fianna Fail's priority, the reunification of the country.

It would be impossible to trace the twists and turns of all that befell Anglo-Irish relationships subsequently, but three events should be noted. One was the attempt by the Irish to raise the Northern situation at the UN, which the Irish knew was a non-starter because Britain as a permanent member of the Security Council had the right to veto discussion on any topic it deemed a vital national interest. However, the publicity value of the Irish initiative caused the British to mount their greatest diplomatic counter-offensive since the Suez War. The second major cause of worsening Dublin–London relationships occurred when the British accepted the unionist analysis of the situation to the extent of introducing internment without trial in August 1971. For many Catholics, this was the final and most unacceptable example of discrimination on grounds of religion – no Protestants were interned. The third turning point occurred on 'Bloody Sunday' on 30 January of the following year, when the Paratroop Regiment received orders that led to the mowing down of unarmed civilians during an anti-internment march in Derry. The genie born of blunder and brutality that bedevils Anglo-Irish relationships was again out of the bottle. Stormont fell and proved devilishly hard to lift up again. Even though on 21 July the Provisional IRA perpetrated an appalling slaughter of the innocents on 'Bloody Friday', when twenty-six badly planned explosions killed and injured civilians all over Belfast, they continued for the next thirty years to maintain sufficient support to mount a campaign that could only be said to have formally ended as this was being written. The support was strong enough to translate to the ballot box and political power, with Sinn

Fein taking over from the Social Democratic and Labour Party (SDLP) to such an extent that Martin McGuinness is now deputy first minister of a power-sharing executive at Stormont where he memorably smiled for the cameras alongside First Minister Paisley.

The pair became known as 'the Chuckle Brothers', after a couple of British comedians. But their metamorphosis was long and painful. It impacted both on Irish society and on my own life and career. Though I was far from being an expert, because of my researches for my books, particularly that on the IRA, I probably had more first-hand knowledge of the Northern situation than most of my Dublin colleagues – with the exception of course of those who had been born in the North like Douglas Gageby. As the situation evolved, it gradually became, apart from my family, the main preoccupation of my life. It affected my writing and outlook to the exclusion of all else.

I realised the extent of that exclusion coming towards the end of Jack Charlton's reign as manager of the Irish soccer team. Knowing that an important era in Irish popular culture was drawing to a close, I felt I should attend at least one match, and went along to Lansdowne Road to see the Republic of Ireland play Denmark. Afterwards in the bar, surrounded by sporting icons like Roy Keane, I met a pleasant, athletic young man who evidently knew most of those around him. He congratulated me on my book on Michael Collins, and showed what I considered to be an unusual interest in, and grasp of, Irish and international affairs for a professional football player. Eventually I apologised for my ignorance and asked him: 'Do you mind telling me where you play?' Before he could reply a friend dug me in the ribs and hissed fiercely: 'Drums.' The intelligent young man was Larry Mullen, the drummer with U2.

Where my writing was concerned I had written short stories, and tended towards becoming a humorist, having humorous op-ed pieces published in the *New York Times*. But there was nothing funny about Northern Ireland. My writings and lectures became devoted to Northern happenings, growing grimmer, and more engaged. I became more and more distanced from the anti-republican Dublin elite. Of course for every friend I lost I gained another for my views. Over the years my attitude to the North crystallised into a settled conviction that there would have to be a degree of imposition in whatever lasting settlement was decided on and that it was essential that some day the British would withdraw, for two reasons. One, the obvious one, so as dry up the wellsprings of the physical-force tradition. The second, to remove the bedevilling factor of having Irish policies yaw wildly depending on who came to power in London, or on the exigencies of political life at Westminster. For example, a) the Tories under Heath so disastrously switching from the reformist policies of Callaghan and Wilson to the onslaught on the Catholics favoured by the unionists, b) Labour, with a slim majority, under Callaghan yielding to unionist demands for an increase in a number of their seats, or c) the Tories under John Major needing unionist support in the House and as a result almost wrecking the peace process by introducing the decommissioning issue to the negotiations.

I also recognised that the sectarian apparatus of the Northern statelet needed to be totally reformed – police, civil service, local government, the lot. The IRA would somehow have to be included in the dialogue despite the objections of unionist sympathisers north and south of the border. After my experiences in Vietnam, not doing so appeared to me like the Americans refusing to talk with the Vietcong. But while agreeing with republicans that they should be spoken to, I disagreed with the republican analysis on two fundamental points: one the use of force, the second the IRA mantra that the British were the only problem and that with them out of the way the Irish, Protestant and Catholic, would easily resolve their differences. The British were certainly part of the problem. But I remember one night advising a republican leader that he should examine the bottoms of those nice, law-abiding men, and their wives with the perms and twinsets, who had voted for Paisley. I told him that he would not find one bayonet mark on any of them. They had gone out willingly to vote for a man they agreed with.

I also came to believe that although most unionists are Protestants, a sharp distinction should be made between unionism and Protestantism. For this reason, coupled with the fact that it was the South that, ostensibly at least, wanted unity, a thirty-two-county Ireland, there was a moral obligation on the Republic to produce a blueprint setting forth legislative guarantees for the Protestant liberty of conscience. This obviously entailed facing up to challenges such as changing the laws on things like contraception and divorce. Of course the Republic hesitated to do any such thing, and the fears of ordinary Northern Protestants at the prospect of being engulfed by Catholic hordes were never addressed. For its part, though it made (and makes) much of 'the Book', Unionism is not based on its ability to provide jobs and a decent standard of living for its followers. In fact it has signally failed to do this. When the great 'smoke-stack' industries of Northern Ireland, heavy engineering and shipbuilding closed down, the unionist political leadership did not stir itself to attract anything remotely resembling the flood of new jobs in more contemporary industries, like computers and pharmaceuticals, that the Republic created.

The Six Counties were, and – though peace has brought and is bringing rapid improvements – to some degree still are, based on a handout economy dependent on the security industry and on doles and subsidies provided by London. Unionist leaders served their followers so badly that one of the keys to Paisley's success was the fact that he literally talked shit. He interspersed his anti-Catholic tirades with fulminations against 'dry closets', which won him many a vote amongst Protestant council-house dwellers. The Unionist Party kept its working-class followers from making common cause with their working-class Catholic compatriots (who also suffered from 'dry closets') in demanding better living conditions by playing the sectarian card. The Protestant working class was told, and told itself, that it was intrinsically superior to its Catholic counterpart because the Protestant had steak on a Friday. Before the Troubles broke out, it was common for Protestant workers to wait to open their pay packets until they came to a street corner where unemployed Catholics could be found. Philosophically, unionism is based on supremacy, on fear and distrust of the natives and a quotient of false righteousness akin to the notion of manifest destiny that their ancestors used to justify their extermination of the American Indians. The fundamental unionist mindset is a provincial one, aping British mores in Belfast bowler hats.

Unionist politicians, like Irish politicians generally, could display a pleasant, friendly persona during their visits to Dublin, London or Washington, but when they got back to the Six Counties, where the votes are, the facility to talk out of both sides of the mouth was exercised and the supremacist hymn sheet was never far away. As the record shows, until Britain began exercising its responsibility in the area, unionists saw nothing undemocratic in denying their Catholic fellow citizens either a job or a house in their native place. Even today it is considered normal for ordinary neighbourly intercourse to be interrupted for about two weeks prior to the Twelfth of July celebrations, when the Orangemen march and dance around their bonfires. It was and is also considered normal for these huge bonfires to be constructed, in city areas, from both politically and environmentally unfriendly materials such as old car tyres. The pyres are normally adorned by an Irish tricolour, a portrait of the Pope or a Celtic football jersey! Whatever about Celtic, if, say, a portrait of an ayatollah, or the Queen of England, were to be treated in this fashion on the 'UK mainland', it would rightly be regarded as offensive and the police would move in. However, in the North such demonstrations are regarded as an integral part of unionist 'culture'.

Although I do not attend church, chapel or meeting, I found such manifestations of intolerance repulsive. I knew that had I been reared in the North, and not being very courageous, I would probably have emigrated, as so many were forced to do. But if I stayed, I would have tried to buck the system by any means possible. I grew up at a time when the UN loomed larger in the world than it does today and I was impressed by the peace-making efforts of Dag Hammarskjöld, the UN secretary general. A saying of his abided with me: 'In our age, the road to holiness necessarily passes through the world of action.' Doing nothing was not an option for a thinking nationalist.

The official-enshrined contempt and hostility with which the apartheid statelet treated its Catholic citizens was probably best exemplified not by the complaints of people living under the system, but by two highly civilised Northern Catholics, a man and a woman, who had got out, one to a senior executive post in a bank in Dublin, the other to a professorship in Atlanta, Georgia. The Dublin-based man, who was then fifty years old, had been born in Omagh, but had spent all of his working life in the Republic. He replied to my question as to how he viewed the fall of Stormont, when the British suspended it in 1972, by saying: 'I feel as though a weight that I didn't know I was carrying had fallen from my heart.'

The lady in Georgia taught Irish at Atlanta University. She and her sister had grown up in Ballymena, Ian Paisley's constituency. She told me that as a child she and her sister were terrified by Paisley. She said: 'I remember when I was only three and a half years old my sister and I used to hide under the sofa when he came on television. Those big blazing eyes . . .'

I think I can fairly claim, at the time of writing, that time has largely vindicated my position. The IRA have been spoken to, and like the Vietcong put down their weapons, but politically the strength of republican support, which I consistently pointed out, has been borne out by the majority of Northern nationalists who support Sinn Fein. Iraq and Afghanistan have made the maintenance of the British presence in the North more onerous for Whitehall. Even with the peace dividend there are still five thousand troops stationed there – at a time when, during the July floods of 2007, the *Daily Telegraph* quoted army sources as saying there were fewer than six hundred soldiers available to deal with any fresh major emergency. Time and demographics will fray the British link. The number of Catholic students in primary school, secondary school and at tertiary level already exceeds that of Protestants.

However, apart from my difficulties with Vivion, my position was complicated by two factors. One as outlined, the fact that partition had worked, and continued to work, despite ancestral sympathies that could burst forth at times of emotion such as the aftermath of Bloody Sunday in which the British embassy in Dublin was burned down. The reality was that throughout the entire decade of the 1970s more people in the Republic marched in protest against the prevailing levels of taxation than ever did for Northern Ireland. The second great inhibiting factor was the lasting effect of the arms-trial affair on Dublin's political life. The arms trial had its roots both in the Northern situation and in the rivalries for the position of Taoiseach which I have already described. When the North blew up, Jack Lynch found himself presiding over a Fianna Fail Party that to my eye resembled one of those Chinese dishes in which duck and prawn are glazed together. There were those who had joined the party out of family tradition, or because of the party's residual republicanism. But there were also those who had simply joined for personal advantage.

However, in the fires of the August burnings the glaze began to melt and the old Fianna Fail republicanism began coming to the surface as Northern delegations poured into Government Buildings bringing word of the apparently imminent slaughter of the nationalist population. On the streets of Dublin nightly protest meetings resounded to the chant of 'Give us the guns'. In answer to those calls, and under pressure from the hawks in his cabinet, particularly Kevin Boland and Neil Blaney, Jack Lynch was forced to sanction the setting of a cabinet subcommittee to 'do something' about the North. He then proceeded to take very good care not to know what that 'something' might be. That is until he was forced to do so. One of the subcommittee members was Charles J. Haughey. I was putting the finishing touches to my IRA book during the end of 1969 and the beginning of 1970 and was very surprised to hear in republican circles that Haughey was taking 'a forward position' on the North.

He had been regarded as the epitome of what I termed 'the Men in the Mohair Suits'. Everyone overlooked the fact that he was also the son of Sean Haughey, born in County Derry and one of those entrusted by Michael Collins with the task of smuggling guns into the North for the IRA, to defend the Northern Catholics at a time when, in the South, Collins had accepted partition and was waging civil war against the IRA. By contrast there was a general acceptance of the republicanism of Neil Blaney, as Fianna Fail's Keeper of the Sacred Flame where Six County policy had been concerned hitherto.

However, when I first heard Haughey's name being mentioned in republican circles, I recalled a small incident that indicated that he might have had a deeper streak of nationalism than people supposed. At a party in the home of a Dublin businessman, Michael Dargan, who at the time ran the national airline Aer Lingus, singing broke out. Someone struck up 'The Bold Fenian Men'. 'Do you know the words?' I asked Haughey jokingly. To my surprise he replied: 'Every word,' and proceeded to sing the entire song, quite fervently.

As we will see, I later came to question the extent of his nationalism, but it certainly appeared that he had been responding to ancestral voices when in 1970 he was charged with illegal arms importation. Writing at this remove, the bringing of this charge appears highly questionable. Jack Lynch was informed by a number of people of what members of the cabinet subcommittee, and of the Irish army, were doing but took no action to stop them. One of these informants was the secretary to the Department of Justice, Peter Berry. Another almost certainly was the minister for defence, James Gibbons, to whom the director of Irish Military Intelligence, Colonel Michael Heffernan, reported on every step taken. The Irish army officer tasked with the attempt to purchase arms (from a Hamburg arms dealer) was a Captain James Kelly, who faithfully kept Heffernan in the loop about his activities. He also liaised closely with Haughey, who, as minister for finance, oversaw the financing of the operation. For his part Berry, the Department of Justice secretary, stated categorically that Lynch could not have remained in ignorance of what was happening for several months 'unless he was wilfully turning a blind eye'.

What Lynch knew or didn't know and why his blind eye suddenly lit up are still matters for debate. He told me himself that he found Berry's accounts confused and unreliable, also that he went to see Berry in hospital, at the secretary's request, and received a disjointed tale about arms being smuggled into Dublin Airport. This resulted in a field near Dublin Airport being dug up by detectives, but nothing was found. He also told me that he visited Charlie Haughey in hospital to put the rumours about arms smuggling to him but discovered that Haughey was virtually non compos mentis. Haughey was said to have fallen off a horse at this critical juncture, but rumours persist in Dublin that his injuries were caused either by a jealous husband or by Special Branch detectives who found him trying to abstract his own files from an office in Dublin Castle. These colourful stories are probably best interpreted as an indication of the climate of rumour and counter-rumour that filled the Irish corridors of power at the time.

It is true that Haughey suffered head injuries some years earlier in a car crash. He was minister for justice at the time and, returning from a function one night, hit a bridge in County Wicklow which was known afterwards as 'Charlie's Bridge'. Haughey, who had insisted on taking the wheel from his driver, was visited in hospital the next morning by Dr Eamon de Valera, a brother of Vivion's, who was one of Ireland's leading gynaecologists. The doctor, who had merely intended calling on Haughey as a matter of courtesy, found him in a state of near unconsciousness with what he described to Vivion afterwards as 'brain fluid trickling from his nostrils'.

Whether or not the crash injury had a bearing on Haughey's powers of judgement is bound to remain a matter of speculation. What is certain is that it was generally accepted at the time that Lynch was forced to take action against his turbulent priests when the opposition leader, Liam Cosgrave, probably briefed by the Special Branch, came to him privately and warned him that action must be taken. There may, however, have been another source of information. Neil Blaney has left a record of the events that states that shortly before the news broke, for the first time in living memory a cabinet meeting was delayed because the Taoiseach was almost an hour late. Blaney was later informed that the delay had been caused by an unexpected visit to the Taoiseach by the British ambassador. In any event the fertiliser hit the fan and the sounds of latter-day Pontius Pilates washing their hands of the affair filled the chambers of Dail Eireann. A very determined effort was made to hang Kelly out to dry, and along with him a number of other people including Haughey and Blaney.

They were charged with attempting to illegally import arms into the state. (A small matter generally overlooked during and after the controversy is that only a trivial amount of either money or arms did find their way north.) The defendants pleaded, rightly in my view, that the guns were to have been imported as part of an officially sanctioned operation. After a first trial had collapsed, Haughey, Blaney, Kelly, John Kelly, a Belfast republican, and a friend of Blaney's Albert Luyx, a Belgian living in Dublin, were all subsequently acquitted. During these proceedings the testimonies of James Gibbons and Charlie Haughey were so conflicting that the trial judge commented that one of them had to be committing perjury. This was obvious to anyone who followed the trial proceedings. What was not obvious was a startling fact that only emerged more than thirty years later, under the Freedom of Information Act. Official documents showed that the state had altered statements made by Colonel Heffernan in May 1970 to suppress the fact that both he and Kelly had kept Gibbons fully informed. Faced with this disclosure, and possibly others not yet known to the public, the Taoiseach of the day, Bertie Ahern, made a public statement stating that Kelly was innocent of all charges. Presumably the cloak of innocence also fits the other defendants, including Haughey.

Unfortunately, Kelly died (in 2003) shortly before Ahern delivered the apology. His family asked me to deliver the oration over his grave. I knew him and found him a decent, honourable man whose version of the attempted gun-running saga I accepted. The man was acting under orders. I felt it no more than just to describe him as 'the Irish Dreyfus'. His army career had been destroyed. Knowing he had no future, he had resigned his commission prior to being charged. However, Haughey bit the bullet and acknowledged that in politics there are two sides, an inside and an outside. He stayed in Fianna Fail and actually joined Gibbons in voting confidence in Lynch at the end of a particularly acrimonious Dail debate. He ultimately worked his way back into the cabinet, finally taking over from Lynch as Taoiseach in 1979 when the latter resigned in a fit of despondency having just lost two by-elections in his native Cork. Lazarus did not have a more remarkable career. However, ever after the arms-trial debacle an odour of sulphur emanated from Haughey, which added to the distrust many people felt for him anyhow.

In the poisonous aftermath of the arms trial, the last thing anyone in official circles wanted to do where the North was concerned was to put their heads over the parapet. This interacted with a general attitude on the part of the public that, while Irish unity, like motherhood, was something admirable, the best thing that could be done with the Six Counties would be to cut along the dotted line of partition, tow the Northern segment out to sea, and sink it. When a former Fianna Fail minister, Kevin Boland, admittedly not the most charismatic of characters, attempted to start a Republican party of his own, it faded without trace after a few elections. Boland, however, did well financially from the arms-trial era. He successfully sued several publishers and newspapers who mistakenly included his name with those who had been fired by Lynch from the cabinet. Boland, who presented himself as the one honest man, wanted it understood that he had not been fired. He had *resigned*.

CHAPTER 10

Northerners

From the time I first began serious research on the North, during the mid-1960s, I had been fascinated by Northerners, and by the Northern situation. For all their seeming dourness, I found the Northerners, Catholics and Protestants alike, friendly, hospitable and, above all, direct. There was none of the circumlocution that one found in the South. Northerners tended to speak their minds. I was under no illusion that they could be a very terrible people in war. Centuries of sectarianism had seen to that where Belfast was concerned in particular. But the countryside was little different. Those seemingly quiet green fields of Fermanagh and Tyrone were likely to have run red with blood during some chapter of the long history of conquest and dispossession. Neighbours might appear to live together in agricultural amity even though the Catholics lived in the small hillside farms, the Protestants in the good low-lying land. But at night the Catholic son of one neighbour might be stopped on his way to a dance by the Protestant son of another. Both might have known each other since childhood. Now in the uniform of a B Special, with a weapon in his hand, the Protestant lad would ask the Catholic for his name and address, probably adding insult to injury by pointedly waving on another Protestant in the car behind. Such confrontations frequently ended in blows. Inevitably the Catholic youth sought a weapon of his own. The outcome of what both sets of families did with their weapons and their explosives was to be seen on the gravestones of the Six Counties.

I became particularly conscious of those gravestones during a moment in the autumn of 1970 when I found myself standing on one in Milltown Cemetery. I had begun a practice – which I continued for some twenty years – of staying in Clonard Monastery during visits to Belfast. Even to this day I can count on the fingers of one hand the number of drinks I have had in Belfast pubs, but it would take a very large measuring device indeed to chronicle the amount of hospitality I received both in the monastery itself and in the homes of people I met through staying there.

Under the duress of the circumstances that drove the Catholic and Protestant communities of the Falls and Shankill Roads into psychological as
well as physical laagers, the monastery returned to the role traditionally
played by such establishments in times of strife. It was a place of sanctuary,
of alms, of worship and, above all where I was concerned, of information.
Over the years I met there Stormont ministers, Republican leaders, IRA
men on the run, prison chaplains, lawyers, doctors, nuns, Protestant
clergymen and ordinary working-class Belfast people who lived in the
surrounding districts.

In October 1970 my Clonard contacts made me aware that a major
shift in Catholic opinion, particularly working-class opinion was taking
place. The Tories' authorisation of the descent on the Falls Road had
exacerbated the situation by pumping up IRA membership, as a result of
which the IRA was literally coming out into the open. I decided to go
to Milltown Cemetery to see for myself what was then Belfast's latest
phenomenon: the black-sunglassed, paramilitary-clad, foot-stamping
young volunteers marching behind coffins and, at public shows of the
tricolour, responding to military commands.

The funeral was a microcosm of what was happening in terms of
republican strength all over the province. The oration over the grave, given
by a man with a Southern accent, was not particularly impressive – a series
of platitudes about our martyred dead and the fulfilment of the dream of
the men of 1916 for a united Ireland, the sort of thing one could easily
have come across at a Fianna Fail commemoration in the South before the
arms trial. However, the speaker was obviously sincere, and the large
crowd around the graveside were equally obviously intent on translating
his sentiments into deeds. From prams and handbags revolvers were
suddenly produced and some of the young men in dark glasses fired three
volleys over the grave before they and the revolvers vanished into the
crowd once more. I didn't feel that a terrible beauty was being born, more
that an old movie was being rerun.

There are two strains of republicanism, the older based on sovereignty
and the expulsion of the British, exemplified by Liam Hanaway, Gerry
Adams's uncle, who had defended Clonard, and a left-wing or social
activist strain. I was witnessing the rebirth of the first strain. For a time
the emerging IRA would look to the South for leadership and deliverance.
In those days nationalists always referred to the Republic as 'the Free
State', its original title under the treaty, not because of its treaty status but
because the South was respected as being literally free. This respect faded
as the struggle wore on. A political vacuum developed. The IRA would

become a Northern-led movement that acted on the meaning of the words Sinn Fein: Ourselves Alone.

As the echoes of the revolver shots died away, a very nice young man touched me on the elbow and enquired in a Belfast accent: 'Excuse me, sir, but are you by any chance a member of the Special Branch?' I laughed and enquired back: 'Do you think I'd be standing up here in front of everyone if I was?' We parted smilingly, but a few years later, close to where I had stood, two British army corporals were lynched when, accidentally or otherwise, they drove into a similar funeral.

To me the significance of the Milltown funeral was the fact that almost every adult male I spoke to told me that he was either a member or a supporter of the Provisionals and that his support began with what they called 'the Rape of the Falls' the previous July. Other sorrowful decades of the rosary followed quickly, notably internment and Bloody Sunday. The tide of Northern republicanism grew steadily.

Meanwhile in the South the after-effects of the arms trial militated against a calm, focused response on the part of the government. The Fianna Fail Ard Fheis, national convention, of February 1971 was the ugliest in the party's history. I had written part of Jack Lynch's speech, which promised that if our Orange brethren were worried about Southern attitudes 'embodied in our laws and Constitution', then steps would be taken to create 'a new kind of Irish society equally agreeable to North and South'. Most of Lynch's audience were drawn from the pros and antis of the arms-trial affair. The most vociferous were those who supported Kevin Boland in a more republican, albeit unspecified, 'forward position' on the North. Light matters such as the Protestant liberty of conscience passed rapidly over their heads.

But as Lynch continued speaking, the question of Catholic and Protestant legislation suddenly ceased to be light matters and became very weighty issues indeed. For the early editions of the *Sunday Press* were distributed amongst those present and it was discovered that the lead story contained an onslaught from the Roman Catholic archbishop of Dublin, Dr McQuaid, designed to spread shock and awe amongst those who might dare to lay impious hands on Catholic legislation. Whatever one might think of the archbishop's views you couldn't fault his intelligence service. Dr McQuaid was particularly exercised by the possibility that contraceptives might become publicly available. He ordered that a letter from him be read from every pulpit in the city stating that access 'to contraceptive devices will prove a most certain occasion of sin'! Changing Catholic legislation would be, he said, 'a curse upon our country'.

Thus I had been instrumental in adding the hierarchy to Lynch's problems at a time when he was contending not merely with his enemies within the party, but with the arrogant and obtuse English prime minister, Ted Heath. Heath's approach was that the correct role for an Irish Taoiseach was to crack down on the IRA in the Republic, seal off the border and keep his mouth shut on matters that Heath saw as being domestic to England, even if they were happening in Ireland. The Tories nearly destabilised the island north and south of the border when they introduced internment in August 1971. No loyalists were picked up in a round-up aimed exclusively against Catholics and based on lists supplied by the RUC. No significant Provisional was arrested. The Provos' intelligence sources had warned them that internment was coming and they had slipped away beforehand. However, many innocent Catholics were subjected to a heightened version of the kind of treatment the Americans have since meted out to Guantanamo detainees, and public opinion eventually forced Dublin to bring the British government before the Court of Human Rights at Strasbourg. But when, in the wake of internment, Lynch protested to Heath, the British prime minister told him not to 'attempt to interfere in the affairs of the United Kingdom' because 'what is happening in Northern Ireland is no concern of his'.

Over the twenty years of my editorship I wrote most, though inevitably not all, the editorials on the Northern issue. Sometimes, both to make an impact and to disguise the absence of much in the way of other columns or feature material, I wrote jumbo editorials that took up four columns, a full half-page. Some critics might argue that these lengthy musings were the worst part of the Northern situation's collateral damage, but they did attract attention to the *Irish Press*. One such editorial, which appeared on New Year's Day 1972, summed up much of my attitude over the whole period of conflict. It was written on the fiftieth anniversary of the year in which the Irish Civil War began and contained the following:

Let us hope that [...] we can learn how to prevent the Northern issue engulfing us all again in the same way [...] Most of us in the South hoped that the border issue had died away, or was beginning to die away with the Lemass O'Neill meetings [...] In a peacetime country we had peacetime interests. Then came the civil rights movement, resistance to it and the slow decline into anarchy and violence that nearly lit a torch in all Ireland in August 1969 [...] This tiny island is now one of the world's trouble spots. In the North the Catholics have said we've had enough. They are not going back under Stormont or the old system.

The IRA are the hard, cutting edge to their grievances and, horrible though many of the deeds which have been done in the North are, the IRA continue to draw support because of the Catholic distrust of Stormont, dislike of the British army, memories of the past and fears for the future.

On the national issue, surely it is not the karma of England and Ireland to be for ever at one another's throats. Yet the daily recitals of death and destruction make today's newspaper reading like turning over the pages of Pearse Beasley and Dorothy MacArdle [two leading authors of the Anglo-Irish War and Civil War]. Irish civilians being shot and maimed on Irish streets by young British soldiers who probably only joined the army because they saw the ads on telly, but whose bullets are as hard as those of the Black and Tans, and who are shot down just as mercilessly, in reprisal.

Policemen leaving widows and orphans behind. This happening in a nation that sends missionaries abroad to Christianise other lands. The old enemy, the old problem – the fresh tragedies – let us end them.

As the situation in the North worsened, the British began putting pressure both on their own media and on the Irish government to restrict coverage of the North. At first Lynch worked on the principle that a lobster doesn't suffer if it is put into cold water under which the heat is slowly turned up until it goes to sleep and dies painlessly. Not being a lobster, I cannot vouch for the truth of this belief, but I do know that one fine day myself, the other Dublin daily paper editors and the director general of RTE, Tom Hardiman, were all called to Government Buildings. Here, speaking gently, as was his wont, Jack had a few 'suggestions' to make about coverage of the IRA. He opined that in some RTE interviews one waited to see if the interviewee was actually going to produce a revolver from their pocket. Where print was concerned, he suggested that we should not 'glorify' the IRA by using terminology such as 'a daring raid', but merely state that a raid had occurred. This would be 'helpful' in preventing the paramilitaries being 'glamorised'. Shortly after this meeting, on 1 October 1971, the electronic lobsters at least had the heat turned up on them. Gerry Collins, the minister for posts and telegraphs, used Section 31 of the Broadcasting Act to order RTE to desist from:

> Broadcasting any matter [. . .] that could be calculated to promote the aims or activities of any organisation which engages in, promotes, encourages or advocates the attaining of any particular objective by violent means.

The following month, in a manner reminiscent of the way he had acted against his political adversaries during the arms-trial affair the previous year, Lynch made another, and this time successful, attempt at a clean sweep of his targets, not merely within RTE but the IRA also. Helped, I understand, by that omnipresent figure in Irish society both then and now, Your Friendly Neighbouring Phone-Tapper, Lynch managed to ensnare the IRA chief of staff, Sean MacStiofain, the entire RTE authority and a prominent broadcaster, Kevin O'Kelly. Kevin, who had earlier been both a film critic and a sub-editor on the *Evening Press*, had taped an interview with MacStiofain in his home, but as MacStiofain drove away from the house in the small hours of November 1971 Gardai stopped and arrested him. They also made a beeline for O'Kelly and his tape recorder. 'Kelly fetched up in court and was sentenced to three months' imprisonment for contempt because he refused to identify MacStiofain as being the man whose voice was on the tape. He actually went to jail for a few days, but was released on appeal, and payment of a £250 fine, after protests by journalists. However, the RTE Authority, the station's governing body, was sacked en masse. Lynch and Heath had previously had a bad relationship, but I was later told by John Whale of the Sunday Times Insight team that when news of the sacking broke – curiously enough, just as Lynch and Heath were having talks in London – that for the first time Heath began to treat Lynch with respect. But there was to be no respect for the consciences of the RTE lobsters.

A new RTE Authority was appointed and the station was ordered not to broadcast any more interviews with either the Official or Provisional IRA. Spokespersons for the political wings of the movements were not aired either. An era of fear and self-censorship that permeated most of the print media too thus began and lasted on both sides of the Irish Sea until the IRA ceasefire of 1994. Amongst other side effects this resulted in practices such as using actors' voices instead of that of Gerry Adams. However, I think the record of the *Irish Press* on matters Northern will show that I managed to maintain a relatively uninhibited coverage of Northern events throughout, although the North generally, and the IRA in particular, took over the space in Vivion's mind formerly occupied by contraception.

Possibly more remarkably, having earned Jack Lynch a fairly stern belt of the crosier, I managed to stay friendly with him and used the friendship to approach him yet again on matters constitutional, this time on behalf of Ian Paisley! The approach was actually set in train by Paisley's arch-enemy Ruairi O'Bradaigh, who had emerged as the political face of the Provisional IRA. I had met O'Bradaigh, before he was cast into the exterior darkness, during an RTE television programme, appropriately enough on the results of the British general election that returned the Conservatives to power and led to 'the Rape of the Falls', and the climate of opinion I encountered at Milltown Cemetery. As the Troubles worsened, an ever-increasing flow of journalists poured into Dublin. I came in contact with many of them and it was obvious that their sympathies and coverage lay with the Catholics, as by then the nature of the Orange state had become widely known and condemned. The B Specials had been disbanded and reform was being introduced. The newly formed Social Democratic and Labour Party (SDLP), led by articulate figures like John Hume, Gerry Fitt, Austin Currie and Paddy Devlin, was winning a great deal of media attention, and as their agenda continued, not merely a reformed but ultimately a united Ireland, violence on the part of the section of the nationalist and Catholic community was, I thought, counterproductive.

I had a meeting with O'Bradaigh to put this view to him. The meeting achieved nothing of what I sought, but O'Bradaigh came up with an interesting proposal of his own, which I seized on. As was to happen several times later over the course of the Troubles, there were feelers being put out from both sides aiming at bringing about loyalist and republican paramilitary contact. O'Bradaigh thought that the man who could help to further this ambition on the loyalist side was the leading Belfast QC Desmond Boal. Several Unionist politicians of the period had close links to loyalist paramilitarism, but Boal was not one of them. It turned out, however, that he did have one potentially influential friend, the big man himself, Ian Paisley.

I eventually got in touch with Boal, who as befitted someone who practised both in Northern law and in politics, proved to be highly elusive, and arranged to meet him in a Dublin hotel. Boal knew the South well. He accepted my assertion that despite the McQuaid debacle and various other manifestations of Catholic power, which aroused hackles north of the border, change was afoot in the South, particularly amongst the young. What he did not accept, however, and was greatly angered by, was what he termed the Republic's 'theocratic Constitution'. However, and most interestingly, he went on to say that he was convinced that the British intended someday to get out of the North, 'stopping only to write a large cheque'. He claimed that if the Republic dropped its 'theocratic Constitution', he was prepared to argue as vigorously in favour of a united Ireland as he had hitherto argued against it.

The relevant sections of the Irish Constitution were its preamble and Articles 1 to 3. The preamble read as follows:

In the name of the most Holy Trinity from whom is all authority and to whom as our final end all actions both of men and state must be referred, we, the people of Eire, humbly acknowledge all our obligations to our Divine Lord, Jesus Christ, who sustained our fathers through centuries of trial, gratefully remembering their heroic and unremitting struggle to regain the rightful independence of our nation, and seeking to promote the common good with due observance of prudence, justice and charity, so that the dignity and freedom of the individual may be assured, true social order attained, the unity of our country restored and concord established with other nations, do hereby adopt, enact and give to ourselves this Constitution.

Article 1 stated that:

The Irish nation hereby affirms inalienable, indefeasible, and sovereign right to choose its own form of government, to determine its relations with other nations, and to develop its life, political, economic and cultural, in accordance with its own genius and traditions.

Article 2 stated: 'The national territory consists of the whole island of Ireland, its islands and the territorial seas.' Article 3 stated that:

Pending the reintegration of the national territory, and without prejudice to the right of the Parliament and government established by this Con- stitution to exercise jurisdiction over the whole of that territory, and the laws enacted by that Parliament shall have the like area and extent of application as the laws of Saorstat Eireann and the like extra-territorial effect.

These articles arose out of the tangled morass of the Irish Civil War, which left de Valera needing to placate both Christ and Caesar, in other words to convince both the Catholic Church and his republican followers that each of them had got the sort of Ireland they wanted. The fact that the country was partitioned of course meant that the constitutional provisions were irrelevant to Ireland's division. But the Protestants of the North did at least have a valid debating point, in as much as they had had no vote on the Constitution when it was introduced in 1937 and they most definitely did not believe that 'the national territory consists of the whole of Ireland', particularly as Article 44 also paid respectful attention to 'the special position' of the Roman Catholic Church. Accordingly I met Paisley at a meeting arranged by Boal in the Europa Hotel in Belfast, to the sound of bombs exploding outside. Initially Paisley himself exploded in bullying fashion, though not at me but at a television PA whom he dismissed in harsh and hectoring tones. Her distress as she departed our table was obvious. Her producer appeared and stated forcefully that she was only acting on his instructions. The TV man's intervention wrought a noticeable improvement in Paisley's manner and we proceeded to have quite a pleasant interlude, apart from the bombs and the fact that Boal rebuked me for the sort of language I used in the presence of the Great Man.

The key point to emerge from our discussion was that Paisley was indeed thinking along the lines that Boal had spoken of in Dublin, and that moreover he intended going public with his ideas via a series of interviews with the Southern media. He duly gave the interviews, condemning the South's Constitution as 'sectarian'. This in many ways was a classic example of the pot calling the kettle black, but he also said that if the Constitution was scrapped and the hand of the Irish hierarchy removed from the levers of power in the Republic:

> then the Protestant people would take a different view – there would be an entirely different set of circumstances. We are not saying that the majority of the people of the South should cease to be Roman Catholic. All we are saying is that they should ensure that rule from Dublin would not be rule from Maynooth.

It seemed to me that given the mounting death toll and destruction, this unlikely straw in the wind should be grasped. Particularly as the response of the IRA to my meetings with Boal and Paisley was also encouraging. Basically they said that if some sort of breakthrough could be achieved, then they were prepared to give it a chance. I made contact with decision-takers in the Republic telling them of the shift in Paisley's thinking that had preceded the interviews. I spoke with members of the hierarchy, to an organisation representing the younger Catholic clergy and to the leaders of the three political parties. At one stage one of the bishops to whom I spoke, Peter Birch, a Kilkenny man remarked: 'Well, I suppose we should thank you for what you are doing.' Unfortunately this pleasantry was about all I ended up with to show for my efforts, though for a time things looked hopeful. When I approached him again, Lynch was as friendly and welcoming as ever, saying: 'You know, I was just thinking recently that it was about time something happened.' He duly set up an all-party Dail committee to investigate the possibility of making changes to the Constitution. Unfortunately what he gave with one hand he took away with the other.

For one of the Fianna Fail appointees to the Constitution was Vivion de Valera. By that stage I was beginning to discover just how reactionary Vivion could be. He had no political philosophy of his own, beyond a fairly blinkered conservatism. He told me once of his disgust at a Council of Europe meeting when he discovered that 'those Liberal Socialists were eroding everything'. Vivion was not about to let anyone erode his father's Constitution. I only discovered later that the report of an earlier constitutional committee, set up under Sean Lemass, had contributed to the resignation of a former editor of the *Irish Press*, Frank Carty. Carty, at the time of the report's publication, had become the editor of the *Sunday Press*. He wrote an editorial supporting the proposed changes. Vivion's reaction was to clip out the editorial, scrawl a five-letter word on it and send it back to Carty. Wisely, Carty threw in the towel shortly afterwards. Not surprisingly Jack Lynch's constitutional committee faithfully conformed to George Bernard Shaw's definition of a government commission, being like a man going to the lavatory. It sits. For a long time nothing is heard; then there is a loud report and the matter is dropped. Not alone did the 'theocratic' elements of the Constitution remain, so did Articles 2 and 3, a prohibition on divorce and the exaltation of 'the special position' of the Roman Catholic Church. And so did the violence in Northern Ireland. So much for extending the hand of friendship, or 'looking anew' to the Protestants of Northern Ireland.

The prospect of Fine Gael moving to lessen the Church's grip on Irish political life was equally remote. The leader of the party, Liam Cosgrave, a trim little man with a toothbrush moustache and a toothbrush mind was no new broom. In fact he was so ultra-Catholic that during 1974 he crossed the floor during a Dail debate to vote against a motion put down by his own government to make contraceptives more freely available. On another occasion he unconsciously demonstrated the centrality of Catholicism in his worldview by stating: 'The Jews and the Muslims should settle their differences in a Christian manner.' Presumably he did not have in mind the manner in which Christians were settling their differences in Northern Ireland at the time.

But in all honesty it has to be conceded that the scepticism that Cosgrave displayed towards Paisley's apparent moderating of his position was well founded. Decades later, referenda having swept away Articles 2 and 3, the Good Friday Agreement having been signed and the IRA disbanded, Paisley was still refusing to share power with Sinn Fein. He did so only as this was being written after two things had happened. One, he had become the unquestioned leader of unionism, having succeeded in his career-long ambition to bring down any leader who stood against him/and had nothing to fear from the right. Two, it had become blindingly obvious that the once rich political vein of 'Ulster says no!' was exhausted and that the overwhelming majority of Irish, British, American and European opinion demanded a little yea-saying. Looking back over the course of the Troubles, from the time of the shooting (in 1966) of the young barman Peter Ward, whose death so moved the waitress when she discovered that I had just shaken hands with Paisley, to the IRA's decommissioning half a century later, I feel now that Ecclesiastes got it right. There *is* a season for all things, and in those days a time for either change or peace had not arrived. The time for killing unfortunately had, and was to remain with us for most of the period under review.

Another brainwave I had around this time also foundered on the rock of Ecclesiastes, as indeed did innumerable other efforts, both public and private, by many well-intentioned people. My idea was to get people from different walks of life in Northern Ireland down to the Republic to stay with their counterparts in Southern society, who would then visit them subsequently in Northern Ireland. Thus (hopefully) would friendships spread. So through my various Northern contacts I arranged for a selection of doctors, lawyers, plumbers, farmers, electricians, carpenters, etc., etc., to come down to Kilkenny, where we all met in the Butler House, a magnificent example of Georgian restoration, before most of the North-erners would fan out to various homes in the surrounding countryside.

At the end of the weekend I asked the group what they thought of the experiment. A Church of Ireland bishop who had come along for the ride remarked that he found the gathering 'too middle class'. In a way he was right, but there were limitations on my ability to go to an interface area and ask people would they be good enough to produce self-admitted, specimen Catholic and loyalist paramilitaries, never mind trying to house the loyalist paramilitary with a Southern counterpart! The experiment came to nothing, but it did provide a valuable microcosm of the overall problem. How was peace to be achieved without doing the unthinkable – talking to the paramilitaries and particularly to the IRA, who increasingly had become the motor force of the situation? Ecclesiastes had got it right once more. It was a time neither for sowing nor reaping. In the crash of a falling Stormont, a disappearing power-sharing executive, there were two unpalatable realities. First, there was no middle ground for middle-of-the-roaders to meet; the only time they did so was as they sprinted across the road to avoid sniper fire from either side. Yet, second, it was generally held that somehow peace could be achieved by excluding the IRA from the negotiating process.

After the Kilkenny meeting, the Protestant people from the North had to go back and live amidst the realities of Paisley oratory and loyalist violence, aggravated by an escalating IRA campaign. The people from the South genuinely liked those whom they met, but for the most part were equally genuinely afraid to go North. Southerners could never hope to understand the extent to which Protestants and Catholics divided, particularly after the loyalist strike of May 1974. The strike was aimed at destroying the power-sharing executive that had been established on 1 January that year. It succeeded only too well and the already deep divide between 'them and us' was greatly accentuated by this episode. Prior to the strike there was at least a semblance of friendliness between Protestant and Catholics at golf and tennis club level. The sight of masked men, supported by units of the Ulster Defence Association (UDA), manning barricades that were openly tolerated by British army patrols though they brought normal living to a stop, seared Catholic nerve endings. There was no going to work, no attending school and no food or petrol deliveries.

As the strike went on, it became known that behind these masks lurked not only paramilitaries but respectable shopkeepers, lawyers, civil servants – neighbours. The thing was a rerun of the Curragh mutiny of 1914 in which the army and navy let it be known that the Liberal government could not rely on their support to introduce Home Rule to Ulster. Just as this defiance led some Irish nationalists to conclude that the British could never be trusted to deliver the result of the ballot box – and so set in train the 1916 Rising, the Anglo-Irish War and partition – so in the 1970s did an increasing number of Northern nationalists come to believe that force was the only solution to the North's problems.

The degree of contact between the Orange paramilitaries and respectable Unionist politicians was far greater than that between the IRA and constitutional politicians in the Republic. This was in part because of networking through the Orange Order and in part due to the very nature of Northern society. Protestant militias had traditionally been an instrument of government policy, organised under the command of local landowners, clergy or magistrates. While ostensibly organised solely for security reasons, these militias also acted to maintain Protestant economic hegemony. During so-called 'arms searches' of Catholic homes they invariably managed to smash up any looms or spinning wheels they discovered. The Unionist politician who defected from the power-sharing executive and so brought down the whole pack of cards was Roy Bradford. He told me himself that he walked away after a visit to his ministerial office from 'two of his constituents' – the leaders of the UVF and the UDA. With the exception of the activities of small inter-church groups, and an appearance of activity without movement, such as a variety of constitutional experiments, conventions, green and white papers, a vacuum existed in the North until after the IRA ceasefire of 1994.

The power-sharing executive was a great opportunity missed, and no less a person than the former British prime minister James Callaghan said as much to me many years later, when he had gone to the House of Lords. 'Merlyn should have seen that thing through,' he said. Merlyn Rees was the secretary of state for Northern Ireland at the time. An old friend of Callaghan's, he bottled out when it came to ordering the army to take down the barricades. Nobody in Ireland was particularly surprised. In those days Labour was not seen as being fully in control of the armed services, certainly not to the extent the Conservatives were. Would Callaghan himself have seen it through? He might have, given the fact that it was he who had sent the troops in the first place. But against that one has to record the fact that it was Callaghan who introduced an infamous measure that increased the Unionist representation at Westminster, hoping to secure unionist support for his rickety government in return. In fact, in what I have always regarded as a curiously under-reported event in British parliamentary history, this manoeuvre cost 'Sonny Jim' his premiership. There was a tie on the vote, which everyone thought would have resulted in the speaker casting his vote with the status quo, but Gerry Fitt, a lifetime Labour supporter, unexpectedly voted with the Conservatives and brought down the government.

Conservatives came to power in Dublin too following the departure of Jack Lynch, and any question of empathy with the position of Northern nationalists disappeared. Political orthodoxy came to mirror the difference between the experience of daily life in Dublin and in Belfast. I was having a cup of tea in the refectory of the Clonard Monastery once, shortly after the change of government, when workmen entered the refectory and began putting up shutters. Information had been received that the petrol bombers who had tried to burn down the monastery in 1969 might be returning soon. I felt as though I was abandoning friends under siege as I headed for safe but uncaring Dublin. The monastery was also under pressure from the British army, which, amongst other things, wanted to place an observation post in the Clonard belfry tower, and who as a matter of course harassed and roughed up the young men and women who attended the social occasions in the hall. During the 1970s, and indeed afterwards, this provided one of the few oases of normal social relaxation in the Falls Road area, whose cinemas and dance halls, like those in any troubled ghetto area, had long been burned out. Apart from external pressures from the army the monks frequently had to contend with those from the hall's patrons, some of whom would first get drunk and then produce their revolvers to impress their point of view on the other dancers.

I organised a concert in the hall once, after Stormont had fallen and normal social life had become impossible in the Falls Road area. The famous group the Chieftains were amongst those who gave their services free, as did Seamus Heaney, who gave a memorable poetry reading. This time there were no revolvers in the hall, but outside it there were a great number of guns as the British army thronged the streets mystified, and not altogether best pleased, by what was regarded by the security people as a demonstration of nationalist strength. The people who attended had to walk home, or to their cars, through a large group of armed soldiers with blackened faces. I tried to use the paper to highlight the difficulties of ordinary life for Catholics in Northern Ireland. I remember an American Jesuit enquiring of one of the monks one day how the community were living, and the monk replied with a nod in my direction: 'By the grace of God and the *Irish Press*.' As a practising atheist, I felt this a nice offset to the tirade of abuse that my common lot from the crypto-unionists in Dublin's anti-republican elite. One of the arenas in which the voice of this elite rang out strongly during the 1970s and 1980s was the British Irish Association, sponsored by the British and Irish governments, which met (under Chatham House rules of secrecy) each year in either Oxford or Cambridge. The changing situation in Northern Ireland means that nowadays spokespersons from Sinn Fein and from the world of loyalism attend these conclaves. But in the period in question the association was rightly described as 'Toffs Against Terrorism'.

I elicited a spectacular torrent of abuse at one of these gatherings (held in Cambridge) when, in the presence of the chief constable of the RUC, Sir John Hermon, I told the audience that senior officers in the Garda were mistrustful of the RUC because of the links between some of its members and loyalism. In fact I was being circumspect, because my Garda informants had told me flatly that members of the RUC were in collusion with UVF and UDA death squads. Various subsequent inquiries, notably those of the courageous police ombudswoman Nuala O'Loan have established the truth of the Garda information. But at the time Sir John was able to mount a display of outrage so convincing that the organisers interrupted the conference to allow a special session to be devoted to his assertions concerning the professional integrity of the force. By a coincidence as I left the hall after speaking I bumped into Chris Patten, whose report into policing in Northern Ireland later led to the abolition of the RUC and the creation of the Police Service of Northern Ireland (PSNI). I boycotted the special session that Sir John had demanded and went punting on the Cam instead. But the Toffs Against Terrorism had the last word. They boycotted me! I received no more invitations to British Irish Association gatherings.

During the 1974–7 coalition period the voice of the Dublin component of the Toffs' Brigade was particularly strong, powerful and continuous. I would blame Dublin's attitude in these years for helping to create a mindset that deepened the political vacuum and helped to prolong the Troubles.

CHAPTER 11

Liberals Bare Their Fangs

The Irish coalition government of 1974–7 contained more liberals to the square inch than any of its predecessors, among them Garret FitzGerald and Conor Cruise O'Brien. Yet I regard it as one of the most repressive administrations of the century. Its efforts to avoid doing anything that might be construed as giving aid and comfort to the IRA were quite extraordinary. For example, the worst atrocities of the entire Troubles were the Dublin and Monaghan bombings of 17 May 1974, which ultimately claimed thirty-three lives. It is now generally accepted that the bombings were intended to weaken Dublin support for the Northern nationalists against the forces of unionism, which, with the aid of MI5, were at the time successfully undermining the power-sharing executive at Stormont. The bombs were put in place by loyalist paramilitaries who neither before nor after the explosions ever again displayed the level of technical expertise involved. The planning and direction of the atrocities is now believed to have been carried out by undercover British agents. The jumping-off point for the raids has been identified as a farm near the Monaghan border.

I walked through Dublin shortly after the bombs had gone off. I never heard a word of hostility directed towards loyalists. The general attitude of Dubliners was: 'Now we know what they've had to put up with in Belfast.' The public's reaction was either to join the long queues that formed outside hospitals to donate blood or to go home quietly and leave it to the government to bring the perpetrators to justice.

In fact the government signally failed to do any such thing. It closed down the inquests into the bombings after only twelve days, and police inquiries were halted within a matter of months. The previous government (Jack Lynch's) had declared a day of national mourning in the wake of the Bloody Sunday shootings two years earlier – shootings, it may be remarked, of persons who lived in another jurisdiction. But the Cosgrave government declared no day of mourning when almost three times as many of its own citizens were blown up and hundreds more injured and maimed. The contrast with the efforts made by the Northern authorities – with of course the active cooperation of the Garda – to bring to justice the perpetrators of the Omagh bombing of 1998, in which twenty-nine people died, was glaring. The Omagh inquiry was not closed down prematurely. Inquiries went on for several years. Even though the charges that were finally brought resulted in an acquittal – and severe criticism from the presiding judge about police methodology – optically at least one got a sense of some official concern and security follow-up to the explosion.

My understanding of the reasoning behind the differences in approach, North and South, was that while there were inefficiencies and harmful inter-departmental rivalries, Dublin's intelligence-gathering units, the Garda Special Branch and Military Intelligence, had provided the government with pretty conclusive information as to who the perpetrators of the explosions were. But the cabinet decided that any effort to provide courtroom evidence against the perpetrators would require cooperation from both the British and the Royal Ulster Constabulary. Reasoning, unfortunately correctly, that this was unlikely to be forthcoming, the government feared that the net result would be to give aid and comfort to the IRA. Accordingly the matter was shelved until 1993, when the controversy was reopened by a damning documentary made by Yorkshire TV. This, after many delays, fuelled the 'Justice for the Forgotten' campaign on the part of relatives of those killed in the bombings. As a result a tribunal of inquiry was set under Justice Henry Barron in 1999. This reported in 2003, and was critical of the Garda and the fact that important documentation had gone missing.

Barron's findings led to discussions by Dail committees and to the setting up of a further inquiry led by a leading Irish lawyer, Paddy McEntee. This reported in 2007 and was also critical of the way inquiries had been handled. However, McEntee was unable to find any evidence of collusion between the British and the Garda.

Commenting on McEntee's report in the Dail, the Taoiseach, Bertie Ahern, said he could never understand why the Garda had shut down the investigation so quickly. Earlier in the year, also in the Dail, the Tanaiste, or deputy prime minister, Michael McDowell, a leading barrister, had said that there was every reason to believe that there had been an involvement between elements in the Northern Irish security forces and people behind the bombings. The eight years of inquiry that ensued between 1999 and 2007 might have been more fruitful if the British had proved more coopera-tive. Even though the two men were personally friendly, Tony Blair, wearing his British prime-ministerial cap, wrote to Ahern in 2005 turning down an Irish request for either a public inquiry into the bombings or even a further search of documentation.

However, as will be evident from the foregoing, stylistically at least Fianna Fail's approach to the atrocities differed markedly from that of the Fine-Gael–Labour coalition in power during 1974. Apart from its almost pathological desire not to do anything that might in any way assist the IRA, the coalition was also seized by a fear that the British might withdraw their troops from Northern Ireland; far from conducting a 'Brits Out' campaign, it was secretly wedded to a policy of 'Brits In'. This sometimes made it difficult for me to decide which of the two governments, Dublin or London, carried passports showing a crown and which displayed a harp. I often wondered at how the liberals in the government could tolerate all that was done during this period. I had to wait until the year 2005 before I found out. In the course of an RTE radio discussion I took part in, Garret FitzGerald, the prime liberal of the day, amplified something he had already revealed in his memoirs. He explained that his, and the government's, real fear had been that Harold Wilson would take the British army out of the Six Counties. One would imagine that this fear would have abated after Wilson resigned, in March 1976, more than a full year before the coalition was put out of office but the 'Brits In' philosophy lasted until the end.

This was an incredibly weak negotiating position for an Irish government to proceed from. Even Jack Lynch would later publicly call for a British withdrawal. It is self-evident that a British uniform on an Irish street is an irritant in the political oyster around which no pearl will ever form. At the time I favoured a bargaining position of a long-term British commitment to withdrawal, not the sort of precipitate pull-out that the Belgians staged from the Congo, and the introduction of UN troops if necessary. But there was not a snowball's chance in Hell of a withdrawal occurring in the way FitzGerald and the others appeared to have feared – i.e. on the whim of Harold Wilson. Wilson did toy with the idea of a British pull-out in the wake of the loyalist strike that collapsed the power-sharing executive, but I doubt that the army would have obeyed him. The evidence of the time, and the existence of the infamous Clockwork Orange plot, in fact shows that, far from acceding to republican demands for a united Ireland, and *ipso facto* a British withdrawal, throughout the strike both the army and MI5 supported the unionist position. The plotters appear to have had the support of Conservative MP Airey Neave and engaged in such tactics as smearing British and Irish politicians and colluding with the RUC to present the victims of British and loyalist death squads as communists and terrorists. Wilson was enraged by the unionists, so much so that he once bypassed his advisers and wrote a celebrated speech in which he suggested that the unionists were 'spongers'. The state of his health also has to be considered. Whether the Alzheimer's disease that ultimately so cruelly consumed him was already present in 1974 is a matter of speculation, but certainly, as at least one serious biographer (Ben Pimlott) has made clear, his powers had noticeably begun to diminish earlier on in the year.

But above all what made the coalition's views on a possible army withdrawal utterly untenable was the fact that in those days the Cold War was still very much in being, with Europe divided, the Berlin Wall standing and Mikhail Gorbachev a long way from the Kremlin. Britain was a member of NATO, which from its bases in the Foyle monitored Russian submarines from Murmansk, and though her soldiers could and should have been reined in, there was very little prospect of a NATO member leaving a hole on Europe's western flank by suddenly pulling out of Northern Ireland. However, in those perfervid days the 'poor, tired child' logic took little active part in matters Anglo-Irish.

Dublin's fear of a British troop withdrawal appears to have been picked up on by the British. No less a person than the British ambassador to Ireland in 1976, Sir Arthur Galsworthy, was shown (by documents released under the thirty-year rule) to have been so remote from the realities of the situation in Northern Ireland that he once solemnly proposed to his government 'that there was only one thing he could think of which would impress the Irish government', a suggestion 'that all British security forces be withdrawn to a line, say, ten miles from the border. The buffer zone thus created would become a no-man's land in which the terrorists could do what they would.'

Sir Arthur was advising his bosses at a time of great sensitivity between Dublin and London. Two groups of SAS men in plain clothes had been arrested on the Irish side of the border with a variety of weapons in their cars, which included a shotgun and a dagger. The arrest came two years after the Dublin and Monaghan bombings, and at a time when citizens of the Republic had been found murdered near the border in mysterious circumstances. The SAS party was questioned about these murders and about the Dublin and Monaghan bombings. The British were furious at the prospect of their soldiers being sent to jail in Ireland, even though the minister for justice of the day, Patrick Cooney, assured them that this was the last thing he wanted to see happen. In an effort to coerce the Dublin government to lean on the director of public prosecutions to drop charges against the SAS men, the British also considered a series of punitive sanctions.

These included measures to put a stop to Irish immigration and to deny the Irish community in Britain either social security or voting rights. In addition the British warned of 'a strong and violent reaction by loyalist paramilitaries' and a trade embargo on Irish goods. This list of sanctions was drawn up at the behest of Prime Minister Callaghan, who wanted a strong reaction should the SAS men be sentenced to prison. Interestingly it emerged from the state papers that guilty conscience also played a part in the British approach to the SAS issue because of what had befallen the Birmingham Six while in British hands. Whitehall believed that consigning the SAS men to an Irish jail was tantamount to a death sentence.

In the event the SAS men were let off with small fines. But the ambassador's suggestion about the 'buffer zone' overlooked the enormous benefit that the zone would have conferred upon the IRA. It would have placed within the IRA's sphere of influence not merely a jumping-off ground for attacks further to the North but important towns like Newry, Derry and Strabane and republican strongholds such as Crossmaglen. The IRA army council's judgement on Sir Arthur's suggestion would have unquestionably been that it was a consummation devoutly to be wished. But such was the atmosphere of incomprehension and threat that permeated London and Dublin relationships during the Troubles. These attitudes make understandable, if not forgivable, the coalition's attitude to the media at the time.

Psychologically this mindset marked off Dublin decision-takers from the North as profoundly as walking on dry land differs from swimming in the sea. I remember the superior of another monastery, that of the Passionists in Ardoyne, an interface area that is still a flashpoint as this is being written, telling me a revealing anecdote. At the time the area was virtually under siege, the scene of almost daily sectarian assassination. But the army was persisting with the policy it had demonstrated during the loyalist strike, of refusing to open a second front by clamping down on Orange as well as on Green. 'The enemy of my enemy is my friend' theory was the order of the day, and as has since been proved, loyalist death squads were supplied with the information that enabled them to make their 'hits' by both British military intelligence and the RUC. Meanwhile, as we shall see shortly, prison populations were increasing to a point where their situation eventually came to dominate the North's political life.

The Passionist priest was a Dublin man, with Dublin contacts. So he got into his car and drove from Belfast to Dublin, where he parked outside

Dail Eireann to gather his thoughts before keeping an appointment with a friend of student days, Declan Costello, now the attorney general, to whom he intended to explain the situation of Catholics in Belfast and elsewhere.

As he sat he studied the people passing by, visiting the Dail or simply walking up and down the street. He saw no strain on their faces, no army presence, no bomb alerts, no similarity whatever to the tension-filled streets around the Ardoyne area. As he sat there he realised the gulf in experience between himself and Costello. He stayed in his little car as the time of his appointment approached and went. Finally he turned on the ignition and headed back to Belfast. In a way I could sympathise with his decision. On a human level he could have made contact with Costello, one of the more enlightened and approachable members of the government, but the coalition's policy was a different matter. I dealt with Costello myself when I was approached in an effort to have Eamonn McThomas, the editor of the IRA paper, *An Phoblacht*, released from prison. He was jailed after seditious documents were found during a raid on the *An Phoblacht* office. While in jail McThomas's already poor eyesight began to fail, a daughter became pregnant and both his wife's nervous condition and her epilepsy worsened.

Costello received me most courteously, and after a number of meetings it finally seemed that the issue of McThomas's release had advanced to the antechamber of concession. The attorney general asked me to confirm with him that he could assure his colleagues that 'If this man is released, he will do no more for the IRA than engage in republican journalism.' I was able to reassure him that not alone would McThomas do nothing more for the IRA, he would have nothing more to do with *An Phoblacht* either. I intended to get him work as a casual sub-editor on the *Irish Press*. However, despite Costello's humane attitude obduracy prevailed elsewhere. McThomas served every minute of his sentence. But he kept his promise to abandon republican journalism and went on to become a well-loved Dublin historian and tour guide. As we shall see, I had been lucky to avoid joining McThomas in jail myself.

While he was in opposition, one of the sternest critics of the efforts to muzzle RTE under Section 31 of the Broadcasting Act, was Conor Cruise O'Brien. Speaking in the Dail (on 23 November 1972), he had said that he did not think that the Irish public would:

like to see RTE brought into line and being made the object of what the National Socialists used to call Gleichschaltung, coordination being brought into line with the party, and being made transmission systems for the party's ideology [...] In any modern democracy autonomy of radio and television is as vital as the freedom of the press.

However, no doubt for the most honest of motives, as minister for posts and telegraphs, he proposed a new legal provision that would have extended the broadcasting restrictions to the print media. Somewhat naïvely I had admired O'Brien during his UN career. I liked his writings and felt that he had been hard done by Dag Hammarskjöld, the UN secretary general who had removed him from his post as UN representative during the Congo's civil war. But as the Northern conflict worsened, I began clashing with him. Joe Mullholland, RTE's head of current affairs at the time, rang me one day to invite me onto a programme with O'Brien, saying: 'The two of you are the outstanding representatives of two opposing but quite decent points of view.' Over the years O'Brien and I had many a radio and TV set-to. Looking back on his decades fronting RTE's *Late, Late Show*, Gay Byrne reproduced one of our debates amongst his list of all-time great rows on the show. O'Brien was generally known in Dublin as 'the Cruiser'. I remember one editorial in which I described him as '*HMS Cruiser*' and another in which I described his contribution to the Northern situation as being akin to that of a lighthouse in a bog, brilliant but useless.

I began to feel that I might have been hard on Dag Hammarskjöld following the installation of the Fine Gael–Labour coalition in 1973 and its rapid departure from the shores of liberalism. Instead of Jack Lynch's rapier, a bludgeon was produced. The police were let off the leash and 'a heavy gang' within the force began maltreating suspects in a manner that created widespread public unease. The Garda's activities scuppered the favourable publicity that the Irish government had hoped to gain from taking Britain to the Court of Human Rights in Strasbourg over the treatment of people rounded up during the internment swoops in the North in 1969.

The court finally reported in September 1976. It found that the 'deep-interrogation' techniques used by the army were a serious breach of the European Convention 'in the form not alone of inhuman and degrading treatment, but also of torture'. However, rather than the scheduled *Panorama* programme highlighting what had happened, BBC viewers instead got an item about the treatment of suspects while in Garda custody. It began to seem that there was very little difference between the Garda's interrogation methods and those of the RUC. Much later, in 1992, a man called Nicky Kelly, who had not alone been beaten up, but unjustly imprisoned on charges arising from a huge robbery from a train at Sallins, County Kildare, in March 1976, would be awarded £750,000 in damages against the state.

Rory O'Bradaigh came to me in connection with the treatment meted out to another suspect in the same case, Osgur Brennacht. He told me that he could reliably inform me that the Provisionals were deeply ashamed of the treatment Brennacht was getting, because they knew he was completely innocent. The train robbery had been the work of the Provisionals. Osgur was a son of the former *Irish Press* features editor Deasun Brennacht. Deasun by this time had become editor of *An Phoblacht*. I was asked would I inform the government as to who was really responsible for the robbery. I did so, but received as little response as I had at the time of the McThomas affair.

Along with being heavily pro the Roman Catholic Church, Liam Cosgrave was correspondingly anti-de Valera and anti-IRA. His deeply ingrained attitudes, widely shared within Fine Gael, stemmed from the Civil War, for which he blamed both de Valera and the IRA, as had his father before him. When I made my futile foray into decision-taking circles at the time of the Paisley–Boal episode, I found Liam in his office reading a book that he intended to use in his speech attacking the government. It was a celebrated anti-de Valera work by Donal O'Sullivan, *The Irish Free State and Its Senate*, published in 1940 – not exactly the best guide to the situation in Northern Ireland more than thirty years later. Government policy was also influenced by the outcome of the loyalist strike that had destroyed the power-sharing executive. The Protestants had won and that was the end of the battle. The only thing to be done was to retreat to Fortress Republic and keep all things Northern Irish safely outside the walls.

One effect of this policy was to create a very unsafe situation in the Republic's Portlaoise Prison, where the Provisional prisoners were kept. The confrontational policy of the government created a situation parallel to that which at the same time was building up north of the border in the H-Blocks. The Portlaoise pressure cooker would have exploded as did that in Long Kesh had not the coalition government gone out of office in 1977. The vast, emotive, political funerals of Northern republican hunger-strikers, which eventually brought Sinn Fein to power in the North, could easily have occurred in the South also. The arrival of the new government brought an end to a violent situation that included a hunger strike that had gone on for forty-seven days. There had been riots, attempts on the life of the governor and, outside the jail, a booby-trap explosion, which claimed the life of a Garda. Basically the cause of the trouble was a familiar one: the IRA's traditional insistence on being treated not as criminals but as prisoners of war, who are entitled to certain privileges. Without announcing the fact, Jack Lynch and his colleagues accepted this position in deed, if not in name. The prisoners were allowed to wear their own clothes, be segregated from other prisoners and retain their own command structure; they also obtained a number of other concessions regarding visits, parcels and freedom of association. In other words Fianna Fail took the pragmatic decision that the object of keeping the men in jail was to hold them, not humiliate them.

The Portlaoise solution so defused the situation that within a matter of months the government decided to allow the editors of the national morning papers to visit the jails to see for themselves how things had improved. It was a shrewd move because it avoided the demand that the republicans had been making for a judicial inquiry, but at the same time gave the public an insight into what had happened. I availed myself of the opportunity to visit not alone Portlaoise but practically every jail in the country. In my subsequent articles I had to report that while the prison buildings dated back in some cases to pre-famine times, every effort was made to render the running of the jails as humane as possible.

But the cost of the Portlaoise situation was still evident even though peace had broken out when I visited the prison. Apart from the normal complement of warders there were sixteen uniformed Gardai on duty on one floor of the republican section of the jail. To keep up a presence of sixteen Gardai for three full eight-hour shifts a day means at least forty-eight men on duty per week. And to maintain this number, heavy additional manpower was required to cover gaps caused by sickness and holidays.

Nineteen seventy-six was a particularly bad year. Even *The Garda Review*, the in-house journal of the police force, protested at what was going on, attacking both the government and the Garda commissioner, Ned Garvey. Garvey, obviously with the support of the government, reacted by referring the offending editorial to the director of public prosecutions in a botched attempt to have the editorial board charged with subversion and incitement to violence! I remember smiling wryly over the incident and thinking of another unsuccessful attempt to influence *Garda Review* policy. This was my father's doing. He had attempted to get Liam O'Flaherty, the Aran Island-born writer, installed as the magazine's editor. Liam, however, proved unsuitable. Apart from a tendency to throw empty 'baby Powers' whiskey bottles out of the window of the deputy commissioner's car, there was the unfortunate matter of his becoming actively involved in attempts to set up communist communes in Holy Ireland. So he never got the job.

However, a bit later in the year I would have occasion to do more than smile wryly at the government's policies. O'Brien and his colleagues had begun their term in office by mounting a very old Irish stalking horse: press coverage of the treatment of IRA subjects in police custody. It was an effort by Liam Cosgrave's father's government to prevent the *Irish Press* printing such articles that gave Fianna Fail the final shove into power in 1932. The state had brought a prosecution against the paper's first editor, Frank Gallagher, as a result of embarrassing publicity given to what was going on in barrack and cell. Liam Junior's government prosecuted every journal within sight on the same issue, successfully bringing contempt-of-court charges against a number of publications, including of course the *Irish Press*. However, the paper won that round, the only one to do so. Garret FitzGerald has recorded the fact that the Republic's anti-republican legislation drew the admiration of the unionists. One of them, he says in an autobiography, sighed sadly that he wished the British would display a similar will to win.

But despite the will to win the government presided over a major lapse in security in allowing the British ambassador, Christopher Ewart-Biggs, to be assassinated in 1976. He had consulted with the Irish security authorities about the risks, or lack of them, of an attack on his car. Being an ex-intelligence officer, he knew what he was talking about. According to his diary, he was assured that he had nothing to worry about. But nine days later a bomb exploded under his car shortly after he had left his residence at Sandyford on the foothills of Dublin. The government reacted by introducing a battery of repressive legislation. Existing emergency power laws were strengthened so as to bring about an increase in the period of lawful detention in police custody from two to seven days. Virtual police powers were conferred on the army, and it was proposed to amend Section 3 of the Criminal Law Bill so that anyone deemed to be encouraging or supporting the IRA in the print media as well as in the electronic could face up to ten years in prison.

Sharing the general feeling of shock and revulsion at the killing, I paid no particular attention to this last. The emergency package as a whole just seemed to come under the heading of 'Something Has to Be Done'. However, living outside of the preoccupations of Dublin, one of the leading journalists of the time took a different and more perceptive view. Bud Nossiter, the London correspondent of the *Washington Post*, knew O'Brien and was intrigued by the apparent intrusion of a man who had hitherto been regarded as a leading liberal into the arena of press censorship. He hopped on a plane and, on 3 September 1976, interviewed O'Brien as to how he saw the legislation working. O'Brien's response was to pull out a drawer filled with clippings of letters to the editor of the *Irish Press*. Some of these espoused a strongly nationalist/republican viewpoint. Others referred to some aspect of the Six County situation, condemned the state of affairs building up between IRA republican prisoners and warders in Portlaoise Prison, or expressed criticism of some aspect of the government's policy. Nossiter pinched himself and enquired if O'Brien really intended to proceed against people whose crime was to write letters to an editor, upholding the well-established Irish tradition of 'If there is a government, I'm against it.' O'Brien reassured him that the target would not be the writers, just the editor! He intended, he said, to 'cleanse the culture' of its nationalist virus.

Decently enough, Nossiter stopped off at the *Irish Press* to warn me to look out for myself. I would like to think that Frank Gallagher would have approved of my reaction. It was greatly assisted by the fact that Vivion de Valera, a bolder man now that his father had died, had just got married for the second time and was away on his honeymoon in Cyprus. Freed of the attentions of Nicodemus, I began by reprinting Nossiter's subsequent interview with O'Brien in the *Washington Post* on page one. Inside, I threw down the gauntlet to the government by reprinting a full page of the offending letters.

My accompanying editorial and many that succeeded it were inspired by advice I remember being given in class in Blackrock to the boy who asked: 'Would it be a sin to kiss a girl?' He was told that it was all a matter of motive. It would not be a sin if he gave the kiss as a sign of his respect for the girl. It would be sinful if he took pleasure out of it. I think that by that standard I would probably have been judged to have committed mortal sin. Some of his spies alerted Vivion to what was happening, and a few days later he interrupted his honeymoon to phone from Cyprus and check anxiously whether all this business about press freedom was being taken too far. I refrained from repeating Brendan Behan's enquiry to me about my own honeymoon, but returned him to the arms of his bride, Vera Rock, a very nice woman, with soothing assurances ringing in his ears.

Inevitably the debate found its way into the Dail, where Fianna Fail, the decapitation of the RTE Authority forgotten, made resounding, and ultimately successful, defences of freedom of expression. However, this took some time to occur, and in the early stages of the debate I felt decidedly lonely. Speaking in the Dail during the debate, O'Brien had said:

I do not believe that those who publish such material as I have quoted will be in any danger under the new law. That may appear to be in contradiction to what I have just said but in fact it is not. They will not be in danger because once the legislation is passed, such people will rightly take good care not to break that law. They are not the stuff of which martyrs are made, although they have published material which may have made martyrs out of other people. This legislation is intended to inhibit that process.

I was interviewed, along with a panel of journalists who included the editor of the *Irish Independent*, Aidan Pender, by Brian Farrell, then RTE's leading presenter. Pender told Brian and the viewers that the legislation wouldn't affect him or his paper because he would never sanction anything that might give aid and comfort to the enemies of the state. Aidan, a former gaucho on the Argentinean pampas, had taken the Franco side of the argument during the Spanish Civil War, and when he got a few glasses into him could be induced to give a spirited rendition of 'Deutschland über Alles', all excellent qualifications for an editor in independent newspapers. I wondered about my own credentials, however, when Brian turned to me on live television and said: 'The legislation is aimed at you, isn't it?'

Fortunately the publicity deflected the aim. The proposal to extend sanctions to the newspapers was dropped. But the emergency powers debate roared on to engulf someone else with *Irish Press* connections. Cearbhall O'Dalaigh, a brother of Aengus O'Dalaigh, the librarian, was a former Irish-language editor of the *Irish Press*. At the time of the censorship debate he was president of Ireland, ex-Irish attorney general and chief justice. Cearbhall, who had all Aengus's gentle, self-effacing qualities, was also a zealous proponent of press freedom. During a spell as a judge of the European Court, he made it a practice to send me photocopies of any proposed European legislation that might affect Irish newspapers. Three weeks after Nossiter's interview with O'Brien, even though the government had backed down on the extension of Section 3, before signing it into law he exercised his presidential prerogative by sending the Emergency Powers package that the Ewart-Biggs killing had elicited to the Supreme Court to be tested for repugnancy to the Constitution.

As O'Dalaigh had been a Fianna Fail nominee, the coalition was somewhat resentful of him anyway. Liam Cosgrave annoyed O'Dalaigh by accepting an invitation as head of government, which O'Dalaigh felt protocol required should have come to him. The invitation had come from the Vatican to be present at the canonisation of Blessed Oliver Plunkett, hanged, drawn and quartered by the English in 1681. Following

O'Dalaigh's referral to the Supreme Court, a member of the coalition then proceeded to lose his head. Patrick Donnegan, a convivial gentleman, in his capacity as minister for defence opened a new canteen at Columb Barracks in Mullingar on 24 October. The officers present had one thing in common: they had all received their commissions from the president, a fact that seemed to have eluded Donnegan. In the presence of both officers and journalists he described O'Dalaigh's 'amazing decision' in testing the Emergency Powers legislation as 'a thundering disgrace'. ('Thundering' was apparently the euphemism agreed upon by the press corps.) More fertiliser hit the fan. The government did issue an apology, but Donnegan did not resign. O'Dalaigh did, however, to establish both his own integrity and the unassailable nature of the presidential office. A crestfallen government decided not to contest an election for his successor and Dr Patrick Hillery was installed unopposed.

The O'Dalaigh incident was to have a profound and lasting effect on Irish politics that is not often discussed. Hillery, who had acquired immense kudos through being the Irish commissioner at the helm when Ireland steered its way through the Brussels shoals and into the Common Market, was generally accepted as being the natural successor to Jack Lynch as head of Fianna Fail and Taoiseach. However, his removal to the presidency created an opportunity that, at a future date (in 1979), Charles Haughey would seize with both hands.

The following June (1977) Conor Cruise O'Brien also departed office, losing his Dail seat in a general election that returned Fianna Fail with a huge majority of twenty seats. With him went the man principally responsible for piloting the Emergency Powers legislation through the Dail, Patrick Cooney, the minister for justice. O'Brien's subsequent career followed an extraordinary trajectory for a former minister in a Republic of Ireland cabinet. He was appointed editor in chief of the *Observer* and began his editorship with a signed editorial in which he described a call by Jack Lynch for a British withdrawal as 'poisoned rhetoric'. Subsequently he sent a memo to the paper's North of Ireland correspondent, Mary Holland, who rapidly ceased to be the paper's North of Ireland correspondent, although her reportage had earned her the Journalist of the Year Award, which said much about his attitude to Irish Catholicism:

It is a very serious weakness of your coverage of Irish affairs that you are a very poor judge of Irish Catholics. That gifted and talkative community includes some of the most expert conmen and conwomen in the world and I believe you have been conned.

Following his *Observer* stint he became a unionist, standing as a candidate for Robert McCartney's tiny UK Unionist Party. He resigned from this grouping in a wave of unionist outrage at an article he wrote in the *Sunday Independent* advising unionists that they would be better off in a united Ireland! The example of people like Havel and Malraux notwithstanding, it is better for writers to keep clear of politics.

CHAPTER 12

Press Freedoms and
Jail Sentences

As a result of the censorship controversy I made an effort in 1978 to cut through the official climate of secrecy that prevailed in Irish governmental circles by campaigning for the introduction of an Irish Freedom of Information Act. I also argued that if a Freedom of Information Act were ever to be introduced, then the newspapers would have to come up with a reciprocal gesture: some sort of press council before which members of the public could air their grievances. I invited Cearbhall O'Dalaigh to chair what should have been a significant gathering. It involved the editors of both the Republic's and Belfast's leading newspapers, some outstanding national columnists, like John Healy, and representation from the provincial press. O'Dalaigh died before the conference, and the historian and subsequent Fine Gael leader of the Seanad, Maurice Manning, took his place. My star speaker was Ben Bradley, the *Washington Post*'s editor who really brought down Nixon, through having the guts to publish Woodward and Bernstein's disclosures. Sean McBride, who won both the Lenin and the Nobel Peace Prizes for his work in founding Amnesty International took Bradley's role the following year. Sean, at the time, was the chairman of a UN committee on journalistic freedoms.

As matters turned out, the event taught me more about my industry than it did about Freedom of Information Acts or press councils. I had persuaded the Shannon Development Authority to sponsor the event. Alas, as the affair progressed over a couple of days, interspersed lavishly with wining and dining in the excellent hostelries and hotels of the Shannon area, I began to realise what Groucho Marx meant when he replied to the invitation to join a golf club by saying: 'I don't want to belong to any club that will accept me as a member.'

It was fascinating to hear Bradley's account of what had gone on behind the scenes in the Watergate coverage, but as I remember it, only Douglas Gageby and the provincial newspapers' representative were really interested in the idea of transforming the climate of Irish journalism. Aidan

Pender of the *Independent* told me that he and the other editors in the group, Independent Newspapers Ltd, had consulted with their managements before coming because there appeared to be some concern about the dangers of an Irish editors' trade union emerging. My own colleagues on the *Evening* and *Sunday Press* only appeared for the second year of deliberations, when reports reassured them that it was safe to come out. But there was no concerted move towards either a Freedom of Information Act or a press council, and the lasting deposit of our convivial meetings was a pile of headed notepaper that Bradley had printed for me, summing up the only basis on which my colleagues would agree. The lettering was in green and read: 'The Loose Alliance.' It proved so loose that a press council was not seriously considered in Ireland thereafter for almost thirty years, and then only for the very worst reasons.

Ironically, in view of the Independent Newspapers' stance at the editors' meetings, the council idea, which was still being debated ineffectually by the industry at the time, was taken up during 2006 by the minister for justice, Michael McDowell. He took advantage of public indignation at the coverage by two of the group's newspapers (the *Sunday Independent* and the *Sunday Tribune*) of the death in Moscow in a car crash of the former Fianna Fail TD Liam Lawlor. Lawlor was wrongly stated to have had a sixteen-year-old prostitute in the car at the time, and to have been coming from a red-light district. In fact the woman, who happily escaped injury, was a respectable mother of two who worked for Lawlor as a translator. Apart from being inaccurate, the reportage was flagrantly in contravention of normal Irish custom concerning respect for the dead and their families. Thus the Irish newspaper industry had reform thrust upon it. (A Freedom of Information Act had already come into operation a few years earlier as a result of EU influences.) Despite its provenance, however, I would expect the council to make its mark because the man placed in charge of it, John Horgan, who, apart from deserving honourable mention earlier in this book for his courage over the contraception issue, for some decades afterwards ran a highly successful post-graduate course in journalism at Dublin City University.

Another crisis of the coalition years involved me in an unusual artistic venture. It had its origins in an IRA kidnapping. Tide Herrema, a Dutch industrialist, was kidnapped during 1975 by an IRA couple, Eddie Gallagher and Marian Coyle. The object of the kidnapping was to trade Herrema for the release of Rose Dugdale, an English heiress who had been jailed for her part in an £8 million (1970s values) art seizure by the IRA from the home of Sir Albert Beit in County Wicklow. During the kidnapping saga Phil Flynn, a leading trade unionist and republican, contacted me to say that he felt that if he could meet Gallagher unobserved, his powers of persuasion might secure Herrema's release. He wanted me to help him by securing a couple of suits of clerical garb, so that he and an associate would be able to make the necessary arrangements without attracting police attention. Could I help in procuring clerical outfits?

Had the query come from anyone except Phil, I would have made alternative suggestions as to what he might do with the clerical outfits. However, Flynn was an impressive man, whose republicanism had so annoyed the coalition that they refused to meet him in his capacity as secretary general of the Public Services Union. He could have resolved the difficulty by stepping down from his role as vice-president of Sinn Fein, but on a point of principle he refused to do this and toured the country explaining his position to union branches. His prowess as a negotiator was such that he received almost unanimous backing and was confirmed in his post. I felt that if Flynn was prepared to risk getting involved with Gallagher, then the least I could do for him was to help him into the Church, however temporarily. Accordingly, I contacted Father Austin Flannery, a leading Dominican intellectual who found nothing objectionable, theological or otherwise, in acceding to Flynn's request. At the time even the slightest hint of involvement in the sorry saga of the Herrema abduction would have brought down an avalanche of publicity on everybody involved. I couldn't be seen meeting Flynn for the clothing handover, so it was arranged that we follow the IRA dictum that the darkest place is under the light. I drove to the car park of the biggest hospital in Dublin, St James's, and left the boot of my car unlocked. A little later, as I watched from a safe distance, Flynn and a friend – both, I thought, looking glaringly conspiratorial – appeared and made off with the clothes.

But despite all the hugger-mugger no contact could be established with Gallagher, because just then he and his fellow kidnapper, Marion Coyle, were discovered in a house in Monasterevan, County Kildare, and a seventeen-day siege ensued, which resulted in worldwide publicity and ultimately the safe release of the kidnapped industrialist. Amongst the representatives of the world's media who descended on Monasterevan was Paddy Barron, a former *Irish Press* photographer and, at the time of the kidnapping, the Irish representative of a number of Scandinavian broadcasting channels. Paddy was nothing if not enterprising. He also ran a video studio production and news agency venture known as Anner Productions, in memory of a lady who, according to the ballad, 'lived beside the Anner, at the foot of Sliabh na mBan'. The armoured car whose safety Michael Collins insisted in getting out of, and thus getting himself killed in an ambush, was also named the Sliabh na mBan, and there were several times during the years that followed when I found myself wishing that Paddy Barron had either stayed beside the Anner or traded places with Collins.

The problem was a familiar one in the Ireland of the time: artistic vision versus shortage of money. Initially Paddy had quite a good deal of money, because the round-the-clock coverage necessitated by the Monasterevan siege brought him some large overtime payments from the Scandinavians. Around the time that the cheque arrived Paddy had noticed two different items in the newspapers, one a paragraph stating that the copyright on Tom Moore's *Irish Melodies* had now expired, and the other an announcement about a number of BBC orchestras being dispensed with because of cutbacks. Taken together, the two stories inspired Barron to get an instrumentalist to produce a score for the melodies, and then to head off to England, where the soon-to-be redundant BBC musicians recorded the score in return for the Herrema overtime. Paddy paid them out of a briefcase, kneeling on the floor as he dispensed the cash.

He then engaged the services of the opera singer Niall Murray to play the part of Moore. By a series of ingenious stratagems, Paddy succeeded in filming the singer, and a small group of actors, in period costumes, both singing the melodies and acting out various scenes from Moore's life. For example, the composer was shown as he walked along the golden sands of the Barbados, where indeed Moore had had a short sojourn. But 'the Barbados' were in fact the shores of the lake at Blessington, County Wicklow. All this provided Barron with a set of beautiful tableaux on his video. What he did not have was a script to either link the performances together or explain to a contemporary viewer who Tom Moore was and why people in nineteenth-century costumes should be involved in a series of outbursts of music and song. So he came to me, saying: 'I just need a bit of a dig out with an ould script, not one with too many actors, though.'

My position was akin to that of an architect who is asked to draw up the plans for a house that has to be built around an existing dozen or so large columns that are both in the way of the design and at the same time indispensable to the support of the edifice. If I do say so myself, I came up with what I thought (and think) was a good solution to the problem. In order to cut down the acting bill and at the same time tell the story of Moore – he was in his day the best-known singer and composer in Europe – I had three patrons and friends of his, Lord Lansdowne and his two sisters, and three Dublin detractors, sitting in Heaven deciding whether or not the composer should be admitted to the Immortals. Whenever one of the critics accused Moore of being overly fond of the British aristocracy or some such charge, one of Moore's supporters would call up one of the pre-recorded *Melody* performances as an indication of Moore's patriotism, artistic talents or whatever. So each of the columns was slotted into its appropriate place in the building. Paddy, however, took a different view: 'Ah, Jaysus, no! Too many fucking actors. Couldn't pay for them!'

To get him off my back, I abandoned my cherished script and played the role of interlocutor myself, in contemporary dress, telling the story of Moore's life and introducing the various songs as the narrative unfolded. This time there was no script and I spoke extempore to the camera at the various locations in Ireland and England. Improbably enough, the result of all this endeavour was a quite impressive video. But one final problem remained: how was the production to be premiered and brought to the attention of the Irish public? I finally hit on the idea of inviting David Kennedy, the then chief executive of Aer Lingus, to a showing in Paddy's studio. David liked what he saw and so we secured if not the highest rating, at least the highest altitude of any premiere in movie history. Travellers on Aer Lingus crossed and recrossed the Atlantic to the strains of Tom Moore's music from the in-flight movie. And, I am happy to say, the video became a collector's item.

One of the few times I was able to record a definite return for my exertions in my self-appointed role as a conduit between the physical-force movements and constitutional Ireland occurred after a particularly terrible IRA atrocity, the La Mon House Hotel firebombing in County Down in February 1978, in which twelve people were killed and many more badly burned. I had arranged to meet Andy Tyrie, the then leader of the IRA's Protestant equivalent, the UDA, and a group of his colleagues for lunch in Comber prior to the explosion. After it I did not feel at all comfortable about keeping the appointment in that fervently loyalist area. However, Andy – who later became the prototype for the character Uncle Andy in the satirical BBC Northern Ireland TV series *Give My Head Peace* – was as friendly as ever and introduced me to a group of his colleagues. To an outsider they appeared to be decent, working-class types who, were it not for the fomented divisions of religion, would have been making common cause with their Catholic counterparts in a quest for better employment and social conditions. As it was, we discussed not unemployment, but the sectarian assassination situation.

The UDA men did not appear to be in favour of shooting Catholics just for the satisfaction of 'stiffing a Teague'. Although the UDA was unequivocally at war with the IRA, I knew of an episode in which Tyrie had been assailed at a meeting of the UDA Supreme Council to do more in the way of killing Catholics. He had demolished his opponents by throwing a revolver and a list of the addresses of known IRA men on the table, daring the bloodthirsty ones to pick them up. Both items remained on the table. Nevertheless, Tyrie told me, the Protestant population was being 'maddened' by the IRA's use of no-warning car bombs, and the assassination campaign was a manifestation of that increased fear and hatred. The group agreed with him that if the bombing stopped, then the assassinations would also. Back in Dublin I contacted the IRA and got a phone call in return from Daithi O'Conaill. I remember thinking that he had probably made the call from a phone box and that, like the exchange of the priests' clothing in the hospital car park, it would be difficult to trace.

In the middle of a busy, brightly lit newsroom I felt it incongruous to be chatting away with a smile on my face, as if I were discussing the coming weekend's rugby, while I informed one of the founders of the Provisional IRA of the effect his organisation's car bombings were having on loyalists. O'Conaill was completely straightforward and decisive. 'Right,' he said, 'if that's the way it is, we'll stop the bombing and they can stop knocking off Catholics. You're the channel, tell them that.' Both O'Conaill and Tyrie were as good as their word and the bombings and sectarian killings ceased for a time. Of course, as happens in such organisations, new personalities and new circumstances arose. The assassinations eventually resumed, but the accident of what was intended to be purely a briefing lunch with the UDA, combined with Daithi O'Conaill's decisive response, did result in several lives being saved.

But the incongruity of discussing an alteration in IRA policy in the bustle and glare of a newsroom was as nothing compared to doing the same thing over bone china in an upper-class, manicured, Dublin suburb. This happened after Eleanor Butler had enlisted my aid. She was a distinguished geographer, a member of the Seanad and head of the Glencree Centre for Peace and Reconciliation, which tried to bring the warring factions in Northern Ireland together. She was married to the earl of Wicklow, who was head of the Catholic publishing firm of Clonmore and Reynolds. Eleanor wanted to know if I could possibly be good enough to prevent the IRA from making an assault on her husband's relatives, whom he intended to visit shortly in Northern Ireland. Billy, she told me, was going to stay with one of the Abercorn family, and as Billy was not in good health, she would be 'frightfully relieved' if she could be assured that the IRA had no plans for shooting Lord Abercorn.

The Wicklows' lovely house overlooked the sea at Sandycove, near enough to my own house for me to walk home. My route lay past the house Roger Casement was born in, and a little further on, past Cherry's grandparents' home, wherein two young IRA men had been shot dead by my father's side during the Civil War. Eleanor's request, and the route, reminded me, if I needed reminding, that because of history, Irish society resembled an electrical cable through which, under a safe enough covering, a deadly current flowed. However, as I knew that both Eleanor and Lord Wicklow used their titled connections, whenever they could, to try to get prominent unionists to take a more benign view of the South, I tried to help. I contacted Rory O'Bradaigh and he called to my house with Joe Cahill, who at the time I only knew through his fearsome reputation.

During the Second World War Cahill had been part of a group of young IRA men who were sentenced to death for the shooting of a member of the RUC. In the event only one of the five was hanged, the leader, Tommy Williams. His hanging is scored into the nationalist folk memory of Belfast. As the time of execution neared, Catholic crowds knelt outside the jail in prayer, while across the road Orange mobs jeered and sang loyalist ballads. It is said that the RUC man was killed by an accidental shot, fired by Cahill, not Williams. Cahill became an internationally known figure in 1971, when he fronted a press conference in Belfast immediately after internment, at which he announced that the swoops had not affected the Provisionals. Outside the unsuspecting British were saturating the street with army patrols, and unionist spokespersons were informing other sections of the media that internment had been a great success and had rounded up all the terrorists.

Cahill also made world headlines through being captured aboard the *Claudia*, off the coast of Waterford, trying to bring in guns and money from Libya's leader Colonel Gadaffi. The Irish authorities got the guns, but IRA frogmen recovered the money. Cahill also later went on a lengthy hunger strike and attracted more world media attention when the Americans arrested him on landing in New York and then deported him. He later told reporters that he had occupied himself by reading my book on the IRA!

Despite his fearsome reputation Cahill was a mild-mannered man. He always wore a cap. Hence the nickname he was given (behind his back), 'Andy Capp', after the *Daily Mirror* cartoon character. I found him to be invariably courteous and prepared to listen to whatever was being proposed. That was one thing about the Provisionals: they would listen, even if subsequently they continued marching to their own drum. I don't know whether the visit to my home had any bearing on Lord Wicklow's subsequent trouble-free visit to the North, but the only time the name Abercorn featured significantly in the Northern troubles was a terrible day in March 1972 when an IRA bomb went off prematurely in a restaurant of that name, killing two people and wounding 130.

Although I did not know it at the time, my path also crossed Cahill's in far-off Libya. I had gone there to interview Colonel Gadaffi and had had to kick my heels for ten or twelve days in Tripoli because a large party of American and European journalists had also descended on the city in an effort to interview Mumar (meaning 'brother' apparently), as I was instructed to address him. Eventually I waited them out and got the interview. Apart from the interest of meeting him in his sumptuous tent, the effect of which was somewhat lessened by its being set up not in the desert sands, but in the grounds of his offices, the interview was quite amusing. Gadaffi was dressed in a tight-fitting leather outfit and gave off a strong aroma of Eau de Something or other. The interview was conducted on the basis that he supposedly knew no English and I had to address my questions to a third party, described as a former foreign minister. He then translated them into staccato Arabic. The translations elicited return fire in the form of even more staccato Arabic from Gadaffi, which was then translated back into English for me by the foreign minister.

This went on for over an hour, during which I in turn was asked a few questions by Gadaffi, chiefly about the level of support in Ireland for the IRA. But as the interview concluded and we moved to leave the tent, Gadaffi caught my arm and led me back to where he had been sitting. I was wondering uneasily about the implications of the leather outfit when the colonel pointed to the ceiling and, speaking perfect English, said: 'This is *sub rosa* – off the record – I have a question for you. Do you think Charlie Haughey will win the next election?' Meanwhile, it later emerged from his book* that in another part of the forest Joe Cahill was also waiting to see the great man. He wanted to discuss the possibilities of getting arms and money for the IRA. But every time he asked to see Gadaffi officials stalled him, saying that the interview would have to wait until after 'a most important Irish visitor' had left Tripoli. Joe duly got his interview after I had left and the identity of the supposedly important visitor was disclosed.

* Joe Cahill, *A Life in the IRA*, O'Brien Press, Dublin.

Over the course of the Troubles I appeared at a number of IRA-related trials in different countries as an expert witness. My two appearances in American courts apparently had some bearing on the verdicts. One involved Joe Doherty, a Belfast republican who, in 1981, had fled to New York, having broken out of the Crumlin Road Jail in Belfast where he had been incarcerated for his part in the killing of a British SAS officer. The British sought his extradition, but after hearing the evidence, this was refused by Judge Henry Sprizzo. However, the British persisted and Doherty was subsequently rearrested on an emigration charge and sent to prison, where he became friendly with John Gotti, the flamboyant Mafia Don. Eventually the authorities became alarmed at what they saw as the potential for a link-up between the IRA and the Mafia, and Doherty was transferred to another jail. In fact Gotti was not seeking a link-up. What he sought was an answer to the baffling fact that Doherty didn't have any money, drive a large car or even own his own home, and yet deliberately put himself in harm's way. And harm's way it certainly was. Although Doherty became a celebrity in the US, having a New York street named after him, not alone did he serve out his immigration sentence, he was subsequently deported back to Belfast and to jail, only being released under the terms of the 1998 Good Friday Agreement.

I remember the Sprizzo trial for one extraordinary moment. The lawyer for the prosecution, who solemnly informed me that his name was Ira H. Block, was accompanied by a gentleman from the British embassy in Washington with whom he conferred from time to time. After one such colloquy he asked me if the proceeds of my book on the H-Block had gone to the IRA, which I promptly denied in outrage. Thinking about Block's question later that evening, I remembered an evening when a woman came to my office asking would I donate some of the royalties from the book to some prisoners' welfare cause. I had turned down the request immediately. (Apart from anything else I had not then received any royalties. And indeed when these did come, they fell far short of my expectations.) But when I got back to Ireland, I checked up on the lady in question and discovered that she was an active republican. So, on that occasion at least, British intelligence about the IRA was clearly superior to my own.

Many years later, again in New York, I appeared on behalf of one Charles Caulfield, from Fermanagh, who was in danger of both jail and subsequent deportation. He had entered 'no' on his immigration papers to a question as to whether he had a criminal record, but he had done a stretch in Portlaoise for IRA activities. The New York judge in the Caulfield case was a very attractive lady, who at one stage in her career had been a bunny girl. She listened sympathetically to Caulfield's lawyer's plea that the defendant had been sentenced in Green Street Courthouse, where Robert Emmet, the nationalist who had led an abortive rebellion against British rule in 1803, had been condemned to death two centuries earlier. How could any young man following in Emmet's footsteps possibly describe his activities as criminal?

I backed up this plea by producing a copy of the Dublin telephone book in which there was an entry under Sinn Fein for 'prisoners of war'. Both judge and jury were suitably impressed to learn that the phone book was published by the Irish government. It bolstered the plea that Caulfield could legitimately consider himself a prisoner of war, not someone who had served a criminal sentence requiring mention on immigration documents. He was acquitted, and for a few years in New York activities on behalf of the IRA were not considered criminal, though I should imagine that that particular viewpoint no longer holds in the wake of 9/11 and all that has either flowed or been manipulated from the atrocity.

In the case involving members of a group arrested aboard the gun-running vessel, the *Eksund*, which was taken into custody by the French navy, some of the defendants owed their extremely lenient sentences to my book on Michael Collins! In this case the Parisian panel of judges consisted of three women. At the end of my testimony I gave the most senior, and best-looking, member of the bench a copy of *Michael Collins* so that she could read about the setting up of the Northern Ireland state, which had led to the presence of Irish republicans in a Paris court. Apparently Collins worked his alchemy, because the three Portias handed down slap-on-the-wrist sentences that, when the time served in custody was taken into account, resulted in the men being set free in a matter of months rather than years, as their lawyers had expected.

I got no such sympathetic hearing at the Old Bailey, however, when I appeared for a team led by Helena (now Baroness) Kennedy on behalf of Patrick Kinsella, whose misfortune it had been to agree to hide a bundle for two Irish gentlemen. Kinsella had been right in one part of his appreciation of the Irishmen's request: the items he had secreted were indeed hot. The bag contained explosive and the men were involved in bombings, shootings and a high-speed car chase that led to the death of a policeman. The principal evidence against Kinsella was an RUC-supplied photograph showing him standing with his son under some Long Kesh artwork during a visit to Belfast. From my own sources I had been able to corroborate Helena's belief that her client had merely gone to Belfast with his son, on a pub outing, to show the lad where his relations had come from.

However, the atmosphere in the court was distinctly hostile to my argument that West Belfast resembled the West Bank in as much as that, whether one detested or supported the IRA or the Palestine Liberation Organisation (PLO), in either setting political slogans and prisoners' handicrafts were an unavoidable feature of the landscape, not an indication of any individual's political beliefs. Kinsella got twenty years. I was able to help him in one respect, however. Far from being regarded as a supporter, he had been getting such pressure from the IRA that he had attempted to commit suicide by cutting his throat with the lid of a Heinz beans can. He would have died had he not chosen to make the attempt in a prison yard, where the cold air congealed the blood flow. Back in Ireland I was able to contact the IRA and intercede, successfully, to have his harassment stopped. He and the other defendants were all subsequently released under the Good Friday Agreement of 1998.

The most bizarre, and horrific, IRA-related aspect of the Troubles that I became involved with arose out of the prison situation north of the border. As we have seen, that in the South was defused following a change of government in the Republic, but ironically the one in the North became manifestly worse after another change of government, this time in London. Even more ironically this in turn led to the present ascendancy of Sinn Fein. My involvement in the prison drama came about through pure fluke. One night, at the end of February 1980, Philip McDermott, a Dublin publisher, called to my office to talk about a novel I was thinking of writing. Philip had the gift of a good editor, of being able to infect those around him with his own enthusiasms. On his way to see me he had passed a procession of barefooted women with blankets draped over their shoulders protesting about something to do with 'H-Blocks' and 'the Dirty Protest'. What was all that about? He wanted me to write a book about it.

I knew in a general sort of way that there were problems in a jail that had been built on the grounds of the Long Kesh, the former Second World War airbase outside Belfast, to house internees from 1971 onward. The H-Blocks took their name from the shape of the prison buildings, which consisted of two long blocks of cells linked in the middle by the administrative offices. I was aware that in the North, as in the South, republican prisoners regarded jail as just another battlefield in which the struggle continued by whatever means practical, but being keener on discussing the prospects of a novel than a book on the H-Blocks, I suggested names of several other writers to McDermott. However, 'persistent', rather than Philip, should have been McDermott's first name, and eventually I promised to look into the situation. It had been a long time since I had visited Clonard anyhow.

Politically, throughout the ending of 1979 and the new year of 1980 the situation in the Republic had been dominated by the ending of Jack Lynch's term as Taoiseach and leader of Fianna Fail and the emergence of Charlie Haughey in both roles.

Privately, for me, 1979 had been an *annus horribilis*. One November night, on the outskirts of the town of Naas, returning to Dublin with Cherry from our daughters' boarding school, where she had been giving final-year students beauty tips, I was involved in a fatal accident. It involved a boy of nineteen. He was riding a motorcycle that his father had given him as an early Christmas present so that he could get to work in his first job, at his father's factory. The lad was approaching the oncoming stream of traffic of which I formed part, when he apparently either touched one of the cars on his own side while overtaking or simply lost control of the powerful motorbike. Either way he was suddenly hurled across the road and under my front wheels. The Gardai, who could not have been more sensitive and understanding in their handling of the tragedy, interviewed witnesses, who described what had happened. I was pronounced blameless and was not even required to attend the inquest. But it was a long time before I could put out of my mind the memory of standing over that boy as he died at my feet. I had children of my own of that age.

Domestically also, it was a bad year. For reasons I am still not entirely clear about, Cherry had decided that it would be a good idea for us to let our own home and move into some of the vast unoccupied space in Tudor Hall. On the surface it seemed like a good idea. My mother would have company, and our mortgage-repayments burden would be lifted. In the early stages of our stay we all lived together in a state of not unreasonable strife. With the aid of a bulldozer I got the vast garden into some sort of shape. With the aid of the lad whom the archbishop had sent to university, the problem of Tudor Hall's lack of central heating was solved, briefly.

The young man had put his academic qualifications to good use by becoming a plumber. One day, in a subterranean basement room in the bowels of Tudor Hall, he found two relics of the 'bedsitter era', a pair of old black iron gas cookers. Drawing on his experience of London 'squats', he attached the cookers to an ancient penny gas meter that still hung on a basement wall. He then somehow 'duffed' this so that the gas flowed, illegally but continuously. He lit every jet on the cookers, including those in the ovens, and a quite astonishing glow of heat wafted through the house for several days. Moved by thoughts of how *Irish Press* reporters would cover my trial on charges of stealing gas, I eventually put an end both to the experiment and to the huge crop of mushrooms that flourished through a combination of the heat and the plentiful water supply from the leaks in the roof.

Earlier in the year I had also witnessed another mushrooming of activity from which I disassociated myself. This also involved water – holy water to be liberally sprinkled as the Pope came that summer to visit the land of saints and scholars. I was possibly the only man in Ireland who had an invitation to meet His Holiness and turned down the invitation (to attend a special papal reception for journalists). I am not a man of faith, but neither do I think I could be regarded as anti-clerical. As I have indicated, at various stages in my career I had reason to be grateful for clerical assistance from figures, like my teachers Father Sean 'Vicki' Farragher and Father Michael O'Carroll. In my private life one of the family's and my closest friends was, and is, Tom Stack, who at the time of writing had become a monsignor. And shortly we will encounter the heroic pastoral work of Father Alec Reid and other priests from Belfast's Redemptorist monastery, which even a practising member of Al-Qaeda or hardened warmongers like Bush and Cheney would have to admire. But apart from specific teachings that I disagreed with – those on censorship, contraception and divorce, for example – I hated the authoritarianism, hypocrisy and triumphalism that dominated much of Irish Catholicism at the time – and this was *before* we heard about the paedophilia.

To me the Pope's visit was literally a Roman triumph, a crescendo of mind-bending triumphal display on the part of one of the most powerful, and cynical, geopolitical multinationals in the world. So anyway, unlike millions of my countrymen, I stayed away from all the ceremonies. And when I say 'millions', I mean millions. At one stage on the day of the Pope's Mass in the Phoenix Park, which my mother, Cherry and some of the family attended, I temporarily left my Sisyphean labours in the gardens of Tudor Hall to drive to a railway station to make enquiries about the likely time of the family's return so that I could give them a lift. There were no trains. There were no people in the streets. Not just around Dun Laoghaire, but all over Ireland. However, while I was chatting with a porter – whom I also knew to be a good pint man himself – there appeared from nowhere a group of youths supporting one of their number who was obviously under the weather. The porter gazed after them in disgust. 'Will you look at that!' he exclaimed, '*Drinking* on the Day of the Pope! And I wouldn't mind but they've all got good educations.'

Even though I didn't go to see him, the Pope's visit caused me problems all the same. On the eve of his visit an explosion of speculation burst out in Dublin society centring on rumours that the president, Dr Patrick Hillery, was having an affair. The explosion was both ignited and fuelled by the descent on the country of a horde of British tabloid journalists. Some of them were absolute thugs. A segment of the pack that believed that the president's alleged lover lived near me entered people's gardens without permission and climbed trees in an effort to spot the phantom lady. They had a photo of a woman with them and they asked locals to identity her, offering them money to do so. Meanwhile, in another part of the city, other hacks had a different photo, which they also sought to identify. All in all Paddy Hillery would have been a lucky (and very busy) man if he had had a quarter of the women ascribed to him. Nevertheless, though nothing had been revealed publicly, with the Totem Pole bearing down on the land of saints and scholars, accompanied by the world's media, the frenzy, which is now thought to have been originated by one of the dark arts sections of the Northern security services, created a serious headache for both the president and the government.

Accordingly, a day or so before Dublin got its full-frontal of the Pope, I got a call asking me to come to meet the president at his residence, Áras an Uachtáráin, in the Phoenix Park. When I got there, I found the other two national newspaper editors and RTE's head of news. Hillery denied to us that he was having an affair and asked what was the best way to go about handling the story. I argued against either saying nothing or holding a press conference, which, in the circumstances would have been a bear garden. Instead I suggested that he give an interview to the political correspondents of the national papers and RTE. The correspondents were all respected and highly professional. Whatever course the publicity rocket took after that, it would at least have got off the launch pad safely. Hillery adopted my suggestion and briefed the correspondents later that afternoon.

But that evening, when I received my political correspondent Michael Mills's report, I found that he had managed to write about interviewing the president without any mention of mistresses or an alleged affair. Then, a few minutes after I had read his initial report, the RTE *Nine O'Clock News* came on and Sean Duignan, the station's political correspondent, announced to an amazed world that the president was not having an affair. Duignan's report was followed by the sound of bums hitting the floors of country kitchens as all over rural Ireland people fell off their chairs. Mills realised that the news was now in the public domain and relaxed his scruples to the extent of writing into his report, in longhand, the gist of what Duignan had told the nation. The Pope's arrival on the heels of the disclosure effectively obliterated the story. Pictures of the president's pleasant wife, Maeve, adorned the coverage, not those toted by the tabloid hacks.

From the time of the Pontiff's arrival and his kissing of Dublin Airport's tarmac – the most succulent of all those he encountered on his travels – he wowed the Irish. One of the highest points of the visit was his address to a huge throng of young people, which he began by saying, in English: 'Young people of Ireland, I love you.' He got a tumultuous response from his audience, a sizeable proportion of whom had spent the previous night in their sleeping bags energetically loving each other. The audience were already in good humour anyhow through the efforts of the Pope's warm-up men, Bishop Eamonn Casey and Father Michael Cleary, who all through the visit kept the crowds, and the country, vastly entertained with their jokes and singing. The Pope left from Shannon Airport in Limerick, after delivering a strong denunciation of divorce. He was seen off by Jack Lynch and Paddy Hillery. Around the same time Maeve Hillery took off from Dublin for a holiday in Spain. The Pope went on to Zaire, where, speaking in Swahili, he told a cheering crowd: 'Young people of Zaire, I love you.' Eamonn Casey was later outed as having sired one offspring, and Michael Cleary two. And may God bring all of us to kingdom come! Irish Catholicism was shaken, though not stirred. But then came the paedophile avalanche and the old authority and certainties were swept away. No more could Rome count on a devout, docile Irish laity.

The Tudor Hall interlude also came to an end after approximately a year as two things became clear. One, the strife levels had climbed well over the acceptability level, and two, the people who had rented our home were not paying the rent. My secretary, the incredible Eileen Davis, rectified this last circumstances by confronting the tenants and somehow persuading them to leave – quickly. We left Tudor Hall equally speedily and matters domestic resumed the uneven tenor of their ways.

In addition to all the foregoing I was beginning to find it harder and harder to put from my mind the suspicion that Vivion de Valera either would not or could not take the steps necessary to halt the creeping decline in the fortunes of the group. As I said earlier, his almost pathological obsession with keeping total control of the firm meant that he would not take out a loan to pay for the extensive remodelling of the *Irish Press* building, which began shortly after I became editor. The inevitable result was that on one hand the work progressed slowly – the staff's working conditions summed up by the 'Short Kesh' banner that greeted Harry Evans – and on the other there was no money forthcoming to help maintain circulation, never mind expand it.

So an escape from Burgh Quay, accompanied by a little re-immersion therapy in the Northern Ireland situation, rather than any burning indignation over the H-Blocks, was my motivation in setting off to Belfast and the real Long Kesh in the first week of March 1980. These priorities speedily reversed themselves after a talk with Father Alec Reid, a man whose career epitomises the truth of Dag Hammarskjöld's aphorism about the road to holiness passing through the world of action. During the latter part of the 1970s Alec had become an increasingly important figure to the Catholics not merely of Belfast but the North generally. His role as a chaplain to Long Kesh had given him an empathy with all sides involved in the situation brewing in the prison complex. The prison authorities had come to accept that here was a good man motivated solely by pastoral concerns, including concern for the families of warders, who were beginning to be shot in increasing numbers, as much as for those of prisoners. The days when it was remarked that Al was losing touch with reality because he was inclined to preach about 'Eeecumenism' were long over. He was now one of the most welcome visitors to the Catholic estates of the Falls Road, Andersonstown, Ballymurphy, the Springfield, Grosvenor Road, Clonard, etc. His outreach included several Protestants also, through a group of Protestant clergy whom he and Father Gerry Reynolds met with at Clonard. Gerry became involved in the peace and reconciliation process following the shooting of a Protestant man who lived on the loyalist side of the peace line, but geographically quite close to the monastery. The dead man had a large family, and learning of the shooting, Gerry felt that he had a duty to do something, anything. So he drove to Shankill Road to the dead man's home and announced himself to the mourners, not knowing whether he would be welcomed or torn limb from limb. In the event he was made welcome, prayed with the bereaved and, afterwards, with Al Reid, became one of Clonard's chief peacemakers.

Father Reid told me that he was afraid that the situation in the H-Blocks was escalating out of control to a point where mass hunger-striking would become inevitable within the jails, and outside them rioting and violence on a scale beyond anything yet seen. In the one sense the situation was quite simple. As in Portlaoise Prison the inmates were making a set of demands. 'The Five Demands', as they became generally known throughout Northern Ireland, were as follows:

1. The right to wear their own clothes.
2. The right to abstain from penal labour.
3. The right to free association. (This didn't mean movement from cell to cell but freedom of association within their own prison area.)
4. The right to educational and recreational activities in conjunction with the prison authorities.
5. Remission restored.

The difference with the situation in Portlaoise lay in the fact that whereas the prisoners in the Republic were seeking to be granted their version of the Five Demands, those in the Six Counties were fighting to have them restored. These concessions had been won as a result of peace negotiations between the British and the IRA in 1972 and had obtained until the building of Long Kesh had enabled the British to begin implementing a policy of 'criminalisation'. By the time I got to talk with Alec Reid the situation in the H-Blocks resembled a pressure cooker with the heat turned high and ready to explode. Things had deteriorated to a point wherein, in a number of selected blocks, prisoners were apparently spending twenty-four hours a day in cells in terrible conditions.

The situation in the jail had a certain symbolism for the faecal society that Northern Ireland had become. The prisoners' protest was rooted in the very nature of the Northern state. The warders were Protestant and unionists, the prisoners Catholic and nationalists. The two sides began to come into abrasive contact, above and beyond that of the always potentially fissionable IRA–warder relationship, as a result of the failure of the power-sharing experiment. The British decided that it had been a mistake to concede a 'Special Category status' to IRA prisoners after the fall of Stormont. As a result of new security policies worked out throughout the mid-1970s, it was decided that not merely should this type of political prisoner status be abandoned but that the IRA were to be 'criminalised', the conflict was to be 'Ulsterised' and a policy of 'normalisation' was to be introduced.

'Ulsterisation' meant, in effect, emulating what the Americans attempted to do in Vietnam and later in Iraq – get the natives to do the fighting. 'Normalisation' meant that everything possible was to be done to give an appearance of normality to the wretched place. To help criminalise the IRA, and curb the organisation, what was known as a 'conveyor belt' system was instituted, hinging on what were known as Diplock courts, after the law lord who recommended them. These courts cut corners where the rules of evidence were concerned and relied on uncorroborated statements obtained (or concocted) at the notorious interrogation centre run by the RUC at Castlereagh Barracks. All this had the effect of considerably increasing the prison population – by some 500 per cent between 1972 and 1980. What the security experts had not foreseen was the effect of this bending of the law on Catholic susceptibilities. Many of the families I met had already felt that they had been reared in a large prison wherein flourished discrimination, gerrymandering, unemployment and violence from the army, the police and loyalist death squads. Now they were being transferred into a smaller prison by unjust laws designed to further degrade and dehumanise them. They were to be treated in a special way but not regarded as being in a special category.

The actual decision to take away 'Special Cat', as it was popularly known, came about as a result of the report of a committee set up under the chairmanship of another law lord, the former lord chancellor, Lord Gardiner. Its terms of reference were, 'in the context of civil liberties and human rights', to consider 'measures to deal with terrorism in Northern Ireland'. The Gardiner report decided that:

> The introduction of Special Category status was a serious mistake [...] It should be made absolutely clear that Special Category prisoners can expect no amnesty and would have to serve their sentences [...] We recommend that the earliest practicable opportunity should be taken to end the Special Category.

When this report was published, in January 1975, the public at large took very little notice; indeed a lot of people thought that what the report meant was that detention without trial was to be phased out. In fact what Lord Gardiner recommended was that internment should be reconsidered by the government, but not as a matter of 'civil liberties and human rights'. Instead Gardiner objected strongly to the lack of discipline within the Long Kesh compounds. By this he meant the lack of control exerted by the authorities. In fact there was a considerable amount of discipline, but it was largely exercised by the paramilitaries. This had not happened by accident. Concurrently with the sitting of the Gardiner Commission and for some time thereafter, the British had in effect been negotiating with the IRA. Following talks initiated by a group of Protestant clergymen, led by the Reverend William Arlow, in Feakle, County Clare, in December 1974, a truce was declared by the IRA a couple of weeks after Gardiner reported.

The truce had been preceded by a ferocious assassination and bombing campaign in England, and there was outrage throughout the North on the part of the Provisionals' opponents, including the nationalist SDLP, when

In Vietnam in 1965 drinking rice wine dressed in a self-designed outfit having refused to wear the official kit issued by the US army to embedded journalists.

With Ronald Reagan, in 1981, at a St Patrick's Day party in the Irish embassy in Washington, Ben Bradlee and Sean Donlon, the Irish Ambassador.

In Libya in 1985 interviewing the supposedly non-English speaking Colonel Ghadaffi with the aid of an interpreter. After the interview concluded, Ghadaffi, speaking perfect English, took the author aside to enquire if he thought Charlie Haughey would win the next election.

The night, in 1987, on which the author announced his retirement. His son
Tom, far right, who knew about the impending announcement, was a
passenger in his friend Billy Harper's car when the news came over the radio.
Billy, right, who did not know, 'nearly crashed the car'. From left, colleagues
Sean Manion, Sean O'hEalai, John Spain and Marie Crowe.

Tom holds the author's coat as he tries to cheer up a rather glum Sean
O'hEalai, the Irish editor, who had a shrewd suspicion that henceforth the
Irish language might not be one of the group's top priorities.

Goodbye to all that. Standing at the door of the editor's office for the last time.

Family group (clockwise): Danielle Delaney (author's niece) and children, Tom, Rachel (on knee), Olwen, Cherry (author's wife) with baby Clara on her knee, Jackie and Thomond. (Colman Doyle/National Library of Ireland)

Some of the author's children and their friends outside the Lodge, the author's former holiday home on the Aran Islands.

Bound for Aran aboard the *Naomh Eanna*, the ferry which used to ply between Galway and the islands, with the author's father-in-law, Michael O'Brien (wearing hat), and the then Minister for the Gaeltacht, Tom O'Donnell.

The author aboard a friend's yacht cruising off the Cork coast with the Fastnet lighthouse in the background.

Catching mackerel off the Glassan Rocks on Inis Mor with Tom.

With the US Ambassador, Jean Kennedy Smith. (Eamonn Farrell/Photocall Ireland)

Enjoying a view of Aran . . . from the window of his daughter
Olwen's house on Inis Mor. (Colman Doyle/National Library of Ireland)

it was discovered that one of the results of the truce was the opening of a series of 'incident centres'. These were supposedly to be used for monitoring breaches of the ceasefire, as each was equipped with a 'hotline' to Stormont buildings that housed the British politicians and the civil servants who ran Northern Ireland. But the incident centres gave Provisional Sinn Fein useful toeholds within the nationalist community from which to develop a lasting political base.

As indicated earlier, the ceasefire had also helped to contribute to a list of concessions to the Provos, which included virtual prisoner-of-war status for the prisoners in the compounds, and all sorts of cooking and recreational facilities. The prisoners were even allowed the right to vet prison staff who would have to deal with them so that the risk of flashpoints could be avoided. In the course of the negotiations that secured these gains, the IRA had also made it brutally clear that any attempt to take away their privileges would be met by a lethal campaign directed against the warders.

However, buoyed up by all the concessions, the IRA leadership of the time did not appear to realise that the British were conning them, preparing, via Gardiner and Diplock, to build the H-Blocks and take away the fruits that had sprouted from Feakle. For example, a proposal that both loyalists and IRA paramilitaries considered seriously for a time was an effort by the British to set up what was described as a 'mini Switzerland' in downtown Belfast. A house in Rosemary Street was designated as a sort of terrorist headquarters in the vicinity of which the Orange and the Green would not attack each other; armed with grants from a benign British government, both sides were supposed to conduct constitutional political and welfare activities under the one roof. Interestingly this shared housing concept would later surface in another and more important guise as a result of the Good Friday Agreement of 1998. The British-Irish Joint Secretariat set up by the agreement shares a building in Belfast's Bedford Square that houses not alone British and Irish officials but important bodies such as the Parades Commission, which adjudicates on contentious parades.

What opportunities Bedford Square offers for electronic surveillance one does not know, but IRA fears of 'bugging' were one of the reasons the Rosemary Street proposal collapsed. However, it served its purpose at the time. It kept the IRA talking and deflected attention from the phasing out of compound detention and its allied concessions. Henceforth, in the eyes of officialdom, H-Blocks would house not IRA 'prisoners of war' but what were known at the time as ODCs, ordinary decent criminals, or HACs, honest average criminals.

Like most people in the Republic, I was completely unaware of this background until well after the H-Block protest started. It began in September 1976, when the first republican prisoner, Kieran Nugent, went 'on the blanket'. He refused to wear prison clothes, making the ringing declaration that 'They'd have to nail them to my back first.' For this defiance he was confined to his cell clad only in a blanket. All articles of furniture were removed – apart from a chamber pot. As other prisoners came off the conveyor belt, they followed Nugent's example. Outside the jail, warders were murdered; inside it, 'the battle of the bowels' commenced. Each side claimed that chamber pots were thrown, the republicans alleging that the warders threw the faeces back into the cells if the prisoners threw them out of the windows. So developed the custom of smearing faeces on the walls: 'You had to put it somewhere,' Nugent told me.

On the street the sense of injustice in the ghetto areas became palpable. Of all the interviews I conducted in Belfast, two particularly abided with me, those with Pauline McGeown and Kathleen Carney. Pauline was twenty-one when I met her. She had been married at seventeen, and her husband, Pat, was 'on the blanket'. She said of him:

> He was always interested in politics and he used to talk to me about what he read. The trouble is, he was too bright. When they sweep the areas, they lift the brains. They know he has got a political mind, that he reads a lot and could see ahead, therefore he is a threat. Talking is not enough to change the system. You must take action. What type, though, is another matter. I wonder does it have to be violence but you can't walk away from it. We are all in a prison here. If you try to run away, you are only running away from yourself. You don't leave H-Block behind you. I worry about Pat's mental condition. I think he is deteriorating, but I know he will stick it out. I am afraid hunger-striking is only round the corner.

Pauline was very frank with me about the other pressures generated by the H-Blocks on ghetto life. For example, the 'valley of squinting windows' syndrome meant that, as the wife of a prisoner, every move she made was observed, every greeting from another man noted. These pressures were to mount enormously. She found herself caught in the crossfire of agonised choices between ghetto code and the life of the man she loved. The year after we spoke a hunger strike broke out. Pat joined it and eventually lapsed into unconsciousness. Pauline braved the hardliners and took the lonely decision to sign the papers authorising the authorities to save his life. Patrick recovered to become a prominent member of Sinn Fein, but his health was impaired by the hunger strike and he collapsed and died under the strain of helping to maintain the IRA ceasefire of 1994.

In the case of Kathleen Carney the life-and-death decision was taken out of her hands. The IRA shot her son dead. Mrs Carney was a deeply religious woman. Her son Michael had joined the IRA without her knowing. She only found out when she noticed the mark of a beret on his forehead and realised that, instead of being at school, he had been on an IRA parade. When she confronted him, he replied: 'Mother, what do you want me to do with them lads on the blanket?' It was a question being asked all over the Six Counties. In answering it, Michael brought unimaginable grief on himself and his mother. One night his twin brother, Sean, got into a fight in a pub. Michael became involved and it later emerged that the man they were fighting with was an important figure within the IRA. Michael was subsequently kneecapped, although he continued within the movement.

Then one day he was 'lifted' and taken to Castlereagh RUC Barracks, where he underwent the dreaded interrogation process. He eventually broke when his interrogators threatened to have his next of kin shot. He gave away an arms dump and the identity of some other volunteers. He was eventually released and, as was standard operating procedure, went to the IRA and told them what he had done so that the damage could be either repaired or minimised. He was taken away for debriefing. After a few days his sister Ann was also 'lifted' by the British army and was told by the soldiers that the IRA were torturing her brother and would shoot him as an informer. For a time his mother desperately hoped that this was untrue. Several volunteers who had broken under duress eventually fetched up working for the republican movement in different capacities. Mrs Carney had a particular devotion to Our Lady of Knock, and was preparing to go on pilgrimage to the County Mayo shrine when, on 12 July 1979, Michael was found near the border shot four times in the head.

Hearing the news, Kathleen travelled to Long Kesh to tell Michael's older brother, Seamus, what had happened. She told me: 'He said I was to forget it. It was just one of those things that happened.' Seamus was 'on the blanket'.

Obviously Kathleen Carney could not forget what had happened, but in a sense Seamus was right. The conflicts that befell his family were not uncommon in Northern Ireland at the time. I decided to write the book as Philip McDermott had suggested. Something had to be done if the H-Block situation was to be prevented from causing a far worse threat to peace than Portlaoise ever did. I decided that the best thing I could do would be to visit Long Kesh myself and see what the situation in 'the Blocks' was like. I had already visited the internment camp in the wake of the introduction of internment some years earlier, before the H-Blocks were built. As I was supposed to be a relation of a prisoner on that occasion, I travelled in a minibus arranged by Sinn Fein, with the parents of Tommy McKearney, a member of one of the most famous republican families in the Six Counties. He was at the time serving twenty years on a charge of murder, but while it was obviously interesting to hear at first hand prisoners' stories, and see what the general layout of the prison was, there was no question of being allowed to visit the compounds where the prisoners were housed. We could meet with them at the visitor centre but could not inspect the conditions of 'the men behind the wire', as they were termed in a famous revolutionary ballad of the period written by Brian McGuigan.

As I could not visit the camps when things were relatively peaceful within the jails, I reckoned it would be a near-impossibility to view 'the Dirty Protest'. No other journalists had been admitted to the cells at that stage, but I was both taken aback and impressed with the cooperation the authorities extended to me. Evidently the British decision-takers, as opposed to the unionist hierarchy within the civil service, made a judgement call that the best way to meet the situation was to be open about it. I interviewed Michael Alison, the Conservative junior minister who had responsibility for the prisons, and found him a pleasant, civilised individual. We got on well, and as we were about to part I cited the dangers of the situation and asked why it had not been decided to do as had been done in the Republic in the Portlaoise situation: hold the prisoners but abandon attempts to humiliate or criminalise them. Alison smiled, a little wanly I thought, and replied: 'There is a lady in the case, you know.'

Indeed there was, Margaret Thatcher, who had become even more of an Iron Lady after the murder of her friend and adviser Airey Neave on 30 March 1979. She wanted a win and that was that. As far back as August 1979 Father Reid had written to Michael Alison setting out the psychology of the prisoners and warning of the effects of the gathering storm in great detail. Alison took four months to reply, before turning down Reid's proposals for settlement. Even then he chose not to reply directly to him, but to Gerry Fitt, the SDLP leader, who had forwarded Reid's letters.

After leaving Alison, and before visiting the jail, I was taken to lunch by a Stormont PR man at his golf club. Approaching the club, we passed a sign pointing towards a place called Knock and I involuntarily exclaimed: 'Knock, the same spelling as the place where Our Lady appeared.' My unionist interlocutor turned to me and replied with feeling: 'I can tell you she won't appear around *here*!' I said nothing, but I thought of Mrs Carney and her futile devotion.

The civilised exchange with Alison, and the visit to the golf club, left me psychologically off-guard for the reality of the Dirty Protest. I was allowed to choose any wing or cell I wished, and stopped outside a door chosen on a whim. The governor of the jail, Stanley Hillditch, whose life of course was then at risk from the prisoners' colleagues on the outside, asked me to wait for a moment while he had a word with the two occupants of the cell. I caught the words 'no conversation' and then two huge warders materialised and stood on either side of the two occupants of the cell, men aged twenty-one and twenty-two, serving sentences of ten and twelve years respectively. This is what I wrote about them and their surroundings:

> When the cell door opened, they both looked frightened and looked anxiously at us for a moment. They were pallid and naked except for a blanket draped over their shoulders. They stood silently, fear hardening into defiance, I felt, as we looked at the cell.
>
> It was covered in excrement almost to the ceiling on all four walls. In one corner there was a pile of rotting, blue-moulded food and excrement, and the two boys had evidently been using bits of their foam rubber mattress to add to the décor as we entered. There wasn't much of a smell but the light was dim and the atmosphere profoundly disturbing and depressing. I felt helpless and angry as I stood, debarred by bureaucracy and by history from talking to two of my fellow human beings who had brought themselves, and had been brought, to this condition of self-abnegation.

As we left the cells someone in our party remarked: 'Well, you certainly picked a good one. I've never seen anything like that. That's the worst one I've seen.' In fact when I checked up afterwards I was assured that there was nothing particularly bad about the cell. Most prisoners, it seemed, woke up in the morning with maggots wriggling in their nostrils, beards and orifices, but at the time I was so unmanned that I could hardly speak, and after walking in silence past a few more cells simply nodded my head at another door. This time I discovered a touch of humanity, creativity, the human spirit, call it what you will, that helped to restore my equilibrium. The prisoner was Martin Meehan, a well-known republican who was subsequently elected to the Stormont Assembly, but who has since died. He wore a white towel round his loins, which literally added a lighter note to the proceedings. Moreover he was attempting to relieve the awful conditions by using his excrement to create a Pacific holiday-island mural on the walls. The faeces only came halfway up the walls to simulate water and then, atop the 'water', palm trees and atolls sprouted within the shitty confines of Long Kesh. Meehan had been using a piece of foam rubber from his mattress to further his artistic experiments. When he recognised me, he transferred the rubber to his left hand and extended his right to shake hands. A combination of that handshake and the maintenance of the smile on my face were two of the bravest actions of my life.

Bad as the conditions were in Long Kesh, I found those in the women's prison in Armagh Jail, where a sympathetic strike had broken out, to be infinitely worse. Again I had allowed myself to be lulled into a sense of normalcy. In jail a curtain of ordinariness comes down over most prisoners, male or female. In Armagh the prisoners wore their own clothes, and could do normal things, like ironing and giving each other hairdos. An outsider looking at the women during recreation periods could well have imagined them to be residents of a women's hostel or a university hall of residence. One of the many pleasant young women I chatted with turned out to have taken part in beating another young woman to death with a brick, because the victim had taken to going out with a warder while her UDA husband was serving a sentence. As the fatal beating took place the victim's six-year-old daughter stood screaming outside a locked door.

But normalcy faded within the cells of the women on the Dirty Protest. The results of the menstrual cycle joined the faeces on the walls and sanitary towels lay about the corridors. Some of the girls had been on the no-wash protest for over three months, and much of their skin was covered in a brownish scaly substance. I met Mairead Farrell, the leader of the women prisoners. She was a sharply pretty, black-haired young woman, inclined to be propagandist and 'on message' where IRA policy was concerned. Unlike most of her colleagues, she had come from a middle-class family and had gone to an upper-crust school. She was teaching the other prisoners Irish. Like all the prisoners male or female, Mairead had a burning sense of injustice. 'We have been treated in a special way and tried by special courts because of the war, and because of our political activities, we want to be regarded as prisoners of war.'

Some years later, after the completion of Mairead's sentence, Mrs Thatcher's government accepted Mairead's analysis that she was 'in a war situation'. On 6 March 1988, in Gibraltar, she and two male companions were ambushed and shot dead by the SAS as they reconnoitred a target at which they apparently intended to plant a bomb.

Very few things in my life have stirred me as did the H-Block situation and, with the help of my treasured secretary, Eileen Davis, who gave her spare time to the project, I wrote a book about the issue called *On the Blanket*, which turned out to be the largest-selling paperback of its time and did a great deal to highlight the situation in Long Kesh. The book took something of a toll on me, because I had produced it between March and the first week of June 1980. During this time the normal demands of the *Irish Press* were being added to by the necessity of attending interminable, fractious meetings with the NUJ.

There is an old Irish phrase '*Tadh idir dhá thaob*', literally 'Tim between the two sides', meaning in effect someone who tries to give the appearance of being on both sides of an argument. The cock-eyed managerial system of the *Irish Press* meant that I was that soldier. On the one hand, as editor, I had to listen to all the special pleadings and defences of the indefensible put forward by union representatives, but on the other I became increasingly conscious that the one great power possessed by managements and not in the keeping of unions, that of initiative, was either not being exercised or if it was, was working in an inefficient and mean-spirited fashion. The experience left me with the settled conviction that, for all their deficiencies, trade unions are essential barriers standing between workers and those who would exploit them.

However, I was not to have much time that year for philosophical musing on the relationships between capitalism and labour. *On the Blanket* failed in its primary purpose: the hunger strike that Father Reid and the prisoners' families had feared broke out in the autumn. Outside the jails, fathers gave up drinking so as to devote all their energies to supporting their sons. Inside, the Dirty Protest was ended and a group of prisoners, led by Brendan 'Darky' Hughes, went on hunger strike.

As mentioned earlier, Charlie Haughey had succeeded Jack Lynch as Taoiseach and leader of Fianna Fail. One day, as I was sitting in Vivion de Valera's office in the throes of yet another interminable meeting about meetings, I got a call from the Taoiseach's office. It came from Pádraig O'hAnracháin, who was at the time both Haughey's guru and political strategist. On the day he rang me O'hAnrachain was serving his fourth Taoiseach. He had previously worked for de Valera, Lemass and Jack Lynch. He later told me that in many ways Haughey had the best brains of the four, which was a remarkable tribute to Haughey, because, coming from a constituency, Clare, that de Valera represented for a lifetime, Padraig had a special devotion to 'the Chief'.

O'hAnrachain's purpose in phoning me was to set up a meeting with

Haughey. When I reached Government Buildings, I found that the Taoiseach was worried about the hunger strikes, although he couched his
concerns in typically arrogant language: 'Look here, I want to put a stop
to this nonsense in the Six Counties.' At the time he was in the antechamber
of a deal with Margaret Thatcher that needs a word of explanation. The
deal was later successfully concluded, in Dublin Castle, in December 1980,
but Haughey completely oversold it as presaging an end to partition and
the gateway to a united Ireland. The communiqué issued after the agreement was signed had spoken about improved relationships and cooperation on all fronts. It contained a phrase, 'the totality of relationships',
which was hyped up to mean that the prime minister of England was
contemplating Dublin's speaking for Ireland North and South. Brian
Lenihan, the foreign minister, and close friend of Haughey's at the time,
said in the course of a radio discussion with me on BBC Northern Ireland
(on 22 March 1981) that the 'totality' phrase meant that there would be
a united Ireland in ten years' time. Far from withdrawing this inter-
pretation, he made it appear to be that of the cabinet by repeating it at a
subsequent press conference, thereby sending Paisley into a paroxysm of
rallies and protest meetings attended by upwards of 30,000 people at a
time.

In the Republic the phrase was assumed to have emanated from the
Irish side, but in fact it had been dreamt up by the British and put to
O'hAnrachain at a dinner given by the British ambassador some months
before the Dublin Castle negotiations took place. Of course the phrase did
contain resonances of a united Ireland – sometime – but as the British
generally, and Mrs Thatcher in particular, interpreted it, the term really
had more to do with a totally united front against the IRA, including
joining in the discarding of the rule book that had led to the hunger strikes.
When Mrs Thatcher met Haughey in London a few months after the
Lenihan interview, she inflicted what Irish diplomats described to me as
one of her vintage 'handbaggings' on him.

However, when Haughey met me two months before the Castle negotiation he was worried that his planned PR coup might be lost in the
fallout from Long Kesh. He wanted some good, first-hand information as
to what was going on. Was this a genuine hunger strike arising out of
matters of principle, or was it just an IRA publicity stunt? What sort of
support did it have amongst the nationalist community of the North? And
above all were the prisoners serious? Would they stick it out? Oh, and by
the way would I go up to Belfast and find the answers to these questions?

Haughey arranged with the British government that I be admitted to

Long Kesh to talk to the prisoners' leader, Brendan Hughes. The visit took a while to arrange because the Northern Ireland authorities were none too pleased with *On the Blanket*. But eventually, in the company of Danny Morrison, the Sinn Fein spin doctor *in excelsis*, I visited Long Kesh again and spoke with Hughes. By the time we met he had been without food for nearly a month. He was pale but still quite forceful and obviously a man of resolution. To keep our appointment, he had had to walk a huge expanse of corridors. We had been searched before being admitted to the room where we talked to Hughes, but I noticed that Morrison still managed to slip him a 'com', a communication written on cigarette paper. Hughes stressed, as had Father Reid, that the strike was not a publicity stunt directed from outside, but an expression of outrage on the part of the prisoners themselves at having what they regarded as their entitlements taken away from them. His attitude was akin to that of a trade unionist seeking to have hard-won conditions restored.

I found Long Kesh and the Hughes visit both depressing and disturbing. I don't know how Morrison bore up through that period and its aftermath. He visited the place almost every other day, but showed no signs of being emotionally affected and never missed a beat as he served up the Sinn Fein line on anything he was asked. Obviously two sets of tough, ruthless adversaries were going to war. A phrase I had heard in Vietnam occurred to me both then and subsequently: 'When elephants fight, it's the grass that gets trampled, and the people are the grass.' All the old clichés of the Anglo-Irish relationship of other days were coming back to life. Inside high walls, behind barbed wire, on red-brick streets, on windswept winter hillsides, anger was growing, body counts multiplying, as bitter men and women clashed again in a conflict of centuries. It was oversimplified and unnecessary, but it was real. Earlier in the year I had seen how prisoners had reduced their conflicts to the elemental: learning Irish by means of words tapped out on heating pipes and passed from cell to cell, which they then etched into their own excrement with the crucifixes of their rosary beads. Language, religion, shite. There was no doubt about the spirit that was seeping through the Catholic ghettos and into the isolated farmhouses of Fermanagh, Tyrone and South Armagh, where fertiliser bombs were being mixed with shovels, and plans were being set in train to shoot neighbours. Neighbours, let it be said, who were also hatching assassination plots with equal venom.

I reported to Haughey on all this and told him that in my view the strike was rooted in the prisoners' grievances and was not an IRA stunt directed from the outside, although it obviously had the potential to greatly benefit Sinn Fein. More to the point, it also had the potential to destabilise not merely the North but the Republic as well. From what I had seen of Hughes, and had been able to glean from various other sources, the prisoners were likely to fast to the death. Haughey was both moved and angered by my report. It accorded with what he had been hearing from other sources – he always tried to have differing sources of information, acting independently of each other, keeping him up to speed on any given situation. However, his efforts to mediate in the hunger strike struck me at the time as bearing a strong similarity to the tactics of the IRA leadership in the post-Feakle period leading up to the abolition of Special Category status and the building of the H-Blocks. Lured by the prospects of the Dublin Castle Agreement, he allowed the surface glamour and publicity of being in negotiation with the British government to blind him to the substance of the British attitude to the IRA.

On the surface, a breakthrough was achieved as Christmas 1980 approached. The deal centred on issuing the prisoners with 'civilian-type clothing' – i.e. tracksuits. The strike would end and normal cooperation with the prison staff in the running of the prison, over matters such as taking showers, etc., would resume. The prisoners were anxious to accept these terms because one of the seven hunger-strikers, Sean McKenna, appeared to be weakening. McKenna's father had been one of those 'lifted' during the internment swoops of 1971 and he never recovered from the 'deep interrogation' treatment he received at the time. McKenna Junior had become an active IRA man and was operating from a base south of the border when one night he was kidnapped by an SAS snatch squad and brought back across the border to a dose of the same treatment meted out to his father. He fetched up in Long Kesh and at the time of going on the hunger strike appeared to regard the prospect of death with indifference.

However, by the time the strike had reached its forty-eighth day his condition had severely worsened. He went blind and began to show signs of psychological as well as physical deterioration. He started to express fears of dying, though he gave no indication of wishing to end the hunger strike. One of the reasons the British gave Haughey for not conceding the five demands was McKenna's condition. It was said that at any moment he would break and the whole strike would collapse. By way of hastening the collapse, on 18 December McKenna was suddenly transferred to a military hospital away from the prison and the support of his hunger-striking comrades. At the same time the prisoners were informed, by a trusted intermediary between themselves, Dublin and London, Father Brendan Meagher, a Redemptorist priest, that a document from the Foreign

Office was on its way to them. It appeared that the document could contain settlement terms.

This placed the leader of the hunger strike, Brendan Hughes, in a terrible dilemma. He was suffering himself and fully understood the health implications for McKenna. If he waited until the document arrived and began a process of consultation, McKenna, whom he now could not contact, could be dead before the consultations finished. Yet if the document met the prisoners' conditions, McKenna would have died for nothing. Accordingly Hughes called off the strike. But when the thirty-four page document did arrive, it turned out to be couched in vague diplomatic language that spoke only of what might occur after the strike ended. Disappointing as this was, however, the prisoners could take comfort from a statement in the House of Commons by Humphrey Atkins, the secretary of state for Northern Ireland, that if the prisoners called off their strike, they would 'get clothes provided by their families'. Perhaps a formula acceptable to both sides had been found? Certainly the news of the hunger strike's ending, especially coming in the mouth of Christmas, was greeted with tremendous rejoicing on both sides of the border. Both the Conservatives and Haughey claimed the settlement was a win for their side.

However, on Christmas Day Father Meagher called to my home for what should have been a festive toast, but as we reviewed the situation, neither of us felt any optimism. For the previous couple of months Meagher had lived through a set of unimaginably nerve-racking encounters between the Northern authorities, Dublin and the prisoners, which had earned him an affectionate nickname from the IRA, 'an Sagart Mait', 'the Good Priest'. One would have expected him to be euphoric at the strike's ending, but in fact he was profoundly pessimistic. He thought that the 'deal' was a chimera. The prisoners were not going to get their Five Demands. And so it proved.

The issue came to a head towards the end of January 1981. Both the hunger strike and the Dirty Protest had ended and the prisoners believed that if they took the final step of going ahead with washing and shaving in the normal way, they would then be given the 'civilian-type clothing'. The clothes were brought to the prison but the prisoners were not allowed to wear them. Another hunger strike was decided upon. This time the strikers were picked with great care both as to their character and their geographical origin, one from each of the Six Counties. Nobody was selected for the strike who might be tempted to come off it before death ended their protest. The PLO was contacted for information about the effects of hunger-striking on some of its members. Thus when the second strike began, the IRA was far better prepared than on the first occasion, and the result changed Irish history.

The strike began on 1 March 1981 when the prisoners' leader, Bobby Sands, refused food. In all the strike was to last for 217 days, with prisoners joining in at various stages between March and 3 October, when the strike was officially called off. By then ten hunger-strikers had died. These included Sands, who was elected to the Westminster constituency of Fermanagh South Tyrone in a by-election. His success, and the sight of the crowds that attended the hunger-strikers' funerals – in some cases over a hundred thousand people attended – combined with Sinn Fein anger at Haughey's ineffectual diplomacy during the strike, resulted in H-Block candidates being put up in the Republic also when Haughey called an unexpected general election in June 1981.

By then Haughey had not one but two albatrosses dangling from his neck. One was his supposedly historic breakthrough agreement with Margaret Thatcher, which appears to have been a determining factor in his attitude to the British government. Publicly there was no condemnation of Thatcher's determination that Airey Neave should be avenged under the cloak of 'crime is crime' and perseverance with the 'criminalisation' policy. Whether or not a public strong line with Thatcher would have made a difference to the hunger strikes' ending is a moot point. Certainly Haughey did seek privately to have a Portlaoise-type solution applied, but unsubstantiated rumours grew that, apart from his Dublin Castle Agreement problem, the British had something in their files that prevented him from speaking out.

The other albatross was the Stardust fire. This appalling catastrophe occurred in Haughey's own constituency at the Stardust Ballroom on a February night while delegates were gathering in Dublin for the holding of the Fianna Fail Ard Fheis the next day. In all forty-eight young people were burned to death and many more injured. The Ard Fheis was postponed. Over the next few days news of the horrific injuries sustained by those who survived circulated throughout the country, mingling with rumours and speculation as to what influences had been brought to bear to allow safety doors to be locked and bars to be fitted over windows, so that escape routes were blocked. As readers will have realised by now, by the time the fire occurred I had had some experience in visiting prisons. When I visited the ballroom some months after the tragedy, the bars on the window struck me as being more suitable for penal institutions than for a young people's disco. However, sometime after the ballroom had reopened again a reader phoned me to enquire whether I would 'have the balls to print the picture'. The picture in question was of a padlock and chain reaffixed to the safety doors. It duly appeared on page one of the *Irish Press*.

No prosecutions were ever brought as a result of the Stardust deaths, but in the wake of the fire Haughey's sense of judgement appears to have deserted him. And, with the economic situation deteriorating, he called a general election before he had to. Sands's success had given Sinn Fein a taste for electioneering and the Party put up ten H-Block candidates. In all they secured 10 per cent of the vote, largely at Fianna Fail's expense, and two of the 'blanket men' were elected. One of them, Ciaran Doherty, thus became the first Dail deputy to die on hunger strike since independence. The immediate result of the election was the replacement of Haughey as Taoiseach by Garret FitzGerald, but the long-term impact, particularly in the North, was something akin to the change in public opinion towards militant republicanism brought by the 1916 Rising. It would be thirteen years into the future before the IRA called a ceasefire, but Sinn Fein were on the way, both north and south of the border.

CHAPTER 13

Aran Interludes

Throughout these turbulent events I did not have time for introspection, interludes for examination of self or consideration of the future, never mind question the present, speculate about choices or try to do something else with my life. Fate had assigned me certain roles and I played them, certainly not perfectly, but as best I could. I did what I could to maintain family life. Our family grew and Cherry and I were soon the proud parents of six children. At the best of times a night worker's job makes family life hard. Being a newspaper editor makes it harder still. My phone at home rang continuously during the daytime, and there were always things to attend to long before I actually set out for the office. One of the factors that affect an editor's role are what Ben Bradley, the *Washington Post's* editor, termed 'the guilts', the feeling that no matter whether you are on or off duty, sick or on holidays, whatever is happening in the world it is somehow your responsibility to oversee its coverage. Shortly after my taking over, one of the assistant editors, Arthur Hunter, reached retiring age and I arranged a party for him. In his farewell speech he said something that abided with me for the rest of my years in the *Press*: 'I spent the last thirty-five years of my life worrying about things – most of which never happened.' The outbreak of the Troubles added to my collateral damage in terms of both family and peace of mind.

Yet even before the Troubles, events outside my control had a way of exploding into some planned moment of tranquillity. For example, I had planned to take the older children away for a week-long horse-drawn caravan holiday in County Cork in the summer after I was appointed. On the eve of setting off Bobby Kennedy was shot. The week was a classic example of the split-level syndrome. On one level I would subsequently always remember the joys of sitting around an open fire at night with the three eldest girls, Thomond, Jackie and Olwen, who either sang or recited poetry. During the day they made friends for us wherever we stopped. Three children provide better social contacts than their weight in bottles of whiskey. In fact one pub owner in Millstreet, County Cork, closed the pub early and brought us, and some neighbours, up to the living room, where the woman of the house played the piano and the convivial group enjoyed both the whiskey and the singing. Appropriately enough, the next day who should pull up alongside the caravan for a chat but the great Irish composer Sean O'Riada.

But on the other level the distracting effect of the unfortunate Bobby Kennedy's fate was emphasised for me on the first morning of the horse-drawn caravan trip. We had spent the night camped in a field owned by two elderly bachelor farmers. As we rumbled off down a lovely, leafy boreen, dappled at intervals by the shadows cast by overhanging trees, I heard somebody calling and pulled up. Behind me was one of the old farmers hobbling awkwardly and waving his stick as he called out: 'Your man's gone! Your man's gone!' Bobby Kennedy was dead. And for the rest of the week I worried about being away from the office as the funeral took place, although of more immediate import was the fact that the holiday nearly resulted in my attending my own funeral.

For our hired horse Charlie turned out to be a) not a horse but a mare, and b) in oestrus. This only emerged as we drove into an ancient convent under a long archway over cobblestones. The sound of the wheels on the cobblestones was magnified by the walls. The already skittish Charlie was spooked and suddenly jumped forward, pulling me off my driver's perch. But somehow I managed to land on my feet and continue holding the reins. I was hauled along in Charlie's wake, acutely conscious that if I didn't keep hold of the reins and at the same time avoid being crushed against the wall by the caravan, then the three children would be killed. I eventually brought Charlie to a halt with nothing worse to show for the incident than a smashed plank on one side of the caravan and indignation on the part of the children. They wanted to know why I had frightened them by jumping off the caravan so quickly!

I don't know whether the Cork air had something to do with it, but incredibly enough Charlie's replacement was apparently also in oestrus. On the night of her arrival the mare managed to clear a huge hedge and made off towards a stallion some five miles away. She was discovered thanks to some excellent detective work by the local Garda sergeant. He guessed where the mare was to be found after taking one look at the track of churned-up earth that the frenzied animal had left behind as she galloped around the field before escaping.

Our third horse conformed to its trade description and the rest of the trip was incident-free apart from a revolt against my cooking by the children. It was sparked by the fact that they discovered that what I had told them was peas and chicken was in fact peas and a couple of hares that someone had given me.

For most of my time as editor the place in which I sought to avoid life's turmoil was the Aran Islands. They formed a background to my own life and that of the family, a place of great beauty, antiquity, enjoyment and refuge. At the time of our first visit there was no electricity and bottled-gas lighting had not been introduced to all the houses. Clerical domination still prevailed. The parish priest visited one local woman a few hours after she had given birth to a child out of wedlock and told her she was in mortal sin. This opinion was so widely respected that, when I first made the woman's acquaintance, the child, then four years old, was still not allowed outside the garden wall. Nor did this deeply pious islander dare to brave the gauntlet of squinting windows by attending Sunday mass.

The pace of life changed slowly. I once took a Ford Escort car onto the island when the children were small, and discovered that I could pack them all into the boot. They used to enjoy the experience hugely, waving at passers-by and singing at the top of their lungs as we cruised slowly from Killeany to Kilronan. Those days are gone, alas. In summer there is so much tourist traffic that one has to think twice about driving by oneself, never mind stuffing children into a car boot. Moreover, although the roads at the time of writing are just as narrow and winding as they were when I first set eyes on the place, nevertheless some bureaucrat has decided that as we're in the EU, European road signs have to be erected, advising drivers that speed limits of eighty kilometres per hour are in force! A far cry from the days when the now thriving Aer Arann first started operations. Then we did not need signs. All one had to do was glance at what in those days was the grassy airstrip. If the donkeys were grazing on the airstrip, it meant no flights were due. If there were no donkeys to be seen, it meant a flight was due and that the donkeys had been temporarily driven off by Colie Hernon, a wonderful man, who, in addition to perennial (unpaid) negotiations with the authorities aimed at improving the island's facilities, was the coxswain of the lifeboat and also ran the airport.

After my initial encounter with currachs I learned how to row the craft properly and had one built for me on Inisheer by a master craftsman, Michael Tom Andy Conneely, whose tools consisted of a handsaw and a sharp axe. He used the axe for both smoothing rough edges and driving nails. The seats of the currach were attached to the thwarts by pieces of twisted fuchsia bush. Rowing off the islands in calm summer weather was one of life's more pleasurable experiences. In those days, before Norwegian harpooners slaughtered them, the seas abounded with basking sharks. I remember rowing up to one of the huge, harmless creatures and unsuccessfully attempting to get the children to follow my example by touching it. Aran nights, when the light never completely faded, and every dip of the oars brought up a coating of phosphorescence, were also incredibly beautiful.

The sea by day brought its own rewards. I used to tell the children that if we followed the path of sunlight on the water, it would lead us to Tir na nÓg, the land of youth. But it was from age that the most tangible rewards came. Two of the old Killeany fishermen, Peter Donoghue and Anthony O'Brien, each of whom could sing Sean-Nós songs containing seventy or eighty verses, also had an incredible stock of lore about fishing grounds. Neither of them knew anything about trigonometry, but they could triangulate a fishing ground with pinpoint accuracy: 'You get the An Dun [fort] down on the point there in line with Tommy Hernon's house, and then you get the white rock open' was the sort of instruction which, if followed properly, could yield a box or two of fish. They showed me how to make up a long line, and how to shoot 'trammel nets'. Sometimes when I returned to Killeany Harbour after a day's fishing, my catch was large enough to feed several families. There would always be children from the village waiting for my arrival. The only place where I wasn't all that welcome was at home. I remember one evening returning to great acclamation from the villagers because I had succeeded in catching, amongst other things, a box of turbot on the long line. Cherry, however, took one look at the boxes, which I, the children and some friends had breathlessly hauled up the hill to our house, and enquired: 'Are those things cleaned out?!' Those turbot taught me that the basis of good fish cookery lies in the possession of sharp knives.

They also contributed to my deepening regret over the thirty-five years that have passed since Ireland entered Europe at the failure to develop the Irish fishing industry. The fertile Irish seas were exploited by the French, the Dutch and the Spaniards, as in effect we traded the mackerel for the bullock. The farming lobby guaranteed that agricultural interests benefited enormously, but the potential for developing marine interests was squandered, along with the advantages conferred by the climate for growing trees. Ironically, climate change, along with the reforms to the Common Agricultural Policy, may yet see bare Aran, and indeed the mainland, once more clothed in forest, but it is doubtful if the fish stocks of the plundered Irish Sea can be regenerated.

Several years later, when the children were much older, Aran also taught me that a boat can sometimes be more dangerous on land than on sea. I graduated from currachs to a beautiful, small mahogany yacht with red sails which, for reasons better imagined than described, I christened *Cherry's Bane*. One day the mast broke, a seemingly irreparable loss on the island at the time. But in the pub that night Colie Hernon suggested a possible solution. There were some spare electricity poles at the airstrip. Perhaps one of them could be converted into a replacement mast? Within minutes the loan of a tractor was organised, along with a team of volunteers to lift the heavy pole. The pub was emptying as we drove from the airstrip. One of the patrons, Joe O'Brien, like his father, Anthony, a famous fisherman and traditional singer, called out: 'Well, you won't break *that* anyway!'

We brought the pole into the workshop of the island school. My daughter Olwen had by this time married and her husband, Michael Gill (now the principal), taught carpentry, and, using a circular saw, attempted to pare down the pole. After about an hour we had accumulated a pile of shavings some six feet high, but the wretched pole showed little sign of conforming to the yacht's requirements. Then there was a loud bang, a flash, and the fusebox blew. Defeated, we withdrew, leaving behind one somewhat attenuated electricity pole and a pile of heavily creosoted shavings for Michael to explain to the then principal when the school opened.

The family fell so deeply in love with Aran that it was hard to get them off it. As well as Olwen, my daughter Rachel was also to marry an Aran man, Michael Connealy, and good husbands and fathers both Michaels turned out to be.

To ensure that the girls did not encounter any of my difficulties with the language, when they were young I enrolled them in an all-Irish primary school, Scoil Lorcáin, in Monkstown, County Dublin. The school principal, Bean Uí Chadhain, was not alone the wife of the famous writer in Irish Máirtín Ó'Cadhain, professor of Irish at Trinity College, she was also regarded by UNESCO as one of the world's experts on the teaching of a language that was not the language of the home. As a result the children learned to play in Irish rather than toil in it and grew up viewing it in its proper context, part of an ancient cultural tapestry into which were woven things like dancing, singing and a lusty enjoyment of life.

The school conferred some ancillary benefits for the girls, which I only realised one day when I found Thomond, Jackie and Olwen 'dressing up' as I thought. In fact they were trying out the dresses they would wear the following Saturday when they acted as bridesmaids for one of their teachers, an inconceivably different circumstance to that prevailing at the time in Church-run schools, which banned the employment of married women. As they spoke Irish, a custom sprang up whereby after Easter they would remain in Aran and go to school there for the summer term. One summer they all stayed on for so long that in order to get the girls ready for boarding school I had to go round the shops in Dublin myself ordering uniforms and guessing at their measurements.

Over the years we rented a number of houses on the island. The most beautifully situated of these was the Lodge. It commanded one of the great views of Western Europe, overlooking Killeany Bay and the North Sound, beyond which loomed the mountains of Connemara. However, the old lady who owned the Lodge, Katie McDonagh, would only agree to lease it, not sell it. 'We are McDonaghs,' she said. 'We don't sell, we buy.'

In fact she did sell quite a lot – of alcohol. Her pub in Kilronan was the largest on the island. Here she held court with her equally spinsterish but less dominant sister, Mary Anne. Over the years Katie had added to the considerable properties she inherited by allowing islanders to run up 'slates' with her. When she judged the time appropriate, she would strike like an expert angler. Reeling in her catch, she would announce the extent of her victim's indebtedness, always far more than the – generally hung-over – unfortunate had realised, and in the same breath assure him that he need not worry: 'Sure I'll just take that ould bit of a crag you have over by Mannister,' and so yet another potentially valuable building site or piece of farmland would be deeded over to the angular little lady with the bun, the knitting needles and the ever-present copy of the *Irish Rosary*.

The Lodge's previous occupants had included a landlord's agent, whose rent-collecting zeal caused him to be frequently attacked by Irish MPs in the House of Commons, and the writers Somerville and Ross, who amongst other works created *Some Experiences of an Irish R.M.* Somewhere along the line the activities of various tenants gave rise to stories of the place being haunted. But I, and all the family, have the happiest memories of it, never encountering anything more ghostly than the creaking of floors and the rattling of windows as Atlantic gales howled. I found the Lodge as fruitful a place for writing as it was idyllic for holidays, particularly so in winter, during nights when my only company was the mice, and one rat in particular, who emerged under the flag floor of the kitchen to nibble the crumbs I fed him. As the winds shrieked outside I would tell myself: You'll either come out of this with alcoholism or manuscript. I think I can claim that manuscript won – by a short head.

In the spring and summer months the Lodge was a paradise. Approximately a mile behind the house, on the western, cliff-guarded side of the island, there lay a low plateau of rock, pitted by the action of the sea and by boulders swirling round in rocky holes. Over the centuries these holes became quite sizeable, and the patch of rock was known as *Datha snámh* (swimming place). Here one could (and can) luxuriate in pools of water warmed by the sun as, on three sides of the plateau, Atlantic breakers crashed against the cliffs.

About two miles to the east of the Lodge lies the Gregory Sound, which separates Inishmore from Inishmaan, the middle island. In fine weather the Inishmaan cliffs shine with green lichens and the sea gently deposits white feathers of foam along the base of the cliff face, but when it turns bad, huge waves crash against the limestone cliffs of the island's breastplate in terrifying fashion.

On the southern corner of Inishmore, at a place called the Glassan Rocks, one can climb down the cliffs to fish in the Gregory Sound from another plateau of rock about fifty metres long and twenty-five wide. In those halcyon days, before the seas around Ireland were so disgracefully denuded of fish, the place was an angler's paradise. I will always remember one sparkling morning of champagne sea and calling seabirds when Thomond caught her first mackerel. I had earlier had a swim from the rocks using an old pair of ragged underpants as swimming trunks. Deciding that these were not worth bringing home with me – and were eminently biodegradable – I had tossed them into the cove alongside the plateau. Later, I noticed vaguely, out of the corner of my eye, that they seemed to float on the water for over an hour, rising and falling with the swell. However, I had better things to concentrate on than an old pair of Y-fronts. The sea teemed with life. I was fishing with a spinning rod and a set of feathers and, along with mackerel and pollock, I frequently foul-hooked small eels, known as 'bells', about twice the size of the sand eels one finds digging along the shore. Shoals of pilchards passed along the rocks splashing on top of the water, and in a large funnel etched into the rock on the side of the cove where I had ditched my underpants we could see a shoal of pollock extending down into the deep as far as the eye could see. I remember thinking as I handed the rod to Thomond, having first cast it out, so that she would not snag herself on one of the six-feathered hooks, that the pollock reminded me of sheep being herded into a pen by a collie.

Thomond suddenly found the rod spring to life as mackerel struck, exclaiming her excitement in both Irish and English. At the same moment I suddenly realised how apt the collie simile was. There, rising and falling with the tide only a few feet from the low plateau on which we stood, were my Y-fronts – the gills of a porbeagle shark finning gently alongside our fishing perch.

After leaving the Glassan Rocks rather precipitously, we headed for Fitzpatrick's pub in Killeany, where I used to run a slate, the consequences of which generally did more to dampen my mood at the end of the summer when I settled my reckoning than did the approach of winter. One of the contributory factors to the total was the children's custom of ordering themselves another Coke, potato crisps, chocolate or whatever, saying: 'But, Da, you've had another so why can't we?' Try arguing with *that* when you're dealing with six children and the various companions that kids on holidays invariably pick up.

Alas, the futility of arguing with my own offspring was to prove to be as nothing compared with tackling that of Vivion de Valera, specifically his son Eamon. For, in what I consider to be one of the worst misjudgements in Irish newspaper history, Vivion handed over control of the Irish Press Group to Eamon.

CHAPTER 14

Birth and Debt of
the *Irish Press*

During a tour of the US at the height of the Anglo-Irish War de Valera collected in excess of $5 million in a bond drive intended to help in the securing of Irish independence. This sum, a large amount in those days, was to be repaid 'one month after the Republic has received international recognition and the British forces have been withdrawn'. The *Wall Street Journal* said that many of the subscriptions came from 'Irish domestic servants, and others of like or lower standards of intelligence'. No one has ever been able to explain why de Valera left some 60 per cent of this money behind him, lying in New York banks, when he returned to Ireland at Christmas 1920. But there it lay until 1927. Then, following a legal battle between de Valera and the Irish government over control of the cash, a New York court ruled that as the parties could not agree, the money should be returned to the bond-holders. De Valera's legal advisers had anticipated this decision and he had made preparations for it. The bond-holders were circulated with documents asking them to sign over their holdings to him for use in setting up an institution that Ireland was badly in need of – a national daily newspaper.

Despite the costs of the legal action there was enough left in the kitty to pay back the bond-holders 58 cents in the dollar. The circulars yielded valuable assistance to de Valera's fund-raising activities and helped to ensure that he got his hands on sufficient money to launch the paper in 1931. It proved to be the most effective Irish journal of the century, and was generally agreed to be the main reason why the following year de Valera became the president of the Executive Council, in effect the prime minister. It was also a major factor in his ceasing to be prime minister in 1959. Dr Noël Browne revealed in the Dail that though de Valera frequently proclaimed that he received no benefit from the paper, he was in fact a major shareholder, as was his son Vivion. His holdings gave him and his family great political and financial strength, but as the shares were not publicly quoted, and at the time paid no dividend, ordinary shareholders were deprived of their value. Ageing and blind, already under pressure to resign because of the bad economic circumstances of the time, Browne's damaging revelations tilted the political balance so that resignation became inevitable. He had also handed over control of the Irish Press plc to his two sons, Vivion and Terry. Typically, even this handover was subjected to a *divide et impera* approach. Vivion got control of the ordinary shares, and of half of the 200 B shares in the Delaware Corporation in America, which carried voting rights. The other hundred went to Terry. What practically no one in Ireland realised at the time was that the Delaware holding was key because the American company was the vehicle through which de Valera controlled the Irish operation.

In his heyday de Valera had placed such importance on the paper that, as one authority has noted, 'For a period in the early 1930s he entrusted most of the responsibility for directing Fianna Fail to others while he was engaged in making the *Irish Press* a successful enterprise.'[4] But the start-up costs were high, and as the circulation soared, so did the bills. Once more de Valera had recourse to the bonds. But this time his target was not the Irish-American domestics of 'low intelligence'; it was the Irish taxpayer.

In a nutshell he used his Dail majority to force through a measure legalising the payment to the bond-holders of the 42 per cent of the monies still outstanding after the payout ordered by the New York court. In addition to this percentage he also decreed that a 25 per cent premium be paid. The total cost of £1.5 million has been estimated at being worth more than €100 million at the time of writing. As a result of the Dail vote de Valera received some £100,000. The opposition was well aware of what he was doing, and mounted a ferocious attack on his ruse, but he had the numbers and he put the measure through, denying as he did so that he was the owner of the *Irish Press*. He said: 'It belongs to the proprietors, who are the Irish people.'

At the time he said this de Valera was the controlling director, as would be his son Vivion and grandson Eamon de Valera. The articles of association of the company say that:

> The controlling director shall have sole and absolute control of the public and political policy of the company and of the editorial management thereof and of all newspapers, pamphlets or other writings which may be from time to time owned, published, circulated or printed by the said company.

[4] Patrick Murray, 'Obsessive historian: Eamon de Valera and the policing of his reputation', *Proceedings of the Royal Irish Academy*, Vol. 101C, pp.37–65 (2001).

But from an editor's perspective the real meat and potatoes were contained in the next paragraph:

> The controlling director can: appoint, and at his discretion, remove or suspend all editors, sub-editors, reporters, writers, contributors, or news and information, and all such other persons as may be employed in or connected with the editorial department, and may determine their duties and fix their salaries and emoluments.

After the *Irish Times* had converted itself into a trust, and Vivion was visibly getting older, I, in my innocence, sometimes tried to suggest that perhaps some thought should be given to the paper's future. Vivion's stock reply was: 'Sure we are the *real* trust.' What he did not say was that he was planning to discharge that trust by installing his son Eamon as controlling director.

Newspapers unfortunately are like any other form of property; they don't have a say in who inherits them. As his father had been generally known as 'the Major', Eamon was nicknamed 'Major Minor', a pretty apt title as matters turned out. One might have ascribed various descriptive terms to him, but 'presence' was not one of them. When he first started coming into my office, he was almost painfully thin, so much so that I thought he looked like a bespectacled stick insect in a pinstriped suit. At the time he had a disconcerting habit of rocking backwards and forwards on his seat when he spoke while emitting unnerving bursts of high-pitched laughter. Initially, however, I was misguided enough to feel protective towards him. His mother had died while he and his only sister were children. As a result a significant portion of his formative years was spent in the company of his octogenarian and nonagenarian grandfather and grandmother in Áras an Uachtárain, the presidential residence. When Eamon first joined the group, Vivion entrusted him to me to show him the journalistic ropes. However, he soon discovered the strongly proprietorial instinct exhibited by both his father and grandfather before him.

Prior to arriving in Burgh Quay full-time, Eamon had virtually no experience of the newspaper world. Vivion had been associated with the paper almost from its inception and he had undergone various pieces of immersion therapy in the newspaper industry such as spending time with the London *Daily Express* to see how a newspaper was produced. In fact when he had come to rebuild the Burgh Quay premises, he had remodelled them on the glass-fronted *Express* building in Fleet Street. But Eamon's only job of significance had been with the Cement Roadstone Company, run by a neighbour and friend of Vivion's, Tom Roche. This was hardly the ideal background for an arrival in the newspaper world in the highly charged atmosphere, both journalistically and politically, of the hunger-strike era – to say nothing of arriving in a newspaper company in which complex modernisation and investment were long overdue. But after Vivion's death in 1982 Eamon, like Vivion, became the newspaper equivalent of the Holy Trinity, that is editor in chief, controlling director and managing director. The title for which he appeared to have most aptitude was the Ghost; one did not have to be a member of Mensa to foresee trouble ahead.

Things became so bad that what should be an absolutely spinal function of any newspaper, the daily conference, became a charade. Ideally a daily newspaper should have two sets of conferences: one around midday to review the previous day's edition and lay down lines of coverage for what is known of forthcoming events, and another later in the afternoon, with of course regular communication between the newsroom and the paper's senior executives about breaking news. Our one conference was held at 6 p.m. There was no midday conference, and what we did have effectively consisted of the news editor reading out a list of the stories already entered in the news diary and the latest RTE news headlines, and we went through a pro forma discussion on the sports, financial and feature content, which was also largely predetermined.

If anybody had any bright ideas for additional coverage, they immediately encountered the problem of finding a reporter to cover the story. The *Irish Press* did not have a newsroom staff of its own and had to rely on the handful of the group's reporters rostered on duty that night. Things were so pared to the bone that most efforts at investigative reporting were a waste of time. Mostly the news coverage was a revamped version of what had already appeared in the *Evening Press*, with reporters or subeditors adding whatever new developments they were aware of to the 'black' – i.e. the carbon copy. David Marcus left to become a full-time writer and publisher and I took over the duties of literary editor. Apart from these tasks I wrote editorials and contributed a weekly column on a Saturday in a vain effort to give our sixteen-page paper something of a competitive edge over rivals who contained several featured columnists in editions more than double our size.

One of the things that made Major Minor difficult to deal with was his belief in his own abilities. Once, while I was trying to redesign the paper, with a view to relaunching it after yet another strike, he told me that he was the only person in the firm that really understood the new technology. He was over-reliant on the opinions of pollsters and such. When I suggested to him that we should develop a publishing arm based on the 'New Irish Writing' feature, he cited some expert's finding to prove that it wouldn't be worth the investment. David Marcus in fact helped to establish the successful publishing firm Poolbeg Press, called after Poolbeg Street, behind the *Press*, which housed David's favourite bookie. Nor did Eamon agree with me that there was any worthwhile revenue to be had from the *Press* developing a radio station. 'We' (a word he used a lot) had discovered that some expert or other could prove that there was no money in radio stations. However, after he married a Tipperary woman this argument seemed to have lost force because he then proceeded to invest in a Tipperary radio station. The Tipperary venture was a success, unlike the purchase of a suburban newspaper, *Southside*, which went into liquidation in 1987.

I naturally resented money that could have gone into developing the *Irish Press* being diverted to *Southside*. But to add insult to injury, somebody connected with *Southside* attempted to conceal the thousands of unsold copies by dumping them in the undergrowth of an open space in front of my house! Eamon also set up focus groups to find out why people were not buying the *Irish Press*. These produced nothing that I had not been telling him all along. The paper wasn't keeping pace with the times in terms of expanding coverage or promotion. Most city people just didn't see the paper, although their fathers may have read it devotedly.

What kept the paper going was a combination of tradition and its excellence as a digest of the news of the day. The skills of the group's reporters and sub-editors meant that the paper, against all odds, remained one of the country's best methods of keeping up with the news. If the paper was made available to people, they tended to like it. I succeeded in persuading Eamon to run an experiment in the suburbs of Clontarf and Blackrock whereby the *Irish Press* was delivered free to a number of households for a couple of weeks. The number of people who continued to buy the paper after the giveaway period elapsed was quite encouraging, but despite this evidence of potential growth Eamon pressed on with his surveys. Apart from the fact that such exercises can be used to produce any answer one wants, life is just not that simple. I warned Eamon that if simply hiring pollsters was the way to newspaper success, then one would soon become unable to cross O'Connell Bridge because of the great number of publishers shoaling along the thoroughfare.

Even now the thought of having to relive the follies that passed for industrial relations puts up my blood pressure. You literally never knew when something was going to occur that would prevent the paper appearing. I remember two occasions involving Galway city vividly. In one I had been giving a talk in the university and asked for a copy of the paper at breakfast the next day. The waitress blithely informed me that on her way to work she had heard on the news that the *Irish Press* was on strike. All had been tranquil when I left the office the previous afternoon, but apparently, later in the evening, some long-threatening storm had burst over the printers. When I rang to find out what had happened, I was informed that there was 'a meeting' in progress. I came to hate those two words above all others in the English language. The amount of managerial and editorial time that was wasted in meetings was colossal. The human resource activity of the company reminded me of the men in white coats one used to see at greyhound races going around shovelling up the dogs' droppings after a race had ended.

The second Galway incident occurred one afternoon as I was crossing Eyre Square. A taxi driver, recognising me from television, hailed me to draw my attention to his morning's work. He had been delivering the *Irish Press* to various newsagents all the way out along the Clare–Galway coast through Kinvara and as far as Doolin in County Clare. He showed me the times at which he had dropped off bundles of papers at the various stops. They began shortly before nine that morning and ended not long before I met him. The paper had been so late in printing that by the time it arrived at the major Galway distribution point, the lorries of the factors who distributed the Dublin and English papers were long gone and taxis had to be employed. The taxi man, who knew something about the cost of getting the papers from Dublin in the first place, showed me his bill, made a calculation as to those of others like him, and enquired: 'Jaysus, Tim Pat, how can youse stick it?' The answer of course was that we could not, no business could.

The conventional wisdom at this stage (mid-1980s) was that the answer to our difficulties was 'the new technology', computerised setting that did away with the services of a number of trades including printers and stereotypers. Alas, the presumed gains of introducing the computers were offset by the losses occasioned by bad industrial relations. Alone of all the Irish national papers, the Irish Press Group managed to generate a damaging strike over the introduction of new technology and all the papers were off the streets for some weeks. I only discovered that the *Irish Press* was not being restored at the same time as the other two publications by accident when I opened the door of what I thought was an empty office and found Eamon de Valera briefing the staffs of the *Evening* and *Sunday Press* on their papers' reappearance. I was stunned. It appeared to me that the *Irish Press* had gone from being the flagship of the group to hind-tit status. But I couldn't voice my anger in front of the staffs of the other papers because the effect on the morale of the *Irish Press* team would have been shattering. As matters turned out, it was shattering anyhow, because the arrangements with the printers did not cater for the extra work involved in bringing out the *Irish Press*. Consequently, when it did reappear, not alone did the *Irish Press* habitually go to press late, there was a damaging knock-on effect on the other publications also.

The theory behind the evolution from hot metal to photosetting was that everyone was equal, the halt, the infirm and the blind, or at least the near-blind. In order to prepare for the return of the *Irish Press*, it was decided that I should redesign the paper's layout and typeface. The man who was assigned to me for the delicate task of cutting up the proofs with a scalpel and then pasting them into place on a make-up easel was an ex-linotype operator who had received little or no training in page make-up.

'Go easy on me, Tim Pat,' he said, 'The ould sight's not too good. I'm going into hospital next week to have two cataracts removed!' In his nervousness, the poor fellow subsequently underlined the force of this statement by accidentally allowing his scalpel to shoot from his grasp. It embedded itself in the band of my watchstrap. It was fortunate it did so, otherwise the scalpel could very easily have cut an artery. The presumption that all operatives were equal inevitably resulted in some of the best people taking their packages and departing. Those who stayed were supposed to have jettisoned the old skills of a lifetime and acquired new ones in a matter of days. It was like asking a grandparent who could barely master the intricacies of the TV zapper to become a PlayStation expert overnight.

These sorts of miscalculations and blunders played a large role in closing down the group, but they were not solely responsible. Inevitably the climate of disorganisation and uncertain chains of command produced a general lowering of standards. The *Irish Press*'s duty of care towards the public, as well as to its own reputation, was gravely neglected. The paper was organised on the basis that the 'back desk', where the assistant editors sat, received proofs of its content well in advance of its being published, so that errors, or potential libels, could be spotted and corrected. But in fact the back-desk arrangement became increasingly irrelevant as mounting deadline pressure and unsatisfactory agreements with the typesetters between them caused much of the editorial content to go straight into the paper unread and uncorrected. The various works departments were uncoordinated. There was no managerial figure on duty in Burgh Quay at night with overall responsibility for the activities of vital but com-partmented works departments – the case room, the stereotype, the printing presses, the transport fleet and the dispatch department that made up the newspaper bundles for their destinations.

The absence of overall executive control made way for a spectacular example of botched communication during one of the 'heaves' against Charlie Haughey's leadership. It was arranged that two pages detailing his career would be preset, complete with pictures, and then kept separate to run should news of his departure come at short notice. But somehow the 'keep separate' stipulation did not travel down the line. By a ghastly application of Murphy's Law (if it can go wrong, it will, and once it does, it will only get worse) not merely were the two pages prepared in the lull after the country edition, but some 16,000 copies of the city edition appeared with 'Charlie's obituary' included.

Libel suits began to increase and typographical errors and spelling mistakes proliferated, even infecting the leading article column, a glaring and shameful public acknowledgement of a lack of respect even for the tabernacle containing the paper's values. Instead of attempting to compete with the services offered by the other papers, there were cutbacks. Every aspect of coverage was affected, from foreign news to drama criticism. In near-despair I suggested to Eamon one day that what he and the company needed was a couple of people with proven media track records, as well as business acumen, on the board of directors. I suggested Tom Hardiman, who had been director general of RTE, and was at the time a director of Ulster Bank, and Michael Fingleton, who had built up the vastly profitable Irish Nationwide Building Society, partly through his ability to attract media coverage. There was a long silence, which I was beginning to take as recognition of a self-evident fact, and then Eamon replied: 'Tim Pat, don't ever utter that thought in public again.' Game lost; set and match to follow.

Another appointment Vivion had made in his last days was that of Donal Flinn to the board of directors. After Vivion's death he became chairman. Flinn was an accountant and businessman whose father had been a minister under Eamon de Valera I. His brother Hugo was also a businessman and a noted nationalist. Flinn was no nationalist. He favoured white linen suits and attendance at Wimbledon each year for tennis and strawberries. By temperament and outlook he was not suited to the media world, let alone to the *Irish Press* and its traditions. I found him arrogant, and in political outlook better suited to the London *Daily Telegraph*. But he did attempt to make the group more businesslike. He succeeded in persuading Eamon to appoint another director with a business background, one Sean McHale, a management consultant. Given the state of the Irish Press Group at this time, I used to wonder subsequently whether subconsciously Flinn was influenced in his choice of McHale by the fact that part of Sean's earlier career had lain with the Arklow Fertiliser Company. In any event so far as the Flinn–McHale axis was concerned, the fertiliser hit the fan after the pair succeeded in persuading Eamon to have the consultancy firm of Cooper and Lybrand conduct an investigation into the running of the company and make recommendations for the future.

By the time the consultant spoke to me he had talked to other executives and had come to certain (as yet unwritten) conclusions. 'You know,' he remarked, 'I've done a zillion of these reports but I've never come up against a problem like this. What I have to do in effect is recommend to the man who is paying for this report that he replace himself with another CEO.' I remember replying that while Eamon was a nice fellow personally, he was also a de Valera, and that the history of the ownership of the *Irish Press* was long and deep-rooted. I gave him some reading material on the subject, an analysis of the *Irish Press* from the Bell of the wartime years, from the 1940s. It had been written by the poet and civil servant Val Iremonger under a pseudonym. Val, who later became an ambassador to India and Norway among other countries, had a keen grasp of the workings of power. The other book was an even older work, a biography of Michael Collins by Piaras Beaslai, which showed de Valera in an unflattering but revealing light. Although both pieces of writing might have appeared irrelevant to a modern Irish newspaper, they had a direct bearing on their controller's psychology. The consultant appreciated their significance and returned them to me with a note saying that he found the material 'a good read'.

As matters turned out, Flinn and McHale would have profited from reading both pieces also. The consultant's report was duly presented to the board. Flinn and McHale pressed hard for its acceptance. Subsequent meetings of the board produced many an old argument but no new CEO. So matters continued until a certain Monday in May 1985. Flinn expected that the day would see the matter of the CEO finally resolved, but before the Cooper and Lybrand report was discussed, another issue was disposed of, the appointment of a new director, which Chairman Flinn had not been informed of. This was Elio Malocco, a solicitor who was married to de Valera's first cousin, Jane. It emerged that Malocco was also taking over the firm's legal business, and furthermore that Eamon de Valera had acquired from his uncle Terry, Malocco's father-in-law, the remaining tranche of a hundred B shares that carried the special voting rights in the little-talked-of Delaware Corporation for £225,000. Control of the B shares, combined with his existing shares, gave him an unassailable grip on the company.

It was a classic de Valera power play in the face of which Flinn and McHale promptly resigned. But the question of what to do with his power could no more be answered by Eamon III than by Eamon I, when in his latter years he presided, omniscient but impotent, over the near-collapse of the Irish economy. The difference was that it had proved possible to remove de Valera I and install someone with ability, Sean Lemass, who turned the country round. Eamon III could not be removed, and there was to be no salvation for the *Irish Press*.

I have alluded earlier to the contribution Jack Dempsey made to building up the company. Psychologically, his role vis-à-vis Vivion had been that of grand vizier to caliph. Vivion put the frighteners on Jack and then Jack frightened everyone else. It was not a role calculated to withstand the stresses and complexities of the modern newspaper industry. For a time Colm Traynor, a son of the Anglo-Irish War hero Oscar Traynor, did his best to fill Dempsey's shoes. He had great experience in dealing with trade unions and, more importantly, all the loyalty and dedication of the classical *Irish Press* executive. However, one day he took me aside to tell me that he had had enough. He wasn't getting on with 'your man' (Eamon) and after a lifetime of attrition intended to retire and take things easy. Unwisely I disregarded something else he said to me: 'Listen, you should think about numero uno. Watch yourself.' He also made a comment that I wondered about afterwards: 'You know, your man is spending a lot of time at British embassy dos.' At this stage the circulation of the *Sunday Press* under the editorship of Vincent Jennings had fallen by almost 40 per cent. From the time he first took over, the *Sunday Press* had been Jack Dempsey's brain-child and he had seen to it that at least a modicum of fresh thinking went into its production. But after his death the paper became increasingly boring, although it was not short of resources. I remember discovering to my astonishment that a book about Richard Nixon had cost the paper £4,000 for circulation rights. I would have counted myself lucky to have acquired £400 to spend on serialising a book in the *Irish Press*.

Nevertheless Eamon saw in Colm's departure an opportunity both to meet the critique of the consultant's report and at the same time to restore the caliph–grand vizier relationship that his father had enjoyed with Jack Dempsey. It was common knowledge that Eamon and Jennings were having regular bust-ups over the circulation situation. Jennings himself told me that these rows were 'horrendous'. Even so, when Jennings, learning of Colm Traynor's impending departure, told Eamon that he would like to replace him, he got the job! And so a man who had proved journalistically unable to stem the slide on one paper was put in charge, both journalistically and commercially, of all three papers.

One of the ideas floating around Burgh Quay as the cure for the ills of the *Irish Press* was to turn it into a tabloid. Larry Lamb, the former editor of the *Sun*, was brought over from London as an adviser. I argued against the tabloid on the grounds that a) it was an obvious hauling down of the flag, b) the company did not have the expertise to produce a tabloid in a market that was ever more saturated with tabloids, and c) what was required was increased expenditure in terms of both editorial content and promotion, not an effort to disguise the lack of either by the contrivance of turning a sixteen-page broadsheet into a thirty-two-page tabloid and pretending that its content (and value) had somehow increased. As things continued to slide in terms of coverage and missed deadlines, advertising and circulation fell with them.

I could clearly see a crash coming, so I took the risk of calling a meeting of the paper's executive journalists in the Galleon pub, close to the *Press*. While I kept my more dire predictions to myself, I did spell out the fact that the paper needed a considerable revamp and needed it soon. I told them that I was drawing up a blueprint for this, which I would circulate to them before submitting it to Eamon. The executives liked the document, but John Garvey, my deputy, suggested that it might have more force coming from the staff. John was the centurion type. His middle name was 'diligence'. If the volcano blew, or the ship went down, you could be certain that the catastrophe would find John at his post, still barking out orders as the lava, or the water, closed over him. I respected his opinion and agreed to his suggestion.

Needless to say, Eamon took no heed. He met the staff's presentation of the document with a bout of instantaneous procrastination that went on for so long that I eventually knocked on the door and was admitted to the meeting. Eamon greeted my arrival with one of his moonlight-on-a-tombstone smiles before placing his hand on the document and saying: 'This is not the answer – a me-too *Irish Times*.' I knew what that meant. Apart from the fact of the inaccurate and offensive dismissal of my blueprint – and he obviously knew that it was my document – I guessed that he and Jennings had decided to go for the tabloid and that the next step would be to go for me. I was right. Appropriately enough, I met the pair at a funeral a short time afterwards and they enlivened the proceedings by telling me there was a letter from Jennings on its way to me. It confirmed the tabloid decision, adding that the company's financial position meant that there was no room for sentiment but that 'It would still be a nationalist paper.' I remember thinking that this probably meant that the tits on the page-three girl would be printed in green. But I kept my cool, at least to the extent of not responding to the document with one of my own, containing my resignation.

I was in a bad state of mind, for reasons, as we shall see shortly, of which the crisis at the paper formed only a part. Nevertheless I was determined that if de Valera wanted to get rid of me, then he would have to be man enough to say so to my face. As matters turned out, he managed to do the one but ducked the other. What he did say, in his office, on a day in August 1987, a few weeks after the letter arrived and I had still shown no signs of voluntarily walking the plank, was: 'I don't think you're the man to edit a tabloid.' I received this piece of seminal wisdom in silence. He then went on to say that I could have practically any other job I wanted in the firm, provided of course that said job was available! I could hold on to my company car, expenses, etc. It was an offer I could not accept. There was not the slightest chance of my opting to stay on, window-gazing in some non-job, as the firm slid to an inexorable collapse. But the good news was that wrong and foolish as the tabloid decision was, it did offer the possibility of my getting back onto the road not taken: becoming a full-time writer. So I told Eamon that, providing there was a bit of generosity involved, I would prefer to resign. The children were reared and, though I still had a hefty mortgage and an overdraft, there was not going to be a better time at which to face the risks of authorship.

A short time later, after I had used that night's conference to inform the staff of my decision, John Garvey decided to run the story across the top of page one. Later in the evening I found Eamon de Valera sitting at the news desk reading a tribute to me he had written for inclusion in the story. 'It's good PR,' he told me. Eamonn McThomas, whose jail sentence I had tried unavailingly to have reduced, called in to wish me well and bumped into de Valera. 'Jaysus,' he exclaimed, 'you're the spitting image of your grandfather.' How right he was.

I should have realised that the words 'generosity' and 'de Valera' taken together were pretty well oxymoronic. I ended up not with a golden but a copper handshake. Not wishing to haggle with him myself, I left the negotiation of my settlement terms to my friend and accountant Joe Charleton. Joe was a contributor to the paper. His proudest boast was that as a boy in Belfast, he had bought a copy of its first edition with two pennies he had borrowed from his widowed mother. Joe was justly revered as a tax adviser, but I should have realised that he was too old and too reverential of the paper's traditions for such a negotiation. I got roughly two years' pay (£76,000), the use of a small car, a Toyota Carina, for two

years, and a very small deferred pension which would not take effect for
ten years. Many a poor devil has been thrown on the scrap heap with less,
but after thirty-five years with the firm it was hard to walk away without
a proper pension. For several years I could not bear to pass the *Press*
building. If I had to do so, I walked on the far side of the Liffey.

Once I had made up my mind to leave, regrets began to develop, not so
much at leaving but at my folly in staying so long in Burgh Quay. Why
had I not taken some of the opportunities that had come my way and
would have given me a career in either broadcasting or another newspaper?
Why had I wasted so much of my time and energy trying to effect improvements in a paper in which I had no stake and whose controllers had so
little commitment to it? Why had I let my interest in the North, and its
coverage, blind me to the reality that the company was headed for disaster?
Had I allowed myself to become institutionalised? At fifty-five, would I be
able to produce the energy and flair needed to make a go of full-time
writing? The energy and emotional scar tissue that I expended on farcical
arguments with Vivion de Valera over issues like contraception alone
would have sustained me through half a dozen books.

The question of energy grew more urgent by the hour. I gave Cherry
£10,000 to invest in her beauty business, cleared off my overdraft, paid
the tax authorities what they sought from my settlement and all of a
sudden had just £30,000 with which to face the future. One of the bright
spots in my departure was the amount of money I was told I could expect
from the state by way of tax rebate and the return of social welfare
contributions. However, most of Joe Charleton's other clients were of a
class that did not have to concern themselves with social welfare issues,
and he, like myself, had not realised that the rebates I had been led to
expect had been whittled away in recent finance acts. Instead of something
of the order of £100 per week, I was entitled to approximately £90 a
month. And I had to sign on for the dole. One day a young woman who
appeared to be in her early twentiies paused as she handed me the money
and, looking at me accusingly, enquired: 'Are you *sure* you are looking for
alternative employment?' I was queuing for my money at Dun Laoghaire
Labour Exchange on another occasion when someone tapped me on the
shoulder and said: 'Imagine meeting someone like you in a place like this.'
It was my son Tom, who also resigned from the paper after I left. We had
a pint together.

After I had gone Eamon continued his PR drive by authorising the
secretary of the company, Tommy O'Reilly, to write to me telling me that:

At a meeting of the board of directors held on Wednesday last, the members present paid tribute to your many years of outstanding service as editor of the *Irish Press* and also expressed their good wishes for your success in the future.

Tommy, who was an old friend, also thanked me personally for 'the many courtesies extended to me personally over the years'. It was a nice note, but I was also conscious of the fact that while the recording of the tributes looked good on paper, it was also cheaper than a presentation, a farewell dinner or anything of that sort. The lack of a dinner was compensated for by the action of my friend John O'Mahony, a cultured Kerry republican (a type, as I tell my Kerry friends, not overly frequently met with) who was also something altitudinous in one of Ireland's most successful banking groups, Anglo-Irish. John arranged that I be the guest of honour at a very grand lunch in the bank's boardroom. Directors and senior executives lurked behind every napkin. The thoughtful gesture, coming at that time, underlined my belief in the value of friendship.

I also received a great number of letters from well-wishers. They came from people of all walks of life: strangers, young people whom I had helped in some way, people in public life, friends of all sorts. They included one from Seamus Heaney, who wrote:

> I just wanted to salute you and your well-timed and finely executed resignation. You have been a real presence and a fortifying one; even though we might not have met that often, it was a consolation to know you were there. And to know you will be.

Another letter that really touched me came from Willy Collins, an old journalistic colleague with whom I had been a sub-editor on the *Evening Press* and who later became assistant editor of the *Sunday Press*. At the time of writing his son Stephen is the political correspondent of the *Irish Times*. Willy wrote:

> I was sad, sorry and bewildered when I heard of your departure while on holidays down the country. When the news bulletin ended, I poured myself a Paddy and went out the back to sit and think and drink to all our yesterdays. I saw a lot of people as I sat there, some of them still with us and others, too many, who are now sleeping the sleep of peace. And I thought, Tim, that you are one of the undefeated because your strength has not gone and your days are not counted and told. So I gave you a toast, went back inside to Mary and the grandchildren, and got on with the business of living.

With regards, good wishes and not a little love.

P.S. If I, or anyone belonging to me can be of any assistance to you in future, don't hesitate to call.

Though I did not know it at the time, other days were to be upon me shortly that would severely test Willy's claim that I was one of the undefeated.

The final reasons for the death of the *Irish Press* could be summed up by a combination of the biblical tale of the Gadarene swine's rush to destruction, and Maurice Liston's dictum that the worst wounds are self-inflicted. A few years after I had left and it was becoming apparent to everyone that things were going seriously wrong at Burgh Quay, I met Brendan O'hEithir on the street. He called out to me: 'Well done! By Jaysus, didn't you get out at the right time!' I didn't feel the slightest satisfaction at my timing. For me every new blow to the *Irish Press* opened an old scar. Liston's saying was particularly applicable in the case of Elio Malocco, the solicitor whom Eamon de Valera had appointed to the board of directors. As noted already, Malocco also took over the handling of the firm's legal business. I remember before I left the *Press*, I spent a frustrating day in court for a libel case and complained bitterly to Eamon about the handling of the case. I told him that we could not have done worse had we deliberately set out to lose. Witnesses I had arranged were not called and we were represented not by senior counsel, which was the normal procedure, but by a junior barrister. Whether or not that particular case had anything to do with later developments I cannot say. But after I left, it was discovered that Malocco had misused his role as a solicitor and that Jennings and de Valera had reported him to the Incorporated Law Society. Accordingly, on another, not quite so bright, May day (15 May 1995) he was sentenced to five years in prison, having been charged with a variety of offences including fraud and larceny. De Valera and Jennings gave evidence for the prosecution. The Law Society subsequently paid out €2.35 million in client compensation and struck Malocco off as a solicitor.

The paper folded ten days after the Malocco sentence was handed down. In a sense the case had only been noises off to the Big Bang that destroyed the newspapers. I chose to leave Burgh Quay, but the staff who remained did not have the luxury of choice and worked on in a climate of ever-increasing misery and uncertainty. The anger and dismay at the prospect of the *Irish Press*'s closure extended to the shareholders. The *Irish Times* edition of 16 May 1995 contained several examples of the wrath expressed at an extraordinary general meeting held the previous day. The most noteworthy being that of the prominent Mayo social and political figure, Loretta Clarke. She walked up to the top table, exclaimed: 'Judas,' and then threw down thirty pieces of silver in front of de Valera and Jennings. The pieces were one-shilling English coins, bearing the head of George V, who had been on the throne when the *Irish Press* was founded. As Professor John Horgan of Dublin City University has written: 'The passion and fury of those final days and weeks were as memorable as the final act was bad-tempered and unworthy of a great institution.' The extraordinary hurt and anger of those days can be traced in the newspaper reportage of the 1995 close-down and in the allied parliamentary and court proceedings. Readers can also be recommended to two good, closely researched books: Mark O'Brien's historical overview, *De Valera: Fianna Fail and the Irish Press* and Ray Burke's cleverly titled *Press Delete: the Decline and Fall of the Irish Press*, on which I have drawn heavily in recording the paper's last days. All I can hope to do within the present compass is to give a brief indication of what happened.

I have previously referred to the de Valera fondness for a formula of control closely resembling the Holy Trinity in which the ruler of the company was also the controlling director, the managing director and the editor in chief. In 1989 Eamon de Valera applied another triple formula to the company he had inherited. Irish Press plc 'hived down', as he put it. This meant that two new *Irish Press* babies were conceived, on 16 June, which, as some of the more Joycean-minded journalists noted, was also the date on which Leopold Bloom was cuckolded. Baby one was christened Irish Press Publications (IPP), baby two Irish Press Newspapers (IPN). The first child, IPP, was granted ownership of the three newspaper titles under licence from Irish Press plc. The second, IPN, was authorised to manage and publish the three papers. In other words the staffs were now employed by IPN. But the babies' parent company, Irish Press plc, retained control of its assets so that when IPN sank, said assets floated free of the vortex and remained in the control of Irish Press plc. The staff of the *Irish Press*, however, had to take their place in a long queue of IPN creditors. It was months before they even received social welfare payments. Baby one, IPP, which controlled the titles, also sold a 25 per cent share to Tony O'Reilly's Independent Group for €1.5 million. In addition the Independent Group made a loan to IPP of €1.3 million as a prior charge on the titles. The Competition Authority later criticised this arrangement as being anti-competitive and designed to prevent any rival to the *Independent* emerging. The point about the loans, which are ring-fenced within IPP, is that they only became repayable if the Irish Press plc titles were sold.

Another unfortunate arrangement made possible by the birth of the additional babies was the introduction of the American Ralph Ingersoll to the Irish newspaper scene in 1989. His company, Ingersoll Publications, acquired 50 per cent of both IPP and IPN, and was supposed to manage and publish the papers. Had Eamon consulted me about the partnership with the American, I would certainly have advised him to think again. This is not a case of hindsight being twenty-twenty vision. Ingersoll, as anyone with a knowledge of America would have known, was an associate of the 'junk-bond king', Michael Milken. Milken's activities finally landed him in jail and Drexel Burnham Lambert, the bank that had financed him (and Ingersoll), in bankruptcy. Facially, Ingersoll had a certain resemblance to Eamon de Valera, but it was in his relationship with his father that Ingersoll bore an uncanny resemblance to that of Eamon with his. Both parents had their flaws, but both could point to the fact that on their watches successful journals had been launched. In Vivion's case it was the *Sunday Press* and the *Evening Press*. Ingersoll Senior had been a major inspiration behind the success of, amongst others, *Fortune*, *Life* and the *New Yorker*. The two juniors, however, will be remembered not for what they founded but for their association with the demise of existing publications. Ingersoll lost millions on his *Irish Press* venture.

During the junk-bond era Ingersoll flew across America in his private jet, swooping down like an aerial predator to acquire long-established local papers, which he then proceeded to gut, firing staff and reducing content, but charging more for advertising. He boasted to *Forbes* magazine that his accomplishments were based on daring to be a son of a bitch. Ingersoll decreed that newsroom costs should not rise above 11 per cent of a paper's budget. In the encapsulated world of the fancy financial footwork, symbolised by Milken's rise and fall, this strategy generated profits – for a time. Eventually, however, some actors made their entrance whom Ingersoll had under-appreciated – the readership. Circulations fell and a publication that Ingersoll attempted to launch, the *St Louis Sun*, failed spectacularly not long after he showed up in Dublin. In Ireland Ingersoll continued on his ham-fisted way, laying clumsy hands on the *Evening Press* in a botched attempt to remodel it and appointing unsuitable American 'experts' to cut the cost of reportage. The effect of the '11 per cent only' approach may be judged from an exchange between one such expert and an Irish executive from the Irish Press Group's art department.

The American wanted to dissuade the Irishman from sending a cameraman to cover one of Ireland's most hallowed religious practices, the annual ascent of the Reek, overlooking spectacular Westport Bay in County

Mayo. Tens of thousands of pilgrims of all ages climb the mountain, often in appalling weather conditions, and sometimes barefooted, to attend mass on its summit. Finally, after much argument, the American accepted the Irishman's assurance that this extraordinary event was of such great cultural and religious significance that it simply had to be covered. Next day, however, the American triumphantly returned to the charge, saying: 'See, I told you there was no need to cover that mountain thing. I checked the files and found out that you already got a picture – last year!'

Unsurprisingly, the Ingersoll–de Valera marriage ended with costly divorce proceedings being brought before the courts. During his brief stay Ingersoll tried unsuccessfully to have de Valera fired, and managed, in 1992, to get rid of Jennings – temporarily. De Valera reinstated him after just twenty-two months. He defended the severance payment Jennings had received, IR£250,000. He told shareholders that Jennings had 'suffered very severely. His pension rights were severely curtailed.' This concern for pension curtailment did not extend to the elderly *Irish Press* pensioners who were receiving tiny *ex gratia* pensions. Some, like Paddy Shanon, who was then eighty-two, and had joined the paper in 1931, were receiving around thirty euros a week. All received a letter from Jennings stating that in view of the impending liquidation of IPN, payments of these pensions would cease from 31 May 1995.

By May 1995 the dogs in the street were aware that there was something seriously wrong at the *Irish Press*. The future of the paper had been the subject of ministerial comment and Dail debate. And there was much publicity about a consortium of the Irish *Sunday Business Post* and the British *Daily Telegraph*, which wanted to buy the papers. As with other would-be buyers, including the tycoon Michael Smurfit, the consortium's proposals were rejected. As the end neared, Jennings and de Valera took the extraordinary step of filling the best part of five pages in the *Sunday Press* with an attack on both the Competition Authority and the consortium. In terms of attractiveness to an ordinary newspaper reader this mass of type had all the realism and appeal of one of Hitler's final communiqués from the bunker to his phantom armies.

Accordingly when a government-sponsored forum on the Irish newspaper industry opened on 8 May, the public already had a pretty fair idea as to where the bodies were buried. De Valera and Jennings refused to join in the exhumation, however, and no *Irish Press* executives attended. Nor did they accept an invitation to contribute to a series of articles that the *Irish Times* ran in conjunction with the forum. The contributors included myself. I said that 'As, managerially speaking, the Ireland of *Riverdance* began to form over the horizon, back at Burgh Quay, the ceilidh band played on.' Colm Rapple, the group's business editor, who also contributed, agreed with me. Rapple was, and is, a much-respected financial commentator on radio and television. He stated that salvation would involve de Valera's transferring his shares to any new ownership and 'an entirely new management culture'. The reaction to this by Eamon de Valera recalled his father's behaviour on the night of the Murrays' affair. Next day, 25 May 1995, Rapple was called in to Jennings's office, handed a letter accusing him of extreme disloyalty and told him to resign by midday.

Leaving Rapple to ponder on this demand, Jennings and de Valera then headed for the Supreme Court, where they discovered that an earlier High Court decision was being set aside and that there would be no millions forthcoming from the Ingersoll divorce proceedings. (Later, in 2002, there would be millions forthcoming, from another source. Warburg Pincus & G. International, the bank which had provided references for Ingersoll, made an out-of-court settlement with Irish Press Plc for €7.6 million, having initially sought almost €60 million.) On the pair's return to their offices Jennings sacked Colm Rapple. By now journalistic morale was at rock-bottom. The climate of industrial relations was indescribably awful. The journalists' lack of confidence in their employers was such that they had taken a High Court action against them so as to receive assurances on their pension fund. Rates of pay had fallen far behind those obtaining in other newspaper offices. There were cutbacks and rumours of cutbacks. Circulations were plummeting. Any fool could have foreseen that Rapple's sacking would lead to a staff backlash. It duly did.

The journalists stopped working. The papers failed to appear. There was a brief sit-in, more *Sturm und Drang* in the Dail and much public bemoaning of the loss of a great Irish institution. But the doors of Burgh Quay were closed and would remain closed. Six hundred jobs were lost. Naturally I found all these experiences painful in themselves, but particularly so during the peace process. I don't know how many times I wished, all personal considerations to one side, that there could have been an authoritative, informed voice from Burgh Quay to back the peacemakers in moments of crisis. The peace-process era was certainly one in which the *Irish Press* could have lived up to the promise of its first editorial with great benefit to Irish society as a whole.

Moreover all this occurred on the cusp of the greatest advertising and property boom in Irish newspaper history. At the time of writing this has faltered noticeably, but in Celtic Tiger Ireland obscure provincial papers have changed hands for millions. Nationally, lured by the soaring advertising revenues and circulations of the city's newspapers, Associated Newspapers, the owners of the London *Daily Mail*, found it attractive to launch an *Irish Daily Mail* in Dublin and to buy *Ireland on Sunday*.

Jennings and de Valera later averred that no suitable investors could be found to relaunch the papers. I cannot say what the pair's definition of suitability was. Speaking for myself, I would have welcomed one particular group who were interested in restarting the *Irish Press* as a nationalist paper, and with it the *Sunday Press*. Amongst those involved were the billionaires Denis Kelliher and Chuck Feeney. So too was Niall O'Dowd, who had begun his journalistic career with the *Irish Press* and gone on to become the successful publisher and editor of the *Irish Voice* paper in New York and, with the help of Feeney, one of the prime movers in bringing about the peace process.

I don't know which factor rendered the deal more unattractive to de Valera, but I do know that the New York group not alone saw no future for him in their intended venture but also planned to engage me as consultant editor. At all events, in his 2004 chairman's statement de Valera solemnly stated: 'It is a matter of continuing disappointment to the directors that it has not proved possible to publish at least one of the titles.'

Eamon once described Burgh Quay to me as a 'dedicated building', meaning that he wanted it known that its value was limited because it was solely adapted for the purpose of publishing newspapers. This assessment sits ironically with the fact that the building now epitomises what the *Irish Press* lacked, new blood. It houses the Irish department of immigration. But it matches the image he tended to project, that of being a man who had only reluctantly become involved with a not very attractive, or lucrative, undertaking through a sense of duty. I once asked him how he saw his future and he replied, with a great air of weariness: 'Oh, I'm probably going to be stuck in this place.'

Far from stuck he turned out to be. On the corner of Merrion Square Park there is a lifelike statue of a reclining Oscar Wilde, with a decided twinkle in his eye. On first sight the twinkle may appear to the fanciful to have been caused by the fact that someone has thoughtfully placed a sculpture of a pair of well-rounded male buttocks just in front of the statue, but Oscar could also be judged to be smiling across the road at number 25 Merrion Square. Here, once the dust of closure had settled, de Valera and Jennings installed themselves in plush offices in one of the most expensive addresses in Dublin.

The only publishing venture now carried on by Irish Press plc would appear to be *Thom's Dublin Street Directory* whose continued publication was said to be 'in considerable doubt'. Under 'Group Undertakings', the Irish Press plc accounts listed a series of 'property' and 'investment companies'. These included what was described as an Irish Press Group 'holding company', incorporated in London, and something called Profinance Ltd, incorporated in Jersey. One of the investment companies that I thought particularly aptly styled was called 'Butville Ltd'. All in all Irish Press plc's assets were listed as being worth €7.325 million at the end of December 2006. Commenting on the accounts, *Phoenix* magazine estimated that the Tipperary radio station in which the company has a 59 per cent share could be worth up to €10 million. The magazine claimed that the Irish Press plc shares would be worth eighteen euros each. The stock-exchange crash would obviously have lessened the value of investments, but nevertheless the company paid a dividend of 15 per cent per share. *Phoenix* commented that the time had come for the company to be wound up so that investors could realise the value of their holdings. It said:

> The substantive issue, however, must be that having overseen its core newspaper business go down the tubes thirteen years ago, it seems pointless to employ Eamon de Valera [...] to effectively manage stock-exchange investments worth €7.4 million.

Will such a realisation occur? I would not hold my breath. Back in 1959 Noël Browne was exercised by the fact that Eamon de Valera Senior and his son Vivion, through operating a buy-in policy, had acquired up to 150,000 Irish Press Group shares. Following the screening of a critical programme in 2005, about the de Valera interest in the *Irish Press*, Eamon de Valera wrote to the RTE Broadcasting Authority listing some 28 complaints, including a claim that his father and grandfather held only 91,983 shares in 1959, some fifty five thousand less than Dr Noel Browne stated when he raised the de Valera connection in the Dail. Eamon de Valera did not mention the fact that, through a continuation of the de Valera buy-in policy, the contemporary Irish Press plc accounts (published 2007) show that at the time of making the complaint, which was rejected, he held 464,803 shares. The accounts also state that the three-man board (himself, Jennings and J.A. Lenehan) 'had decided' that he should henceforth hold the position of Chief Executive. The de Valera fondness for a form of control based on the Three Divine person in One was once more demonstrated. Eamon was now the largest shareholder, the Chief Executive and the Chairman.

The *Irish Press* story had evolved a long way from the days when those 'Irish domestic servants' had subscribed to a bond drive so that Ireland might be free.

CHAPTER 15

Hard Times

I come now to a chapter in my life that I wish did not have to be written. In fact I did not much like having to write the previous one either, but when sorrows come, as Shakespeare said, 'they come not single spies, but in battalions'. The deepening ridge of depression centring over the *Irish Press* contributed to another dark cloud which had been gathering – that over my marriage. Like that over the *Irish Press*, it formed over a period of several years and its portent was obscured by the rush of events. There was a great deal of noise and jollity, caused by the seemingly incessant parties for our friends and the constant comings and goings of the children and their companions. My mother used to remark that the children had 'an idyllic childhood'. I sometimes used to wonder darkly whether she meant compared with her own or mine, or what the children would say if they were consulted. I know what my bank manager's views were. He explained them to me frequently in lengthy monologues about my finances.

Apart from family and social traffic the house was also stuffed with waifs and strays of one sort or another. So far as costs were concerned, nothing that my bank manager might do to me could inhibit Cherry from following the dictates of an unusually kind heart. There was commonly either an expectant, but unmarried, mother or a boy whom some religious had found either sleeping rough or in trouble with the police. The sort of young people involved were a pretty good reflection of the gaps in the welfare system of the time.

For example, a boy who would have given no trouble during his stay in one of the industrial schools of the period could find himself in difficulty with the law shortly after leaving. The sort of trades learned at these schools – cobblering, tailoring, elementary farming skills – were precisely those in decline. So a lad without family support could leave an industrial school all spruced up in a decent suit, but with no job and no prospect of getting one. The often brutal disciplinary code in which he would have been reared for several years was not conducive to initiative or learning to think for oneself. Such a lad could soon be found sleeping rough, his suit and shirt no longer pressed and clean, and his chances of gaining employment lessening by the day. I remember one young fellow we took in who had discovered a seemingly sure-fire way of overcoming these difficulties. He stole a chequebook and went along to a bank, wherein he cashed a forged cheque. Unfortunately for himself, he knew so little about the banking system that a week later he came back to the nice man who had given him the money to repeat the performance.

Though the house was always full, the faces were constantly changing. The unfortunate unmarried mothers generally went on their way after their babies were given up for adoption. In those days a single mother received not support but hostility from Irish society. When their babies were put up for adoption, they had to sign a form which included the following:

> I hereby relinquish full claim for ever to my child and surrender the said child to Sister ... [Nuns generally ran the adoption process.] I further undertake never to attempt to see, interfere with, or make any claim to the said child at any future time.

'Spooner', as she was known, was our longest visitor. She had cystic fibrosis and had been placed in care. She came to us at the age of six. It was not expected that she would last for more than a year or two, but in the event she managed to eke out six years before she died. The children regarded her as a sister. She was like a little sparrow, so thin and small that when I gave her a piggyback her weight seemed about that of a light schoolbag. She would stamp her foot and cry: 'Mind your patience' when someone said or did anything to annoy her. Poor Spooner, had she lived to the time of writing, her life expectancy would have been more than double what it was in those days, although cystic fibrosis treatment in Ireland is still disgracefully far from what it should be. I think of her death as marking the end of an era in Cherry's and my relationship.

As the children grew up, Cherry had ceased bringing home waifs and strays and begun looking for other outlets for her energies. As I indicated in the previous chapter, she qualified as a beauty therapist, and she carried over into her new world her old sympathies for the troubles of others. Her looks, new skills and her personality, combined with the fact that most women attending beauty salons and suchlike are secretly hoping to find an understanding confessor/analyst, rapidly made her first the senior tutor in the beauty school she had trained in (Bronwen Conroy's), next a partner in a salon and then the owner of one, situated in Dublin's most prestigious hotel, the Shelbourne. I think I can fairly claim to have as many interests in life as most men, but I'm afraid that beauty therapy is not one of them. I was once voted Dublin's Worst Dressed Man by the *Evening Herald*. Nor would either the world of newspapers or the affairs of Northern Ireland figure at the top of Cherry's Most Favoured list.

A serious problem was the difference in our working hours. When I left for work at the *Irish Press*, Cherry would not have arrived home. And when she went out of a morning, I was often still asleep. There was also the loss to family life caused by the time given to writing and to matters Northern Irish. All of this exacerbated the inevitable stresses of marriage, stresses that were compounded by living in the Ireland of large families, small incomes, high taxation, and interest rates that at one stage reached 23 per cent on my overdraft and 18 per cent on the mortgage. In such an atmosphere there could well develop all the sad downward steps that life sometimes creates, even for childhood sweethearts.

The powder train that finally blew the relationship apart was laid down in 1985 by an event whose jollity was in binary opposition to the sadness it ultimately led to. The occasion was the launching of a novel, *Nothing Happens in Carmincross*, by Benedict Kiely. Ben was an old friend, as was (and are) the Kenny family who owned the famous bookshop and gallery in Galway where I spoke at the launch, saying with more prescience than I realised that, despite the title, a great deal happened in Carmincross. The book was well received and was subsequently issued in paperback at another launch, this time in the Tailors' Hall in Dublin. As I had been present at the birth of the parent book, I also attended that of the son's book. What happened next is simply stated.

At the paperback launching I met Barbara Hayley. We left together and commenced a relationship that lasted for almost six years. Barbara was some seven years younger than me, approaching her fifties. In the Ireland of the time she held an unusual position, a Protestant and a woman, she was professor of English at St Patrick's College, Maynooth, which was then far more of a pontifical institution than the largely secular college it has since become. Dublin-born, she had won scholarships to Alexander College and to Trinity, after graduation from which she went into new product development in a London advertising agency. She then went back to academia and became a fellow of Lucy Cavendish College, Cambridge, before returning to Ireland, as a lecturer in the English department at Maynooth, in 1981. Her researches into the life of William Carleton, the nineteenth-century Irish writer, caused scholars to look in a new way not merely on Carleton, but on nineteenth-century Ireland itself. A few years after being appointed a lecturer she was raised to the chair of English.

Interested in the arts, a prominent critic and broadcaster, Barbara cut a striking figure. Above average height, black-haired, with a smiling open face and a strong, carrying voice, she exuded a powerful force field and seemed the epitome of the successful modern professional woman. But there was a darker inner reality, a font of fear and unhappiness welling from a deeply unsatisfactory marriage. For all sorts of reasons Barbara hesitated for several years before obtaining a separation. (Divorce was not available in the Republic at the time.) She was concerned for the effect on her children, two girls, her position in the college and then, ironically, after we had met, because she did not wish to create a scandal for me and my family. But despite the secrecy we had a few idyllic years – September roses bloom sweetly. Our relationship played a part in helping to save both my life and my career.

For some years I had been having difficulties with my right eye. The consultant who attended to me said that the dark brown spots and the soreness were caused by macular cystic oedema. I knew what the words meant individually, but there was no indication as to what underlying condition was giving rise to the problem. A few years before I met Barbara, the consultant decided to treat the problem by using laser surgery. It worked in so far as the spots disappeared, but so too did a significant proportion of the sight in the right eye. This became a worry when the spots made a reappearance in the left eye, and in the months before and after I left the *Press* an increasing soreness and a noticeable reddening developed. I attended the consultant and, disquietingly, he blew out his cheeks, shook his head and said: 'You're forcing me, you're forcing me.' He did not say what I was forcing him to do, but it sounded disturbing. Half of me wanted to find out, the other half didn't, and I left the consulting rooms, with another appointment scheduled months into the future, troubled but with no idea of what was wrong.

I told Barbara what had transpired and, without telling me, she phoned a contact in Moorfields, the famous London eye hospital, and enquired: 'Who is the best eye specialist in Ireland?' The answer was 'Peter Eustace'. She then phoned Peter and arranged that, if I told my existing specialist that I was seeking a second opinion, he would see me later in the week. Like Barbara herself, Peter was a polymath. Apart from being the country's leading eye specialist, he held the chair of ophthalmology at University College, Dublin, was a poet, a student of archaeology and a first-class golfer and yachtsman. He had me on the operating table less than a week after seeing me. Though he did not tell me until some fifteen years later, he had diagnosed me as suffering from what in Latin is described as *melanosis oculi*, in English as melanoma of the conjunctiva. In any man's language it meant that, if the disease took its normal course, malignant melanoma would carry me off in between three and five years. Not the sort of condition one would recommend to a man in his mid-fifties embarking on the risky career of authorship, but as the pathology confirmed, it was the condition that had developed: malignancy had already been detected.

I was kept in the Mater Private Hospital, where Peter had operated, for a week before being allowed home. This was in October. The following July Peter had me back in the Mater for another, longer, operation, which necessitated a two-week stay. While the conventional wisdom would simply have been to eviscerate the left eye, the amount of vision remaining in the right one militated against this. As Peter remarked to me later, attempts to learn Braille by seniors are usually unsuccessful. He decided to try to save both my sight and my life by chipping away at the spots whenever they appeared. To ensure that he noticed the nasties in time, he arranged to see me every three months. As a result a sort of ocular roulette developed. I never knew at which visit Peter would find something and a trip to the operating theatre would ensue. The eye would be frozen under local anaesthetic and, ignoring the odd scraping sound, I would attempt to chat away with Peter about Northern Ireland, or whatever, as though I was at the barber's. Once, I did my John Wayne bit by telling a joke as he worked, but the panicky realisation that laughter might cause something unfunny to happen with the scalpel put a quick end to the jokes. In all, over the coming fourteen years, before he retired, Peter carried out more than a dozen procedures, of varying degrees of severity, removing the telltale tiny brown spots before the melanoma could develop.

Years later he told me that my case had 'beaten the books'. He said it was one of the cases that made him glad he had taken up medicine. To which I may add, with heart-felt sincerity, not half as glad as I am. I was fortunate too that Peter's practice was taken over by another first-class surgeon, a younger man, Tim Fulcher, who also removed some tissues before they got a chance to do harm. Tim and I also developed a friendly relationship, even though the first time I rang his mobile number, to make an appointment, I discovered that I had interrupted him as he prepared to ski down a mountain slope in Austria! Another continuing piece of good luck was the fact that over the years I had maintained a high level of medical insurance cover, so that my health situation did not create an economic disaster for me. However, economic disaster would have struck, for other reasons, had not Barbara again helped me over a stile, this time by helping me to resume writing. My eye condition caused, first, interruptions in the work, and then, after the second big operation in July 1989, a complete cessation. For several weeks my sight was so blurred that I could not use my computer. Family demands, and the cost of research, were rapidly reducing both what little was left of the *Press* money and the advance I had received to write the book on Michael Collins.

I had IR£7,000 left in the bank and was forced to make various economies – cutting out the Clarence Lunch, for example. The Clarence Lunch was held more or less weekly. It was organised by Sean J. White, man of letters and former *Irish Press* columnist. The regular table included Barbara, Ben Kiely, Tony O'Riordan, Brian Fallon and whatever guest a member of the table wished to invite. It was a valuable Dublin institution, which provided visiting firemen from academia, the media or the diplomatic world with a hospitable listening post during their Dublin stay. Initially, on leaving the *Press*, I had found the Clarence an invaluable oasis of friendship, but by late 1989 I was beginning to dread the regular phone calls from Sean J. White, in his capacity as convenor, and had run out of excuses for missing the lunch. I was at the time writing my book on Michael Collins, to coincide with the hundredth anniversary of his birth, in October 1990, and it began to appear inevitable that I would miss the spring deadline this necessitated.

Then Barbara intervened. One fine day in October 1989 she invited me to her mother's house in Clontarf, where she had installed a computer. I remember the sun streaming through the French windows, and the hint of autumnal chill, as she sat at the computer and said: 'Dictate something to me, anything to begin with.' I had some notes in my briefcase and used these to dictate a passage about Cathal Brugha and the opening session of the First Dail. We repeated this routine for three or four more days until I decided that if I could read notes – especially in my handwriting – then I could force myself to use my own computer. I did so and found that as the days passed, though things swam a bit, and gazing at a computer for too long caused a certain amount of pain, I was able to resume the production of my manuscript. I managed to achieve the deadline by setting myself a target of a chapter every two weeks.

By May 1991 Barbara had obtained a legal separation from her husband and bought a house in Londonbridge Road, Ballsbridge. Where I was concerned the gamble in leaving the *Press* appeared to have paid off. My first book had been a success and I had been given a contract for two more. The compass of life seemed to be set reasonably fair. However, the impossibility of conducting an affair in secrecy in Dublin was about to be forcibly brought home to me. Cherry was told about it and decided on a separation.

At the time I was preparing to visit San José, California, for the second time. The former lord mayor of San José, Tom McEnery had arranged a series of talks and arranged for me to spend some time at his holiday home on the beach at Santa Cruz. This last appeared a particularly attractive idea at that moment of emotional crisis. My flight from Dublin Airport left around midday on 15 May. Barbara picked me up and drove me to the airport. The journey was long and tiring, requiring stops at Shannon and New York and a change of planes. Tom met me at the airport. We drove straight to the hotel and I collapsed into bed without bothering about dinner. At two o'clock in the morning, California time, the phone rang. It was my son Tom ringing from Dublin to tell me that Barbara had been killed in a car crash. She had gone driving in the country after seeing me off, and hit a wall. 'I wish I could be there with you, Dad,' he said. Lines from a favourite poem went through my mind:

> Break, break, break,
> On thy cold gray stones,
> O Sea!
> And I would that my tongue could utter
> The thoughts that arise in me.

But under the constraints of generational inarticulateness, what I actually said was: 'Don't worry, Tom, the stomach is fairly round but the shoulders are pretty broad.'

My immediate reaction was to try to open the window to jump out. Then I sat for some hours on the floor, weeping, in a corner of the room, as far from the window as I could get. For a long time morning did not appear to be coming. By the time it did I felt I understood the meaning of the expression 'a dark night of the soul'. Tom McEnery proved himself a good and understanding friend, accepting the cancellation of his speaking arrangements without a murmur and helping me to make arrangements to fly home the day after I had landed. Afterwards I could only remember two incidents from the journey. One was that a minibus picked up passengers between the hotel and the San Francisco flight, making so many detours and stops that we got to San Francisco an hour after our scheduled arrival time. My nerve ends were screaming, but the flight itself was delayed for some reason and I was allowed on moments before take-off. The second incident was banality itself. There were two very badly behaved children sitting behind me on the Aer Lingus flight from New York. For a short time they were kept in some sort of check by their parents, who sat in the row in front of me, even though their constant turnings backwards, to shout admonitions over my head, did make napping impossible. But then, after about forty-five minutes in the air, the couple were bumped up to first class and the children were left to run riot until they eventually collapsed and went to sleep.

But at least I achieved my purpose in returning to Dublin so precipitately. Barbara's widowed mother, Mabel, had gone on holiday to Cuba with Barbara's cousin, Olive Buttimer, and the news had been broken to them there. They too had had to make a sudden rush home from a far meridian, and I wanted to be in Dublin to do what I could to comfort Mabel when she arrived. Mabel, who was then eighty-three, epitomised for me the qualities of a Southern Irish Protestant: cheerful, durable and hard-working, thrifty but generous, she was, and is, the sort of person who makes an ideal friend or neighbour. She bore up wonderfully in the days after Barbara's death and funeral, demonstrating perfectly what Hemingway meant when he defined courage as grace under pressure. She had had a particularly happy marriage, and often quoted sayings of her late husband, Jack Fox. One that abided with me, and that I have since practised, was 'Project yourself forward.' In other words look forward to the time ahead when the crisis of the moment will have abated. Mabel's example, and friendship, helped me through the valley of despond. I'd like to think that I helped her to cope with the loss of her only child. Certainly Olive Buttimer did. Like her late cousin, she is a particularly able person and had also made a successful career switch, becoming first a barrister, after a spell as a social worker, and then being appointed a circuit court judge.

It was a tragedy for all of us – Barbara, Mabel, Cherry, myself, our children, grandchildren and Barbara's two daughters. But that awful year of 1991 passed and family wounds healed with the passage of time.

Such was the physical and emotional background to my abandoning editorship and attempting a second professional career as an author. After a lifetime in journalism I decided I had enough of newspapers and did not attempt to write any articles for several years. Then I was approached by the *Examiner* to write a weekly column. While I was still writing this, sometimes sending it from the other side of the world as I conducted my researches into the diaspora, another development occurred. A group of businessmen headed by one Pascal Taggart, who had revolutionised the Irish greyhound industry, got together. They decided that the closure of the *Irish Press* had left a gap that should be filled and founded a new Sunday paper, *Ireland on Sunday*. The editor of the new paper was Liam Hayes, a legend of the Gaelic football field who had captained Meath to win three All-Ireland titles. He asked me to write a weekly column. I found Liam to be a most sympathetic editor, my copy was never touched by the sub-editors, except when they had to make sense of my syntax, and they phoned me before doing this.

For some years I enjoyed myself enormously bringing comfort to causes I approved of, such as the peace process, and confusion to my enemies, generally opponents of same. However, just as the paper was on the cusp of making a significant breakthrough, it was sold to a Scottish conglomerate, which in turn passed it on to Associated Newspapers, which ultimately used the paper as a springboard to launch the *Irish Daily Mail*. Needless to say, this publication's philosophy was in direct opposition to that of the *Irish Press*. My column was dropped, causing an instant loss in circulation variously said to be between 10,000 and 25,000 copies. After my experiences in the *Irish Press* I decided that there would be no more Mr Nice Guy and successfully sued the paper.

While the world of book publishing is neither more sedate nor more honourable than that of journalism, as people on the outside often mistakenly believe it to be, it is unquestionably psychologically more satisfying, conferring as it does far greater freedom of expression on an author than does a newspaper. The practical details of my exploration of the world of authorship were as follows: first I had to learn how to use a computer. This nearly drove me insane. I was forever losing copy that ought to have been saved, forgetting which controls moved copy and which cut it, and as for learning how to keep related materials in the same folder, forget it. If I had never doubted the wisdom of trying to teach the *Irish Press* typographers to move from hot metal to computerised setting with only a few weeks' training, my own searing experiences of learning how my simple Amstrad worked would have convinced me of its folly The first six months of computer use so highlighted the risks of authorship for me that I took the codename 'Daring' for my email.

The road to full-time authorship ran as follows. After leaving the *Press* I went to Aran, to finish writing a novel. I had been pecking at this work, inconclusively, ever since Philip McDermott had come to my office in 1980 to suggest I write it, but had ended up instead getting me to write *On the Blanket*. Latterly, however, things had picked up. I had shown the manuscript to Mark Barty-King, then head of Transworld Publishing. Mark had suggested a number of changes, some of which I agreed with, some not. But the crucial factor was that, having left the *Irish Press*, I was now able to devote a chunk of uninterrupted time to the manuscript. Mark was both pleased and surprised at how much improved the text became. Truth to tell, so was I, and Barbara, who as I have indicated was much respected as a literary critic, was not merely supportive but enthusiastic. However, the path of creation never runs smooth. Murphy's Law began to apply. Mark passed me on to one of his editors with whom I had a pleasant dinner in London. We agreed that I would continue my rewriting and that he would come to Aran when the final draft was ready.

The history of publishing is littered with stories of manuscripts mislaid, but in my case it was the editor who got mislaid! It happened in Galway, where we had a convivial evening – which may or may not have had a bearing on what happened. At all events I went ahead of him to Aran, on a pre-booked flight to the island, but he failed to arrive after me, either on a later flight, as arranged, or on one of the ferries. I heard afterwards that a man answering his description had been noticed in Galway trying to find out how one got to the Aran Islands. However, the familiar problem of the difficulties of a shared language in Anglo-Irish communication would appear to have arisen, because he seems to have decided ultimately that one place he could get to easily, without braving wind and wave, was London. Certainly he returned there with some speed. Not unsurprisingly, we subsequently differed on the merits of the changes he wished to see made. I wouldn't make them. In an outburst of what one could describe either as wounded integrity or foolish pride, I told myself that I hadn't left the *Irish Press* to be told how to write by a bloody Englishman, even if one of his authors was Anthony Burgess! The entirely predictable outcome was that no changes meant no novel. But meanwhile, in another part of the forest, something else had stirred.

Century Hutchinson had retained the services of Frank Delaney as a sort of minister for Irish literary affairs and it was he who suggested to the company that I write a biography of Sean Lemass and arranged that I be made quite a generous offer. I admired Lemass and, coming in the immediate post-*Irish Press* period, Frank's initiative was a lifeline, particularly after the novel debacle. But Lemass's prosaic businessman persona did not enthuse me as a subject.

Then 'Doc' Carroll touched my life again. I was sitting at my writing (and kitchen) table in Aran and, finding it hard to write, decided instead to make a belated attempt to answer the file of congratulatory letters that had arrived after I resigned from the *Press*. I found that the Doc had actually sent two. The first, written before my resignation, congratulated

me on what I had done with the paper! The second said: 'Keep going; the
best is yet to be.' It went on to suggest that I should make my next writing
project a biography of Michael Collins, whose centenary was approaching.
'Doc' said he had been discussing the idea with Michael Collins, the Big
Fellow's nephew, and he quoted to me what Robert Bolt had said when he
was asked to do a script for a film about Collins: 'It will be an honour; I
know him from having read the parliamentary debates in Ireland and
England. He is one of the great achievers of our century, unrecognised.'
Reading that letter worked like switching on a light bulb.

I had been to school with Collins's nephew Michael (Michael Collins's
brother Johnny's son by a second marriage), and we had both been
members of the same swimming club, Sandycove. But, most importantly,
Collins was a more colourful and romantic figure than Lemass, even
though he was cut down in his early thirties and Lemass lived on to become
the most successful Taoiseach of the twentieth century. So I contacted
Frank and suggested the change of subject. Both he and the publishers
were amenable, even enthusiastic when they discovered that Collins's
centenary was less than two years away, in October 1990. Publishers
set great store by centenaries, because they automatically create media
attention. So the good news was that I now obtained a contract, for
UK£25,000, payable in three tranches, signature, delivery of finished
manuscript and on publication day.

I have already described the problems that arose with my eyes and how
these were resolved, but I should also mention a particularly fine editor,
Annelise Evans, who helped me to produce the finished text in time. Like
the battle of Waterloo, it was a damn near thing. As I was posting new
chapters to Annelise, she was posting me copies of earlier ones containing
editorial queries. We thus produced a lengthy, serious biography as though
it were an instant book. On top of these pressures, while we were at the
proofs stage a crisis occurred that almost destroyed the printing schedule
and could have destroyed the credibility of the book.

I was sent a copy of the dust jacket, which featured a drawing of
Michael Collins that did not look like any picture of Collins that I had
ever seen. I discovered that it had been obtained from the National Gallery
of Ireland, who had not been informed what it was needed for. The gallery
very decently arranged that I see their collection of Collins memorabilia
and I discovered that the drawing was catalogued with a question mark
as to its provenance. It was apparently a sketch of a young man who had
been active in the Irish literary revival while Collins was engaged in
revolution. On a holiday weekend I managed to contact Richard Cohen,

who was at the time a senior editor with Century Hutchinson. Several thousand copies of the jacket had already been printed and had to be destroyed. I selected a replacement picture, this time a photograph of the real Collins.

But at least, after all the alarms and excursions, the book was a tremendous success by Irish publishing standards. For several years thereafter I enjoyed a mutually beneficial relationship with Hutchinson. Annelise Evans was succeeded by another particularly fine editor, Tony Whittome. I became friendly with him and his wife, Martha, and I also liked and respected the company's chief executive, the legendary Gail Rebuck.

Part of the success of the Collins book could be explained by a remark made by a heavily pregnant lady from the *Cork Examiner* (as the *Examiner* was then called), who battled her way out to the Aran Islands on a pitching ferry, on a very bad day, to do a laudatory interview: 'You know,' she said, 'all these years a great injustice has been done to Michael Collins.' By this she meant that the success of de Valera and his Fianna Fail Party, the effects of the patronage that the party had been able to dispense, of the books and articles published by the *Irish Press*, all had combined to obscure Collins's contribution to modern Ireland. The timidity, and low productivity, of Irish historians had facilitated the creation of an image of Collins as the man who, in signing the Anglo-Irish Treaty of 1921, had betrayed his leader, de Valera, and partitioned the country.

Civil War bitterness was such that it was not until his centenary was commemorated that a Fianna Fail Taoiseach (Bertie Ahern) allowed the army of which Collins was the first commander-in-chief to officially attend the ceremonies at the place where he fell, Beal na Blath, County Cork. I almost fell there myself on that historic occasion, coming within an ace of disrupting said ceremonies. I had been given the honour of delivering the centenary oration, and set off from the West Cork Hotel in Skibbereen in good time in a crammed car. It contained Cherry, my mother, one of our oldest friends, Father Tom Stack and the driver, Cherry's friend, Mary Anderson. Earlier in the day, another old friend and a former *Irish Press* colleague, Tom O'Mahony, had led a band of followers to the hotel. After leaving the *Press*, Tom had become an icon of the Cork-based *Examiner*, so quite a number of his colleagues had accompanied him for our large liquid interview/lunch.

Unfortunately each journalist had had his or her version of the best route to take to the ceremony. Inevitably, with all this helpful advice ringing in our ears we took a wrong turning. After a lengthy spell of driving through deserted countryside, as the minutes ticked away terrifyingly, I spotted a man walking along the roadside and enquired whether I was on the right road for 'the ceremony at the monument'. 'Oh, begor ye are,' was the answer. 'The monument's only a quarter of an hour from you down that road there.' And so it was, but two things were wrong: a) the monument site was completely deserted, not a uniform in sight, and b) the inscription on the monument explained why. It had been erected not in memory of Michael Collins, but of the Kilmichael Ambush of 28 November 1920, led by Tom Barry during the Black and Tan war. 'Really,' observed my mother, 'they do seem to have an awful lot of monuments in Cork.'

I have a good sense of direction, and relying on that, rather than on incomprehensible Corkonian instruction, we hurtled towards Beal na Blath through bog and boreen at impossible speeds, in an impossibly short space of time. 'This is great,' opined Father Stack. 'Very Irish. I love all this sort of stuff. It'll be great to look back on!' We got as close to Beal na Blath as the huge number of parked cars would allow and, ten minutes late, I ran the rest of the way. I had to pass Lynch's pub, where the fatal Collins ambush was planned. It saved my life, however. I dashed in, ordered that three small brandies be placed in one glass, downed it in a swallow, had a pint of water, and raced on to deliver what I was told afterwards was the speech of a lifetime. It had to be to take my mind off some of the sights I registered as I arrived. Apart from the daunting effect of the largest crowd ever to attend the Beal na Blath Ceremony, and a bank of TV and newspaper cameras, there was Michael Collins's anguished (and angry) expression as he sat on the platform beside an empty speaker's chair. I remember also the exhausted face of a young officer as he stood to attention in a near-fainting condition under a boiling sun, holding a staff that bore a huge tricolour. But all's well that ends well, and as Father Stack said, it was a great occasion to look back on. In paying tribute to a great man, Ireland was healing its wounds.

The actual launch of the book was held in Kilmainham Jail, and the place was packed to suffocation. The attendance was such that even Jack Lynch was left waiting for a drink. The rocket thus launched was boosted into outer space by a *Late, Late Show* discussion a few days later. Like Beal na Blath, this could have been a disaster, because by way of setting the scene for discussion of the book Gay Byrne had included amongst his guests Gordon Wilson and his wife, who had lost their daughter in the IRA bombing atrocity at Enniskillen on 8 November 1987. And the lady to whom Byrne had assigned the role of critic, a trade union official, clearly did not share my viewpoint. The conversation could very easily have gone crashing off the rails into an indictment of contemporary terrorism.

However, I was genuinely moved by the nobility of the Wilsons, their lack of bitterness, and said so. The audience applauded, as did the country, and the debate moved on to a discussion of the Danton and Robespierre of the Irish Revolution, Collins and de Valera, and to the issue of who was right and wrong over the treaty. I had had the benefit of the passage of time when I came to research the book: papers were more readily available; survivors of the period were prepared to talk in a way that would have been unthinkable even a short while earlier. Not alone did Collins's life prove interesting and exciting in itself, but the issues he confronted helped to make contemporary events in Northern Ireland explicable if not forgivable. What the research also did was to show that de Valera's behaviour in not going to London to negotiate the treaty had been highly duplicitous.

Nobody was more keenly aware of this than Frank Delaney. He pulled me aside in Kilmainham on the night of the launch in October 1990 and said: 'Your next book will have to be on de Valera.' I hadn't wanted to write another state paper, National Library-bound book. My intention had been to chronicle the story of the Irish diaspora, thus fulfilling an urge to travel and at the same time to do something about one of the subjects closest to my heart: the nearly criminal neglect on the part of decision-taking Ireland of its diaspora. The Department of Foreign Affairs in Dublin calculates that worldwide some 70 million people are of Irish origin. If the dots were joined up between America, Africa, Argentina and Australia, the clout of the Irish would at least equal that of the Israelis.

However, the reality is that as far as the bulk of those who left Ireland were concerned, until comparatively recently the well-to-do would be fêted around St Patrick's Day in a swirl of embassy parties and festive marches. Those who did not do so well were left to die unnoticed, often in depressing bedsitters or doss houses. I had had an interest in the diaspora long before I came to write *Wherever Green Is Worn*, some years after *Michael Collins*. In part this interest was sparked by the sight of the shabby hordes I saw as a boy daily pouring onto the mail boat in Dun Laoghaire. These men and women sent home the money that kept their families housed and fed. The men, lacking in formal education, lonely, drinking too much, would sometimes resort to guilt-drenched interludes with what one of them described to me as 'filthy creatures'. Very often these 'creatures' would come from the ranks of the unfortunate female emigrants who left with them. Though the strain of emigrant life felled many of that far-off shabby horde both physically and psychologically, I knew from experience that many more of those unsung heroes, male and female, still managed to display an enormous sense of responsibility and family commitment. From a different type of emigrant, my uncles Tim and Frank in Australia, I had experienced at first hand the benefits of that commitment. Schooldays in Blackrock had also helped to further an interest in Irish missionary activity.

The idea of writing a book about the impact of the Irish on the world had been with me on and off since I had visited India as a guest of the Indian government in 1972. My preliminary reading had made me aware of the fact that in the early part of the century Indian (and Egyptian) nationalists had kept a keen eye on political developments in Dublin. Culturally also there had been links, due largely to the work of Ireland's Yeats and India's Tagore. But it was not until December 1972, when I landed in New Delhi, that I acquired a more homely insight into such bygone contacts – the important role played by Irish landladies in the formation of the economic and political thought of at least one Indian leader, President Varahagiri Venkata Giri. I met the president, who was at the time a fast-talking seventy-eight-year-old, in a magnificent, awe-inspiring palace, where he received me with great warmth and courtesy. He described to me how, as a young law student in Dublin, he had become a friend of James Connolly, the Labour Party founder who was executed in 1916. Through his association with Connolly and his Citizen Army he had come to the attention of the British and was deported back to India after the Rising. He also knew Sean O'Casey, the playwright, but the Irish people who most influenced him were neither revolutionaries nor playwrights, but the landladies of Dublin.

Seated in surroundings of extraordinary opulence, the president told me how, in his poverty-stricken Dublin days as a law student, he had lived for a time in every one of the city's postal districts. 'You see,' he explained, 'I had no money, so I used to have to keep changing my digs. I would stay in one part of the city for about two weeks and then, when the landlady would start looking for her money, I would have to find a new landlady, in a part of the city where I was not known. I cycled all over Dublin and I got to know the place very well!'

In Heathrow Airport on the way home I was reminded that the British-Irish revolutionary tradition was still alive and virulent. My name was called out over the loudspeakers asking me to contact Information. I did so to discover that my luggage had been cordoned off and my Indian Christmas presents were being examined by armed policemen. That little problem was soon solved, but I often wondered, as the North of Ireland situation worsened, how many of the young men from the Middle East and the Basque region who visited Ireland during the Troubles would turn out to be the Giris of the future.

For throughout its history Ireland has acted as an extraordinarily important colonial laboratory for all sorts of experiments in policing, education, constitutional development and counter-insurgency. This was brought home to me during a visit to Korea in May 1979. I was received in Seoul by one of President Park Chung-Hee's principal advisers, a fascinating man who had been South Korea's ambassador to Washington. He had a considerable grasp of Irish affairs and could quote Yeats at will. The official Korean guidebook which I had been given opened with the statement that 'The Koreans are the Irish of Asia' and went on to describe the similarities between the two 'hard-working' races in their shared respect for culture, education, the aged and, very properly I thought, feasting and the enjoyment of life.

However, it was not merely these similarities that impressed President Park and his circle. It was the fact that before the Japanese invaded Korea in 1910 they had sent four professors to the British Museum in London to study the methods of what the Japanese regarded at the time as the world's most efficient colonial system, British rule in Ireland. The Japanese found that it was based on the extirpation of native dress, language and culture, destruction of the existing system of land-holding and the inculcation of feelings of inferiority towards the master race, notably by teaching children in state schools that they were not Irish, but British. All these lessons, combined with the emulation of British efficiency in quelling revolt, were subsequently applied in Korea. One result of the Japanese experiment was that it created in Koreans an admiration for the Irish success in resisting the process. Tragically, before our friendship had time to develop, both the former ambassador and President Park were assassinated later in 1979.

Eleven years later, Frank Delaney suggested to me how I might achieve my ambition of drawing together the threads of the tapestry of the Irish diaspora and at the same time accomplish the de Valera project. 'It's simple,' he said. 'Write both books. Just do de Valera first.' I was duly given a contract for the two works, and *De Valera* appeared in 1993. In all honesty I found that my researches into the latter part of de Valera's life confirmed the unfavourable impression I had formed of him while compiling the Collins book. His character did not improve after 1922, when Collins was killed. He became more serpentine, more Machiavellian, the manner in which he founded and controlled the *Irish Press* being a prime example. De Valera more than any other Irish politician of his lifetime knew how to acquire and hold on to power. The Fianna Fail Party at the time of writing is still the most successful political machine on the island.

But in de Valera's era, after an initial burst of social progress when the party took office in the 1930s, all became stultification, rhetoric and a lack of substantive policy that manifested itself in poverty and emigration. Ill fares the land where initiative decays and emigration thrives. Writing with these beliefs, it can be imagined that the picture I painted of the once almighty de Valera was not a flattering one, but it was a widely popular one if the hardback sales of the book were anything to go by and, like *Michael Collins*, it has had a continuing shelf life in paperback. However, it created one very disgruntled reader – the then Taoiseach, Albert Reynolds.

Albert had very decently agreed to loan me Dublin Castle for the de Valera launch and in addition promised to launch the book himself. The invitations duly noted that the launching ceremony would be performed by Taoiseach, Mr Albert Reynolds. However, the *Irish Times* serialised extracts from the book, and one fine morning Martin Mansergh walked into the Taoiseach's office to enquire if he was aware of what the book contained. Albert was not and Mansergh's enlightenment horrified him. What was to be done? The invitations were out, the event was much discussed, and it was common knowledge that the acceptances read like a Who's Who in Dublin's media, social and political life. Backing out at that stage could land the Taoiseach with more unfavourable publicity than would appearing to countenance the dreadful things I had unearthed about *der Führer*.

Albert solved the problem with the same sort of country cuteness that he was at the time bringing to bear on John Major over Northern Ireland. My daughter Jackie works in the Taoiseach's office, so a message was conveyed to her to 'tell your dad the Taoiseach won't be able to launch his book because he has got to go to an important meeting in Vienna'. Then the government jet took off to some obscure European bunfight, which someone had pulled out of the EU ministerial calendar at short notice, and at equally short notice I was faced with the problem of getting someone to perform the launching ceremony. Protocol demanded that this should have been either the Taoiseach or a cabinet minister. With Albert hightailing it, cabinet ministers were out of the question, and for some time there existed a possibility that the permission to use Dublin Castle might be withdrawn.

Then, with the launch less than a week away, I took part in a radio discussion involving Tom Garvin, professor of politics in University College, Dublin, with whose father I had been involved in another conflict over my writings, all those years ago in the *Evening Press*. We adjourned for a pint after the programme and Tom asked me who was going to launch the book. 'You are,' I replied. Tom could, would and did perform the ceremony. The launch was a huge success, one of the biggest ever seen in Dublin. Unfortunately it turned out to be too successful for my peace of mind. So many people bought books, and I had to do so much signing, that the speeches were delayed for almost two hours. During this time the wine flowed copiously, and a charming lady from the Department of Foreign Affairs saw to it that my glass was continually replenished. So was everyone else's and, forgetful of the fact that I had a leather-bound copy of the book for him, the one I had intended to present to Albert, Tom Garvin also bought a copy. When he loomed up in the crowd, his face beaming like a full moon in a fog, unexpectedly seeking my autograph, I incautiously inscribed my brainchild to 'Tom Garvin for courage in the face of a retreating dog-food manufacturer'.

The wine had made Tom equally carefree, and when he stood before the microphone, he prefaced his otherwise entirely appropriate, if unduly flattering, speech by reading out the inscription, which was picked up by a gossip columnist in the *Irish Times*. I patched up the difficulty with Albert subsequently by sending him another leather-bound copy, which he graciously accepted. Not a man to hold a grudge, he was also good enough to subsequently launch another one of my books (*Ireland in the Twentieth Century*), even though in the meantime I had inadvertently given him further grief. A few years after he resigned as Taoiseach we had bumped into each other in a Dublin hotel as Albert waited to be picked up by his driver. Some miscommunication had occurred and the minutes ticked by as Albert waited to be driven to a meeting in Government Buildings. I offered Albert a lift in my old Volvo, which had bars between the front and back seats so that Thor, my overgrown Dalmatian, was prevented from sharing the driving with me. Albert accepted the lift and got to his meeting in time, but as he headed up the steps of Government Buildings, I noticed to my horror that somehow Thor had recently managed to satisfy his desire to sit in the front seat. Albert's magnificent suit, tailored in some sort of shiny black material, was covered in white hairs.

Though I was very proud of the fact that I had thought of writing about the diaspora before President Mary Robinson was elected (in December 1990) and placed a candle in her window as a symbol of recognition and welcome for the emigrants, I was again delayed in putting my idea into practice. Publishers, as I have said, are intrigued by anniversaries. The twenty-fifth anniversary of the British troops being sent to Ireland in 1969 approached after the publication of *De Valera*, and Hutchinson thought it would be a good idea for me to put the diaspora on the back burner and instead produce a history of the Troubles. This duly appeared in 1995 and was followed by the diaspora book, *Wherever Green Is Worn*, in 2000 and by *Ireland in the Twentieth Century* in 2003. *De Valera* and the diaspora book were over 750 pages in length, the *Twentieth Century* history more than 850. By comparison *The Troubles* was a minnow, only 480 pages in length. In between producing these volumes I also wrote the text for two illustrated books, on the Irish Civil War and on 1916, and extensively updated the IRA book.

Researching the diaspora necessitated extensive travel, from America to Africa, the Argentine to the Caribbean, from Scotland to Newfoundland, Australia and New Zealand and many places in between. Between the travel and incessant interviewing and note-taking I developed two permanent conditions, tiredness and anxiety. Would I make this flight, or that connection? Would so and so be at the airport? I realised how deeply the tiredness had sunk in while visiting Perth. There was a nude beach less than half a kilometre from where I was staying, its patrons renowned for their arresting displays of beach volleyball, but in a week-long visit I never mustered up the energy to walk to a game, never mind take part in one! Not surprisingly the reading and writing involved took its toll on my eyes, and I had to learn to cope with a more or less permanent state of headache, punctuated every three or four months by a visit to Peter Eustace and sometimes the scalpel being produced yet again.

However, work is the best therapy, and particularly work that involves not merely interviewing fascinating people, but researching fascinating original documents such as correspondence or memoranda, in the handwriting of people like Collins, Lloyd George or Churchill. The good news was that I managed both to establish a mental equilibrium after the upheavals in my personal and professional life and at the same time to generate sufficient revenue to eventually meet the considerable costs of the separation agreement with Cherry. The bad news was that the effort involved in researching *Wherever Green Is Worn* had unpleasant health consequences.

A striking feature of my research was the welcome I received all over the world. The peace process hung in the balance for most of the time I was travelling, and everywhere I went I found myself invited to give talks and get involved in discussions on how things were going. The common denominator could be summed up in two words 'interest' and 'hospitality'. These qualities probably saved my life in Africa, where I generally stayed either with friends in the Irish Diplomatic Service or with various members of the GOAL humanitarian aid organisation. In Nairobi I stayed at the home of the GOAL representative Noreen Prenderville and her Swedish husband, Goti.

One of my best sources of information in Kenya was the Loreto nuns, who had originally concentrated on education but were now increasingly involved in justice and peace issues. A couple of days before I was due to leave Kenya for Rwanda, I arranged to take the head nun, Sister Catriona Kelly, and one of her colleagues to lunch. Catriona casually asked me a few questions about my health. How was the travel affecting my energy, was I sleeping, etc. I thought she was just making conversation, but after lunch she announced that a Dr Meyerhold would see me in the morning! In vain did I splutter objections. Sister Kelly literally took me by the arm and led me through the throbbing Nairobi traffic to a tall office block, to show me where I was to meet Dr Meyerhold, who turned out to be the doctor to the Loreto Order.

He had been in Africa for a lifetime and was despondent about the prospects for the schools, hospitals and orphanages which the Irish missionaries had built but which increasingly now had no Irish clergy or nuns to run them. 'The Irish came to work and pray; I'm afraid the others just pray,' he said. He told me that the department in the local hospital where my blood samples would be tested cost as much to run as did an entire hospital under the care of the nuns.

My blood pressure produced a marked change in the tone of our conversation. Meyerhold took my blood pressure a second time, refusing to believe what the first attempt showed. Then he literally paled and sat down. When he told me the reading, I too paled. I didn't have blood pressure, I had a cricket score – something of the order of 205 over 118 as I remember it. (I've lost the scrap of paper noting the reading which I used to carry in my wallet as a sort of memento mori.) If I had flown on to Rwanda the next day, as I had intended, I would more than likely have had a stroke. Certainly I would have been in a very, very bad place in which to seek hospital care. As it was, Meyerhold grounded me for three weeks and prescribed a lot of blood-pressure tablets and no alcohol.

At first Noreen, the GOAL representative with whom I was staying, could not believe my blood pressure levels were so high. She was a qualified nurse and I remember her saying: 'That's impossible! You could not be smiling like that if your diastolic was a hundred and eighteen.' She tested my blood pressure on a home monitoring device, which she tested by taking her own and Goti's (normal) blood pressures, but for the first few days this could not cope with mine. The little screen danced with a combination of jumbled numbers and the letter E. However, after three weeks of rest, healthy eating and no alcohol both the machine and myself returned to normality. The unfortunate Noreen and Goti were the real victims, having to put up with me unexpectedly for an additional three weeks. The same fate would later befall my friends Charles and Wilma Mooney in New York. Various unexpected interviewing delays greatly protracted my stay with them also, but as with Goti and Noreen, our friendship survived the ordeal. Fair play to them! The African delay played merry hell with my African schedule, causing me to lop a number of countries off my itinerary. It also caused me to forget to have my Kenyan visa extended. This omission was pointed out to me by two enormous Kenyan detectives who were checking passports before allowing people into the departure area at Nairobi Airport. I explained that I had been sick. 'Are you too sick to stand up in court, Mr Coogan?' enquired one of the cops. However, after the pair had laughed mightily at this witticism, they allowed me to board a flight to Kigali.

Ironically, after all the travel and effort involved, *Wherever Green Is Worn* missed much of the Christmas 2000 sales period because a libel suit caused it to be temporarily withdrawn. It was amended, and at the time of writing, almost seven years later, it continues to tick over quite satisfactorily. There is no great money involved, but I do have the consolation that it, like at least two of my other books, was a 'first'. *Ireland Since the Rising* was the first work to chart Irish history for the fifty years after the 1916 Rising and *The IRA* was the first in-depth study of the movement. All of which, according to *History Ireland* (summer 2004), added up to make me 'one of Ireland's most prolific writers of history, certainly one of the most widely read'.

Libel is not the only hazard faced by a writer. Eternal vigilance is the price of survival. Writers, and creative people generally, are too preoccupied with either their next work or with money problems to keep a proper eye on the business side of creativity. When my long-term agent Murray Pollinger retired, I discovered that he had sold on my contract for the IRA book to another agent, David Higham. I have never laid eyes on anyone from this agency, who do not act for me in any way, but they now receive Pollinger's percentage of my royalties from that work. It's profoundly irritating, but quite legal. Indeed I had stupidly signed a contract for a new edition of the book without even reading it and did not realise that Pollinger had put in wording that allowed him to sell on the contract.

Nor did I receive any money from the 1996 film *Michael Collins*, which clearly showed the influence of my book. A hitherto unpublished quotation of de Valera's, which I had revealed in the book, was used to link de Valera to Collins's death.

De Valera, at the end of his own life, refused to lend his name to a scholarship fund set up to commemorate Collins, saying that 'in the fullness of time' Collins's greatness would be recognised – at his expense. However, the film transposed the quotation back in time by over forty years in such a way as to make it appear that de Valera gave the go-ahead to an ambusher to shoot Collins. In fact he had made strenuous efforts to have the ambush called off, and I had been at pains to point out that, whatever else one might accuse de Valera of, he had nothing to do with the fatal ambush and in fact had tried to prevent it.

The Collins book made one significant contribution to man's happiness – it fathered a whiskey! One day I was phoned by a member of the Collins family, Michael O'Mahony, a solicitor, asking me if I would take a call from a Lee Ensidler, the CEO of a New York importing and bottling company, who wanted to engage me as a consultant. Ensidler told me: 'We got an old guy here. He's got all his marbles. He's a great reader, but he's eighty-six so he ain't ordering too many green bananas.' The 'old guy' turned out to be the legendary Sidney Frank, who had made billions out of developing Grey Goose vodka, America's favourite. I went to New York to meet him and found him holding court in bed, surrounded by his staff, while outside the house there waited a retinue of young golfers whose careers the great man was sponsoring.

Frank indeed had possession of his marbles. He was an omnivorous reader and told me that when he finished my book he put it down and said: 'We gotta have an Irish whiskey and we gotta call it Michael Collins.' What Sidney Frank wanted, Sidney Frank got. His staff went to the Irish distillery Cooley for the whiskey, to China for the unusual large, fluted bottle, and to me for publicity material. And so, since St Patrick's Day 2006 the Frank organisation have successfully marketed what I called Michael Collins's 'heroic spirit' with the slogan 'the Big Fellow'! Sadly the 'green bananas' comment proved apposite. Sidney died a few months before Michael Collins was launched.

CHAPTER 16

The Peace Process

After the years – no, the decades – of seemingly fruitless effort directed at getting the IRA into politics and the North out of the headlines, witnessing the Good Friday Agreement of 1998 come about was one of the happiest occasions of my life. It was *the* classical example of the split-level syndrome. On the one hand there was delight at the achievement of the Agreement itself, even though with an obvious cloud hanging over it – at that stage Paisley and his party were still refusing to have anything to do with it. On the other I got a sudden insight into what Tom Moore meant when, on hearing that Catholic Emancipation had been passed, he exclaimed: 'Good! Now I can stretch my Protestant legs!' Now there could be an end to polemic and propaganda, a catching up with other aspects of life. But whatever my, or anyone else's, reaction to the Agreement, was there can be no doubt that it was a great and significant occasion, a turning point in Irish history.

I have written extensively about the peace process in other books. Here my intention is not so much to give a step-by-step history of events as to offer an impressionistic account of the process as it involved myself. In a nutshell the Agreement came about because both Ecclesiastes and Jean Kennedy Smith, US ambassador to Ireland, rode into town. Ecclesiastes, as already noted, had been travelling for some time. Jean arrived in Dublin on a June day in 1993 as the new American ambassador, sister to Senator Ted Kennedy and to the two murdered brothers President John F. and Attorney General Robert Kennedy. Another boost for Ecclesiastes and the struggling Irish peace process was the fact that Albert Reynolds had already arrived in Government Buildings as Taoiseach, a position in which he had prioritised the Northern issue. As Taoiseach he was also well placed to judge the importance of having an ambassadorial Kennedy in his bailiwick.

I first met Jean shortly after she had arrived, at a Fourth of July garden party in the embassy at which she invited me to a dinner that she was giving for some of Dublin's decision-takers a few days later. Said decision-takers were kept waiting as Jean subjected me to a viva voce on the Northern Ireland situation. She became so engrossed in the subject that she overlooked the fact that we had all been called to dinner quite some time earlier. As Dick Spring, the minister for foreign affairs, commented as we went to our places, 'That was intense!' 'Intense' barely described the zeal and enthusiasm with which Jean set about her Irish mission. Apart from a certain *pietas* towards her ancestral homeland, her posting afforded her the opportunity to put behind her some wrenching experiences from her recent past. One was the nursing of her husband, Stephen Smith, in his last illness. Smith had been in charge of the Kennedys' personal finances. His death was followed by the ordeal of the protracted trial of their son William on rape charges, of which he was ultimately cleared.

Welcoming her on the night of her dinner, Albert Reynolds had wound up a felicitous speech by saying: 'Welcome home, Ms Ambassador.' It sounded like the sort of graceful platitude one heard uttered at such occasions, but both Jean and Albert certainly acted over the next few years as though they were serious. Jean's contribution in particular would enrage the British, outrage the unionists and help to change Irish history for the better.

Here a brief word is necessary about how Anglo-Irish relationships were regarded from Washington before the Kennedy descent. I had been on friendly terms with a number of Jean's predecessors. Three in particular had impeccable Irish connections: Pete Earlie and John Moore, both of whom were Republicans, and William V. Shannon, a Democrat appointee under Carter. Moore, as a boy of twelve, had been brought by his father to the Democratic Convention at which Al Smith was elected and a prized boyhood memory was of being photographed with 'Dev'. He later went on to become a sort of mercantile foreign affairs minister to the Latin American interests of John Grace, also an old Irish-American stalwart and founder of the giant Grace Corporation. The family interest in things Irish may be gauged by the fact that his brother Richard also became a US ambassador to Ireland. Earlie too was at home in the corridors of both commerce and politics. A successful Madison Avenue figure, he had overseen Reagan's first presidential election media campaign. Bill Shannon in his day was the top Irish-American journalist, being a member of first the *New York Times*'s and then the *Boston Globe*'s editorial boards. He later became a professor at Boston University, teaching Irish history and politics, and was a close friend of Democrat luminaries such as Ted Kennedy and Thomas 'Tip' O'Neill, whom he most credited with getting him the Dublin posting.

All three were first-class men at their jobs. With Shannon in particular few would quarrel with the proposition that in the combination of himself and his wife, Elizabeth, a former *Washington Post* journalist, Ireland got two ambassadors for the price of one. After Bill died many people in Ireland, including myself, had hoped that she would get the ambassadorial call.

Unquestionably, all of the foregoing would have liked to have done something about Northern Ireland, or helped to bring about a united Ireland, but their instructions precluded them from taking any steps in this direction. Washington saw the problem very largely through London's eyes, and the American embassy in London regarded the Dublin embassy as a sort of minor sub-office. Apart from the 'special relationships' there were practical day-to-day relationships between powerful Washington agencies such as the State Department, the Pentagon, the CIA and the FBI, which involved, on the British side, MI6, Scotland Yard, the British armed services and Whitehall. In addition British commercial interests in America were, and are, immense. There was also the influence of the old blood and old money of aristocratic British families, like the Cecils, who were traditionally pro-unionist. One of the family, Lord Robert Cranborne, now the 7th Marquess of Salisbury, became an important figure in Anglo-Irish affairs in the latter days of John Major's rule. Cranborne had shrewdly backed Major when John Redwood mounted a leadership challenge against him. He was rewarded by being appointed to the cabinet sub-committee on Northern Ireland. Thereafter, when Irish initiatives were proposed, Major's reaction tended to be: 'See what Robert says'!

However, Jean set about discharging her Irish duties in the spirit of the sentiments taken from George Bernard Shaw, in a speech written by Bill Shannon, and delivered by her brother JFK, during his Irish visit in 1963. She asked not 'Why?' but 'Why not?' She, and the Irish government, were helped by a number of factors. Reynolds had built on Haughey's policy of ending the policy of cold war that had existed between Irish-Americans and Dublin's 'heavy-gang' government. To a degree this policy had carried over for a time under Jack Lynch, who in 1978 was persuaded for the first time in Irish diplomatic history to write a letter attempting to discredit an American congressman, Mario Biaggi, who ran what was known as the Ad Hoc Committee, which comprised some eighty-four congressmen and senators with an interest in Ireland. The letter accused Biaggi and his committee of giving aid and comfort to the IRA, something which, inci-dentally, he emphatically denied to me. It was the brainchild of two prominent Irish diplomats who had come to prominence in the FitzGerald era: Michael Lillis, who was attached to the Irish embassy in Washington, and Sean Donlon, head of the Anglo-Irish section.

It's difficult at this remove in time to recapture the wasteful degree of hostility that built up between Dublin, its emissaries and rank-and-file Irish-Americans, but I always think of one incident in particular that helps to encapsulate it. The annual centrepiece rite of identification for the Irish in America has traditionally been the St Patrick's Day parades, particularly that in New York. One incident, or set of incidents, involving that parade exemplifies the atmosphere that prevailed at the time.

Judge James Comerford, who was also a leading figure in the influential American Ancient Order of Hibernians, which traditionally controlled the parade, was such a stickler for detail that he consulted with the United States Military Academy, or West Point, and the archivist of the famous Irish regiment the Fighting 69th, to ensure that the parade programme was printed in authentic Kelly green. But he also ensured that the name of Sean Donlon, who by then had become the Irish ambassador to the States, was omitted from the list of dignitaries. The rank but not the man was to be honoured. Donlon for his part continued his campaign, stepping down off the reviewing stand every time a Noraid, the Irish Northern Aid Committee, banner was seen approaching! A good way to lose weight perhaps, but not to win friends and influence people.

However, when Haughey tried to replace Donlon in Washington, during his interlude as Taoiseach (in 1979–81) he found the Donlon–FitzGerald axis too strong for him. Figures like Ted Kennedy, 'Tip' O'Neill, Hugh Carey and Pat Moynihan had been mobilised. Haughey was informed that moving Donlon would be thought of as caving in to pro-IRA pressures. Donlon stayed and, under FitzGerald, subsequently became secretary of the department of foreign affairs. He became the first Irish governmental department secretary to resign his post (for a job in industry) in January 1987, as Haughey neared the Taoiseach's throne once more. Speaking in New York, Haughey had pointedly stated: 'Where there was antagonism and suspicion we must now create a whole new atmosphere of constructive dialogue.'

The detritus of the 'heavy-gang' government's policy remained in being for some time, however. I wrote a piece for the *New York Times*'s op-ed page pointing out that whereas St Patrick was said to have driven the snakes out of Ireland, 'the snakes of dissension' were now manifesting themselves in New York during the saint's feast day. I advocated dialogue between the warring Irish factions. For this I received a warning letter from Senator Pat Moynihan's office on the well-worn theme that recognition of their existence would give aid and comfort to terrorists. But gradually, as the tone from Dublin changed, so too did a quiet revolution begin to take place in Irish-American circles.

This originated not with Northern Ireland, but on the issue of getting Green Cards for the thousands of Irish immigrants illegally working in the US, and bore fruit in the provision of first the Donnelly and then the Morrison visas, which enabled tens of thousands of Irish immigrants to legitimise their existence in the US. One of the moving spirits in the campaign had been Niall O'Dowd, publisher and editor of the *Irish-American Voice*, who like most of the better journalists of the era had had his first writings published by the *Irish Press*. Niall, realising the potential of the immigration reform movement, had enthused people like Bill Flynn, the chairman of Mutual of America, and Chuck Feeney, the philanthropist who had pioneered duty free shopping, the Democratic congressman Bruce Morrison and the Republican Peter King to continue their involvement in the Irish arena, this time with a view to ending the violence in Northern Ireland. Other vitally important forces that came together at this time included two particularly able Irish diplomats Dermot Gallagher, the ambassador, and Brendan Scannell, the number-two man at the embassy, who had earlier served as consul general in Boston. Coming from County Leitrim, one of Ireland's most impoverished areas, Gallagher's guile and manoeuvrings were such that even Israeli diplomats came to envy his access to Bill Clinton. Scannell, for his part, had all the charm and forcefulness of his native Kerry with an additive not always found in that area, tact. And supporting all these initiatives was the single most powerful figure on the Irish-American scene and in the Democratic Party, Ted Kennedy.

With Kennedy aboard, the Clinton administration got around the institutionalised objections of the pro-British Washington bureaucracy by making a number of key changes to the manner in which Dublin–Washington relations were handled. The direction of Irish policy was withdrawn from the State Department and given to the National Security Agency under Tony Lake and, importantly, to another Kennedy loyalist, Nancy Soderberg, who became the conduit and adviser to the White House. This outraged the British and reactivated the turf war between the London and Dublin embassies. The war had become but a distant memory under Jean's predecessor, William Fitzgerald. A charming man and a particularly spry octogenarian, Fitzgerald arrived in Dublin with some unfortunate baggage. Asked about his views on the solution to the Irish problem at his confirmation hearings, he had replied that the answer lay in bringing the loyalists and the unionists together.

But Jean was a Kennedy, a fact that had consequences on two levels. One, the political: the Kennedy political dynasty had grown from, on Jean's mother's side, the quintessentially Irish-American politician John Francis 'Honey Fitz' Fitzgerald, mayor of Boston; and on her father's side, the even more astute and wheeler-dealeresque Joe Kennedy, ambassador to the Court of St James's and founder of one of the great fortunes of America.

The other consequence was at a deeper, psychological, level. The White House side of Jean's character saw no harm in occasional mention of the fact that Brian Boru, the High King of Ireland, credited with breaking the power of the Vikings in Ireland, was a Kennedy! But in her thatched-cottage background she was conscious of the fact that her ancestor Patrick Kennedy had left Wexford as a famine emigrant, and she maintained contact with the Wexford relations whom she had first met on that day in 1963 when her brother JFK came to Ireland as president. The significance of this visit could only be fully understood by people who were alive at the time. To the Irish public it meant that the stench of the coffin ships had given way to the scent of the rose garden. 'One of their own' had made it. Now, almost a lifetime away from her brother's murder, another member of the family had arrived in Ireland determined to establish a reputation in her own right.

The other central figure without whom the Irish issue could never have taken centre stage, or Clinton and Blair functioned as they did, was Albert Reynolds, who had dethroned Haughey in 1992, the year before Kennedy Smith arrived in Dublin. Reynolds was absolutely central to the peace process. If the Irish Taoiseach cannot, or will not, act over Northern Ireland, nothing will happen. Ever since the power-sharing executive had collapsed in the mid-1970s, constitutional activity on Northern Ireland could be characterised as activity without movement. A Convention that was set up in the wake of the power-sharing executive's collapse had proved to be nothing more than a ploy on the part of the Whitehall mandarins to keep the Paddies talking while efforts continued in another part of the forest to lure the IRA into a ceasefire that led only to the H-Blocks. Ironically the hunger strikes within the H-Blocks changed the North's political landscape and made for the emergence of Sinn Fein as a political force. In an effort to prevent the nationalist support swinging completely away from the SDLP, Garret FitzGerald, who had succeeded Haughey in 1981, after his first stint in office, set up what was known as the New Ireland Forum in Dublin Castle. All the constitutional nationalist parties on the island took part, and for almost two years the Irish political system turned its energies to finding a formula to resolve the conflict.

Being an Irish political forum, it found not one formula but three. The options were a united Ireland, joint authority between London and Dublin or a confederal Ireland. I was driving my friend Aidan Hennigan, the London editor of the *Irish Press*, to Dublin Airport after a funeral when, on 19 October 1984, we heard over the car radio Mrs Thatcher deliver her considered opinion on all three proposals. She listed them and, speaking with great deliberation, said after each one: 'That is out.' More than twenty years later, in 2006, Aidan would receive an honorary OBE in the New Year's honours list. The prospect that Aidan Francis Bernard Hennigan from the County Mayo, former London editor of the *Irish Press*, would one day receive the Order of the British Empire with the blessing of Her Majesty Queen Elizabeth II was not more remarkable than the fact that said Aidan Francis Bernard survived the effect of Mrs Thatcher on my driving.

Granted that La Thatcher might have been allowed a certain personal animus towards militant Irish republicans, given the fact that the Feinians had blown up her friend Airey Neave, and would subsequently attempt to blow up herself and her colleagues at the Grand Hotel in Brighton. Nevertheless, politically, it was as if the British Labour Party, the Conservatives and the Liberal Democrats had spent a year and a half doing nothing else except attempting to resolve some major Anglo-American difficulty, only to have the American president dismiss its proposals out of hand. After decanting Aidan at the airport, I returned to the office to write one of my more sulphuric editorials. Its bitterness was no doubt wasted on the desert air of Downing Street, but the Irish public's general reaction was much like my own. Importantly, the feeling transmitted itself to Irish America. This impacted on the White House, where Reagan had already come out in support of the New Ireland Forum's proceedings. His advisers told the president that Thatcher's reaction to the Forum Report had had the opposite effect to what was intended. It was Sinn Fein, not the SDLP, who had benefited from the 'Out! Out! Out!' speech as it became known.

To the horror of the unionists the Iron Lady was forced into a mini U-turn. After further London–Dublin negotiations the Anglo-Irish Agreement, also known as the Hillsborough Agreement, was signed at Hillsborough Castle, County Down, on 15 November 1985. This confirmed the North's position within the UK, but it also allowed for the setting up of a joint Dublin–London secretariat at Maryfield in Belfast and for an inter-governmental conference at which it was expected that the Irish government would be putting forward 'views and proposals on matters relating to Northern Ireland'. The secretariat meant that the Irish flag now flew openly over Maryfield, a far cry from the days when it was so illegal and so anathematised that Paisley was able to launch his political career by protesting against its display in a Belfast backstreet window. Another distasteful morsel for unionist digestive systems to swallow was the mention of the fact that if a majority in the North ever sought a united Ireland, the UK would not stand in the way.

The unionist outrage at these developments resulted in riots and, more importantly, their withdrawal from the Northern Ireland Assembly, which had continued to totter along at Stormont as a sort of parliamentary fig leaf. Paisley literally had to be carried out for the benefit of the cameras. And there, so far as the public was concerned, matters constitutional seemingly rested (or languished) until Albert Reynolds became Taoiseach in 1992, William Jefferson Clinton became president of the United States in 1993, and Jean Kennedy Smith packed her bags for Dublin.

However, under the surface a peace process was actually making some progress. There is an Irish phrase '*uisce faoi thalamh*', which means 'water under the ground', secret stirrings, and this is what was happening in republican circles. One can take a number of starting points. For example, the Pope's visit to Ireland in 1979, during which he delivered a speech carefully crafted for him by Cathal Daly, the then bishop of Down and Connor, in whose diocese Belfast lay. The speech contained severe condemnations of IRA violence, but it also contained references to the responsibilities of politicians to take the steps open to them to remove the conditions in which violence flourished. Gerry Adams began a sort of on-off public dialogue with Bishop Daly arising from the Pope's speech. In an open letter to Daly he wrote: 'You call on republicans to renounce violence and join in the peaceful struggle for the rights of nationalists. What peaceful struggle?' Father Reid, after reading his utterances and consulting with the Redemptorists' leading theologian, Father Sean O'Riordan, decided that Adams's queries were legitimate and that the question of political initiative should be pursued.

Father Alec Reid's health had broken down some years earlier as the result of the many pressures on him and he had withdrawn from the Northern situation. I called to see him in hospital in Drogheda one day and found him lying on his bed with eyes closed, fully dressed and seemingly drained of all energy. By coincidence Gerry Adams and his wife, Colette, also called to see the priest while I was visiting. I don't think any of us would have bet on the spent figure on the bed ever having the energy to resume normal living, never mind become a central figure in a nerve-racking and protracted process. But after a spell in Rome, and then some time in Redemptorist monasteries in different parts of the country, as remote from the stresses of Northern Ireland as his superiors could arrange, Reid gradually became involved again in Northern Ireland matters. The murder by the IRA in South Armagh of an Ulster Defence Regiment (UDR) man whom he tried unavailingly to save was the catalyst that caused him to rejoin the peace process along with a number of other priests and Protestant evangelicals who felt they were called on by their religion to make some sort of response to the Troubles. Prominent amongst the would-be peacemakers was another Clonard Redemptorist, his friend Father Gerry Reynolds.

Like Father Reid, Reynolds was a Southerner, from Limerick, and an ecumenist. Like Reid, he had decided that something, anything, had to be done after hearing of a murder, this time of an RUC man. The dead man had lived on the Protestant Shankill Road, not far from the monastery. So, not knowing whether he would be lynched or not, Reynolds called to the dead man's house to offer his sympathies. He was made unreservedly welcome and thereafter, with Reid, devoted himself to doing what he could to prevent any more such deaths.

Both priests knew Adams and his character. Adams attended Sunday mass at Clonard Monastery, generally accompanied by his son Gearoid. Reid knew that, along with a keen sense of humour, Adams had a political calculator implanted in his thinking processes. I rarely met anyone who could analyse any given political situation with the same acuity. Along with these qualities Adams had gravitas, exuding a force field that made people instinctively defer to him. Reid decided that Adams was sincere in seeking a political rather than a military route and that he had the qualities needed to travel that road. With a view to getting the republicans into mainstream politics, Reid began making contact with a number of people, including myself. A debate had already begun within the republican camp on the way forward. Possibly one of the most important turning points in this had occurred one night back in the early 1980s on the M1 motorway outside Belfast as three men were driving towards the city after attending a Sinn Fein meeting. They were Gerry Adams and two other prominent republican leaders and theoreticians, Tom Hartley and Jim Gibney.

Adams had been holding forth on his ideas for involving Fianna Fail and Irish America with Sinn Fein in an unarmed strategy, which would advance the movement's goal of a united Ireland through the use of the ballot box rather than the bomb or bullet. He had emerged as the leading republican intellectual in the wake of the IRA ceasefire of 1975 and the recriminations that followed its disastrous outcome for the IRA. He had feared a similar debacle would follow a more notable republican attempt to dabble in politics – the selection of the hunger-striking Bobby Sands as a Sinn Fein candidate in a Westminster by-election – and at first had opposed the idea. However, on seeing the huge surge in nationalist support that the candidacy elicited, Adams swiftly became enthusiastic about the value of the political route. So did Hartley and Gibney. Probably had the three men in that car been ten or fifteen years older at the time of the Sunningdale experiment they would have opted to support it. As it was, Hartley, who was driving, pulled over to the side of the motorway and exclaimed to Adams: 'Why don't you go to the IRA and put that strategy to them?'

At the time Adams had to be careful about discussing such a policy (which by definition necessitated a ceasefire) with the IRA, or anyone else in Irish politics. The republican movement was riven by a debate over whether or not to drop its traditional abstentionist policy (which Adams favoured) and take any seats it might win in elections. The fact that he, and other prominent leaders, like Martin McGuinness, owed their ascendancy in the republican movement to having opposed the 1975 ceasefire was both a stepping stone and a millstone. However, he and, crucially, Father Reid persevered along the political route. Reid's motivation, as he said several years later, in the draft of an important letter to Haughey (dated 28 November 1986) was not political but pastoral and moral.

Given its republican background, Fianna Fail might have appeared the logical conduit between Sinn Fein and the Republic's political system. But Reid's early efforts to make meaningful contact with the party had proved unsuccessful. He tried and failed to get in touch with Haughey through various people. One was the popular Belfast priest Father Des Wilson, who could fairly be described as a Belfast version of a worker priest. He was also a cousin of John Wilson, a prominent Fianna Fail frontbencher and a former minister. But John proved unreceptive to Des's overtures because he mistrusted the avant-garde priest's socialism. Other doors having remained closed also, Father Reid turned to me. He phoned me to say that he wanted me to 'tell Mr Haughey that there now exists a real possibility of Irish unity'. That got my attention! He went on to say that he wanted me to help with putting Adams in touch with Haughey.

Reid could hardly have come at a worse time, because Haughey and I had recently had one of our periodic fallings-out, this time over the recently concluded Hillsborough Agreement of November 1985. We used to meet fairly regularly for lunch in the Berkeley Court Hotel in Ballsbridge, where a table was always kept waiting for him, as was a bedroom wherein he used to entertain Ms Terry Keane. As he was wont to do when people either crossed him or told him things he did not want to hear, Haughey had flown into a rage. He got up and walked out of the restaurant, leaving me sitting there by myself. My offence had been to say that I thought that it was a mistake for him to have criticised and apparently rejected the Hillsborough Agreement out of hand as he had done a few days earlier. To my way of thinking, it contained some positive aspects and might be built upon. My assessment was that the tide of Irish nationalism had reached a higher level on the quay wall of Northern Irish history than ever before. Certainly the fact that the unionist community had exploded in riot and protest march against its provisions indicated that it favoured nationalists. The *Irish Times* political correspondent, John Cooney, shared my view, observing (on 16 November) that the Hillsborough Agreement had given the Republic 'a foothold in decisions governing Northern Ireland'.

Speaking in the Dail and on television, however, Haughey greeted the signing of the Agreement by criticising it for giving away the Irish constitutional position on the North – that contained in Articles 2 and 3 which Paisley had objected to (see Chapter 10) – and said that he was opposed to the recognition of British sovereignty over the North. A day or so later, however, came the one and only time he rang me concerning a speech of his. He rang me to say that I would find 'interesting' a speech he had just given. It was indeed. At a Friends of Fianna Fail dinner he in effect rowed back on his criticism of the Hillsborough Agreement, saying that while he maintained his objections to it, he nevertheless would not 'impede or obstruct' any benefits it might provide for nationalists. But things were still edgy between us. Accordingly, when a few weeks after the Berkeley Court walk-out, Father Reid suggested that I, 'as a friend of Mr Haughey's', was in a position to help end the killing and bring about Irish unity, I got a sudden keen insight into the meaning of the term 'conflicting emotions'. It was indeed, as the American humorist Bennett Cerf once observed, like 'watching your mother-in-law back your new Cadillac over a cliff'.

Though left to myself I would have judged it wiser to stay away from Haughey for a few weeks more, out of respect for Reid I contacted Haughey again and our skirmishing lunches resumed. I asked Reid to get me some sort of written authorisation from Adams, to prove to Haughey that my approach was well grounded. When the letter arrived, via Father Reid, Haughey told me with great glee that it contained an endorsement of his position on the Hillsborough Agreement! Adams was under pressure at the time and he had scribbled the undated note in a hurry, in pencil, on lined, loose-leaf jotter paper. Ironically, in view of the fact that such items would become synonymous with bribery and corruption when Haughey became Taoiseach again, Adams's letter was contained in a brown paper envelope. However, its importance lay not in its presentation, but in the fact that it was the first direct written communication of the Troubles between the leader of militant republicanism and a mainstream political leader who had been, and would again be, an Irish prime minister.

Though visibly cheering Haughey up over Hillsborough, Adams's letter also contained some alarming news. After stating that the purpose of Hillsborough was really to consolidate Britain's hold on the Six Counties and to undercut Irish nationalism, it said that both the British and Irish governments were actively considering the reactivation of internment to further the Agreement. Internment appeared to be a crazy suggestion, particularly in view of what had happened when it had been introduced earlier, but, with Mrs Thatcher in London and Fine Gael, the party of the 'heavy gang', back in power in Dublin, this time under Garret FitzGerald, anything was possible. Certainly there could be no doubting that Adams had good sources of information. Fortunately, however, as the days passed the internment threat did not materialise. Of the many reasons why it did not, probably the most cogent is the fact that the unionist population turned out to be much more inflamed about the Hillsborough Agreement than the republicans. If internment had been introduced, it would have had to be extended to unionists also, and even in the unlikely event that the British army would have agreed to this opening of a second front, the combined reaction from the unionist and nationalist camps would have been uncontrollable.

The letter was not what I had been expecting. I had thought it would contain an indication of the new thinking in the republican leadership. Sometime later Father Reid did give me such a blueprint, signed by him, but then he contacted me to say it should not be handed over just yet. The final document which I was cleared to hand over took almost a year in preparation, and it was signed by Father Reid. He had asked me to tell Haughey that there now existed the real possibility of a path to a peaceful united Ireland. 'A glittering prospect indeed,' said Haughey. However, the glitter soon faded. Internment did not materialise, but neither did any progress towards a united Ireland or an Adams–Haughey meeting. When he wanted to be, Haughey was faster at getting decisions translated into action than any other politician in Ireland.

I remember a particular demonstration of this in the case of Tom McEnry, the former lord mayor of San José, California. Tom's ancestors came from Kerry, one of them being executed during the Civil War. He had done his MA thesis on Michael Collins and, more importantly, had sought for several years, during the late 1970s and early 1980s, to have San José twinned with Dublin, without, as he told me himself, 'even receiving a postcard in return'. One day he phoned me at the *Irish Press* to tell me about his difficulties. On investigation I found that, in their wisdom, Dublin's city fathers had decided that San José, the gateway to California's Silicon Valley, was not worthy of being twinned with Dublin, which, be it remembered, at the time was a shabby, run-down city suffering from emigration and unemployment.

I contacted Haughey, who uttered a few expletives, within a few weeks had McEnery in his office and shortly thereafter gave the go-ahead for the twinning. That was Haughey's style; he either turned down a project then and there or ensured that it went ahead.

But he proved to be uncharacteristically indecisive over the Adams–Reid initiative. Some republican critics have attributed this to the effects of the arms trial, saying that he was afraid that if word of IRA contact got out, old memories would be stirred and used against him by both his enemies within the Fianna Fail Party (of whom there were many) and the opposition. Yet, as against this, when he had first become Taoiseach back in 1979, he had sent word to the IRA that he was prepared to hold *uisce faoi talamh* talks with their representatives in a Carmelite monastery in New York. On that occasion Southern IRA leaders had been in favour of the proposal, but the Northern IRA leadership had baulked. Now, when the movement was Northern-led and had become conscious of the need for dialogue, it was Haughey himself who was baulking.

He continued to baulk throughout 1986 and the years that followed his again being elected Taoiseach (for the third time, in February 1987). In fact, after becoming Taoiseach, he was even firmer in his refusal to meet Adams. One day in his office I suggested to him that even though he had reservations about doing a full-frontal with Adams, it would be helpful if he were to make a strong speech about the North, showing that he regarded the issue as a priority. He replied by picking up a thick report, compiled by the financier Dermot Desmond, and saying: 'This report by Desmond is going to take all my political energy. I can't do what's needed and take on the North at the same time.' The Desmond Report was certainly important. The reforms to the public finances and other steps that it recommended were implemented by Haughey and were essential to the creation of the Celtic Tiger. But for a man who once told me that he had advised Margaret Thatcher that she would never get into the history books because of her economic policies but could become venerated for showing statesmanship over Northern Ireland, he remained curiously wary of acquiring such veneration himself.

Haughey did not lack courage. Years later he was treated for prostate cancer in the Mater Private Hospital. He was informed that his prostate was cancerous but that once it was removed he would be all right. The only side effect would be that he would become impotent. Haughey promptly refused to have the operation. His surgeon remonstrated with him, warning him that the cancer could spread to his bones. But Haughey, then in his seventies, shook his head and replied: 'No, there's life in the old man yet!' The cancer did spread and it eventually killed him.

Nor was his hesitancy based on any undue deference towards the British. During one of our Berkeley Court lunches I happened to mention the Grand Hotel bombing in Brighton. He reacted by counting off on his fingers the names of the Tory dignitaries who, along with Thatcher, had escaped the blast. 'Think of it,' he said. 'What an operation! If it had come off, they'd have got nearly the whole British cabinet. It would have been greater than 1916.'

His private money problems may have had a bearing. It would later be revealed that his extraordinarily lavish lifestyle was funded not out of his own pocket, but those of wealthy businessmen, and he would die, in 2006, before a tribunal set up to investigate payments to politicians (the Moriarty Tribunal) issued its extraordinarily damning report on his behaviour. Perhaps his involvement in the Northern issue was simply political. He once showed me a list of electoral statistics and pointed out: 'There's a core five per cent republican vote – that should be coming to us.' By 'us' he meant Fianna Fail. But he hesitated on making any contact with Adams which might have led to that republican vote coming his way. Once, at the Berkley Court, he told me: 'You couldn't do something like that without the Special Branch finding out. For their own reasons they don't always tell what they know. But they know everything.' Again, the reason why he should fear the Special Branch must remain a matter of speculation.

Some republicans suggest that the special branches of intelligence involved may have been British ones. That the hesitancy goes back to the British devaluation of 1967 while Haughey was minister for finance. On the eve of devaluation the British informed key players – the Americans, the International Monetary Fund (IMF) and, because they were then in the sterling area, the New Zealand and the Irish Departments of Finance – of what was coming. Subsequent heavy forward buying of sterling was allegedly later traced back to Dublin. Whatever the extent of secret service knowledge on either side of the Irish Sea, it is highly unlikely that anyone outside of a very small circle of republicans did know the magnitude of the seismic shift in policy direction that Adams and his confidants were planning.

Reid set down the new vision, on Clonard Monastery notepaper, in the draft of a potentially explosive letter to Haughey dated 28 November 1986, which curiously enough was the date of my parents' wedding anniversary. The document was in fact Gerry Adams's blueprint for the successful peace process that emerged from it. It advocated a common approach by all the nationalist parties on the island towards dealing with the Northern issue. It stated that the aim of 'the armed struggle' was to establish the right of all Irish people to decide their own political future through dialogue among themselves and that the establishment of a thirty-two-county socialist republic was not the aim of this struggle. This was a political ideal to be pursued by political means only. Sinn Fein sought a declaration from the British that the existing unionist veto over political progress could be set aside so that Irish political parties could sort out the future amongst themselves. More importantly, the Sinn Feiners wanted the British to make a public declaration that if the Irish succeeded in reaching agreement, then the British would not interfere, as they claimed the right to do under the Government of Ireland Act of 1920. Most explosively the document said that Sinn Fein were not seeking a British withdrawal from Ireland at that stage and in fact would insist on their remaining there until constitutional arrangements necessary for peace had been put in place. Very much the same strategy for long-term British withdrawal that I had been advocating for decades. No Congo-style pull-out.

The fact that, under the leadership of Gerry Adams and those in the movement who shared his views, Sinn Fein was not pursuing a thirty-two-county socialist republic and, like the anti-republican Fine Gael, would insist on the British remaining in the country were two points whose importance it would be difficult to exaggerate. The statements would have been seized on like manna from Heaven by Adams's opponents in the republican movement. I would go so far as to say that if the contents of the letter had been generally known in the IRA, Gerry Adams could very easily have been shot. Instead, in the months of October and November

1986, he succeeded in persuading first a secret IRA convention and then a public Sinn Fein Ard Fheis to open a political path by allowing Sinn Feiners to take seats in Dail Eireann, while at the same time apparently supporting a continuation of the 'armed struggle'. Suffice it to say that the serpentine diplomacy with which Adams advanced on his objectives without providing either a physical or a political target for his enemies, both inside and outside the movement, was one of the major diplomatic feats of Irish politics in the twentieth century.

He and Reid were frequently pressed to the point of exhaustion, and there were times when he had to conduct his discussions with the cleric from his bed. Clonard Monastery and Adams's own home in Andersonstown were (and probably still are) bugged. If matters of particular delicacy had to be discussed, the pair would go to the bathroom and turn on the taps (to foil the bugs) before talking.

Adams angered Haughey in May 1987 by bracketing him with Garret FitzGerald as a 'shoneen' (polite version: a British toady) while speaking at an IRA funeral. I had gone to Haughey's office to give him the copy of the Reid–Adams document, which had finally been cleared for handing over. By now it was dated 11 May 1987. The funeral practically coincided with his reading of it – not the best backdrop for my attempts to persuade the Taoiseach of the country that a revolutionary opponent should be brought in from the cold. Haughey told me that what I was telling him and what Adams was saying did not add up.

Nevertheless, after reading the document Haughey invited me to another lunch, at which he agreed to meet Father Reid. And, by way of setting some sort of a test, I thought, he asked me to find out through Reid what was the story behind the event that had given rise to the funeral, the biggest single IRA loss of the period. This was the wiping out of Michael Lynagh's much-feared active service unit at Loughgall earlier in the month (on 8 May 1987). So, a short while later I brought Reid to meet Haughey at his luxurious home in Kinsealy, North County Dublin, and in this somewhat incongruous setting Reid duly gave Haughey the explanation of what had befallen Lynagh.

The raiding party was expected and walked into an SAS ambush, not an arrest. Those members of the group who survived the initial fusillades were placed lying face-downward and shot through the head. Two people who were unlucky enough to be passing in a car were also shot, one fatally. Apparently the IRA, in Reid's words, thought their comrades' fate was 'fair enough' – they would probably have done the same in the SAS's place. However, at the risk of digression I must say that judging from various things I heard afterwards, I wondered if the IRA leadership's attitude was partly conditioned by relief at the fact that Lynagh was now out of the way. He had been something of a maverick who often acted on his own without waiting for directions from Belfast.

The Haughey contacts over the peace process were all very interesting – phone calls and meetings going back and forth and so on. The only problem was, we never seemed to get anywhere. Padraig O'hAnrachain died in 1986. His natural abilities, his vast experience of the dark-arts side of politics and his influence with Haughey would have made him an ideal negotiator with the republicans, but the state of his health ruled him out. Haughey did appoint another adviser, Martin Mansergh, to liaise with Father Reid. Mansergh, who wrote speeches and position papers on the North for Haughey, had a very different background to O'hAnrachain. He had served in foreign affairs and had a family background in Anglo-Irish relationships, his father, Nicholas, having been one of the more benign and influential British civil servants concerned with Ireland. I remember a BBC journalist to whom Martin had given a briefing saying wonderingly afterwards: 'I went in to meet the Fianna Fail spokesman on Northern Ireland and I was met by this upper-class Brit!' Mansergh eventually became an important player in the peace process negotiations and their aftermath. But in so far as tangible Haughey initiatives were concerned, very little of substance occurred beyond a *sub rosa* meeting involving Brian Lenihan, who was then Haughey's foreign minister, Dermot Ahern, who subsequently held the same office, and republican emissaries, which took place in the secrecy of the Redemptorist monastery in Dundalk.

A central point of the Reid–Adams initiative was the involvement of the Church in the peace process. The Reid document had suggested that 'Leading Church figures would invite both Fianna Fail and Sinn Fein to meet under Church auspices. The idea being that the talks would result in the creation of a political alternative to the IRA.'

During the years 1987–90 the single most influential figure prepared to take the initiative in furthering this objective was Cardinal Tomas ÓFiaich. Tomas knew that he would bring a torrent of criticism down upon himself but he decided that his pain would be slight compared to the gain involved in getting Adams into mainstream political dialogue and showing republican hawks that politics led somewhere worthwhile. He did meet a republican delegation privately, and was planning to go public on the need to get Sinn Fein into the loop, when he collapsed and died as he was leading a pilgrimage to Lourdes in May 1990.

Prior to ÓFiaich's appointment as cardinal and the 1977 *Sunday Times* article (discussed in Chapter 8), some British Foreign Office approaches had been made to the Vatican suggesting that the red hat go to someone else. Probably the British had divined, quite correctly, that he could not be counted on to toe their line at moments of crisis in the Six Counties. ÓFiaich was to confirm their anxieties on at least two occasions. One of these would occur during the H-Block saga, when he described the condition of the prisoners on the Dirty Protest as being more revolting than those he had encountered in the slums of Calcutta. Another was to involve myself. I had been angered by the *Sunday Times* article and wrote a fiery editorial for Monday's paper in support of ÓFiaich. Sometime after midnight my phone rang. It was Tomas to say that he felt he just couldn't go to bed without expressing to me his appreciation of the support at a difficult time. The incident later had a bearing on quite a significant episode in Irish Church history. Out of gratitude he agreed to do a major interview with me in the course of which he said he favoured a united Ireland as the long-term solution to Ireland's difficulties.

It was the first time in the history of the state that an Irish cardinal had made such an announcement, and it attracted widespread attention, including that of Daithi O'Conaill, the Provisional IRA leader. He rang me up to congratulate me 'on getting that historic commitment from the Church'. I in turn rang Tomas and told him that we had both better examine our consciences! O'Conaill of course had not averred to the fact that the interview had contained a very strong denunciation of IRA violence. The incident helps to illuminate the difficulty of showing sympathy with an aspiration without espousing the methods of those pursuing the same goal. I once met an IRA man who underscored this difficulty for me in brutally stark terms. He was describing a visit that ÓFiaich had paid to Long Kesh.

Tomas had stuffed the pockets of his cassock with cigarettes, and the prisoners, in time-honoured Irish political-prisoner fashion, had picked his pockets of the contraband while other prisoners circled him in the exercise yard to block the warders' vision. It was a technique used by Irish MPs visiting political prisoners as far back as the days of the 1916 Rising and beyond. But I commented to the IRA man that this was an unusual and risky gesture on the part of a cardinal. He replied: 'Och aye, surely. He was great. We took it that he was telling us to carry on killing.'

I got another insight into the perils of Church leadership where killing was concerned at the end of a memorable day-long visit to ÓFiaich. He had great enthusiasm for local history and genealogy and, partly because of this and partly out of friendship, he set aside a day to show me around the Moy and other places in Armagh and the adjoining County Tyrone, from where my grandfather, Patrick Toal, and his ancestors had hailed. We created a sensation when we called into a pub owned by distant relations of Patrick who I had not known existed until the cardinal told me who they were. Two old men in a corner recognised the cardinal, and the next thing we heard was a thunder of feet on the stairs as the relatives, who had been at their evening meal, descended to bring us up to the best room in the house. It was musty-smelling, obviously having been opened for the first time in months, and contained an unusual amount of fine silverware. It turned out that at one stage my new-found relatives had operated a pawnbroking business.

Later in the evening, as midnight approached, I accepted the cardinal's invitation to join him 'for a last pipe in the grounds'. He had a habit of smoking a pipe as he took a turn in the grounds of his residence before turning in. As we walked he told me that this was his last midnight pipe. Sometime earlier 'a well-doing man in the parish' had come to him, against his wife's wishes, accompanied by his daughter to say that the daughter had information concerning a recent murder of Catholics by security forces as part of the ongoing but unacknowledged 'shoot to kill' campaign. An accident of circumstances had enabled her to identify members of the security forces both going to and shortly afterwards coming from the scene of the crime. Her car had developed a flat tyre, and as it was being fixed, a lorry containing the killers had pulled up on the way to their mission to fix the tyre for her. She told her father, who, although it created 'great trouble between husband and wife', felt it his duty to bring the matter to the attention of the one person in authority he felt he could trust, the cardinal.

ÓFiaich had reacted by first getting a canon lawyer to interrogate the girl as thoroughly as would any Queen's counsel. Satisfied that she was telling the truth, he arranged what was intended to be a secret meeting with the chief constable of the RUC to tell him what he had learned. Shortly afterwards another RUC officer turned up to see ÓFiaich at Ara Coeli. He opened the meeting by saying: 'I understand you were in with the Chief.' ÓFiaich was shocked and pointed out that the meeting had been arranged under promise of the strictest secrecy, to protect the lives of the father and daughter. The RUC officer brushed aside his protest by claiming airily that no breach of secrecy had occurred. 'One of the local lads' had allegedly recognised the cardinal's car in the compound at RUC Headquarters, he averred. However, purely coincidentally, and with no

bearing on the cardinal's interest in the matter of the murders, he wanted
to inform Tomas that intelligence had been received that a loyalist hit
squad was planning to assassinate him shortly, during one of his late-night
pipe-smoking strolls in the garden. As a result, our tour of the gardens
that night was the last undertaken by Tomas ÓFiaich.

ÓFiaich apart, the other figure of stature who did show himself willing
to stand up and be counted publicly during this period was John Hume,
who from the outset had also been privately supportive of Father Reid.
Throughout most of the Troubles Hume, a former Maynooth seminarian
and a teacher at St Columb's College in Derry, was the main nationalist
political philosopher. For him to enter into talks with Adams was both an
act of political courage and a recognition of the fact that the Sinn Fein sun
was rising and that of the middle-class SDLP setting. This fact was easier
recognised than acted on. On one level as leader of the SDLP he was
seeking to legitimise his main political rival in a manner that was bound
to damage his own party. On the other he exposed himself to real physical
danger. There was always an understanding in the Six Counties that
political leaders were not to be assassinated. (This did not apply to 'the
UK mainland', where the Brighton bombing took place and the MPs Ian
Gow and Airey Neave were assassinated.) In fact it was the IRA who
broke this agreement, the Provisionals murdering the Unionist MP the
Reverend Robert Bradford, and the Officials being responsible for the
death of the Unionist senator Jack Barnhill. But one never knew from
moment to moment when the unacknowledged agreement might change.
There were several murder gangs at work at the time. Apart from those of
the IRA, the British had the SAS, the 14th Field Reconnaissance Unit,
MI5 and MI6, and into the bargain were using elements within the UDA
and UVF as proxy assassins.

Hume had always been regarded as the sane voice of moderate Northern
Ireland nationalist opinion. He struck a considerable chord in both Dublin
and Washington, where he was admired by Ted Kennedy. It was a given
of all mainstream political discussion that Hume and the SDLP had to be
supported in order to prevent the pursuing wolves of Sinn Fein and the
IRA from gaining ground on the middle Ireland troika. When he began
talks with Adams in 1988, it appeared to some that he was turning the
horses round towards the pack, and a torrent of criticism broke over his
head, the attitude of the *Sunday Independent* being particularly infamous
in this regard. However, Hume persisted despite a swelling chorus of
dissent within his own party, notably from his able deputy and chief rival,
Seamus Mallon.

As Hume was of course briefing Dublin and his London and Washington contacts on the talks, the dialogue, apart from lending an aura of respectability to Adams and Co., did help to further the concept of negotiating with the IRA in the public mind. Privately of course the British while publicly condemning all contact with terrorists, were also conducting their own discussions through officials. The Hume–Adams dialogue also provided a channel through which British and Irish decision-takers could convey to the IRA what would play in Peoria and vice versa. One of the principal fruits of the Hume–Adams contact was a statement in November 1990 by the secretary for Northern Ireland, Peter Brooke, which was in fact a reassurance sought by Gerry Adams. Brooke stated publicly that the British had no 'selfish strategic or economic interest' in Northern Ireland and would not stand in the way of a united Ireland if a majority wished for it. The speech had a profound effect on republican thinking.

Nevertheless the political time zone in which all of this transpired continued, in Ecclestiastes' words, to be 'a time to kill'. Then, in 1992, the 'time to heal' began with the advent on the stage of Albert Reynolds, in succession to Haughey, and with Jean Kennedy Smith preparing to step from the wings. The economy was perking up and everyone expected that this would be Reynolds's main focus of attention. However, he surprised his colleagues and officials when on taking office he announced that his main priority was going to be Northern Ireland. They reacted much as I did when I heard him speaking at the dinner in the American embassy the following year, saying to Jean Kennedy Smith: 'Welcome home.' Felicitous phraseology was expected, but no follow-up action. The officials were just as wrong as I had been.

Reynolds had decided before taking office that he was going to do what he could to achieve a settlement. He had a 'feel' for the situation. He lived near the border, did business with unionists, was appalled at the human cost of the Troubles, and by background and instinct was one of nature's deal-makers. His antennae and his contacts told him that the times were right for change. He told me himself that one of his first acts was to phone a close friend of Paisley's with whom he had once done a lot of business. He said: 'I told him that we had made a lot of money together and we could make a lot more for our children and grandchildren if we got the Troubles over with. Both economies would benefit enormously. I asked him did he think his man [Paisley] would deal. I told him I didn't want to waste his man's time, or my own, if there was no possibility of a deal. My man said leave it with me for a bit and I'll come back to you. He came back within a week and said his man didn't want to waste my time either and that there was no deal possible.' Reynolds told me that he replied: 'Fair enough. At least we know where we stand.' But the businessman interrupted him: 'No! No! Hear the second part of my message. My man says he will deal – but *only when he gets the top job.*'

Reynolds didn't wait until the day came when Paisley was returned electorally as the leader of the largest segment of unionism. He abandoned the shilly-shallying of the Haughey years and began using his personal friendship with John Major to find a settlement. Major and he had become friendly in their roles as finance ministers during EU meetings. The Englishman had no baggage where Ireland was concerned – the issue simply was not on his radar screen – but as Reynolds told me afterwards, the problem was, he got a good deal of misinformation from the security services. Major was not informed, for example, that a group of German clergymen had succeeded in persuading the IRA to call off its European campaign against British military and diplomatic targets until Reynolds informed him of this.

The prime minister was astounded when Reynolds was proved right. Unfortunately, he was also right when he complained to Major that British intelligence sources bugged Reynolds's conversations with Clonard and eavesdropped on meetings that Reynolds had set up between his representatives and the republicans in the monastery. The pressures exerted on Major by his situation in the House, where he had to rely on the unionists for vital votes such as that on the Maastricht Treaty, as well as by the disinformation he received from some of his informants, stiffened him against Reynolds at some junctures. Meetings between the two men were so abrasive that on one occasion Reynolds called the British prime minister an 'eejit'. And the sight of pencils being thrown across Dublin Castle and Downing Street tables was not uncommon.

In Chapter 11 I mentioned the attitude of the coalition government of 1974–7 to the IRA and the speed with which the file on the Dublin and Monaghan bombings was closed. The coalition extended this attitude across the Atlantic, successfully lobbying against attempts to hold Congressional hearings on British human rights abuses in Northern Ireland.

As Jack Holland wrote: 'To the Irish authorities it was more important that the IRA be given no opportunity to enhance its credibility than that the British be criticised for their violation of human rights.' When Jimmy Carter espoused Irish unity and the protection of human rights in his presidential election campaign, Dublin's initial reaction was frosty. Incredibly enough Carter had to explain to Garret FitzGerald, as minister for foreign affairs, that he was not supporting violence and point to his credentials, as a democrat and human rights campaigner. The Lilliputians found themselves in an awkward position when Carter entered the White House and it became necessary to lobby him for a statement of support for the Dublin/SDLP position. However, Dublin got no thanks from London for its activities. Despite all the toadying to London that had gone on, as the Irish ambassador to Washington at the time, Sean Donlon, later wrote:

> We reckoned without the British influence and the skills of British diplomacy in exploiting to the full the special relationship between London and Washington. It took six months of patient and at times painful and bruising Irish diplomatic effort to overcome the many obstacles created by the British.

If this was the experience of the blatantly anti-republican Cosgrave government, it can be imagined how Reynolds's efforts to centrally involve the IRA in Anglo-Irish affairs was viewed by the British. Martin Mansergh would later write:

> There were an extraordinary series of diplomatic crises behind the scenes. The Taoiseach resisted enormous pressure to drop the initiative, making it clear that he would proceed with it in some shape or form, if necessary recast it as a purely Irish initiative regardless of whether he had the British government or not, and of course in those circumstances he would not be prepared to cover for them in America or elsewhere.

One unwelcome legacy of Reynolds's encounters with Major, and of the prime minister's domestic political situation, whose significance was not realised at the time was the introduction of the idea of IRA decommissioning to the process. I can say with complete certainty from my own knowledge of what went on that it was not pressed before the ceasefire. Had it been, there would have been no ceasefire. But apparently, with the prospect of peace seemingly guaranteed, Major became alarmed that the Irish issue might result in the Euro-sceptics within his own party making common cause with the unionists. He saw the decommissioning issue as a retarding factor which would allay fears that the thing was going too fast. The net result was that they went too slowly for the IRA militants, and the ceasefire was dealt a mighty blow with the IRA's bombing of Canary Wharf in London in February 1996. Even after the effects of this disaster were overcome, decommissioning continued for almost a decade to affect the process like a toxic knitting needle stuck in an elbow joint.

The most important issue for those working for the peace process during the early 1990s was making real the question of the American dimension for the republicans. One of the principal planks of the doves within the IRA had been the appointment of an American peace envoy to Ireland, but Adams and the others had been persuaded to drop this idea because of its counterproductive effect on the unionists. Instead their interest centred on getting a visa for Adams to enter the US so as to mainstream Sinn Fein and reap a rich publicity harvest by putting the republican case in person. The British fought the idea like a rearguard action in the field. If Adams, technically a citizen of the UK, had had to rely on getting a visa by applying for it in his native Belfast, he would not have succeeded. But Brendan Scannell, then on the Anglo-Irish desk in the Irish Department of Foreign Affairs, suggested that the Kennedys be inveigled into play by making the application through Dublin. As Jean Kennedy Smith had come to Ireland determined both to be in effect the peace envoy personified and to take whatever steps were needed to make this role a meaningful one, she immediately engaged with the visa project. After the Phoenix Park dinner I prepared a lunch in my house so that Jean could meet Father Reid. He underscored what I had been saying about the value of the visa to the peace process and, as he had done for Haughey, gave a very credible and lucid account of republican thinking. The difference was that this time substantive action would follow his briefing. The priest, or 'the monk' as she called him, had clearly impressed Jean.

One aspect of the lunch that didn't impress her quite so much was the fact that I had not provided shell-cracking equipment for the lobster. Ever the gentleman, I forbore from telling her that most women I invited to my home would count themselves lucky to be served lobster. However, for the even more important Lunch Number Two I pressed my daughter Jackie into service as my housekeeper and she ensured that everything was above reproach.

This time the third guest was not to be Father Reid but her brother Ted. Ted, like Jean, as an individual had no side to him or any sort of pretence. Either in their official capacity could be rigidly formal and protocol-upholding, but not privately. I remember that when the ambassadorial car drew up outside, Jean wasn't quite sure whether this was the house she had visited earlier. Ted hopped out to ring the doorbell and to get as far as enquiring 'Is this Mr Coogan's house?' before I welcomed him in.

Under Jackie's aegis, we had a somewhat more elegantly served meal, and one moreover conducted without the restraining presence of the Pioneer-pinned Father Reid. But the purpose of the visit remained fundamentally serious: should the visa project be backed? I gave Ted the same answer I had given Jean. Albert Reynolds and the others whom he met during the rest of his two-day stay provided more weighty corroboration: granting the visa would immeasurably improve the prospects of getting an IRA ceasefire and a peaceful settlement in Northern Ireland.

Apart from being one of the more pleasant people I had encountered for many a long day, Ted turned out to be one of the most resilient. He had had virtually no sleep, having crossed the Atlantic that morning, and Jean was hosting a dinner in his honour at the embassy that evening. But he had a theory that even if one didn't sleep, if you can lie down for an hour, you get all the rest you need. He had managed such an interlude before coming to lunch. Accordingly he accepted my suggestion after lunch that we drive to Killiney Hill to see the view of the Vico Bay from the Green Road, which is a pathway originally cut along the side of the hill to allow an English monarch to savour the delights of 'the Irish Naples'. As it doesn't do to get stranded on the side of a hill, even a small one, far from a pub (approximately one mile) should a sea mist blow in suddenly, I had thought it only prudent to slip a bottle of Paddy into my waxed jacket before we set off. The odd drop of Paddy and the friendly greetings from people, who seemed to emerge from the furze bushes to tell Ted that they had sons in Boston, or admired his family, or both, made the sight-seeing trip a huge success. Unfortunately, the surprising numbers emerging from the furze bushes also made it impossible for Ted to answer a call of nature. 'God,' he groaned. 'I'm carryin'. I gotta get to a restroom.' So we shot off to another local beauty spot, Bullock Harbour, where the rocks behind the harbour afforded Ted a little more privacy.

The foregoing may read simply as a description of a light-hearted post-luncheon excursion, but it is worth noting also that, apart from the view, one of the principal landmarks of South Dublin is the obelisk standing on top of Killiney Hill. It was erected as a relief work by a local Catholic landlord during the great famine of the 1740s, which occurred a hundred years *before* its better-known successor drove Jean and Ted's ancestors out of Ireland to America, and before the nineteenth-century famine there had befallen ten other similar catastrophes. History had moved on, so that Jean was now an ambassador to a sovereign Irish Republic and Ted was one of the most influential figures in the world's only superpower. *Pietas* ordained that now both become involved in removing the last vestiges of the shadows cast by obelisk and famine on the land of their forebears.

When Ted got back to Washington, he threw his weight behind the visa project. No Irish policy would have stood a chance of succeeding with the White House if Jean and Ted Kennedy had opposed it. As it was, it would appear that the last step in swinging Bill Clinton behind the idea was a round of golf with Ted's close friend and political ally Chris Dodds. Dodds maintains a house in the west of Ireland, but more importantly he was at the time the chairman of the Democratic committee charged with getting Clinton re-elected. Approaching the final tee, Clinton, as Dodds (and Kennedy) had expected, asked what should be done about the visa. Dodds's advice was: Grant it.

Thereafter Clinton became an advocate of the peace process to a degree that, even to this day, appears incredible. In the teeth of a howling gale of criticism from the pro-British elements in Washington, not alone did he grant the Adams visa, he subsequently accepted Jean Kennedy Smith's advice that one be granted to Joe Cahill as well. The significance of this was that on 31 August 1994, when the news of the ceasefire broke, the respected figure of Joe Cahill – who had been one of the founders of Noraid – was in the US reassuring Sinn Fein and IRA supporters that there had been no sell-out. This averted a damaging split, and the inevitable canalising of resources from Sinn Fein to those who continued in the physical-force camp. One would have thought that the British would have wished for this outcome. In fact they fought so hard to block the visa that the announcement of the IRA ceasefire was put in jeopardy for some days while Jean Kennedy Smith conducted a campaign of her own to ensure that Cahill would be allowed to speak and the guns to fall silent.

She was on holiday at the home of the former Conservative chief whip Michael Jopling when Albert Reynolds managed to track her down. She immediately left the bewildered Jopling sitting beside the swimming pool and returned to Dublin to begin trying to find the Washington players on the Irish scene. They too were mostly on holiday, but she succeeded in finding out where, and eventually, over the objections of the US attorney general, who pointed to Cahill's previous record, a visa was conceded. However, British protests resulted in various restrictions being attached to it. Albert Reynolds was apoplectic. First, the whole purpose of the visit was to allow Cahill to move around freely, so as to be able to speak to any group or individual required, and second, and the second was like unto the first, Reynolds felt that it was outrageous that an Irish passport should have conditions attached to it at the behest of the British. Jean spent most of the night of 29/30 August on the phone to Washington. Alec Reid rang her on the hour every hour. Finally, on the direct instructions of Bill Clinton himself, the way was cleared for Cahill to turn up at the American embassy in Ballsbridge, pick up his visa and head for Dublin Airport. While he was still en route to America, the wording of the IRA ceasefire declaration was handed to Reynolds. He promptly read it over the phone to Messrs Clinton and Major. Both were suitably impressed, as were the Irish public when the following day, 31 August 1994, at 11.25 p.m., the statement was read over the airwaves. A long and bloody chapter in Anglo-Irish relationships was seemingly closing.

But the closure was to be agonisingly slow. The outrage that the Adams and Cahill visas elicited was as nothing to the response to Clinton's decision to invite Adams to the White House and allow him to collect funds for Sinn Fein, which, as the process evolved, became recognised as a legitimate political party. 'Robert' was not pleased. And the sense of personal anger that this particular concession occasioned in John Major was such that for a full week he refused to accept a phone call from the president of the United States. Allied to the political exigency of Major's dependence on the unionists, ancestral Irish prejudices were reawakened in the British establishment. Their outrage found resonance not alone in the various American departments of state that dealt with the British but in the Republican Party also.

Without Clinton's backing for the Dublin government's policy, and the Kennedys' assistance in translating this policy into meaningful action where it counted, in Washington, there would have been no IRA ceasefire and no peace process. Without the appointment of Senator George Mitchell as the chairman of the Good Friday Agreement talks, the negotiations that followed the ceasefire would never have achieved a result. He really was a peace envoy, sticking to his task as chairman and, somehow, achieving consensus in an atmosphere that he afterwards described to a friend as being 'like Selma in the 1960s'.

But Mitchell would withstand the climate of Selma, as would the Kennedys and Bill Clinton. The White House policy towards the potentially destabilising Canary Wharf explosion was described off the record by one irreverent staffer as 'Shit happens.' The explosion certainly was one very large piece of 'shit'. I inspected the damage myself shortly after it happened and was shocked at its extent. Symbolically, I thought, as I gazed at the destruction, a sizeable group of mounted London policemen and women cantered by – a picturesque but archaic method of dealing with modern policing requirements and the equally archaic approach to Anglo-Irish relationships that lay before me. The decommissioning issue continued to dog the peace process for a decade.

The year after Canary Wharf, in May 1997, Tony Blair won his huge majority and was able to deploy his latent Irish sympathies, honed on holidays spent in Donegal as a child with his Protestant grandmother, to reinvigorate the peace process. Jean Kennedy Smith had remained invigorated throughout the entire period, and not merely on the political front. Socially, she was one of the most active, and discriminating hostesses ever seen in Dublin. Poets, politicians and film stars poured through the embassy. I think that one of these last, Lauren Bacall, felt herself lucky to be able to pour back out again after I attempted to teach her 'the spin'. This particular spin is not of the political variety, but an Irish dance step in which the woman (or women) is spun off her feet and whirled round. Lauren may be comforted to know that nowadays I leave that sort of thing to Michael Flatley.

At times it appeared as if Jean's activities had thrown the British into a spin of their own. Their hostility was expressed in all sorts of ways. On one occasion a visit she had planned to the North was called off because, the RUC averred, they 'could not guarantee her safety'. Another story told of her is that she was actually heading north, to Whitehall's displeasure, when her mobile phone rang. It was Warren Christopher, the US secretary for foreign affairs, to tell her that the Brits were raising Cain over the fact that she was crossing the border. According to the story, Jean's reaction was to inform the secretary that his line was breaking up and that she couldn't hear what he was saying and accordingly she was handing over the phone to a younger person, with better hearing, her assistant, Amy Sigentaler, who was with her in the car. Seemingly, however, Amy could not hear too well either. The car continued northward.

But there can be collateral damage to the exercise of power, as I found out. Some of Jean's embassy staff objected to her policies also, saying that she was damaging US–British relationships. They later went at least semipublic on their displeasure, voicing their opinions in a journal of dissent in which the State Department allows its employees to let off steam. The article was couched in diplomatic language but it contained a pretty strong hint that I was the villain of the piece.

So too did a piece in the *Sunday Times*, which on 3 March 1996 printed a montage of pictures of Jean, her cousin, Father Michael Kennedy, and myself with a caption that read: 'Kennedy Smith and two of her retinue, Father Michael Kennedy and Tim Pat Coogan, with whom she has a close friendship. Now the State Department is investigating her.' Charming! The article by Richard Woods that accompanied it lamented that 'The embassy has traditionally adopted a pro-British stance,' and went on to inject a snide note into the debate:

She has become most talked about for her relationship with Tim Pat Coogan, a journalist (separated from his wife) who has become something of a fixture at the embassy. The two socialise and have a close friendship, though they deny anything deeper. He is the author of *The Troubles*, a history strongly sympathetic to the republican cause. He previously wrote a book about the IRA.

It also quoted my old sparring partner Conor Cruise O'Brien, who said of Jean: 'She has nothing to contribute to reconciliation. She is wholly aligned with one side. The idea that you can get peace in Northern Ireland by catering to the IRA is wrong, and I'm afraid that's what the Kennedys are after.'

Toby Harnden, the Ireland correspondent of the *Daily Telegraph*, took up the theme (on 10 February 1997) when he noted disapprovingly of Jean that 'Her close friends include the author Tim Pat Coogan, who wrote a history of the IRA that was highly sympathetic to the republican cause.' The article quoted a 'disclosure' from a book by the *Irish Times*'s Washington correspondent Conor O'Cleary that:

> Mrs Kennedy Smith was code-named '*spéir bhean*' or 'woman of mythology' during contacts with Sinn Fein. Mr Adams was known as 'the chairman of the board' and the IRA was referred to as the 'local football team'. President Clinton is said to believe that Mrs Kennedy Smith and Mr Hume allowed themselves to be duped by Mr Adams. In O'Cleary's book she is quoted as telling a friend: 'I was convinced the ceasefire would hold for ever.'

The thrust of the article was that Jean was 'expected to be recalled by President Clinton because her strongly pro-nationalist views are now at odds with White House policy on Ireland'. Over a year later, the Good Friday Agreement was signed and Jean Kennedy Smith was still the US ambassador to the Republic of Ireland. However, her opposite number in London, Raymond Seitz, was not. He too had fallen to the Kennedy juggernaut, and in his memoirs, which unsurprisingly were serialised in the *Sunday Telegraph*, claimed that the previous British government had 'stopped passing sensitive intelligence to the White House because it often seemed to find its way to the IRA'. *The Times* greeted Mr Seitz's remarks by thundering:

> Britain deserves not only an apology from the White House but credible assurances that such episodes will not occur again. There is one move the president can make as belated compensation. He must show that there is more to his stance on Northern Ireland than pandering to the Kennedy clan. To that end, Mrs (Jean) Kennedy Smith should cease to serve as her country's ambassador to the Republic of Ireland.

It is an interesting comment on the allegations of spying that the terms mentioned in the *Daily Telegraph* article, '*spéir bhean*' (readers will remember my animadversions on such creatures in my ill-fated Matriculation Certificate examination), 'the chairman of the board' and 'the local football team', were not used by the IRA but by me, in telephone conversations with Father Reid in which we used a private code. 'The chairman of the board' was not Gerry Adams but God! Reid, a keen Gaelic football and hurling fan, would describe progress, or lack of it, by saying where the chairman of the board was on the field of play at the moment. If He was in the forwards, things were going well. If in the backs, things were bad. If He was on the subs' bench, things were at their worst. The long arm of Cheltenham had evidently reached into Glenageary, but did not appear to understand what it had picked up.

However, the Irish people understood very well what had happened, and when the dust of the Good Friday Agreement settled, there was a countrywide welcome for the Irish government's action in rewarding Jean Kennedy Smith by making her an honorary Irish citizen.

Earlier in this chapter I mentioned my dislike of Irish dependence on the vagaries of English politics and English decision-takers. The manner in which the allegedly autonomous power-sharing Executive at Stormont rose and fell like a whore's knickers after the Good Friday Agreement was signed in 1998 confirmed me in this view. I happened to be in Stormont during most of the day on which it first collapsed, in February 2002. We now know from the memoirs of Jonathan Powell, Tony Blair's chief of staff, and a man who would make Sir Humphrey Appleby, the senior civil servant in the TV series *Yes, Minister*, look like an amateur, just why it came down. The Dublin government under Bertie Ahern, who both then and subsequently had laboured mightily for the peace process, had brought the IRA to the point of putting its commitment to finally resolving the decommissioning issue on paper. But Blair and Powell decided that the IRA statement on 'finally and completely' putting arms beyond use would be insufficient to convince David Trimble's enemies at a forthcoming Unionist Party conference of its worth. They decided, to Dublin's and Sinn Fein's outrage, to suspend Stormont rather than put his support to the test. In vain did Bertie Ahern and his top aide, Paddy Teahon, who had been in contact with the IRA until three o'clock in the morning, argue with Blair and Powell that the statement was genuine but could not be published as matters stood because Gerry Adams and the republican peaceniks were in danger of a violent backlash from their rank and file. As Powell notes, Adams risked the backlash by 'rather sneakily' publishing a version of the statement late that afternoon. But, despite renewed pleas from Ahern and President Clinton, Powell writes: 'We decided to apply some Nelsonian blindness by applying the telescope to the wrong eye and said there was nothing we could do because the suspension order was already beyond recall. Then we rushed it out.'

Some might call that rather sneaky. Not surprisingly Powell notes that a phone call from Ahern which the Irish Taoiseach then handed over to Paddy Teahon later in the evening was said to be 'in danger of coming very close to the outer limits of what is unacceptable from officials of another government'. I can understand Teahon's feelings. Around the time that call was being made, I was in the company of a group of IRA activists away from Stormont in another part of Belfast. Previously I would have described them as strong Adams supporters, but now they were disturbingly angry. They made it very clear to me that they thought that the IRA had already gone too far in return for too little concession towards republican aims and the sacrifices that had been made. If any more slippage occurred, Adams, Martin McGuinness and their senior supporters would be in serious risk of their lives. It was a very chilling reality check after the false smiles and the self-important comings and goings at Stormont.

However, a diplomatic formula was subsequently worked out whereby the Executive was temporarily restored. But another republican whom I met that day was central to its being suspended again the following October. This was Denis Donaldson, whose public role could be thought of as being the office manager of the Sinn Fein operation at Stormont. With some glee Denis, an intelligent, affable man, had discussed with me a letter which had recently been sent by Sinn Fein to the *Irish News* seeking a meeting to complain about the paper's coverage which, the letter claimed, was biased in favour of the Sinn Fein. Later that afternoon, as I left the Stormont building, I bumped into Noel Doran, the editor of the *Irish News*, arriving. During our brief chat he told me he intended to 'meet some people'. I said nothing about the letter but, as we shook hands, I said silently to myself 'and you think you had troubles at the *Irish Press* ... I left Stormont thinking of another incident involving the *Irish News* some twenty-five years earlier when a gentlemen from the Official IRA had called into the newsroom to discuss matters of press freedom – carrying a submachine gun.

The following October the television screens were filled with pictures of police pouring through the doors at which I had encountered Doran. They were carrying out a raid on the Sinn Fein offices during which they 'discovered' some disks in Denis Donaldson's desk. These were alleged to contain evidence of a 'Stormontgate' spy ring headed by Donaldson. In a welter of unionist outrage, and Sinn Fein counter-claims that the police raid was a baseless intelligence sting operation aimed at keeping Sinn Fein from power-sharing, down came Humpty Dumpty once more. The Assembly was suspended. A new daily newspaper appeared, *Daily Ireland*, decidedly sympathetic in tone to Sinn Fein. But it soon folded, one ironic reason being the fact that it failed to attract sufficient public service advertising: such things as vacancies in the prison service, the police, the British army and so on.

The next time I was in Stormont it was to attend a lavish dinner hosted by the *Irish News* to honour its legendary political correspondent Jimmy Kelly. There was no talk of biased coverage that night. Realpolitik had set in, and among the dignitaries who attended, from all over Ireland, were Gerry Adams and Martin McGuinness. Forty years earlier, standing on the steps of Clonard Monastery's Church, where he, like Gerry Adams, attended mass, Kelly had told me: 'Whatever settlement is arrived at, it's going to have to contain a degree of imposition.'

Kelly was right. To be fair to Blair and Powell, despite the cock-ups over the Stormont suspension they continued working for a settlement with Bertie Ahern, Adams and the rest of them. As the world knows, that settlement arrived in the shape of the St Andrews Agreement, concluded five years after Stormont's Second Going and after the British had willed it back into existence once again to set the scene for the talks. But this time Blair combined with Ahern to twist arms sufficiently both to convince the IRA that it could safely go out of business and to satisfy the unionists that the republicans would keep their promises. Ecclesiastes also played an important role. Paisley agreed to power-sharing, having previously so decimated his unionist opponents in a general election that the only light Orange bottle left standing was Sylvia Hermon, the attractive wife of Sir John, my old RUC sparring partner of the Toffs Against Terrorism occasion in Cambridge. To me at least, that election demonstrated convincingly what I had always believed, that Trimble and his like were a cosmetic non-event in terms of being able to deliver a majority of unionist voters. These people like their Orange to be stronger, and of a deeper hue. And so, with nothing to the right of him and the 'top job' in his pocket, on 8 May 2007, Ian Kyle Paisley became first minister of the Stormont Assembly with Martin McGuinness as deputy first minister.

Denis Donaldson did not witness this development. In December 2005 he had announced that for several years he had been a spy for the security forces. The following April, lonely and haunted, living alone in a cheerless cottage in a remote part of Donegal, without electricity or running water, he was blasted into eternity by a shotgun-carrying hit man.

The Chuckle Brothers era was also cut short. Irony of ironies, the Book was used to help dethrone Paisley. Firstly his Free Presbyterian Church voted to remove him as moderator, ostensibly on the grounds that he could not be the North's first minister and the Church's leader at the same time. To some, Bible thumping meant thumping Catholics, not spreading Christian ecumenism and thereby helping Fenians into power. Paisley's smiling joint appearances in public with McGuinness widened cracks – in part occasioned by his age and autocratic style of leadership – that had visibly opened between himself and members of his party during the St Andrews negotiations. Theologically weakened, the political *coup de grâce* was administered in the wake of allegations that his son, Ian Junior, nicknamed Baby Doc, had used the St Andrews negotiations to lobby Blair on behalf of a businessman friend of the Paisley family. Ian Junior denied these allegations but resigned his ministerial portfolio. Then Papa Doc himself announced his resignation, which took effect in May 2008, as did that of Bertie Ahern, albeit for different reasons. Ireland had come a long way from the days when Paisley fired up a huge rally, declaring in tones of thunder: 'Where do the terrorists go for sanctuary? To the Irish Republic. And yet Mrs Thatcher tells us that that Republic have some say in our Province. We say, never, never, never, never.'

Never say never!

Paisley's reinvention of himself as a kindly, grandfatherly figure, an Orange version of Mandela in his latter days, reminds one of the image de Valera sought to portray in his final years. It is a performance that certainly adds weight to his friend's statement to Albert Reynolds that the Big Man would deal when he got the top job. Perhaps his changed policies are attributable to the fact that he had had a brush with cancer. Perhaps, as some say, he was influenced by his wife, Eileen, now Lady Paisley, but certainly, like de Valera, his rabble-rousing speeches diminished in direct proportion to the amount of responsibility he had to take for their consequences. But whatever one thinks of the motivation of either the Orange or the Green components of the historic compromise that now forms the basis of the Six Counties' administration, it has to be conceded that the present is better than the past. Paisley, Blair and Ahern have departed political life, leaving behind a vastly improved Northern Ireland and a far better Anglo-Irish relationship.

The pity is that to get to this point, on a *per capita* basis, compared to America, Northern Ireland first had to suffer a death toll equivalent to five Twin Towers a year for the thirty years of the Troubles.

Epilogue

Near my home, arching over the quaintly named Atmospheric Road, a laneway running alongside Eventually, which was once the Atmospheric Railway, built to transport granite from Dalkey Quarry for the construction of Dun Laoghaire Harbour, there grows my luxuriant clock. It is a chestnut tree by which I have measured time throughout the writing of all my books and the growing of my family. Sometimes the spring would be accusatory: 'Oh, God, the blossoms are out and I've three chapters to go.' Sometimes the autumn: 'The chestnuts have arrived. I'm not nearly finished' and so on. As I write this, the tree is particularly beautiful, as it (and I) approach autumn. Who knows whether the arboreal clock will be needed again? But certainly my family have blossomed and grown. Thirty-one of us, including Cherry, sat down to dinner last Christmas in Eventually. The twelve grandchildren have grown and produced three great-grandchildren, Molly, Ruby and Poppy, who is currently two and a quarter years, and whose status in the family may be deduced from her nickname, the Pop Star. Though time seems to go faster these days, I try to spend a little more of it with all of them and in cultivation of not merely my horticultural garden but the human one, wherein flowers friendship.

That garden's inhabitants are as worthwhile as they are diverse. To hand in Dalkey and its environs are John O'Mahony, a banker and author, and his wife, Angela. There is Brian Brennan, a celebrity plumber, and his wife, Catherine. There is Peter Caviston, a restaurateur and a devout fishmonger. Another Peter, Peter O'Halloran, is a singer and organiser of the several events that brighten the lives of those of us fortunate enough to live near his beloved Bullock Harbour. Others who might also be said to add to the gaiety of nations are Michael McEvilly, his wife Ursula, an accountant; Ian Flood, an electrician, and his wife, Susan; Miceal O'Siadhal, a poet, and his wife, Brid; Joe Wildes, a retired harbour constable; and Ian McDonald, an undertaker, and his wife, Margaret. Further afield are people like the lawyer Charles Mooney and his wife, Wilma, of

New York and Florida. In Toronto, Mary Durkan, whose Bloomsday celebrations are linked each year to ours in nearby Sandycove. And, further away still, in darkest Kerry, there is the former All-Ireland Gaelic footballer and present-day poet, combatant and entrepreneur Jo Jo Barrett. And last, but far from least, flourishing in a special niche of her own, there is Mabel Fox, ninety-seven on the calendar, twenty-one in her heart. My experience of these people, and of many others, really does make it a source of pleasure, and of pride, to be able to say the list could go on for pages.

Not quite so unmixed were my feelings at New Year 2008, when I read *The White Book of Interiors*. It is a leading Dublin journal of furniture and design. It contained the following:

> A charming portico flanked by mythical dogs marks the entrance to Tudor Hall. Two steps rise to the front door which opens on to a large hallway paved by classical flag stones. The walls have been subtly hand-painted to recreate the ambience of old stone, an effect known as sandstone blocking. The paintwork runs into the basement [...] The main entertainment quarters lie to the rear of the hall. Light pours into the vast double room through the huge, deep wooden windows at either end.

Describing the history of Tudor Hall, *The White Book* noted that in the 1920s the house:

> became home to the Coogan family, from whom descend the distinguished historian Tim Pat Coogan. His mother, Beatrice Coogan, was author of *The Big Wind*, winner of the Frankfurt Book Fair's Novel of the Year in 1969. As such there is a somewhat genteel and intellectual ambience, well captured in the intimate but spacious sitting room.

If my mother had lived to see that, it would have killed her!

She died in 1997, in her ninety-third year, having sold Tudor Hall during the housing slump of the 1980s. Lacking the resources of subsequent owners, who benefited from the Celtic Tiger boom, the sale brought her only IR£76,000 (curiously, the same fateful figure with which I left the *Irish Press*). Refurbished, the house entered the millions bracket. But her final days were not uncomfortable. She had at last secured a Garda pension and, as nature took its course, had lived first with my sister, Aisling, finally moving to the nursing home wherein she died. Her funeral mass at the nearby St Joseph's Church, Glasthule, a parish or so away from Tudor Hall, was attended by an overflowing congregation, which spontaneously burst into an unusually loud and sustained burst of applause when I concluded my eulogy with her favourite Shakespearean quotation. It was from *Antony and Cleopatra*:

> *So, fare thee well.*
> *Now boast thee, death, in thy possession lies*
> *A lass unparalleled.*

The transformation of Tudor Hall could be taken as a paradigm of the transformation of the Irish economy, which Beatrice did not live to see. But the memory of the house's poor days could also be taken as a metaphor, to be borne in mind as we contemplate the global credit crisis, the rise of China and the fall of the dollar. Economies, like houses, can fall into decay. In fact, in gloomy moments, looking at America's national debt, the weakened dollar and above all its bloody foreign policy blunders, I am inclined to ponder whether we are all living in the shade of the contemporary version of the Fall of the Roman Empire. Certainly the gulf between America, the country I know and love, and America as empire is widening viciously.

The international scene and Ireland's fall from European grace caused by her rejection of the Lisbon Treaty are compelling reasons for Ireland to look to its last great unexploited resource – her diaspora. Geographically, Ireland is but a speck on the world map, but emigration has meant that in three of the G-8 nations and in Australia, there are huge numbers of well-doing, generally prosperous Irish. If all the dots were linked up as part of a planned policy, directed from Dublin, the Republic would have the potential to create a lobby in the US and the world to rival that which supports the state of Israel. Unlike Israel, such a lobby would have no military aspect, but it would immeasurably strengthen Ireland's place in the world. As this was being written, Bertie Ahern was justifiably honoured for his role in the peace process by being asked to address the joint houses of the American government in Washington. The media coverage played well in Ireland, but the reality was that part of his address was a new fruitless plea on a very old issue: the plight of undocumented Irish emigrants to the US. A properly organised Irish lobby exercising even a fraction of the clout of the Israelis would have ended this situation years ago.

The Irish should view America as a continent rather than a country. It has different time zones, foods, attitudes, climates, state governments. Few in Idaho comprehend what Washington doeth. Only a fraction of its people ever leave its shores. Approximately a fifth of its legislators hold a passport. Its foreign policy is largely controlled by lobbies, on behalf of oil, the industrial military complex, Israel. Ireland bobs like a tiny cork on such vast seas. Yet at census time 43 million people give their ethnic origin as Irish. The unspoken political latency behind the millions who annually celebrate St Patrick's Day is self-evident. The Irish are a hugely well-educated, wealthy segment of society. We have seen what the Irish-Americans could achieve when they put forth their strength for the peace process. That strength should not be allowed to die away. We gave away our fish when we joined the EEC; we should not give away our diaspora because they have joined the world.

In so far as the Republic can be viewed in isolation, so long as it forms part of the knowledge economy its future seems relatively assured. Compared to the position that obtained when my mother sold her home just twenty years ago, never mind the days of my youth, the wealth of Ireland has grown incredibly. I don't know how reliable such estimates are, but at the time of writing official statistics say its citizenry own assets of more than €1 trillion.

Granted, an over-reliance on the construction industry and on property development meant that the backlash of the sub-prime debacle in the US cut some deep stripes from the Celtic Tiger's fat. One indication of their depth being the fact that the once soaring Irish Stock Exchange turned down through the later part of 2007 and the beginning of 2008 to become the worst performer in Europe. In addition to this, in Ireland, as elsewhere in the West, the flow of manufacturing jobs towards the East continues inexorably. Also there is the unpleasant dark cloud forming on the horizon of future inward investment in Ireland in the shape of growing EU attacks on the Republic's low corporation tax rates. It was these rates that helped to bring the multinationals to Ireland. Will they stay if, in the next five to ten years, the EU rules that multinationals may no longer use the Republic as the base from which to declare their worldwide profits?

There are other serious socio-economic problems: the drug-fuelled crime wave that has lowered respect for human life; the diminished quality of life, particularly in rural Ireland has led to a troubling rise in suicide rates; and the corruption in public life and the disconnect that one senses growing between the governing and the governed are dangerous challenges for the Irish. Income disparities are increasing. On the one hand, there are fat-cat exclamations of satisfaction at evidences of wealth such as the ever-increasing number of privately owned helicopters in the Republic. There would be no trouble getting poor Nurse Folan to the Aran Islands these days. But on the other, there are signs of crassness like the fact that, as this was being written, the government and senior officials were awarded huge pay increases, at a time when the unions were being told that they would have to lower their expectations from forthcoming talks on social partnership that are vital to the continued industrial peace – and growth – of the country. In some cases the rises, which the government were ultimately forced to forgo, amounted to *three times* the total of the state old-age pension. Ireland still has work to do in developing a greater sense of public outrage in order to prevent such crassness.

But a nation's wealth is not assessed solely in terms of stock exchanges and multinationals. The durability, flair and imagination of the Irish people have carried them through far worse times than those we now live in. Those qualities remain, long after the empires of Church and state, which once towered over the Irish people, have departed. I have particular faith in the younger people. Firstly there is the fact that I can still hardly believe – the burden of probability is that they will not have to worry too much about emigration. Whether they wish to make their careers in Ireland or to go abroad, the choice, absent a world slump, seemingly will largely, if not completely, be theirs. Secondly, to me, Ireland's younger generations appear educated, confident and caring. They haven't lost the traditional Irish aptitude for fun and the celebration of life either. Economic forecasts are being revised downward, but population projections are not. Both the native birth-rate and the healthy admixture of foreign immigration are set on an upward trajectory.

Demographics, combined with immigration, are also the factor I look to for a final healing of Ireland's worst and longest-running sore – the Northern situation. Masked by the sound of bomb bursts, the cries of the bereaved and a general, and very natural, concentration on the peace process, a quiet revolution has been taking place within the Six Counties area. For some time it has been obvious that the number of children from nationalist backgrounds in both school and university has been exceeding those of unionist origin. Neither Dublin nor the nationalist parties want to make much of this for fear of frightening the horses in the street. The unionists, for obvious reasons, don't want to trumpet the fact either. A loss of supremacy is no more welcome in areas of the North than it was in America's Deep South.

But the reality of the situation is that the old two-third Protestant and one-third Catholic population ratio, maintained by discrimination and gerrymandering, is a thing of the past. A glance at the nationalist *Irish News* tells the story. It is bulky and packed with ads. By contrast the unionist *News Letter*, the oldest paper in Ireland, indeed in the English-speaking world, appears skinny and lacking in advertising. Recent years have also seen the emergence of flourishing nationalist-based publications such as the *Anderstown News*. The possibility of something of either a nationalist majority or at least something of the order of a fifty-fifty divide within a decade is not remote. The concept of power-sharing thus has a built-in native dynamic to it, not merely the galvanic effects of pressures from Dublin, London and Washington. One, to me unwelcome, evidence of this force is the trend among unionist families of going abroad, mainly to Scotland, for university education. Demonstrably, a high percentage of these young people, who should be regarded as the natural future political elite of their class, do not return to Ireland on completion of their studies. This is a loss to political life in the area as a whole, for both nationalists and unionists.

But unionism, which has not shown itself to be an adaptable creed in the past, seems certain to pay the highest price for this loss. Education is the bread of the future. By contrast, members of the growingly confident and assertive nationalist population either show a strong tendency to return to Ireland after a few years abroad or don't emigrate in the first place. As the Republic's population is also increasing, the consequences of present demographic trends would appear therefore to be moving inevitably towards more and more cooperation with the South and, down the line, a united Ireland.

Some Sinn Fein supporters have occasionally been guilty of atrocious deeds. Episodes like the McCartney and Quinn murders or the Northern bank robberies have deservedly made headlines. Undoubtedly from Carlingford Lough in the east to the Foyle in the North, the Border, the Troubles and the smuggling have spawned a culture of warlordism in some places. One can still encounter an arrogant illegality and profiteering. It is also a given that, on the republican side, organised dissent to the Good Friday Agreement still exists in the form of the Real IRA and the Continuity IRA. The Irish physical-force tradition won't die out that easily.

Nevertheless, from a historical perspective, the settling-down process in the Six Counties after the Good Friday Agreement has been far more peaceful and far less bloody than the comparable ten-year period in the Twenty-six Counties following the ending of the Civil War. There is a much more broad-based acceptance of the value of the peace dividend and a correspondingly widespread willingness to build on it.

From my perspective, Father Alex Reid and the peace-makers have wrought well. I wish him the best in his more recent endeavours. Since the Good Friday Agreement he has turned his attention to attempting to bring the Basque separatist movement ETA and the Spanish government into negotiation. Impossible? Never say never. Even if the Holy Spirit has temporarily left the stadium, if anyone can get him back into play it is Al Reid.

And, in valediction, what more is there to say about my own life? Nothing really, except, I suppose, that if I lived long enough, and Molly, Ruby, or Poppy were to ask me one day what I did in the war, I could at least reply: I tried.

Index